Docum

United States Brewers' Association

With a sketch of ancient Brewers' gilds, modern Brewers' association, scientific stations and schools, publication, laws and statistics relating to Brewing. Throughout the world, Brewers in public life, &c.

G. Thomann

Alpha Editions

This edition published in 2020

ISBN : 9789354004933

Design and Setting By
Alpha Editions
email - alphaedis@gmail.com

As per information held with us this book is in Public Domain.
This book is a reproduction of an important historical work. Alpha Editions uses the best technology to reproduce historical work in the same manner it was first published to preserve its original nature. Any marks or number seen are left intentionally to preserve its true form.

CONTENTS.

PAGE.

ANCIENT BREWERS' GILDS.—Brewers among the oldest craft-gilds; historical value of their records. Connection between brewing and the earliest gilds. Beorscipe, sacrificial banquets and gilds. Prominence of brewers' gilds in Germany, England, Flanders, etc.; their sturdy defense of freedom of trade. The London Brewers' Company, a typical gild; chartered in 1445; their curious and interesting record; evidence of antiquity; importance as compared with twelve great livery companies. Status of craft-gilds at time of brewers' incorporation. Nature of prerogatives and privileges, economic and political. Martial spirit of gilds; participation in civil wars. Extent of brewers' company's jurisdiction. Regulation of trade, apprenticeship, freedom, etc.; market rights. Citizenship and craft-membership synonymous. Sir Samuel Starling, a brewer, Lord Mayor of London. Educational and charitable institutions of brewers' company; munificent bequests and their management up to date. Social and religious duty of gild brothers. Pageants, feasts and festivals; sumptuous dinners, a sample of them. Prices of beer fixed by Government; injustice of this course; brewers' futile protest. Introduction of excise on beer; effect of same. Illicit brewing. Brewers' charter, 1685. Decadence of craft-gilds. Status of Brewers' Company to-day....... 3–24

MODERN BREWERS' ASSOCIATIONS.—Origin and objects of modern brewers' associations. Germany, Bavaria, Baden, Wurttemberg, Thuringia, Saxony, Great Britain and Ireland, Scotland, Austria-Hungary, Belgium, Sweden, Italy, etc., etc.. 24–33

THE BREWING INDUSTRY OF THE WORLD; LAWS AND STATISTICS.—German beer-tax territory, Bavaria, Wurttemberg, Alsace-Lorraine, Great Britain and Ireland, Austria-Hungary, Belgium, France, Russia and Finland, Denmark, Switzerland, Holland, Sweden, Norway, Roumania, Spain, Servia, Italy, Greece, Bulgaria, Canada, India, Japan, Australasia, Mexico, Barbados, Jamaica, Salvador, Brazil, Chili, Hawaiian Islands 34–67

SCIENTIFIC STATIONS AND BREWERS' ACADEMIES.—Scientific methods of modern brewers. Science more than a mere handmaid to brewing. Brewers' schools subsidized by Government. Experimental station and school at Berlin. Scientific station at Munich. Subsidized schools at Weihenstephan, Nuremberg and Angsburg, Bavaria, and at Hohenheim in Wurttemberg. Schools and stations at Worms. Schools and stations at Moedling, Vienna and Prague. Public brewers' academy at Donai, in France. Institute at Ghent. Hansen's laboratory at Copenhagen. Laboratories at London. Brewers' school at Zurich. Brewers' academy and scientific stations at New York and Chicago....... 68–79

II CONTENTS.—Continued.

PAGE.

BREWING TRADE PERIODICALS.—Germany, Austria Hungary, Great Britain and Ireland, France, Belgium, United States, Miscellaneous.......... 79–82

BREWERS IN PUBLIC LIFE.—Brewers in the German Reichstag and Belgian Senate. Status of trade in Great Britain. Brewers in Parliament. Titled Brewers. Bequest of Brewer Jacobsen, of Copenhagen. Munificent gifts by Lords Iveagh, Burton, Hindlip, Sir Andrew Walker, Sir William Gilstrap. Annual expenditure by American brewers for works of mercy. Educational, social and charitable institutions founded or endowed by Vassar, Massey, Bergdoll, Ballantine, Krueger, Trefz, Voigt, Busch, Burkhardt, Bechtel, Horrmann, Finlay, Pabst, Uihlein, Schandein, Schlitz, Seipp, Schoenhofen, Wacker, etc......... 83–91

HISTORY OF THE UNITED STATES BREWERS' ASSOCIATION—CHAPTER I.—Status of American brewing before 1862. Three periods of development and two periods of decadence. Brewing encouraged and extensively practiced in Colonial days; its flourishing condition. Unfavorable conditions and vascillating fiscal policy conspire with growing rum-habit to stay growth of brewing. Decadence. Revival of brewing under first Federal excise system. The era of free-rum; decadence of brewing. Introduction of lager-beer. Rapid development of brewing from 1842 to 1862; a few comparative data as to its growth. Outbreak of the Rebellion. Revenue-question. Proposed internal revenue system. Report of Committee on Ways and Means. Brewers feel need of organizing. John N. Katzenmayer's agitation and consequent organization of the New York brewers. Call for national convention of brewers. Text of law of 1862. First convention of United States Brewers' Association. Permanent organization. Discussion on revenue-questions. Correspondence with Treasury Department as to several important points. Appointment of committees. Resolutions and remonstrances as to payment of certain taxes and regarding bonds, entries, etc. Character of permanent organization. Adjournment.. 92–116

CHAPTER II.—Character of first convention's work; its impression upon the trade. Ale-brewers willing to co-operate. Why German was used exclusively at the convention; the Associations' subsequent attitude in regard to the two languages. Second convention meets at Philadelphia; its composition. Local association of Philadelphia; its character. Patriotic appeal to members by President. Appointment of committees. Efforts to organize local associations. Drawbacks of representative system and compromise necessitated by it. Biographical sketch of members of Agitation Committee; their significant experiences and efficient work at Washington; great courtesy shown them by eminent statesmen; Government appreciates brewers' loyalty and integrity. What brewers asked for and complained of. Delegation of ale-brewers offer assistance and are made honorary members; effect of this move... 117–129

CHAPTER III.—Third convention; its composition. Work of committees. Justice of brewers' claims. Congress passes several amendments asked for by brewers. Ale-brewers recognized as members and take active part. A new committee created; important labors assigned to it; is to work for reduction of tax; internal trade affairs; the need of a newspaper and of a substitute for pitch. New committee composed of excellent men. Fourth convention; new departure in many respects; parliamentary usages begin to be observed; first Nominating Committee and Special Convention Committees; the latter's excellent reports. Joint Executive Committee embracing ale-brewers. Membership and financial status. Permanent Agitation Committee. The association adopts its present title. Agitation for tax-reduction abandoned for patriotic reasons. Magnificent arguments submitted to Congress prevent increase of tax. Treasury Department confers with association; welcomes its offer of assistance in collecting tax. Patriotic speech by Collins. Resolution expressing loyal sentiments and providing for action against delinquent tax-payers. Presentation of handsome gifts to Laner and Katzenmayer. Election of officers. Another new departure........................ 130–145

CHAPTER IV.—Mode of tax-collection defective. Secretary McCulloch seeks brewers' advice; their motives appreciated, and complaints attended to. Proposed revision of revenue-law; special commission appointed. Brewers' resolve to assist Government and appoint a committee to study the excise question in Europe. Secretary of the Treasury approves the plan. Composition of the committee; its departure for Europe. Agitation Committee defeats tax-increase; old tax cheerfully borne. Fifth convention meets at Baltimore; its composition and vital importance. Relations to Revenue Office. Court decides against taxing beer consumed by brewers. Propositions relating to scientific improvements in brewing; dawn of progressive era. A war incident. Special Revenue Commissioner Wells represents Government at convention; his reception and his speech. Collins reads report of European Commission; the Special Commissioner's opinion of it. Special Committee confers with Government's representative as to change in mode of taxation; recommends adoption of revenue stamps. Another Special Committee appointed to agree with Commissioner Wells upon details of stamp law. Commissioner Wells embodies brewers' memorial in his report; extract from the latter. Extracts from brewers' memorial............... 146–176

ANCIENT BREWERS' GILDS.

BREWERS AMONG THE OLDEST CRAFT-GILDS; HISTORICAL VALUE OF THEIR RECORDS. CONNECTION BETWEEN BREWING AND THE EARLIEST GILDS. BEORSCIPE, SACRIFICIAL BANQUETS AND GILDS. PROMINENCE OF BREWERS' GILDS IN GERMANY, ENGLAND, FLANDERS, ETC.; THEIR STURDY DEFENSE OF FREEDOM OF TRADE. THE LONDON BREWERS' COMPANY, A TYPICAL GILD; CHARTERED IN 1445; THEIR CURIOUS AND INTERESTING RECORD; EVIDENCE OF ANTIQUITY; IMPORTANCE AS COMPARED WITH TWELVE GREAT LIVERY COMPANIES. STATUS OF CRAFT-GILDS AT TIME OF BREWERS' INCORPORATION. NATURE OF PREROGATIVES AND PRIVILEGES, ECONOMIC AND POLITICAL. MARTIAL SPIRIT OF GILDS; PARTICIPATION IN CIVIL WARS. EXTENT OF BREWERS' COMPANY'S JURISDICTION. REGULATION OF TRADE, APPRENTICESHIP, FREEDOM, ETC.; MARKET RIGHTS. CITIZENSHIP AND CRAFT-MEMBERSHIP SYNONYMOUS. SIR SAMUEL STARLING, A BREWER, LORD-MAYOR OF LONDON. EDUCATIONAL AND CHARITABLE INSTITUTIONS OF BREWERS' COMPANY; MUNIFICENT BEQUESTS AND THEIR MANAGEMENT UP TO DATE. SOCIAL AND RELIGIOUS DUTY OF GILD BROTHERS. PAGEANTS, FEASTS AND FESTIVALS; SUMPTUOUS DINNERS, A SAMPLE OF THEM. PRICES OF BEER FIXED BY GOVERNMENT; INJUSTICE OF THIS COURSE; BREWERS' FUTILE PROTEST. INTRODUCTION OF EXCISE ON BEER; EFFECT OF SAME. ILLICIT BREWING. BREWERS' CHARTER, 1685. DECADENCE OF CRAFT-GILDS. STATUS OF BREWERS' COMPANY TO-DAY.

Among the ancient craft-gilds* those of the brewers' have from the earliest beginning of the co-operative movement, which subverted the thraldom of skilled labor, occupied a very conspicuous and in many of the Germanic countries an exceptionally prominent position. Their gilds certainly belong to the oldest craft-organizations, and both in England and in Germanic Europe their gild-records are regarded by historians as the most valuable sources of information concerning the origin

---

*Although the word is frequently spelled *guild*, we prefer to use this form, adopted by all modern lexicographers.

and antiquity, the aims and objects, the privileges and customs of craft-gilds in general.

It is universally assumed upon the authority and concurrent opinions of gild-historians that craft-gilds were first organized in the eleventh century, a long time after the merchants'-gilds and many centuries after the organization of those earliest religious and secular bodies of that name, the origin of which is hidden in the mysterious obscurity hovering over that border-land where tradition and legend, fable and folk-lore intermingle with written history. A wide historical gap and broad space of time separate these latter gilds from the mediæval unions of handicraftsmen and there is no evidence of a genealogical link between them, *except in the case of the brewers.*

Strange as this may seem at the first glance, it is nevertheless a historical fact, sufficiently interesting to warrant a brief digression. The meetings of the earliest gilds were styled *Beorscipe* or *Gebeorscipe* which, literally translated, means beer-ship or, freely rendered, beer-drinking meetings—hence, the latin term *convivium,* which the Roman historian applied to the gatherings he had witnessed among the Germanic tribes. The student of history need not be told that these meetings were not mere drinking-bouts; nor that it is, in fact, rather difficult to over-rate the deep political, social, religious and ethical significance of these feasts, which signalized all the more important events, in peace and war, that made up the life, public and private, of that people.

In all of them, as even in Northern mythology, the brewer and his art played an indispensable and significant part. Wilda, in his excellent work on Gilds (pp. 12, 13 et seq.) demonstrates beyond peradventure that these feasts were also called gilds; for "gild meant' originally the sacrificial meal composed of the common contributions, then a sacrificial banquet in general, and, finally, a society." When in later ages the North yielded, more or less reluctantly, to the civilizing influence of Christianity, the sacrificial banquets, with all their rituals and ceremonies christianized, remained in existence fostered and even commanded by the church; but the libations were then offered in honor of Christ, the Virgin Mary and the saints, instead of Odin and Freya and the other indwellers of Asgard. Wilda cites several examples of this amalgamation of Heathen feasts with Christian festivals, and among them that of King Hakon who ordained that Yule-tide should be celebrated on the day of Christmas and that every freeman should brew the third of a tun of good malt and continue the celebration as long as his beer lasted. The ancient Scandinavian *samburdar-öl*, *i. e.*, festival-ale, thus becomes a means of determining the origin of many of the customs which the conservative spirit and tenacity of the German and Anglo-Saxon nations have helped to preserve even up to our time. The Whitsun-ales, lamb-ales, leet-ales, mid-summer-ales, &c., and the social and religious customs connected with them betrayed in a palpable manner the ancient usages from which they arose.

In the exceedingly interesting history of the struggles by which the craft-gilds finally succeeded, in the fourteenth century, in establishing for themselves civic rights, privileges and powers equal and, in very many instances, superior to those of the patrician gilds, we find the brewers among the foremost of the stanch champions of what was then considered to be freedom of trade. They successfully maintained their standing wherever their industry flourished to any considerable extent, and both their social status and their share in

municipal government demonstrate conclusively the
power they wielded and the esteem in which they were
held by other crafts and their fellow-townsmen.

At a time when there existed a very rigid social and
political classification of crafts, when even certain handicraftsmen were excluded from gild-rights and any participation whatsoever in the government of towns, the
brewers generally ranked next to and often out-ranked
the most distinguished gilds, such as those of the goldsmiths, the armorers and the drapers.

The German oldburghers, many of whom belonged
to the gentry or lower order of nobility, frequently
engaged in and sometimes monopolized brewing within
their towns, as for instance, at Ratisbon where a powerful brewers'-gild flourished in the thirteenth century.
In the fierce and often sanguinary struggles of the
towns against the rapacity and brutality of the nobles,
the brewers distinguished themselves in many ways.
The brewers'-gild of Dantzig, for instance, renowned
for the great number and wealth of its members, was
noted throughout Germany for the prowess and daunt-
less courage with which they defended, by force of arms,
the rights and safety of their city. It was a brewer,
Johannes Lupi, who in 1416 organized the gilds of that
city and by force of arms wrested the government from
the privileged classes who for many years had tyranni-
cally oppressed the burghers and handicraftsmen.
Among the German Gilds who in the reign of Charles
IV. opposed, with varying success, patrician mis-rule
and the depredations of the robber-knights, the brewers
everywhere participated in and often initiated and led
the liberating movement, and wherever success crowned
their efforts their gilds were invariably named among
those entitled to seat and voice in the municipal councils. Thus we find the brewers at Nuremburg among

Their Origin, Development and Decline. 7

the eight craft-gilds of that city, to whom, in 1378, after many hard-fought battles, was accorded the right of representation in the lower branch of the municipal legislature. We find a brewer among the seven leaders, who secretly organized the craft-gilds at Augsburg and by the united efforts of their armed followers compelled the authorities to recognize their civic rights. In Munich, Cologne, Hamburg, Bremen, Magdeburg; in all the larger cities of Flanders, Brabant, Bohemia, etc., the brewers'-gilds occupied eminent positions. A large volume might be written on the subject of these brewers'-gilds and their successful work in the various countries; but as it is the object of this chapter merely to present an outline of the antiquity, objects, rights, privileges and customs of such ancient corporations, our purpose will be fully accomplished if we select a single typical gild and narrate its history as briefly as possible. To this end no better selection could be made than that of the Brewers' Company of London.

This company—still in existence under the official title of "The Master and Keepers or Warden and commonality of the Mystery or Art of Brewers of the City of London"—is doubtless one of the oldest craft-gilds whose records have been preserved in unbroken continuity from the time of their first authentic charter, granted by Henry VI. on the 22nd of February, 1445, up to the present time. It is impossible to determine when this gild was first organized, but there can be no doubt that it had existed for many years before the last-mentioned date. This may be inferred from the wording of the charter which incorporates the company as "one of the ancient mysteries of the city of London" and further from a book entitled the "Records and Accounts of the Brewers' Company from 1418 to 1440."

Pre-eminence in point of antiquity and importance is

usually claimed for the Twelve Great Livery Companies of London,* to whom the brewers do not belong; but this claim, we apprehend, cannot successfully be maintained in the face of an array of significant historical data the correctness of which has never been disputed. Even the historian of the Twelve Great Livery Companies, William Herbert, who from the very choice of this subject may be supposed to have had a slight leaning towards a bias in favor of these gilds, animadverts disparagingly upon this claim in these words: " It is but candid to remark that notwithstanding the ancient rank of the Twelve Companies, many of the others are, on various accounts, of equal or superior importance." After mentioning several other companies more ancient, wealthy or important than any of the Twelve he states: "The brewers are distinguished for their ancient and curious records and yield on that point, perhaps, only to the leather-sellers."

That the Brewers' Company must have been an important gild, in prosperous and flourishing condition, long before the granting of their first charter may conclusively be inferred from the fact that as early as 1422 they owned their own hall, which many of the other gilds, among them some of the Twelve Companies, had hired at various times during the year named. Many other evidences equally strong and conclusive support our assumption. Their records for the year 1418, for instance, note the death of their clerk, John Morey, who had faithfully served them for many years; this fact proving that the company must have been thoroughly organized and systematically governed many years before the reign of Henry VI. By a comparison of the

---

* The twelve companies are those of the fishmongers, goldsmiths, skinners, merchant tailors, haberdashers, salters, ironmongers, vintners, clothworkers, mercers, grocers and drapers.

amount of money subscribed by the various companies for the purpose of celebrating the second arrival of Henry V. from France, in 1422, the conclusion becomes inevitable that the Brewers' Company, although not yet incorporated by royal charter, was even at that time one of the wealthiest of the London craft-gilds. Another rather entertaining bit of evidence, frequently cited in other prints, may also be quoted here. It is derived from the same source to which gild-historians are indebted for much of their information, i. e., the books of the Brewers' Company, which for the year 1421 contain an account of the insubordination of brewer William Payne, at the sign of the Swan, by St. Anthony's Hospital, Threadneedle Street, who refused to contribute a barrel of ale, to be sent to the king (Henry V.), whilst he was in France. For this refusal he was fined 3s. 4d., for a swan for the master's breakfast; and failing to pay, was imprisoned. He afterwards refused to wear the company's livery * and was therefore brought before the mayor. He eventually conformed, but, it is added, "was very long before he could be humbled and brought to good behavior." This clearly indicates that the company exercised, even as early as 1421, all the more important prerogatives granted to chartered gilds.

As we have seen, the incorporation of the Brewers' company occurred about a century after the period when the universal ascendency of the trades had imparted to the craft-gilds such a degree of importance that Edward III, in whose reign were granted most of the charters legally sanctioning the privileges which the gilds had theretofore exercised only on sufferance, himself sought and obtained membership in the linen-armourers' com-

---

* The brewers' livery, which females were also entitled to wear, consisted of a party-colored gown of "blood color parted with rayes; green & cours cloth for vestments."

pany. The adoption of the gild-dress, called livery, which subsequently became, and up to the present time serves as, a distinguishing mark between the higher and lower grades of gild-members, dates from this period. The prerogatives and privileges, as well as the duties and obligations of the craft-gilds were of a two-fold character, namely, industrial and political. The gilds possessed absolute control over their trade in an economic sense, and their participation in and influence upon the city government was paramount. Freedom of the city and membership in one of the companies were in one sense synonymous terms.

Their trade-regulations embraced every conceivable subject connected with the manufacture and sale of their product; the quality both of the raw-materials and of the finished commodities; the economic and social relations between gild-brothers and between apprentices, freemen and liverymen; trade competition within the jurisdiction of the company and all similar matters. Besides this, the gilds watched over and sought to secure the physical and spiritual welfare of their members and in many matters touching the public weal the chosen officers of the gilds, with the consent and sanction of their associates, acted for and in behalf of the entire body of handicraftsmen. Disputes arising from trade-matters were settled exclusively by gild-courts. They established schools and charitable institutions, and for the spiritual welfare of their members founded churches, chapels, altars, memorial windows and mural decorations. In time of peace they organized themselves into military companies, and in time of war undertook the defense of their city. In this particular, English history offers abundant evidence of their sturdy bravery and martial spirit. Indeed, in all the internecine wars the contending parties strove to enlist the support of the London craft-gilds, sure of winning if in this they succeeded. The barons would probably never have secured the Great Charter without the aid of the militant gilds; if Henry III. had not palpably betrayed his intention of despoiling the gilds, the armed handicraftsmen might not, perhaps, have gathered under the banner of De Montford. The House of Lancaster succumbed under the opposition of London, and to the gilds' loyalty to Parliament may in part be ascribed the victorious termination of the war which popular rights waged against despotic rule.

This was the status of craft-gilds in the century before the Brewers' Company of London obtained their first charter. From the report of the Companies' Commission, presented to Parliament in the year 1884, it appears that "the great extent of the trade and the large number of persons exercising it in and about the City of London led to the incorporation of the company." This really means that the company perceived the difficulty of lawfully enforcing its trade-regulations beyond the confines of their own organization without the exercise of that judicial, political and police power which could be obtained only under and by virtue of a charter or act of incorporation. Subsequent charters granted to them in the reign of Elizabeth, Charles I., Charles II., James I. and James II. had the tendency and effect of enhancing the economic prerogatives and extending the jurisdiction of the company, and also of expanding the territorial limits of such jurisdiction. At first confined to the city, the company in 1579, under their third charter (21 Elizabeth), brought under its control the entire trade in the suburbs and within two miles of the city. Under Charles I. this limit was extended to four, and under James II. to eight miles.

One of the essential levers of trade-control consisted

in the compulsory membership of every person engaged in brewing; another, in the power vested in the gild to make and enforce rules and exercise supervision over *all* members of the trade and inflict penalties for non-observance of trade-regulations. The charters gave the company the right to inspect brew-houses; to search for unlawful utensils, measures, materials and product; to exact quarterage according to the number of persons employed; to bind apprentices, prescribe the time of servitude and the necessary qualifications for admission to the trade and for election to its freedom and livery.

Certain rights, which under changed economic conditions became a standing menace to the freedom of trade and commerce, as well as to individual liberty, were deemed quite essential in the earlier stages of the development of craft-gilds. As prominent among these may be mentioned, so far as the brewers are concerned, the right to regulate the sale of barley and malt. Thus, for example, an ordinance provided that no foreigner, burgher or other person should buy barley or malt in the market until the resident brewers and maltsters had been served. This exclusion of outsiders usually ceased at stated hours, generally at 11 o'clock in summer and 12 o'clock in winter; or, as the old text reads, "by xj of the belle in somer season and yn wynter by xij of the belle."

As in other gilds, admission to the brewing-trade depended upon moral conduct, stainless honor and respectable parentage. The rigid regulation, which in most trades and towns debarred any one not "born to the trade" from being admitted to apprenticeship, seems to have been adopted by the company in a limited measure. Membership could be obtained either by inheritance (patrimony), redemption or servitude. The question of servitude has at all times been a prolific subject of gild-legislation and in later days aggravated the evils growing out of the gild-system after it had outlived its legitimate purposes and economic usefulness. The apprentice, being regarded as a member of the family, owed filial devotion and respect to his master and was wholly subject to the latter's guidance and control in moral and social matters. Brentano justly styles this apprenticeship a novitiate to citizenship, for with the freedom of the trade that of the city was inseparably connected; it was for this reason that the initiation of apprentices always took place in the town-hall. Having faithfully served his stipulated term and acquired the requisite knowledge of his art, the apprentice was advanced to full membership in the gild and thus, upon payment of a fee, became a citizen of London. His political rights and privileges were then identical with those of the members of the other craft-gilds who jointly elected the lord-mayor of the city.

It may as well be stated here that the brewers' company gave to the city, among many other meritorious officers, at least one very efficient lord-mayor, in the person of Sir Samuel Starling. When visiting the court-room of the brewers' hall some years ago, the writer's attention was directed to the following inscription conspicuously placed over the mantle of the spacious hearth, viz.: "The Right Wor. Sir Samuel Starling, Knight and Alderman of London, a worthy member of the Brewers' Company, did wainscott this parlour in the year 1670, the said Sir Samuel Starling being then Lord Mayor of the City of London."

The stubbornly defended right of the company to prescribe the number of apprentices has often been characterized as the offspring of narrow selfishness, but this reproach—well founded in a much later period when gilds had degenerated into tyrannical monopolies—is

totally undeserved so far as the earlier periods of the
development of craft-gilds is concerned, when the gilds
supported the indigent and defective members of their
trade, cared for the widows and orphans, assisted needy
gild-brothers pecuniarily, attended to the education and
moral and physical training of the children, and provided
for the spiritual welfare of all. (While the gilds
flourished, England had no poor-laws and no need of
them.) The obligation thus assumed by the companies
necessarily required some safe-guards against an undue
increase of the number of persons entitled to the benefits
arising from membership. So long as the gilds were
permitted to shape their own destiny without royal interference, prosperity perched upon their halls, their
trades flourished and labor found ample reward for its
efforts. But the towns in which they dwelt naturally
shared this prosperity, and some of the beneficient
results of this healthful state of affairs are manifest even
to this day. Some of the older colleges connected with
the universities of Oxford and Cambridge, for instance,
were founded by craft-gilds, and England to-day has
many excellent educational and charitable institutions
which owe their existence to the munificence of gild-
brothers and the wise and provident management of
trust-estates by craft-companies. The Brewers' Company of London even to this day maintains, as we shall
presently see, schools and eleemosynary establishments
founded by members of their gild. The brewers were
no exception to the rule in this particular, but it deserves
to be mentioned that their charitable bequests were made
during the period succeeding the temporary suppression
and spoliation of the gilds in the country-towns by
Edward the Sixth's uncle, Somerset, and the confiscation
of all gild-lands by Henry VIII.

The oldest brewers' charity is the one founded by

Alderman Richard Platt on the 18th of February, 1596; it consisted of 20 acres of land in the parish of St. Pancras, Middlesex; a house in Great Knight Ryder Street and the Medburn Farm in Hertfordshire; its objects were the erection and maintenance of a grammar-school and almshouses at Aldenham. The grammar-school, together with two lower schools at Aldenham and Medburn and six almshouses at Delrow still exist, but the control of them has been transferred, in part, to the parish authorities. In 1875, a portion of the trust estate was sold to the Midland Railway Company, part of the proceeds being used to endow elementary schools, and $100,000 to endow the North London and Collegiate Schools for Girls. In 1609, Dame Alice Owen purchased lands at Islington and Clerkenwell and conveyed them to the Brewers' Company in trust for the use of an almshouse for poor widows, and a school, for both of which institutions she had erected suitable buildings. In 1878, two hundred and sixty-nine years after this noble benefaction, a scheme for the administration of the Dame Owen charities was approved providing for the establishing of two new schools on the site of the old almshouses and school, viz: 1, a school for 300 boys, with facilities for future extension, and 2, a school for a like number of girls. Since then the new buildings for the former institution have been erected and the school is in a flourishing condition.

By far the most munificent charity is that of Alderman James Hickson, founded in 1686. By his will Hickson gave to the Brewers' Company the Manor of Willwotts, many houses and parcels of land in London and elsewhere, on the condition that they maintain certain schools and almshouses founded by him. The Company managed this estate very successfully, and in 1852 erected a new school-house and master's residence in Trinity Square, Tower-Hill.

In 1794, Samuel Whitbread conveyed to the company what is known as "The Great Barford Estate," the object of the benefaction being to support "decayed master brewers and their widows." Another bequest for a similar purpose, i. e., to support and relieve poor freemen of the company and their widows, was made by the same Samuel Whitbread in the same year. There are many other trust-funds of various kinds and for various purposes, the main objects in each case, however, being either educational or purely charitable. Among the minor bequests we find one which to the modern mind may appear a little singular. It is that of Robert Hunt, who gave the company $1,000, on the condition that $100 be paid annually to the Vicar of St. Giles', Cripplegate, for "holding a catechising."

In the course of nearly 300 years the value of the lands thus conveyed to the company has enormously increased in value and, naturally enough, every bit of ground is now utilized for buildings. Thus the St. Pancras estate consists to-day of 73 houses in Aldenham, 36 houses in Pancras Road, 67 houses in Barclay Street, 84 in Charrington Street, 11 houses and a chapel in Goldington Crescent, 11 houses in Goldington Street, 40 houses in new Goldington Street, 30 houses in Medburn Street, 18 houses in Pennyn Street, 22 houses and the Police Station in Platt Street, 45 houses in Stanmore Street, 8 houses, a cottage and other buildings in Werrington Street. The Clerkenwell estate, to cite but one more example, now consists of 260 houses, Brewer Street and Brewer Street, North. The total annual rental value of the company's property probably amounts to more than $160,000. By way of comparison it may be stated that the aggregate income of *all* the London companies is estimated at $2,500,000 annually.

The duties of gilds and gild-members in regard to

pageants, holidays, public feasts, state-dinners, &c., were regulated with the utmost precision and the observance of them was a matter of compulsion. In many ceremonials and feasts, particularly those of a religious character, females (whose rights, by the way, in the case of freedom by patrimony and other respects were fully secured) participated on equal footing, not as a matter of choice, but because the gild rules prescribed it. Thus, for instance, in case of burial services for dead "brethren and sisteren" the company's beadle notified all sisters and brothers of the day of sepulture and required them to be present at the dirge in full livery. Attendance at divine service was also demanded of all, and this will not be deemed surprising when it is recollected that the brewers' charter required all freemen to be communicants.

In like manner the ceremonies attending the initiation of members and officers were minutely described and religiously observed. On becoming a freeman by redemption the new gild brother had to give a breakfast; the officers also gave dinners celebrating their election; in fact, any event deviating in any way from the ordinary occurrences of every-day life was gladly seized as a welcome opportunity for such dinners, and that they must have been exceedingly sumptuous affairs is evidenced by some of the bills of fare preserved in the records of the Brewers' Company. The following gives in detail the courses served at an election dinner of the Brewers' Company on the 5th of September, 1419:

First Course :—Brawn with mustard; cabbages to the pottage; swan standard; capons roasted; great custards. Second Course:—Venison in broth, with white mottrews; cony standard; partridges with cocks roasted; leche lumbard; doucetts with little parneux. Third Course:

—Pears in syrop; great birds with little ones together; fritters, payn puff, with a cold baked meat.*

Swan seems to have been a delicacy in those days, calculated to arouse the envy of gourmets. The Brewers' Records perpetuate the fact that in 1419 Mayor Whityngton of London expressed his dissatisfaction with the Brewers' Company for having had fat swan at their feast on St. Martin's day.

It has been stated that the brewers'-gilds possessed the same prerogatives, rights and privileges as all the other livery-companies; doubtless, in a general way, this statement accords with historical facts, but in one respect there existed between them a very essential difference. While in the matter of prices those gilds which produced commodities the use or consumption of which is a matter of individual choice, taste and means, were at liberty to avail themselves of whatever advantage the condition of the market afforded them, the brewers, like the bakers and other producers of necessaries of life, were obliged to sell their product at a price agreed upon between them and the town authorities, or fixed by the King. Prof. Thorold Rogers, in his "Six Centuries of Work and Wages," gives the following lucid explanation of the cause of this seemingly unjust rule: "In the middle ages, to regulate the prices was

---

* As an interesting evidence of the then prevailing prices we quote from the same source the following account showing services and materials required for this dinner and the cost of them, including a compensation of 1s. 4d. to the minstrels and of 3s. 4d. to the cook, viz.:

For 2 necks of mutton, 3 breasts, 12 marrowbones, with porterage of a quarter coals, 2s. 5d. For 6 swans, 15s. 4 doz. pigeons, 4s. 4d. 12 conies, 3s. 200 eggs, 1s. 6d. 2 gals. frumenty, 4d. 2 gals. cream, 8d. Hire of 2 doz. earthen pots, 4d. Hire of 2 doz. white cups, 1s. 4d. 1 qt. honey, with a new pot, 4d. Divers spicery, 2s. 4d. Porterage of water, by the water bearers, 4d. 1 pottel of fresh grease, 8d. 100 pears, 7d. 11 gals. red wine, 9s. 2d. 4 gals. milk, 4d. White bread, 2s. Trencher bread, 3d. Payn cakes, 6d. Half a bushel of flour, 7d. 1 kilderkin of good ale, 2s. 4d. Given to the minstrels, 1s. 4d. To John Hareley, cook, for him and his servants, 3s. 4d. To William Denerysshe, panter, 6d. 1 qt. vinegar, 1d. Packthread, 1d. Hire of 2 doz. of pewter vessels, 1s. 2d. Salt, 1d. Washing of the napery, 4d. Total, £2. 15s. 3d.

thought to be the only safe course whenever what was sold was a necessary of life or a necessary agent of industry. Hence our forefathers fixed the prices of provisions. The law did not fix the price of wheat or barley. It allowed this to be determined by scarcity or plenty; but it fixed the value of the labor which must be expended on wheat or barley in order to make bread and ale. Not to do this would have been to the mind of the thirteenth century, and for many a century afterwards, to surrender the price of food to a combination of bakers and brewers or to allow a rapacious dealer to starve the public."

In the earlier years of its existence, the Brewers' Company had a determining vote in fixing the price of ale, which was usually "assessed at law-day," and there probably was no cause for complaint on their part; but a very disastrous change took place when Henry VIII.—inveterate enemy and persecutor of the mechanics' gilds, and in this respect the very antipode of Edward III.—not only prescribed the quality of the beer, but also arbitrarily fixed the price of it, in utter disregard of the high price of barley, caused both by a scarcity of the material and the depreciation of coin—the latter one of his nefarious schemes for raising revenue. The brewers remonstrated in vain and came near being amerced for jeopardizing the public weal. This unfavorable turn in their affairs occurred at about the time when hops, used a long time before on the continent of Europe, were just beginning to be used pretty generally by English brewers. The introduction of this healthful bitter element and preservative had been retarded by a prohibitory edict issued by Henry VI. and now Henry VIII. fond of spiced ale, when Burgundy was not to be had, again forbade the use of hops. Unnecessary and harmful intermeddling of this sort harassed the trade considerably.

The injustice of fixing the price of ale became manifest in 1591, when the company, in an able remonstrance, clearly proved the hardship to which they were subjected by being compelled to sell their product at a price fixed sixty years before, although every material employed in brewing had since then vastly increased in price. Although Elizabeth generally evinced a strong disposition to remedy the injury done to the trades by her predecessors, her government turned a deaf ear to the brewers' "prayer," and the company was compelled to rescind their order advancing the price of ale. In the reign of Elizabeth, however, two new charters were granted to the company conferring upon the masters, wardens and commonalty further powers to regulate the trade. It is difficult to determine whether these additional powers served to offset the effects of the serious restraint just described; but there can be no doubt, judging from the enormous increase in the consumption of ale, that the injury sustained by the trade by reason of the hardship before-mentioned, was counterbalanced to some extent by the growing popularity of the beverage. So common was the use of ale in England during Elizabeth's reign that it formed part of the rather substantial breakfast of that time. A quart of beer at breakfast was the usual allowance for each man and woman. English brewers had an excellent reputation in those days, and great quantities of their product found a ready market in foreign lands. Queen Elizabeth herself engaged in this export commerce, securing the needful material by purveyance.

The company had a charter from James I. and another from Charles I. confirming in the main the rights and privileges exercised by it under previous charters. The period between the granting of the latter charter and the decapitation of Charles I. was productive of many measures affecting the trades in general and among them one which could not but be particularly injurious to brewing. We refer to the introduction by the revolutionary Parliament (1643) of excise-duties upon beer and ale, the very kind of taxes which Charles I. was prevented, in 1626, from introducing by the determined opposition of Parliament. This tax-law, rendered more severe and oppressive in subsequent years, undoubtedly caused a change of drinking-habits among the English people. As a war-measure the imposition of this tax, like that of all the other taxes upon the necessaries of life, such as bread, meat, salt, sugar &c., seemed justifiable enough and for a time, the promise of an abolition of the taxes after the war being held out, was borne by the people without any signs of discontent. The whole scheme of what we at present style the "internal revenue" soon became very unpopular, however, and gave rise to riots and other public demonstrations of opposition. The greater part of excises were then abolished but those upon beer, malt and hops remained, increased from year to year until malt-liquors, enormously enhanced in price, yielded to the cheaper spirits, causing in after-years what is known in England as the "gin epidemic." At first this beer-excise proved to be an exceedingly prolific source of revenue, yielding an income for England and Scotland of $1,632,280 in 1659. But subsequent increases of the tax-rate soon diminished the production of beer by gild-brewers and naturally led to surreptitious brewing by outsiders. An illustration, taken at random from among many, may serve as an example. In the year 1690 the quantity of beer brewed by the licensed brewers of London amounted to 2,088,595 barrels. In 1692 the tax, which in 1650 had been 2s. 6d. per barrel of strong beer, was doubled and, as a result, the production of strong and small ale decreased in the following years to 1,523,123 barrels.

A great number of persons not members of the company engaged in brewing as soon as the upward tendency of the excise-rates began and in order to elude the legitimate control exercised by the chartered company, they carried on their business beyond the limits of the company's sway. This fact, doubtless, led to the extension of the company's jurisdiction to within 8 miles of the city and suburbs of London, under their charter granted by James II., in 1685. We quote from the official abstract before referred to the following synopsis of this last charter:—

After reciting the charter of 16 Henry VI., and 4 Elizabeth, 1563, and the surrender of their charter by the company it orders all brewers within 8 miles of the City or suburbs of London to be of the corporation. Provides for the election of a master, three wardens, and 22 or more assistants, limiting the number to 28. Ordains the manner of holding the elections, orders the offices to be held for life, unless such persons as above stated be guilty of misbehaviour, or be obliged to retire from some unforseen cause. Provides a clerk. Orders that the master, one warden, and nine assistants shall form a court. Orders brewers to be admitted to the company. Establishes search and quarterage payments according to the number of servants employed. Gives the company power to make laws or set penalties. Grants a license in mortmain to purchase lands up to the value of £60. Orders every master, warden, assistant, and clerk to take the oaths of allegiance and supremacy, and to subscribe the declaration. Orders each person elected to be a communicant. Orders the clerk to be approved by the King's sign-manual before election. Sanctions the removal of any master, warden, assistant or clerk by an order in council. Orders the corporation to be obedient to the lord mayor. Confirms previous privileges. *Gives freemen the power to distil!!*

The right of freemen of the Brewers' Company to distil ardent spirits had already been conferred in the

Their Origin, Development and Decline. 23

charter granted by Charles II. To the student of the liquor-question this fact throws a flood of light upon the sad conditions and circumstances which in the subsequent century tended to put gin in the place formerly held by malt-liquors.

In 1739 the company adopted new by-laws, which are virtually in force to-day. Toward the middle of the eighteenth century, however, the brewers' company, like all other craft-gilds, entered upon the era of gradual decadence. Yet, some of these gilds, particularly in Germany, survived, in a fashion, for more than a century and a half, until in our age of inventions they succumbed to the new system. It is needless to describe their downward course; every student of economic history knows how these institutions, after serving a most excellent purpose in the earlier periods of their existence, gradually degenerated into tyrannical and selfish monopolies, at war with each other, opposed to every progressive tendency of more enlightened ages, stubbornly clinging to, and brutally asserting, antiquated rights, prerogatives and privileges totally at variance with liberal views and aims as well as with the demands and requirements of more advanced and continually advancing political, social, economic and commercial conditions.

The London Brewers' Company still exists, it is true; but, considered industrially, it is a mere shadow of its former self. It still shares indirectly in the government of the city; freedom of the company must still be obtained by patrimony, servitude or redemption; the company still gives its state-dinners; its members of higher grade still wear livery; its liverymen, like those of all other gilds, with the lord-mayor and four aldermen still constitute the Court of Common Hall; its many educational and charitable institutions secure to this day inestimable advantages to many persons; all freemen by redemption must still "enter into a bond in $2,000 with the company against any expenses that may be incurred in the event of their being elected to the office of sheriff or lord mayor;" in short, the show and semblance of the thing still exists, but as a trade-organization, the Brewers' Company amounts to nothing and might as well be dead, like all brewers'-gilds in other lands, whose places have been taken by journeymen's organizations and modern brewers' associations.

MODERN BREWERS' ASSOCIATIONS.

ORIGIN AND OBJECTS OF MODERN BREWERS' ASSOCIATIONS:—GERMANY, BAVARIA, BADEN, WURTTEMBERG, THURINGIA, SAXONY, GREAT BRITAIN AND IRELAND, SCOTLAND, AUSTRIA-HUNGARY, BELGIUM, SWEDEN, ITALY, &c., &c.

The organization of brewery-owners' associations is not, as some ill-advised writers hold, an outcome of the modern labor-movement; in fact, the determining motives in each case can be traced with unerring precision to causes entirely foreign to any question whatever connected with this movement. In all beer-producing countries the paramount considerations in organizing national brewers' associations were of a purely ethical and scientific or of a fiscal character. The objects sought to be obtained were either the advancement and elevation of the trade by joint deliberation and action in matters relating to the art of brewing as viewed from the scientific level to which the industry has been raised by modern inventions and the works of such eminent scientists as Pasteur, Hansen, Delbrueck, Jorgensen, Van Laer, Will, Schwarz, Lindner and others; or the protection of the trade in the matter of fiscal legislation. In the latter respect there exists a striking similarity between all modern brewers' associations. In Great Britain co-operation began earlier than in any other country and, when fairly started, received a powerful impetus from the rapidly-growing movement in favor of so-called temperance measures.

In the following pages we shall endeavor to enumerate all the more important brewers' associations, with such particulars concerning their origin, location, objects, membership, &c., as are likely to prove of general interest.

GERMANY.

German Brewers' Union, the national organization of members of the brewing and allied industries in the German Empire, was founded in 1871, at a convention assembled on July 27th of that year in the city of Dresden. Its objects, as set forth in its constitution, are the consideration of the common interests of the trade and their protection; the special advancement and elevation of the craft by the aid of free discussion. The constitution further defines as follows the object of its " brewers' congress," to be held, if possible, annually: " To afford its members, and those desirous of becoming members, opportunity to become acquainted with each other, to guard and promote the interests of the Brewers' Union and to encourage the exchange of views and opinions in friendly discussion." Members representing breweries using more than 5,000 hectolitres of malt per year pay 10 marks annual dues; those using 5,000 or less pay 5 marks, the expenses of the annual congress being defrayed by the sale of tickets to participants. The Union, which has a membership of 636, has its headquarters at Frankfort-on-the-Main, its president being Mr. F. Henrich, a brewer of that city.

The Brewermasters' and Forman-Maltsters' Association of Germany, with headquarters in Munich, was founded in 1888, and has for its objects, in addition to the promotion of good-fellowship among colleagues, 1, the support of members who may become disabled and needy through accident; 2, financial assistance to the needy family of a deceased member; 3, to aid a member out of work to obtain employment. Membership in the Association is open to German brewery managers, brewmasters, foremen-maltsters, brewery presidents, directors and owners, directors and owners of malt-houses and master-coopers; also retired members of the foregoing trades. Dues, assessments and initiation fees constitute the income of the organization. The President of the Association is Jos. Wild, brewmaster of Munich, Bavaria, and its membership is about 800.

The Bavarian Brewers' Union is composed of owners, lessees or managers of breweries located in Bavaria. Its object is the unification of the brewers of Bavaria as common representatives of the interests of the Bavarian brewing industry. The affairs of the union are directed by a National Committee of thirty, elected by the annual convention, who choose a board of officers six of whom, with the counsel of the union, elect a president, vice-president, secretary and treasurer. The annual dues are three marks; the union, of which Joh. Sedlmayer, Spatenbrauerei, Munich, is president, has a membership of 135.

The Association of Brewery Proprietors of Munich succeeded, in 1868, the old gild-like body of brewers of that city. The purposes of the organization are primarily the promotion and representation of general trade interests; also the assistance of impoverished Munich brewers and their widows, other commendable works of benevolence and the maintenance of the ancient religious rites and ceremonies. It is supported by an assessment on the product of the members fixed by the annual congress and by an admission fee of 20 marks. The membership, amounting to about twenty, consists of members of Munich brewing firms producing bottom-fermentation beer.

The Brewers' Union of Baden, which has a membership of about 130 and headquarters at Carlsruhe, is composed of brewery proprietors in that State, its object being to afford to its members opportunity of personal acquaintance, to discuss trade affairs and interests and to secure its advancement by a mutual exchange of views and experiences. To accomplish these purposes annual meetings are held at which members have the right to introduce colleagues, the place of meeting, with the headquarters of the union, changing each year. Members are pledged to contribute 5 marks annually to the support of the organization. The Union was established at Carlsruhe in July, 1876.

The Wurttemberg Brewers' Union, which has its headquarters in Stuttgart, accept as members brewery proprietors, directors, managers and brewmasters of irreproachable reputation, who must pay annual dues of three marks. The objects of the Union are the promotion and representation of the general interests of Wurttemberg and Hohenzollern brewers and the elevation of the industry by the mutual exchange of experiences and views, which it is aimed to accomplish by biennial conventions, by meetings and discussions in the general committee, and by the use of the press. The membership of the Union is about 400; its president is G. Munz, brewery director at Stuttgart.

The Thuringian Brewers' Association has its headquarters in Salzungen.

The Leipsic District Association of the German Brewers' Union has headquarters in the city of Leipzig. Its objects are as follows: To promote in every direction the interests of the brewing trade, to discuss and exchange views on scientific questions relating to the art of brewing and generally to direct its efforts in the lines of the German Brewers' Union. The members, comprising brewery proprietors, lessees or directors, brewmasters and foremen-maltsters, hold annual meetings at which association matters are considered and subjects closely related to the brewing trade discussed. The officers, consisting of president, secretary and treasurer and a deputy for each office, are elected every three years. Members pay an entrance fee of five marks and annual dues, the amount of which is determined at the annual meeting. In addition to the ordinary duties of membership, the affiliates must notify the association of the name, birthday and birthplace of their apprentices, with the time of apprenticeship, which must not be less than two years, except under special conditions. Apprentices are received and those who have completed their course examined twice a year, in spring and autumn. The Association has about 100 members; Director Franz Reinhart, of the Leipsic Brewery of Rendintz, Riebeck & Co., is its president.

GREAT BRITAIN AND IRELAND.

The Country Brewers' Society, established in 1822, with headquarters in London, consists, as its name implies, of owners of breweries and brewing firms located in England and Wales, outside of the city of London. Its objects, briefly defined, are to watch legislation and other public matters affecting brewers, to obtain for its members free of charge the most immediate and reliable advice on all questions connected with the licensing laws, to furnish pecuniary assistance in appeal cases of general importance or where it is necessary that the law should be ascertained, to give business advice of a general character, as, for instance, with regard to assessments, unreasonable demands of excise officers, or any matter arising out of the general conduct of the trade; finally, to furnish to members advice of a technical character through the Society's professional staff, at special rates. Members also receive all the publications of the Society, including the *Brewing Trade Review*, its monthly organ, and have access to the Society's reading room. The annual subscription of members varies between 25 shillings (about $6.25) and a fixed maximum of £26 5s. (about $130) and is calculated at the average rate of £2 2s. ($10.00) for each 8,000 bushels of malt, or its equivalent, brewed annually. H. H. Riley Smith is chairman and H. A. Newton secretary. The Society has a membership of about 650.

Affiliated Associations.—There are in England and Wales 43 local brewers' associations affiliated with the "Country Brewers;" namely, one each in Bedfordshire Berkshire, Birmingham, Bradford, Bucks, Bury, Cambs, Cheshire and Shropshire, Cumberland, Derbyshire, Devonshire, Dorset, Durham, Essex, Gloucestershire, Hampshire, Herefordshire, Hertfordshire, Huntingtonshire, Kent, Leicestershire, Lincolnshire, Liverpool, Middlesex, Norfolk, Northamptonshire and Durham, Nottinghamshire, N. Wales, Oxfordshire, Sheffield, Shropshire, Somerset, S. Wales, Staffordshire, Suffolk, Surrey, Sussex, Westmoreland, Wigan, Wiltshire, Worcestershire, Yorkshire. In addition to these there is an independent Brewers' Association at Bolton.

The National Trade Defense Fund was established in 1888, and represents all branches of the trade in alcoholic liquors, the brewers being its most influential members. Its objects are "to watch at all times the general interests of the whole trade in and out of Parliament; to secure by all legal means, regardless of party politics, the return to the House of Commons and other elected bodies of candidates favorable to trade interests;

to federate existing societies; to decide upon the general policy of defense and generally to do all things that the committee shall deem to be for the interests of the trade." The management of the affairs of the Fund is vested in a General Committee, comprising delegates from the various sections into which the country is divided for representation, the presiding officers of the leading organization of manufacturers of, and dealers in, alcoholic beverages being ex-officio members. This Committee must meet at least three times a year, and elects an Executive Committee of not more than 20. Any firm, company or individual can subscribe to the fund, there being no limit to the amount of the subscription. The Secretary of Committees, Henry A. Newton, is manager of the Fund, with headquarters in London.

The Federated Institutes of Brewing, the headquarters of which are in London, was organized in December, 1894, by the federation of the Institute of Brewing in London, the Midland Counties Institute of Brewing and the Yorkshire Institute of Brewing. In February, 1895, these three were joined by the North of England Institute of Brewing, forming the present body. It is purely a scientific and technical organization, its object being to prosecute research and advance the knowledge of the art of brewing and to disseminate such knowledge among those less informed. This has been done by holding meetings of the different institutes, which still preserve their separate organization, at which papers are read dealing with the practical and scientific operations of the brewing industry, by the most eminent authorities, followed by open discussion, both papers and discussions being subsequently published in the "Journal of the Federated Institutes of Brewing" together with abstracts of papers that appear in other journals. The officers of the Institute are Frank Wilson, President; Edgar B. Pymar, M. A., LL. D., Secretary.

IN SCOTLAND

the brewers form part of the Scottish Trade Defense Association, of which a brewer, Mr. George Younger, of Alloa, is president. The object of this body is similar to the National Trade Defense Fund of London, in which this Scottish organization is represented by delegates.

AUSTRIA-HUNGARY.

The Austrian Brewers' Union, organized in 1887, with headquarters in Vienna, has for its objects the discussion of the general interests of the trade, their protection by petition and all legal methods, and the advancement and elevation of the industry by means of free discussion and the use of the trade press. Annual dues are five florins; members who donate twenty florins for the first year are designated "founders." Regular general meetings of the Union are held every two years, the management of its affairs being entrusted, in the interim, to a General Committee of nine or eleven members, elected at each general meeting. This body elects an Executive Committee, including the president, vice-president and at least two other members. The Union has a membership of about 150, its president being Mr. Johann Medinger.

The Brewers' Association of Vienna and Vicinity was founded in 1885; its object is to combine all owners and representatives of breweries in Vienna and vicinity for the protection of their common interests. At periodical meetings the means of elevating the brewing industry are discussed; these means consist of petitions to the government and legislative bodies, the institution of investigations concerning trade and industrial progress and the proper representation of the craft in the daily press. Under certain circumstances, assistance is given to those who have been employed in breweries and their relatives. The annual dues are adjusted in proportion to the relative production of the breweries and are fixed by the general meeting, which must be held not later than March of each year.

There is also a *Brewermasters' and Foremen-Maltsters' Association* for Austria-Hungary, with headquarters in Vienna, and a *Styrian Brewers' Association*, located at Gratz.

BELGIUM.

The General Association of Belgian Brewers, of which M. Vanden Molen of Antwerp is President, has its headquarters at Brussels.

SWITZERLAND.

The Swiss Brewers' Association is composed of proprietors, lessees and directors of breweries in Switzerland and of brewmasters of Swiss breweries. It aims to bring its members into closer union; to consider and protect trade interests and promote the advancement of the craft by the mutual exchange of views and experiences, and to disseminate among the members, through addresses by competent authorities, a knowledge of the science of brewing. The Association, which dates from 1877, has a membership of about 230; G. Feller being its President and G. Strelin its Secretary. Members pay an initiation fee of three francs and annual dues of five francs.

SWEDEN.

The Swedish Brewers' Union, having its headquarters at Stockholm, represents the industry in that country and has a membership of about 325. The objects of the Union are to "promote the general interests of the trade and to labor for the elevation and advancement of the brewing industry."

ITALY.

There is in Italy a brewers' organization entitled "*Unione Italiana Fabricanti Birra*," of which almost all the Italian brewers are members and which has for its object "application by common accord to the government for better facilities or such modification of the taxes and regulations as may be considered necessary." The President of the Union is Angelo Poretti, Varese, Lombardy; its Secretary, Charles Michel, Alessandria, Piedmont.

CANADA.

The Ontario Brewers' and Maltsters' Association is a body of brewers and allied manufacturers originally organized for purely industrial purposes, but subsequently compelled by the untiring efforts of unreasonable opponents to engage in political agitations similar to those successfully carried on by the trade associations of the mother-country. The present favorable status of brewing in Canada, in spite of prohibitory movements of a local character and the constant menace of adverse legislation, must be attributed to the excellent work of this association. The constitution of this body resembles very closely the fundamental laws governing brewers' organizations in the United States; it admits to membership all maltsters, hop-dealers and representatives of kindred trades upon an equal footing with the brewers. The executive work devolves almost exclusively upon the Secretary-Treasurer (Mr. E. O'Keefe), whose office is located in Toronto. The association was regularly organized in 1894; previous to that year the members of the trade met whenever economic, commercial or political events required it.

THE BREWING INDUSTRY OF THE WORLD;

LAWS AND STATISTICS.

GERMAN BEER-TAX TERRITORY, BAVARIA, WURTTEMBERG, ALSACE-LORRAINE, GREAT BRITAIN AND IRELAND, AUSTRIA-HUNGARY, BELGIUM, FRANCE, RUSSIA AND FINLAND, DENMARK, SWITZERLAND, HOLLAND, SWEDEN, NORWAY, ROUMANIA, SPAIN, SERVIA, ITALY, GREECE, BULGARIA, CANADA, INDIA, JAPAN, AUSTRALASIA, MEXICO, BARBADOS, JAMAICA, SALVADOR, BRAZIL, CHILI, HAWAIIAN ISLANDS.

A great number of glowing pæns have been written of late on the "triumphant progress of the great civilizer King Gambrinus," but neither from these nor from the extensive literature on the subject could one deduce as good an idea of the extent of beer's present dominion and of the rapid development of the brewing industry, even in those countries where the produce of the grapevine has theretofore held undisputed sway, as can be gained from a statistical summary, presented, not in dreary tables, but in the form of a brief and concise narrative. The following pages contain all such information as it has been possible to obtain from official sources during a period of about two years. The figures are not all of the same date and in fact cannot be, owing partly to the slowness of communication with far-distant lands and partly to varying methods of compiling statistics in the different countries. Such as they are, however, they present, we venture to assert, a very clear summary of the laws relating to brewing, the production of malt-liquors, the number of breweries and capital invested and men employed in them, wages, production and prices of raw materials, exports and imports, and many other equally interesting data.

GERMAN BEER-TAX TERRITORY.

The German Beer-Tax District includes Prussia with Waldeck-Pyrmont, Lippe-Schaumburg, Saxony, Hessia, Mecklenburg-Schwerin, Mecklenburg-Strelitz, the Thuringian provinces, Oldenburg, Brunswick, Anhalt and, since Oct. 1st, 1888, by reason of their incorporation in the German Tax Union and consequently in the beer-tax district, the free cities of Bremen and Hamburg, and also the Grand Duchy of Luxemburg.

The beer-tax throughout this district is levied on the unit of 100 kilog. of the following substances when used in the manufacture of beer: a, cereals (malt-grist, etc.), rice (ground or unground) and green starch, 4 marks; b, starch, starch meal (including potato meal), dextrin and syrup of all kinds, 6 marks; c, sugar of all kinds, as well as sugar solutions and all other malt surrogates, 8 marks. All commercial breweries are liable for this tax; also all private breweries making beer exclusively for household purposes, where the household comprises more than ten persons over fourteen years of age.

The tax may be levied on a brewing permit, which is, in fact, the rule. In this case, before he commences to brew, the brewer must furnish the tax officer with a written notice, stating the kind and quantity of material to be used with each brewing, the day and hour of mashing and the quantity of beer it is designed to brew. The official enters these notices in the book he keeps for the purpose, receipts for the tax in the tax-book, which he returns to the payer, and, at the time appointed for mashing, presents himself at the brewery, where, after the material has been weighed in his presence, mashing is commenced. After-mashing may not, as a rule, be permitted. To ensure more complete control of the process and a supervision of the beer product, at least eight days before commencing operations, the place occupied as a brewery, including the fermenting rooms, the mashing, boiling, cooling and fermenting vessels (the capacity of which must be given in litres) must be described to the tax officer.

A second method of collecting the revenue is provided by the law in the shape of a "mill" or "grinding tax," according to which the mash-material that requires grinding or crushing before mashing is taxed in proportion to its weight as determined in the mill before grinding. The adoption of this method is optional with the authorities and may be permitted on request, provided the officials possess sufficient confidence in the applicant, who must keep a set of books and use annually at least 50,000 kilogrammes of malt. The mill in which the grinding is done is under official lock. At the appointed time for grinding, the proper official is present to open the mill, and the previously declared brewing material is weighed and ground in his presence. After grinding, he again locks the hopper of the mill. The brewer must never grind any brewing material except in the mill officially registered; he must not have on his dwelling, mill or brewery-premises brewing material that has been ground elsewhere, nor must he have or permit, within the limit of the brewery-premises, any mill in which brewing material might be ground, under a penalty, although no actual fraud may have been committed, of 300 marks for a first and 600 marks for a second offense.

Finally, by an arrangement with the officials, in place of paying the tax separately on every brewing, the payment of a lump sum for a certain time may be arranged for. The brewing of tax-free household beverages must be conducted by those having the privilege according to a prescribed formula, which must be recorded at the tax office with a statement as to the number of persons over fourteen years of age in the household and the period for which the permit is to be in force.

Besides the foregoing, the law and accompanying regulations contain a number of rules regarding the storage of malt-grist and malt-surrogates, the records to be kept of saccharine surrogates for use in brewing and their introduction into the brewery, etc.

A drawback is paid on beer in cask or bottle exported from the beer-tax district, amounting to 1 mark per hectolitre; but the shipment must amount to at least 2 hectolitres and a minimum of 25 kilogrammes of grist, rice or green starch must have been used in brewing the beer exported; or, in case of the use of material paying a higher tax than 4 marks per kilogram, a proportion of such material, equivalent to a tax of 1 mark, must have been used for each hectolitre of beer. A re-imbursement of the tax may also be obtained, should the materials set apart for the mash be destroyed by accident before mashing or so damaged as to be useless for brewing purposes, or in the event of any unforseen occurrence preventing the proposed brewing. In all cases the claim for re-imbursement must be made to the tax official within twenty-four hours after the time set for mashing.

The penalty for fraudulent violation of the law consists of a fine equal to four times the amount of tax unlawfully withheld; for a second offense, eight times this sum. Subsequent violations are punishable by imprisonment for not more than two years.

The duty of collecting the beer-tax in the beer-tax district, which amounted in 1894 to 32,133,418 marks, is entrusted to the various constituent States; the amount of the same, less the sums legally disbursed for drawbacks and re-imbursements and the cost of collection and supervision, being paid by them into the Imperial treasury. The same applies to the duties collected on beer imported into the district from Bavaria, Wurttemberg, Baden or Alsace-Lorraine.

An increase in the malt-tax to double the present

amount is contemplated in the entire German Customs' Union and is vigorously opposed by the Brewers' Union. A similar increase in the duty on imported foreign malt has also been suggested. At present the customs-tariff is 4 marks per 100 kilogrammes.

The number of breweries in the beer-tax district in 1894, the latest period for which returns are available, was 8,243, and their output amounted to 34,384,547 hectolitres, representing a per capita consumption of 84.6 litres, which is steadily increasing. In spite of the growing production of beer, the number of breweries decreases annually, the falling-off being largely in the class of breweries producing top-fermentation beers and paying annually less than 1,500 marks in taxes. The number of those paying between 1,500 and 15,000 marks on the other hand is steadily increasing. The average number of brewers for private consumption during the ten years 1880–1890 was 800 to 900, which are included in our total. The aggregate value of the commercial breweries is estimated at 750,000,000 marks, and the amount of capital invested in their operation in 1890–91 was about 300,000,000 marks.

Drawback was paid in 1890 on 378,000 hectolitres of beer exported from the beer-tax district. The exports reached their maximum in 1889–90; since then they have decreased. On the other hand, the importation of beer into the German beer-tax district shows a steady increase, most of it coming from Austria-Hungary, which furnished in 1890 nine-tenths of the beer imports, amounting to 1,868,000 hectolitres.

The number of persons employed in breweries in the German Empire in 1891–92 was 72,517, and the wages paid averaged for that year 984.50 marks. These figures, however, apply only to establishments affected by the accident insurance law of July 6th, 1884, including breweries using steam machinery or paying tax on at least 1,000 hectolitres of malt. All the others, and they are numerous, are not subject to the insurance law. According to the census of June, 1882, there were in the beer-tax district about 28,000 males and 400 females employed in breweries and malt-houses.

In spite of rising prices for hops and barley and a material increase in wages, the price of beer has undergone no change and tends, if anything, to decline. Top-fermented beer costs on an average 8–10 marks per hectolitre, bottom-fermented beer 15–18 marks, and strong beer of the latter kind 19–21 marks per hectolitre.

The consumption of malt and malt surrogates, keeping pace with the growing production of malt-liquors, has steadily increased, and amounted in 1891–92 to 6,134,000 *meter-centners*, about 67,000 *meter-centners* of malt surrogates being also used; the price of malt during the year in question ranged from 26 to 29.50 marks, and all but $\frac{1}{3}$ or $\frac{1}{4}$ of the malt used was employed in bottom-fermentation breweries. Rice, wheat and sugar were the principal surrogates employed. The average price of hops, of which 13,251 *meter-centners* were produced in 1891–92, was 142 marks per *meter-centner*.

BAVARIA.

The most important regulations governing the taxation of malt-liquors in Bavaria may be summarized as follows: All malt which is used in making beer or vinegar is subject to taxation, the owner of the malt being liable for the tax. Malt surrogates are not made the subject of taxation and cannot be used in the production of beer, which must be produced from kilned malt, hops, yeast and water. The tax collected is 6 marks per hectolitre on all malt ground for use in making beer or vinegar, whether dry or sprinkled, calculated according to the quantity measured in the mill. Where more than 10,000 hectolitres of malt are used annually in a brewery, an additional tax is levied, amounting for the next 30,000 hectolitres to 25 pfennigs per hectolitre, and where the quantity used exceeds 40,000 hectolitres, to 50 pfennigs per hectolitre. On the other hand, breweries which were in existence before October 1, 1889 and did not brew more than 6,000 hectolitres of malt, as long as this consumption does not exceed 7,000 hectolitres, pay only 5 marks per hectolitre of malt. The total amount of beer-tax collected in Bavaria in 1894 was 31,755,551 marks.

Beer brought from other German states into Bavaria, where it has not been imported from a foreign country and paid customs duty, is subject to a tax of 3 marks 25 pfennigs per hectolitre.

All breweries are subject to the tax, even those brewing for private consumption, and every brewery must have been officially recorded at some time, the annual renewal of the record not being necessary. The measurement of the quantity of malt in the mill is recognized as the sole basis of determining the tax by the government. All malt must be ground in public mills or properly authorized private mills, which must not be transportable; green-malt can only be worked with the aid of proper crushing machines. Persons wishing to grind malt must notify the tax office of their district of the fact in writing. Private as well as public mills having cylindrical crushing rolls *must*, other public mills *may*, be furnished with automatic measuring devices. This must be officially locked; the mill may remain open. Trafficking in ground malt in Bavaria is prohibited. The tax, as a rule, is collected quarterly.

The malt tax may be remitted or, if already paid, refunded, if it can be proved that malt or its products in transportation to or from the mill, in the mill, during the brewing process, in transportation from the brewhouse to the fermenting cellar or in the cellar, have been damaged in such a manner as to render them valueless or unfit for use. The tax paid on beer exported is also refunded, provided the shipment amounts to at least 60 litres. The drawback, without regard to the form in which it is shipped, is 2 marks 60 pfennigs per hectolitre for brown and 1 mark for pale beer. Where a brewery paying tax, exports in any year more than 12,000 hectolitres of brown beer, the drawback allowed on the following 48,000 hectolitres is 2 marks 75 pfennigs, and where the quantity exported exceeds 60,000 hectolitres, an allowance of 2 marks 85 pfennigs per hectolitre is made.

Where the laws relating to the taxation of malt do not specifically apply, the general regulations set forth in the tax laws of the German Empire are observed. The first-mentioned laws provide that failure to observe their separate provisions shall be punished, according as the case is one of intentional fraud or only of more or less culpable carelessness, by fines of 300 to 900, 180 to 540, 90 to 450, 90 to 180, 36 to 180 and 18 to 54 marks, with double the penalty for a second offense. For fraud in connection with the remittance or re-imbursement of the tax, the penalty is fixed at ten times the amount wrongfully obtained. There are also laws regulating the collection of a local tax (a communal impost in addition to the State tax) the levying and collection of which by local officials must first be authorized by the State government.

While the production and consumption of malt liquors in Bavaria is steadily increasing, the number of breweries is steadily decreasing, those producing brown beers being most affected by the movement, there being a slight increase in the breweries producing pale beer.

In 1894 there were in Bavaria 6,622 breweries, their product for the year amounting to 15,019,297 hectolitres, representing a per capita consumption of 282 litres.

The quantity of malt consumed in Bavarian breweries was 438,991,000 kilogrammes in 1894, and of hops 6,157,800 kilogrammes. The number of persons employed in breweries in Bavaria, according to the census of 1882, was 11,367, including 85 women, and their average wages in 1891 was 900 to 1,200 marks a year, as compared with 800 to 1,000 marks in 1886. The average price of beer increased during the same period from 22 to 24 and from 24 to 26 marks per hectolitre.

While Bavaria's imports of beer, which amounted in 1891 to 49,000 hectolitres, have gradually increased of late, her exports of malt-liquors have advanced much more rapidly, amounting in 1891 to 2,199,000 hectolitres, three times as much as in 1881.

WURTTEMBERG.

The source of beer-tax revenue in Wurttemberg is malt of every description made from grain for use in brewing, as well as malt surrogates used for the same purpose. The unit quantity for taxation is the double-hundredweight, on which, in 1889–91, a tax of 10 marks was levied; the tax on imports from other States is 3 marks per hectolitre for brown, 1 mark 65 pfennigs for pale beer.

The taxpayers are all those who for their own account grind malt or have malt ground for the preparation of beer, or for whose account malt surrogates are delivered at a brewery, the tax being payable as soon as the malt is delivered at the mill or the surrogates at the brewing place. The tax is collected in four quarterly instalments; it may be remitted or refunded where ground malt, before use, or its product, is destroyed or so spoiled that no use can be made of it; when beer on which tax has been paid is made into vinegar, or when ground malt or finished beer is shipped out of the country.

Malt, as a general rule, must be ground only in a public place. Private mills, where their use is permitted, must be so arranged that they can be securely locked by the tax officials, and the hopper must be large enough to contain the malt for one brewing. The possession of a feed grinding-mill, that might also be used for grinding malt by farmers and other persons who do not brew beer, is permitted.

Those who propose to use malt surrogates in brewing are bound, before bringing them into the brewing place, to see that a tax officer is present, who must take due note of the quantity and character and prepare the declaration on which the amount of tax is calculated.

Violations of the various provisions of the law are classified as follows: (*a*) Tax frauds punished by a fine of four times, or when the offense is committed at night of five times, the amount of the tax withheld; for a second offense the fine is increased to eight times, for a third to sixteen times, and for a fourth to twenty times the amount of the tax fraudulently withheld, together with the forfeiture of the right to brew. (*b*) Obstructing the supervising officers in the performance of their duty is punishable by fine not exceeding 200 marks. (*c*) For other violations fines not exceeding 60 marks are prescribed.

In Wurttemberg, the number of private breweries, *i. e.*, those operated only to meet household requirements, is very large, the number of commercial breweries showing a steady decrease. In 1891, out of a total of 6,748 breweries, no less than 4,568 were private establishments. In 1894 Wurttemberg had 6,141 breweries, which produced 3,478,065 hectolitres of malt-liquor, equivalent to a per capita consumption of 236 litres. For the past decade there has been a decrease in the output of beer. The number of brewery employés is estimated at 3,300, and their earnings average 1,000 marks a year, including board and lodging and 6 litres of beer daily. During the year 1894, the total beer tax collected was 8,198,657 marks. The price of beer, which has somewhat declined during the past eight years, was 16–18 marks per hectolitre in 1891.

The consumption of malt and its equivalent in the production of the above quantity of beer was 84,342,500 kilogrammes and of hops, 1,519,500 kilogrammes. The value of the breweries in Wurttemberg may be estimated at 120,000,000 marks, a capital of about 35,000,000 marks being employed in their operation. In 1891–92, Wurttemberg harvested 155,905 tons of barley and 3,091 tons of hops.

BADEN.

In Baden, the tax on beer is levied on the worts, calculated according to the capacity of the brewing apparatus. The firing arrangements of the brewing vessels are under control of the tax officials. One hour before firing is commenced, the declaration of the brewing must be made and the tax paid. The tax may be refunded where the brewing on which the tax has been paid is through any cause a failure; or when the beer is spoiled during brewing, provided that the spoiled beer is left in the brewing vessels, on the surface-cooler or in the fermenting vessels without interference and is pronounced by the tax officials unfit for use as beer. A drawback is also allowed on beer exported under supervision from the State. The tax amounted, in 1891, to 2 pfennigs for each litre of the total capacity of the brewing vessels. The same tax is collected on beer imported into Baden from the other four tax States of the

Empire. The drawback allowed on beer exported from Baden is 2 marks 50 pfennigs per hectolitre.

Violations of the tax law, according to the gravity of the offense, are punished by fine or imprisonment. The former amounts for the first offense to four times the amount of the tax withheld, for a second offense, eight times the amount, and so forth.

In Baden, as in the remaining German States, the number of small breweries is decreasing, in spite of increasing production and consumption of malt-liquors. In 1894 there were 1,721 breweries in the grand duchy, the output of which amounted to 1,710,172 hectolitres (100 litres per capita of the population). The tax paid was 5,644,620 marks. The amount of capital employed in Baden's breweries was estimated in 1891 at 20,320,000 marks, their workpeople numbered 2,557, earning on an average 1,200 marks per year, an increase in wages of about twenty per cent. in five years. The average price of beer per hectolitre was 17 marks, a decrease of nearly ten per cent. in five years.

Baden's imports and exports of beer have steadily increased during the past ten years, the former to a notable extent. In 1891, her exports amounted to 162,000 hectolitres, with imports about equal in quantity.

The production of hops in 1891 was 2,270,000 kilogrammes, and their average price 136 marks per 100 kilogrammes. The average price of malt per 100 kilogrammes during the same year was 29 marks.

ALSACE-LORRAINE.

The union of these provinces with the German Empire had not been attended up to 1890 with any change in the system of beer taxation. The tax, which amounts to 2 marks 30 pfennigs per hectolitre for strong and 58 pfennigs for light beer, is now collected at the end of each month. On exports of beer the full amount of the tax is refunded, but is allowed only to brewers exporting beer they have brewed themselves and on which they have paid tax. The duty on beer imported from any of the other four German States is 2 marks 30 pfgs. per hectolitre, making the tax, the import duty and the drawback on exports equal, at 2 marks 30 pfennigs for strong and 58 pfennigs per hectolitre for light beer. In other respects, the beer-tax-system of Alsace-Lorraine is identical with the kettle-tax-system of Baden.

The number of breweries in operation in Alsace-Lorraine has steadily decreased since 1871. In 1873 there were 318, in 1894 but 106 breweries in the provinces. Their output, on the other hand, has shown a tendency to increase during the past few years, amounting to 907,386 hectolitres in 1894, compared with 836,700 hectolitres in 1891, a per-capita consumption of 52 litres. The quantity of brewing material used in 1894 was, malt 27,021,500 kilogrammes, hops 313,750. The amount of tax collected was 2,808,908 marks.

The imports of beer into Alsace-Lorraine from the remaining German States is steadily increasing, whereas the exports are falling off, the former having increased from 188,000 hectolitres in 1886–7 to 265,000 hectolitres in 1890–91, while the exports decreased from 146,000 hectolitres in the former to 80,000 hectolitres during the latter year.

The number of employés in breweries in 1882 was 1478, of whom 15 were women.

The harvest of 1891–92 included 87,119 tons of barley and 4,682 tons of hops.

GREAT BRITAIN AND IRELAND.

Brewers in Great Britain must take out an annual license, under penalty of a fine of £200 and the confiscation of all worts, beer, utensils and vessels. The tax is based on the supposition that every brewer produces 36 Imperial gallons of worts of a specific gravity of .1055 from each 2 bushels of malt consumed; 42 pounds by weight of malt being considered, with the same quantity of grain of any other kind or 28 pounds of sugar, equivalent to a measured bushel of malt. The tax is levied on each 36 gallons of beer of a specific gravity of .1055 produced by commercial brewers (termed "brewers for sale"), the amount collected on each 36 gallons (an English barrel and the unit of taxation) being 6 shillings and 6 pence, and in the same proportion for beers of higher specific gravity, calculated either according to the entries made in his books by the brewer or based on the results of measurements made by the revenue officials, and according to the highest results of either of these methods of calculation. In determining the quantity and gravity of all worts a certain saccharometer prescribed by the government and an accompanying table must be employed.

The tax, which amounted for the year ending March 31, 1895, to £10,494,329, is payable to the revenue officer immediately on the determination of the amount due, but arrangements may be made whereby commercial brewers may pay the tax on all the worts made by them during one month on the first, or on the fifteenth of the succeeding month. Every brewer for sale must keep a book in prescribed form, open to the inspection of the revenue official at all times. The mash must remain undisturbed in the mash-tub for one hour after the time announced in the book for drawing off the worts, unless the revenue officer has previously made the necessary measurements. Every "brewer for sale" must keep the product of each brewing, for twenty-four hours after its completion, separate from the product of any other brewing, except where the official inspection of such brewing has been previously completed.

Should the specific gravity of a wort exceed by 5° the figure entered in the book, it is regarded as a new brewing and so treated officially. The concealment of the quantities of worts or beer, or the addition to either of sugar after measurement by the inspector, is punishable by fine of £100 and the confiscation of the worts or beer in question with the vessels in which they are contained. Private brewers, subject to tax, pay on the quantity of wort produced, which is calculated according to the material employed.

The tax may be remitted (*a*) in cases where taxable materials, worts or beer, while contained in the building in which they were measured, are destroyed by fire or other unavoidable occurrence; (*b*) on the exportation of beer manufactured by a brewer for sale, in which case the tax is refunded in full. Imported beers or ales, which are found on test to be produced from worts of a specific gravity not exceeding .1055, pay a tax of 6 shillings 3 pence for 36 gallons, and more in proportion where the specific gravity of the original worts is found to be higher than .1055. On other beers (mumme, spruce-beer, Berlin white beer), which show a gravity of original worts not exceeding 1,215°, a duty of £1. 6s. per barrel is collected, and on beers the gravity of whose original worts was upwards of 1,215° a duty of £1. 10s. 6d. per barrel.

Under the present law the number of commercial breweries in Great Britain and Ireland has steadily decreased, their output having, however, increased in quantity. The total beer-tax paid by the brewers of those countries for the year ending March 31st, 1895, was £10,494,329, the total number of brewers licensed for the year being 26,091, of which 9,050 were brewers licensed to sell at wholesale only, the remainder being saloon keepers having small breweries and private brewers. The total number of English barrels of malt liquor brewed in Great Britain and Ireland during the year in question was 31,879,397, equivalent to about 44,000,000 American barrels.

The capital value of the breweries and distilleries and their properties in 1891 was estimated at £200,000,000, and in malting and brewing in Great Britain and Ireland about 66,000 persons were employed, their average annual wages being from £25 to £30. During the year 1894 1,906,101,300 kilogrammes of malt and corn, or their equivalents in sugar, etc., were used in brewing, with 29,580,250 kilogrammes of hops. The production of hops in 1891 is placed at 436,716 cwts., and 195 cwts. of hops were imported, the average price per cwt. of English hops being £5.12s. The total number of licensed retailers of fermented and spirituous liquors in England and Wales during the year ending March 31, 1891, was 135,837, or 4.6 per 1,000 of the population. Of these 32,497 were "beer houses," selling malt-liquors only.

During the year ending March 31st, 1895, Great Britain's exports of malt-liquors amounted to 497,059 barrels.

AUSTRIA-HUNGARY.

In Austria-Hungary, according to the present law passed in 1890, a tax of 16.7 kreuzers is collected for each degree on the saccharometer and each hectolitre of the beer worts produced in breweries. Beside this, in the enclosed cities there is an extra tax of 7 kreuzers for each hectolitre and degree on the saccharometer, except in Vienna, where the tax, levied without regard to saccharometric gravity, amounts to 1 florin 68 kreuzers for each hectolitre of beer worts produced.

When the brewer receives a receipt for the taxes paid,

or is in possession of the "polette" embodying the necessary advance notification of the tax to be paid, he is entitled to commence at the stipulated time the proper brewing process for producing revenue beer, which is held to commence with the firing-up of the kettle or, in steam breweries, with the admission of steam to the mash-kettle. During the greater part of the time required for the brewing process, the revenue watchman is required to be present in order to observe the quantity and saccharine value of the worts produced; their value, *i. e.*, their saccharometric gravity, being determined with the aid of the saccharometer. No dilution of the quantity of worts declared or produced is permitted. Before leaving the brewery, after completing his tour of duty, the revenue officer must officially and securely seal the means of heating the kettle.

Re-imbursement of the beer-tax is allowed (*a*) where a brewing is unavoidably interrupted or the beer spoiled before the process is completed; (*b*) where beer is shipped out of enclosed cities; (*c*) where beer is exported beyond the customs' limits. In Vienna, the drawback allowed amounts to 1 florin 47 kreuzers, and in the remaining cities to 74 kreuzers. Where the beer is shipped out of the country, if, when deprived of its carbonic acid, it has a saccharometric gravity of at least $2\frac{1}{2}$ per cent. and is exported in quantities of not less than 1 hectolitre, a drawback is paid (*a*) without reference to the extract contained in the worts from which the beer is made, of 1 florin 50 kreuzers; or (*b*) taking the minimum percentage of extract of all beer-worts produced during the preceding six months by the exporting brewer, a drawback of 16.7 kreuzers is allowed on each hectolitre and each degree of saccharometric gravity of such shipment. Imports of beer into Austria-Hungary pay a duty on each hectolitre, in cask, of

3 florins, and in bottles or jugs of 8 florins. In this duty the internal revenue tax is included.

Violations of the tax-law in making returns of tax-beer are punished by fine equal to four to eight times the amount of tax illegally withheld; irregularities in the revenue brewing-process, by a fine of from 2 to 200 florins.

Between 1872-73, when 13,500,000 hectolitres of beer were produced in the empire-kingdom, and 1889-90, no material increase in the production of malt-liquor was reported; the industry apparently then started on an upward movement and the output amounted for that year to 14,117,000 hectolitres, while in 1894 the 1,775 breweries of Austria-Hungary (less by 28 than in the preceding year) produced 18,357,000 hectolitres of beer, an increase of 845,413 hectolitres compared with 1893, and equivalent to an average per capita consumption in all the constituent States of 58.99 litres. The malt consumed in this year was 396,754,000 kilogrammes, with 7,204,250 kilogrammes of hops, and the amount of tax collected was $17,474,029.

The exports of beer, amounting in 1891 to 552,373 hectolitres, also displayed a considerable increase, the imports during the same period being 51,977 hectolitres.

BELGIUM.

The tax on beer may be paid by the brewer either in the form of a tax on the capacity of his mash-tub of 4 francs per hectolitre, or on the amount of ground malt used, at the rate of 10 centimes for the kilogram. The smallest mash-tub capacity permitted in a taxable plant is 10 hectolitres, and where the thick-mash process is employed a tax is also levied on the product. The tax is paid, as a rule, at the end of each month.

The drawback paid on exports of beer is 2 francs 50

centimes per hectolitre and is allowed only when a single shipment amounts to 5 hectolitres in cask or 2 hectolitres in bottles. The duty on imported beer is 6 francs per hectolitre in cask and 7 francs per hectolitre in bottles.

In 1894 there were 2,900 breweries in operation in Belgium, the product of which amounted to 9,571,746 hectolitres, equivalent to a per capita consumption of 146.1 litres. The amount of tax collected during that year was $3,539,248.

The census of 1890 gave the number of employés in 2,574 breweries as 9,857, of whom 118 were women. The daily wages then paid for employés under 14 years of age was 0.50 to 0.25 francs, from 14 to 16 years 0.50 to 3.50 francs, over 16 years 0.50 to 7.00 francs. On an average, the wages paid amounted to 25 centimes per hour, and the daily earnings to 2.91 francs, or 654.75 francs per year. In 1891 the capital invested in 21 joint stock breweries in Belgium amounted to 7,892,000 francs; no other data as to invested capital could be obtained.

The consumption of malt in 1894 was 210,578,400 kilogrammes; of hops, 3,923,500 kilogrammes were consumed, the total product of hops being 2,980;000 kilogrammes; the hop imports in 1891 amounted to 1,488,-000 kilogrammes.

Belgium imports more beer than she exports; in 1891, her brewers shipped 8,000 hectolitres of their product to foreign markets, and the imports of malt liquor amounted to 53,000 hectolitres.

FRANCE.

The tax on beer is levied on the worts and is calculated on the official measurement of the kettle capacity with an allowance of 20 per cent. The amount of the tax is 3 francs 75 centimes per hectolitre for strong, and 1 franc 25 centimes for light beer worts. Besides this, the brewer must take out a license each year, costing from 75 to 125 francs, and is also liable for a local tax. Violations of the law and ordinances are punished by fine of 200 to 600 francs, and persons brewing for private consumption pay the same tax and are subject to the same restrictions as commercial brewers. Any material not injurious to health may be used in brewing. The tax is collected at the end of each month, and a drawback of the full amount paid is allowed on exports. Imports of malt-liquors pay customs duty of 7 francs 7 centimes per hectolitre.

In 1894 there were in operation in France 2,611 breweries, most of them located in the northern departments. Their output amounted to 8,443,685 hectolitres, on which a revenue of $4,536,562 was collected, representing a per capita consumption of 25.2 litres. The amount of malt or its equivalent used was 216,592,100 kilogrammes, of hops 2,912,000 kilogrammes, and the quantity of hops produced was 3,500,000 kilogrammes. In 1891 France exported 41,000 and imported 169,000 hectolitres of malt-liquor.

RUSSIA AND FINLAND.

Beer in Russia is subjected in the course of production to a double-tax, a license tax and a beer-excise. The license tax is collected annually from all breweries having a mash-tub of 100 wedros (1 wedro = 12.3 litres) capacity. These establishments are taxed in St. Petersburg and Warsaw 150 roubles, with an extra 1 rouble 50 kopecks for each additional wedro capacity; in other cities, 50 roubles for 100 wedros, with 50 kopecks additional for each extra wedro-capacity. Breweries with a mash-tub of less than 100 wedros capacity pay in St. Petersburg and Warsaw for the first 35 wedros 55 roubles, and 1 rouble 50 kopecks for each additional wedro; in other cities and the provinces 20 roubles if under 35 wedros capacity and 50 kopecks for each additional wedro. The beer excise is also calculated according to the capacity of the mash-tub, amounting to 20 kopecks for each wedro of its capacity at each mashing. When beer is exported, the entire duty is refunded, and imports of beer in cask pay a duty (in gold) of 1 rouble 30 kopecks per pud. (= 16.4 kilogrammes) and in bottles of 20 kopecks per bottle.

In the manufacture of beer, only cereals, yeast, hops and water can be used. A drawback equal to the amount of the tax can be obtained where a brewing is spoiled by accident.

Violations of the law are punished in part by a fixed fine of 25 to 500 roubles, and also by a fine amounting to double the amount of the tax or beer-excise involved.

In 1894 there were in Russia 1,161 breweries, which produced that year 4,621,270 hectolitres of beer, a per capita allowance of 5.6 litres for the entire population. The amount of revenue collected was $4,069,661; the amount of malt or its equivalent in other grain used was 115,531,800 kilogrammes; of hops, 1,490,000 kilogrammes. The production of hops for the same year was 3,050,000 kilogrammes.

Finland has its own system of beer taxation, which is patterned after that of Bavaria. Reliable figures are not easy to obtain, but the number of breweries and their product shows an increase. In five years, 1886–1890, the number of breweries increased from 83 to 89, and their product from 12,739,000 litres to 19,846,000 litres. In 1891 the exports of beer amounted to 28,945, the imports to 2,501 litres, and the price of beer averaged

32 francs per hectolitre. During the same year 3,633,782 kilogrammes of malt and 128,973 kilogrammes of hops were imported, and the total revenue derived from the brewing industry was 782,486 francs. In 1889 there were 1,306 people employed in breweries, of whom 268 were women.

DENMARK.

Until October 1st, 1891, beer paid no tax in Denmark; since that date an impost of 7 crowns per tun has been levied (6.98 francs per hectolitre) on all beer containing more than $2\frac{1}{4}$ per cent. of alcohol.

The industry has made notable progress since the establishment of Jacobsen's Carlsberg brewery, and a flourishing export trade has been established. In 1894 there were 231 breweries in Denmark, which produced 1,978,765 hectolitres of beer (91 litres per capita of the population), and paid a tax of about $2,568,216, consuming 51,447,900 kilogrammes of malt and 660,000 kilogrammes of hops, of which 225,000 kilogrammes were of home production.

Denmark's exports of beer in 1891 amounted to 22,259 hectolitres; imports, on which a duty of 10 öre per pott (0.966 litres) was paid, aggregated 1,505 hectolitres. The quantity of malt produced was 157,313 *meter-centners* and 33,412 *meter-centners* were imported. The average price of beer for the same year was 18 francs 54 centimes.

SWITZERLAND.

No State tax is levied on beer in Switzerland; the number of breweries in that country in 1894 being 327, and their product 1,584,216 hectolitres, equivalent to a per capita consumption of 44.2 litres. The malt consumed in these breweries amounted to 32,189,600 kilogrammes, with 460,750 kilogrammes of hops, of which 90,000 were of home production. In 1888 there were in Switzerland 22,008 retail liquor-saloons, nearly all of which sold beer, or about 7.1 per 1,000 of the population. This proportion had increased to 7.2 in 1890. In 1891 the price of beer was 23–27 francs per hectolitre; malt sold then for 34 francs per *meter-centner*, hops for 190 francs per 50 kilogrammes. The imports of malt in 1890 amounted to 233,000 *meter-centners*, of hops to 3,734 *meter-centners*. The wages paid to employés in breweries that year ranged from 700 to 1,100 francs.

HOLLAND.

The malt-liquor tax is levied on worts made for brewing exclusively from raw or unbolted cereal meal or from crushed or ground cereals (malt), either according to the capacity of the mash-tub used for brewing at the rate of 1 gulden per hectolitre, or according to the weight of the material used at the rate of $3\frac{1}{2}$ centimes per kilogramme. It is not permitted to make several brewings on the same day, selecting the capacity tax for one and the tax on the volume of material used for the other. The tax as a rule is paid as soon as the declaration is made to the revenue office. The remittance or return of the tax paid is provided for in case of accident to a brewing or when beer is exported. A duty of 3 gulden per hectolitre is imposed on imports of beer.

The production of beer in Holland, although not large, shows a tendency to increase in proportion to the population, and in 1894 the 471 breweries produced 1,496,288 hectolitres of beer (about 30 litres per capita of the population), using 38,903,400 kilogrammes of malt and 555,000 kilogrammes of hops, of which the total production was 1,490,000 kilogrammes. The amount of revenue derived from the brewing industry was $547,446.

In 1891 Holland exported 59,000 hectolitres and imported 27,000 hectolitres of malt-liquor, and imported

92,415 *meter-centners* of malt and 15,496 *meter-centners* of hops. The exports of malt and hops for the year in question amounted, respectively, to 18,344 and 6,127 *meter-centners*.

SWEDEN.

No tax is levied on the production of malt-liquors in Sweden, but imported beers in cask pay duty as follows: Ale and porter, 7 öre per litre; other kinds per litre, 5 öre. In other packages porter pays 12 öre, other beers 8 öre per litre. The average annual imports of malt-liquors amount to 4,800 hectolitres, the exports to about 700 hectolitres.

Sweden, in 1894, had 546 breweries, which produced 1,317,176 hectolitres of beer, equivalent to a per capita consumption of 44.2 litres. The quantity of malt consumed was 34,296,500 kilogrammes, of hops 557,500 kilogrammes, the production of the latter in Norway and Sweden for the year in question amounting to 320,000 kilogrammes. The average price of beer for the five years ending 1891 was 12 to 15 crowns per hectolitre, and the number of employés in breweries in 1890 was 4,550, of whom 950 were women. The average rate of wages paid to men was 780, to women 540 crowns per year. The imports of malt during the year in question amounted to 15,234 *meter-centners*, the exports to 1,199 *meter-centners*, and 4,841 *meter-centners* of hops were imported. The average price of hops for the year 1891 was $65 per *meter-centner*.

During the year 1891 the imports and exports of beer were above the average, the latter amounting to 6,467 hectolitres in cask, with 2,884 litres of porter and 34,156 litres of other beers in bottle; the imports amounted to 19,188 hectolitres of porter and 279,578 hectolitres of other beers in cask and 11,120 hectolitres of porter and 78,302 hectolitres of other beers in bottle.

NORWAY.

In Norway the barley used for malting is the object of taxation in beer production, 17.1 öre per kilogrammes being the amount of the tax. The steeping tanks are under official seal. The brewer must keep an accurate record of the barley used, and the tax is payable when the barley is weighed out.

In 1894 there were 46 breweries in Norway, the combined output of which was 529,705 hectolitres of beer, representing a per capita consumption of 21.2 litres. The tax collected amounted to 527,819 dollars; the consumption of malt was 11,772,300 kilogrammes, of hops 151,000 kilogrammes; Norway and Sweden together having produced 320,000 kilogrammes of hops. In 1891 the imports of malt amounted to 30,396 *meter-centners*, with 1,971 *meter-centners* of hops. The number of work-people employed in the breweries was 1,494, of whom 277 were women, and their average daily wages in 1890 amounted to 2.24 crowns.

The exports of beer, on which, when shipments amount to at least 4 hectolitres, a drawback of 6.6 öre per litre is allowed, aggregated, in 1891, 8,044 hectolitres. The imports, on which a duty of 17 öre per kilogramme is charged when in the wood, and 21 öre per litre in bottles, amounted, in 1891, to 581 hectolitres.

ROUMANIA.

The beer-tax in Roumania is levied on the product. No beer can be removed from breweries without the necessary permit, and a ticket or stamp must be pasted on the package, showing that the tax on the contents has been paid. The tax is paid when the removal certificate is issued, and a heavy fine is imposed for any violation of the law. The tax amounts to 1 lei 50 bauni (1 franc 50 centimes) on each ten litres of beer, without regard to quality. Beer for export is tax-free, as also that brewed for household consumption.

In 1894 Roumania had 28 breweries, which produced 271,670 hectolitres of beer, or about 2.8 litres per capita of the population, and paid 815,010 dollars tax. The consumption of malt was 6,520,000 kilogrammes, of hops 110,000 kilogrammes, all of which were imported.

The imports of beer into Roumania, averaging about 1,200 hectolitres annually, pay a duty of 30 francs per hectolitre; the exports average about 700 hectolitres a year.

SPAIN.

In 1894 there were 51 breweries in Spain, which produced 132,560 hectolitres of malt-liquors (1.3 litres per capita), and paid 55,465 dollars in beer-tax, using 3,050,900 kilogrammes of malt and 50,600 kilogrammes of hops, all imported. There is a duty of 12.50 pesetas per hectolitre on beers imported from countries with which Spain has no commercial treaty, and of 9.75 pesetas on imports from treaty nations.

There are a few small breweries in Portugal concerning which no official figures are published. The duty on beer imported into that country is very high.

SERVIA.

Servia taxes the finished product of the brewery at the rate of 12 dinar (1 dinar = 1 franc) per hectolitre, and no beer can be removed from a brewery without the proper stamp being affixed to the package.

The number of breweries in the principality in 1894 was 11, their product amounting to 101,860 hectolitres, or 2.2 litres per capita of the population. The amount of beer-tax collected was 244,464 dollars. The consumption of malt during the year was 2,695,500 kilogrammes, and of hops 37,250 kilogrammes, all imported. The value of the breweries in 1891 was placed at 2,523,000 francs, and they employed 152 persons, including 6 women.

In 1891 Servia imported 4,000 hectolitres of beer, on which a customs duty of 5 dinars per hectolitre is collected, besides the excise tax of 12 dinars.

ITALY.

The tax on malt-liquors in Italy is levied on the worts, the gravity of which is determined by the centesimal saccharometer; it amounts to 1 lire 20 centimes for each hectolitre and each saccharometric degree, 12 per cent. being deducted for loss on worts. Beer of lower gravity than 8° cannot be brewed, or if it is, will be taxed as though of this gravity, no matter how much less it weighs; the maximum gravity permitted is 16°.

Although Italy's brewing industry is in its infancy, there were in that country, in 1894, 121 breweries, in which 101,766 hectolitres of beer were produced, a per capita equivalent of 3.5 litres. 2,671,200 kilogrammes of malt were consumed and 35,400 kilogrammes of hops, all of foreign origin. The imports of malt were 12,098,000 kilogrammes, the exports 2,182,000 kilogrammes; the imports of hops 930 *meter-centners*, and the exports 238 *meter-centners*. Between 1,100 and 1,300 work-people, including about 100 women, were employed in the breweries in 1891, ordinary workmen receiving 1.75 to 2.50 francs daily and free beer; foremen, maltsters and mechanics 4 to 5 francs, and women 1 franc per day. The price of malt was about 33 to 40 francs per *meter-centner* during the year in question, without duty; hops cost from 300 to 1,200 francs per *meter-centner*, according to the harvest in Bavaria and Bohemia. In 1893 the price of beer varied from 40 to 50 francs per hectolitre.

In 1891 Italy imported 94,481 hectolitres of beer, on which, besides an impost of 9.60 lire per hectolitre, as an equivalent to the inland tax, a duty of 12 lire per hectolitre in casks and 20 lire per 100 bottles was levied. The exports of beer during this period amounted to 164 hectolitres.

GREECE.

A tax of 30 lepta (30 centimes) per oka (1.28 kilogrammes) is collected on all beer brewed in the 6 breweries of Greece, the combined output of which, in 1894, was 51,652 hectolitres, or 2.5 litres per capita. The aggregate amount of tax paid was 252,190 dollars; the brewers consumed 1,349,600 kilogrammes of malt and 22,250 kilogrammes of hops, all imported.

In 1890 Greece imported 112,203 oka of malt liquors, on which, in casks a duty of 35 lepta per oka, in bottles 60 lepta per oka, was paid in addition to the inland tax. On the exports of beer, which are inconsiderable, the tax is remitted.

BULGARIA.

In 1894 Bulgaria had 17 breweries, with a total output of 44,857 hectolitres (1.8 litres per capita). Beer is subject to a local tax only, the amount of which is 5 lew per okka (1 lew = 1 franc; 1 okka = 1,278 kilogrammes). The breweries consumed 1,186,700 kilogrammes of malt and 23,000 kilogrammes of hops, all imported, although an attempt is being made, with good promise of success, to cultivate hops in some parts of the country. The average annual imports of beer amount to about 1,500 hectolitres, on which an *ad valorem* duty of 8 per cent., with ½ per cent. added for shipments of over 200 francs' value, is collected. The exports are nominal.

CANADA.

Official reports for the year ending June 30, 1895, give the number of breweries in Canada for that year as 128, distributed as follows: Province of Ontario, 69; Province of Quebec, 19; Province of New Brunswick, 3; Province of Nova Scotia, 5; Province of Prince Edward Island, 1; Province of Manitoba, 9; Province of British Columbia, 21. The combined output of these breweries was 17,628,815 gallons, and the quantity of malt used 48,242,465 pounds. In 1891 it was estimated that the entire capital invested in plant, buildings, etc., of Canadian breweries, amounted to $6,676,682, and that 2,056 men were employed in these establishments.

The only tax on the brewing industry in Canada is levied on the malt, which pays since 1890 (when it was raised from one cent) two cents per pound. The amount of revenue derived by the Dominion government from the malt tax, for the year ending June 30, 1895, was $766,080, and the quantity of malt imported was 1,826,252 pounds. Canadian brewers must take out a wholesale dealer's license, for which they pay $50 per year, the revenue derived by the government from this source last year being $6,536.

Malt-liquors imported in bottles (6 quart or 12 pint bottles reckoned as a gallon) pay 24 cents per gallon; imported in casks or otherwise than in bottles they pay a duty of 16 cents per gallon. For 1894 Canada imported 192,752 gallons of malt-liquors in bottles, valued at $138,479, and 117,507 gallons in casks, valued at $23,705. The larger proportion of the beer in bottles came from Great Britain, most of the imports in the wood from the United States. The per capita consumption of malt-liquors in the Dominion is 3.471 gallons.

Newfoundland, which is under a government separate from that of Canada, has three breweries.

INDIA.

In British India, in 1894, there were 22 breweries, 12 of which are located in the northern mountain districts. Their product for that year amounted to 6,121,905 gallons, of which the larger portion was purchased by the government for the English troops serving in India. A tax of one anna (one cent) is levied on each gallon of beer brewed, and a low-priced license is issued to retailers of domestic beer; dealers in imported beer and alcoholic beverages pay a higher license fee. There is no import-tax on malt-liquors, and about 3,000,000 gallons are imported annually, almost wholly from Great Britain and principally on account of the military establishment. The first brewery in India was established in Mussooree in 1850; the largest brewery in the country is at Murree, and produced in 1894 upwards of 800,000 gallons of beer.

In 1893 the amount of capital employed in Indian breweries was estimated at 17,000,000 rupees. In 1891–92 there were 3,474,877 acres reported under barley, the product per acre being estimated at about 15 bushels. In Cashmere, one of the native tributary states, a commencement has been made with the cultivation of hops.

JAPAN.

The brewing industry, as we understand it, first found a footing in Japan about ten years ago, when an English stock company established the "Yokohama Brewery" in Yokohama. There are now four breweries in Japan, located, respectively, at Yokohama, Tokio, Osaka and Sappora, their combined output approximating 100,000 hectolitres. Plenty of good barley is grown in Japan, but so little hops that they are not referred to in statistics. Japan exports beer in considerable quantity to other Asiatic countries, the value of these exports in 1893 amounting to $62,595.

The breweries above mentioned are equipped with modern appliances, but they are not working to their full capacity, although the demand for their product is steadily increasing and there is a growing market in Japan for malt-liquors.

AUSTRALASIA.

New South Wales.—In 1892 there were in operation in this colony, besides some smaller establishments, 49 breweries employing more than three hands, the capital represented by their buildings, plant, etc., amounting to £702,889. They employed 745 workmen and paid wages ranging between £4. 17s. 5d. per month for brewmasters, to £2. 1s. for ordinary brewery hands, and £1. 7s. 1d. for bottlers.

An excise duty of 3 pence per gallon is levied on all beer manufactured, besides which brewers within the metropolitan area (Sydney and vicinity) pay a license fee of £30 per annum, and elsewhere £20 per annum. During 1892 the output of beer was 9,980,785 gallons.

The quantity of barley produced in the colony during the year in question was 91,701 bushels, imports were 49,248 and exports 607 bushels. No malt was made in the colony, but 369,744 bushels were imported, of which 10,308 bushels were re-exported. The imports of hops amounted to 886,982 pounds, of which 122,326 pounds were re-exported, no hops being raised in the colony.

Queensland.—During the year ended June 30, 1894, there were 19 breweries in operation in this colony, with an estimated invested capital (in 1892) of £350,000. The combined output of these establishments, 13 of which are located in the southern portion of the colony, was 3,540,132 gallons, an increase of 400,255 gallons compared with the preceding year, and they employ 212 workmen, whose average earnings are £2 per week.

No inland revenue tax is levied on malt-liquors in Queensland. Malt, of which but a very small quantity is made in the colony, pays a customs duty of 4 shillings and 6 pence per bushel; the duty on hops is 8 pence per pound. During the year 1892 the various breweries consumed 124,776 bushels of malt and 300,037 pounds of hops, none of which was raised in the colony. The production of barley was 6,969 bushels, the imports 3,559, and the exports 933 bushels. Of hops the colony imported 293,381 pounds and exported 25,826 pounds.

Western Australia had in 1893 six breweries. No revenue tax being levied on breweries, a record of their production is not available. The census of 1891 showed 36 persons employed as brewers or beer bottlers, and their average rate of wages was 6 to 8 shillings per day. In 1892, the acreage under barley was $3,665\frac{1}{4}$ acres, with a yield of about $15\frac{1}{2}$ bushels per acre. No barley was exported, but 14,461 bushels were imported. No hops were raised; the imports amounted to 75,393 pounds. A general licensed victualler's license costs from £10 to £50, according to circumstances and locality; a wine and beer retailer's license costs only £5.

South Australia.—In 1893 there were 35 breweries in operation in South Australia, but there being no special taxes on brewing or malt-liquor, the records of the industry are very incomplete. About 350 men are employed in the various breweries, their wages being approximated at 10 to 12 shillings per diem. During the year 1891 the colony produced 175,468 and imported 1,018 bushels of barley, 68,626 bushels being exported. There were also 21 acres of hops under cultivation during that year, but the results of the experiment were not made known ; 297,918 pounds of hops were imported, of which 61,555 pounds were re-exported. No licenses are required by vendors of alcoholic liquors, beer, etc., who sell exclusively in quantities of more than 5 gallons.

Tasmania had in 1892 eleven breweries employing 83 persons, the machinery and apparatus of which represented an investment of £38,097, the entire plant having been appraised in 1891 at £84,800. The output of the breweries was 1,430,932 gallons during the year in question, and the beer-duty, at the rate of 4 pence per gallon for the entire output, yielded £17,676. Besides this tax, brewers have to take out a license, annually renewable, at a cost of £12. The per capita consumption of beer for 1892 was 8.88 gallons. The average rate of wages paid to brewery employés was about 6 shillings per day of ten hours.

During the season 1892–93, Tasmania produced 80,205, imported 385,679 and exported 1,146 bushels of barley. During the same period the hop-yield was 377,885 pounds ; 65,858 pounds of hops were imported and 741,822 pounds (partly the product of previous seasons) exported.

Mexico had in 1894 several breweries, some of large capacity, located in Chihuahua, Monterey, Tolucca and Orizaba. According to a decree of May 19, 1893, a yearly sum is collected from all manufacturers of alcoholic beverages, including brewers. It amounted for the first year to $50,000.

Barbados in 1894 had one small brewery, established in 1892 and located in or near Bridgetown. There is an internal revenue tax, but no data as to the amount is available.

Jamaica.—There was a small brewery at Kingston in

1894, brewing ale, porter and ginger ale. There is no internal revenue tax.

Salvador had two small breweries in 1894 producing ginger beer and "chicha," a fermented drink made from molasses, water and pineapple juice. There is no internal revenue tax upon beer.

Brazil.—In Rio de Janeiro in 1894 there were 20 breweries, 10 of fair size, the remainder small. No internal revenue tax is collected on malt-liquors.

Chili.—In the consular district of Valparaiso there were in 1894 six breweries, mostly small plants and paying, in common with all industrial establishments, a tax levied for each year by a commissioner appointed annually by the municipality.

Hawaiian Islands.—The only brewery on the islands, located at Honolulu, was not in operation in 1894. An internal revenue tax of 5 cents per gallon is collected on malt-liquors brewed, and brewers pay an annual license fee of $150.

There are several breweries in the Argentine Republic; some owned by European companies are quite large and well-equipped; all are located in or near Buenos Aires. There are one or two breweries in and near Montevideo, Uruguay.

SCIENTIFIC STATIONS AND BREWERS' ACADEMIES.

SCIENTIFIC METHODS OF MODERN BREWERS. SCIENCE MORE THAN A MERE HANDMAID TO BREWING. BREWERS' SCHOOLS SUBSIDIZED BY GOVERNMENT. EXPERIMENTAL STATION AND SCHOOL AT BERLIN. SCIENTIFIC STATION AT MUNICH. SUBSIDIZED SCHOOLS AT WEIHENSTEPHAN, NUREMBERG AND AUGSBURG, BAVARIA, AND AT HOHENHEIM IN WURTTEMBERG. SCHOOLS AND STATIONS AT WORMS. SCHOOLS AND STATIONS AT MOEDLING, VIENNA AND PRAGUE. PUBLIC BREWERS' ACADEMY AT DOUAI, IN FRANCE. INSTITUTE AT GHENT. HANSEN'S LABORATORY AT COPENHAGEN. LABORATORIES AT LONDON. BREWERS' SCHOOL AT ZURICH. BREWERS' ACADEMIES AND SCIENTIFIC STATIONS AT NEW YORK AND CHICAGO.

In the brewing industry, more than in any other trade devoted to the production of a necessary of life, the process of manufacture has been systematically adjusted to the scientific and technical progress of our age. In this case science is vastly more, indeed, than the mere handmaid of industry; it first revolutionized antiquated methods insufficient in theory and practice, and then built up an industry as different from the former trade as the modern product is superior to the old. Formerly a slow, most conservative and easy-going tradesman, the brewer, under the influence and impetus of scientific discoveries and mechanical inventions, has become one of the most progressive, enterprising and energetic of modern manufacturers, ever ready to consult science and eager to seize upon any mechanical contrivance designed to raise the standard of his processes and product.

In this respect individual and corporate enterprise has been enhanced in many countries by material assistance freely extended by wise and enlightened governments. More fortunate than their American confrères, the European brewers, instead of being constantly harassed and persecuted by adverse legislation, enjoy the hearty support both of the people and the government, who recognize beer as one of the most wholesome beverages, a necessary of life and, withal, an efficient temperance agent. Hence, in many countries brewers' schools and experiment-stations for brewing are being assisted by munificent government subsidies, while in others the chemistry of brewing is embodied in the *curriculum* of many State institutions of learning. The reader will find below a fairly complete list of such educational and scientific establishments.

GERMANY.

Berlin.—The Experimental and Scientific Institution for Brewing has been established by German brewers under the sanction and with the assistance of the government. Fifteen hundred members of the trade contributed one million marks towards the fund required for this purpose. This exceedingly efficient institution comprises not only a laboratory for chemical analysis and research, but also a completely-equipped experimental brewery, which was erected, in 1891, at a cost of 700,000 marks, and is of such a capacity as to admit of the production of 7,000 hectolitres of beer annually. In connection with this brewery the institution operates an experimental malt-house, so that all the more important results obtained in any one of the various scientific departments of the establishment may at once be put to a practical test in the actual process of brewing and malting. The institution consists of: 1. an analytical department, conducted by Dr. O. Reinke; 2. a department of pure cultures, under the direction of Dr. P. Lindner; 3. a department of machinery, where modern inventions and improvements in the line indicated are scrutinized and tested; 4. a department of raw-materials, devoted to the improvement of hops, malt and grain;* 5. a glass-

---

* This department is in close touch with agricultural experiment stations, where scientific suggestions may be practically demonstrated and tested as to their usefulness to the trade.

blowing establishment; 6. a bureau of information; 7. a library; 8. a weekly journal, edited by Dr. Windisch and devoted to the interests of the institution and the trade. The whole of this magnificent scientific establishment is governed by Dr. M. Delbrueck.

Munich.—The Scientific Station for Brewing, founded by the German Brewers' Union in 1876, is an incorporated organization, having for its object the development of the scientific principles of brewing by systematically-conducted investigations. It also includes in its functions the analysis of brewing materials for its members, the testing of scientific instruments used in brewing and consultations concerning technical defects in the brewing practice, as far as they come within the scope of its work.

The affairs of the station are conducted and its rights and property are vested in an organization, of which brewers, brewery-managers, maltsters and other manufacturers whose business is specially connected with the equipment of breweries may become members, on payment of an entrance fee of 50 marks and annual dues of at least 100 marks. Officers and directors are elected annually at a general meeting; they have immediate charge of all operations carried on at the station and, jointly, constitute the executive committee.

The results of the investigations and experiments conducted at the station are regularly published in its organ, which is sent free to all members, and through its columns enquiries relative to brewing processes, etc., are answered. Members can also obtain the special advice or assistance of the station, for which a schedule of fees is established by the directors. Prof. Dr. Lindner, Jr., Dr. H. Will and Prof. L. Aubry, whose names have become familiar to brewers throughout the world, hold prominent positions in this institution.

Weihenstephan.—The Scientific and Technical Experiment Station, transferred to this town from its former seat at Memmingen, is subsidized by the government and subject in a measure to official supervision. Its director is Dr. Hans Vogel. This station is placed at the disposal of every Bavarian brewer. No charges other than tariff-rates are made. Lectures on important subjects of the trade are given annually in the fall and winter. Inspections of Bavarian hops and malt are made and their fitness for use in breweries are discussed. The annual dues of members are at the rate of 1 pfennig for every hectolitre of malt used by them. The minimum dues are 1 mark and the maximum 25 marks a year.

Nuremberg.—The Experimental Station in this quaint and ancient city virtually occupies the position of a public institution of learning; it is managed by Dr. Eugen Prior, under the direction and supervision of the Department of Finance of the Bavarian government. The object of the station is to promote the interests of the brewing trade by the dissemination of useful information concerning scientific research and mechanical improvements in all the various branches of the industry. The dues here are also 1 pfennig per hectolitre, not to exceed 25 marks, and not to be less than 1 mark. Foreign brewers may become members on payment of 50 marks yearly.

Augsburg, Bavaria, has a Brewers' School, founded in 1877 and conducted under municipal supervision by Dr. E. Leyser. A completely-equipped brewery and a malt-house, both on a diminutive scale, form the principal features of this very efficient establishment.

Hohenheim, Wurttemberg.—The Technological Institute of the Agricultural Academy maintains an experimental station for brewing and distilling, subsidized by the government. A chemical laboratory operated in connection with brewing and distilling establishments is so conducted as to admit of the most effective work in each branch. The officially promulgated object of this institution is to assist brewers and distillers, particularly the smaller ones, in adopting methods and processes more in harmony and keeping with scientific requirements than had theretofore been in use. The institute also analyzes raw-materials and products; tests and advises upon the usefulness of technical improvements; gives gratuitous advice to manufacturers and permits brewers of Wurttemberg (under a privilege reserved to them) to conduct experimental brewings with their own raw materials. A physiological department, recently established, enhances the great usefulness of the station. The scientists are Prof. Dr. Behrends, Drs. Schuele and Lafar.

Worms.—The Brewers' Academy at this place was founded in 1861. With the exception of the school at Weihenstephan, it is the oldest institution of the kind. Here, also, the course of study runs parallel with practical brewing and malting, and the principal tutors are practical brewers, acting under the general supervision and guidance of Dr. Schneider. There is also a brewers' school in this city, established in 1865 by the late Dr. Lehmann, and an Experimental Station for Brewing, constituted on lines similar to those of the Stations before described. "The Beer-Brewer" is the organ of this establishment.

AUSTRIA.

Moedling, near Vienna, is the seat of the Austrian Brewers' School; it is connected with the Agricultural Academy Francisco-Josephinum. Its director is Dr. Theodore v. Gohren. Theory and practice supplement each other in this, as in all the other institutions of learning before referred to. At

Vienna, Dr. Victor Grieszmayer, a recognized authority, superintends a very efficient Experimental Station for Brewing and Malting.

Prague, Bohemia.—A public school for brewing was first established in this city in 1869. In harmony with the composition of the population (German and Bohemian) and as a result of the constant friction between the two elements, this school could not but become a bi-lingual institution; but even this was not deemed a sufficiently clear demarkation and the school was, therefore, divided into a German and Bohemian department, with separate instructors for each, under the joint management of Dr. Joseph Berndt. Naturally enough, there are also two separate and distinct publications, one in German, *Der Boehmische Bierbrauer*, and another in Bohemian, *Kvas*.

The Association of the Brewing Industry of Bohemia, organized in 1873 and located in this city, devotes a great part of its means to the support of the school and an experimental station.

FRANCE.

Douai.—In 1893, after many futile efforts, a brewing academy was established in France and dedicated with appropriate ceremonies on November 12th of that year. The ancient college at Douai, having been disestablished by the government and its buildings confiscated, was devoted to the purposes of the new institution, largely endowed by popular subscriptions. A considerable part of the necessary fund was raised through the personal efforts of Mr. J. Paul Roux, publisher of the *Revue Universelle de la Brasserie et de la Malterie*. The Academy is under government control. It is devoted to the interests of the brewing, distilling and sugar manufacturing industries, and is advantageously located in the section in which the most important establishments of this character are situated.

BELGIUM.

Ghent.—The Superior Institute of Brewing, in this city, occupies a distinguished position among the famous European brewing institutions. Prof. Henry Van Laer, of the Institute, has devoted special attention to the science of fermentation, on which he is a recognized authority.

DENMARK.

Copenhagen.—At his death in 1887, J. C. Jacobsen, Sr., the philanthropic proprietor of the Alt-Carlsberg brewery, near Copenhagen, left the entire establishment, to the development of which he had devoted his life, to the Carlsberg fund, one of its objects being the maintenance of the Carlsberg Laboratory which, with the assistance of Prof. Hansen, he had founded and made famous. The laboratory was to be "devoted to scientific investigations and particularly such as might prove of value to the brewing trade." Indeed, under the able direction of Prof. Dr. E. Chr. Hansen and Joh. Kjeldahl, it has rendered the most eminent service in promoting the science of brewing.

It was as the director of the Carlsberg Laboratory that Hansen prosecuted his studies of the biology of ferments and developed his system of pure-yeast-culture that has practically revolutionized the art of brewing, thus turning to eminently practical account the investigations Pasteur had so brilliantly initiated.

The Laboratory for the Physiology and Technology of Fermentation, established and conducted by Alfred Jörgensen, at Copenhagen, also merits special attention.

Following in the footsteps of Pasteur and Hansen, the founder has made a life-study of fermentation and its organisms as applied to the fermentation industries. His writings on the subject are exceedingly valuable. Students trained in these and other branches of the science of chemistry, under his direction, are to be found in prominent breweries throughout the world.

GREAT BRITAIN AND IRELAND
have no established institutions for the study of the brewing science, their places being taken by the classes and laboratories conducted as private ventures by distinguished chemists and scientific brewers.

The Federated Institutes of Brewing, mentioned in a preceding chapter, may, in a measure, be regarded as a scientific corporation. Originally founded as the Laboratory Club (1886), its objects are: to afford facilities for intercourse between the scientific and practical members of the brewing trade. During the session (November to May) essays on suitable subjects are read and discussed. These essays, as well as abstracts and translations of technical or scientific works, are published by the Institutes' editor, Dr. A. R. Ling, under authority of the council. The corporation comprises the London Institute, the North of England Institute, Midland Counties Institute and Yorkshire Institute.

The Country Brewers' Society of England has secured the services as consulting chemists of Dr. E. R. Moritz and Dr. G. Harris Morris, both well known in connection with recent scientific works on brewing, whose advice on technical questions is freely given to members of the Society, and who, associated with Mr. Horace T. Brown, conduct an educational and analytical laboratory in London.

Similar establishments are conducted in that city by

Messrs. John Heron, Alfred C. Chapman (formerly chief demonstrator of applied chemistry at University College, London), Lawrence Briant, Dr. Salomon and others, and by Charles George Matthews (well known as one of the authors of "The Microscope in the Brewery") at Burton-on-Trent.

These and other establishments of a similar character, at which thorough instruction in chemistry as applied to brewing can be obtained, are not the only opportunities for acquiring a theoretical and practical knowledge of the art. The principals of many of the leading breweries gladly receive pupils who pay a stipulated sum for a thorough course of instruction in brewing, completing their education at one of the laboratories above referred to, or in one of the continental brewing academies.

Switzerland has an excellent Experimental Station for Brewing at Zurich, where ample means are offered for scientific research and investigation, this city being the seat of a university and technological academy.

UNITED STATES OF AMERICA.

During the Columbian Exposition at Chicago many of the scientists mentioned in the preceding educational review as authorities on the subject of brewing, visited America with a view to studying the status of the American brewing industry. Some came of their own accord, impelled by a desire to enrich their own knowledge; others, like Dr. Delbrueck, were sent here by their governments with the special instruction to familiarize themselves with and report upon the American system and its results. Their opinions, as expressed in their published works, bear testimony not only to the progressive spirit of the American brewers, but also to the purity and excellent quality of their product. It need scarcely be said that here, too, such progress would have been impossible without the aid of science.

Before the year 1880 American brewers depended more or less upon local experts, and frequently engaged graduates of European Brewers' Academies. In that year, however, Mr. A. Schwarz, even then favorably known to the trade as the translator and commentator of a standard work on brewing, established at

New York the First Scientific Station for the Art of Brewing in conjunction with a National Brewers' Academy and Consulting Bureau. The main object of the Station, as stated by the present Director, Mr. M. Schwarz, is to examine disturbances in brewing, to locate their cause and determine upon suitable remedies; also to analyze all raw materials.

The curriculum of the Academy embraces chemistry and chemical experiments; natural philosophy; technology of brewing; microscopical investigations; mechanical technology; fermentation; science of saccharometer and attenuation; mathematics.

A complete model brewery of a daily capacity of ten barrels of beer, and a pneumatic malting plant serve as adjuncts to the Academy and enable the student to combine theory with actual practice, the course of instruction being so regulated as to demonstrate and test in the brew-house what has been taught in the lecture-room. The organ of this institution is "The American Brewer."

New York.—The National Brewers' Academy and Consulting Bureau was established in 1888, by Dr. Francis Wyatt. Its objects, as briefly stated by its founder, are as follows, viz.:

"To instruct young men of good education in the modern science and art of brewing. The course includes the fundamental principles of the chemical and physical science generally; mechanics and mechanism; the practice of brewing; modern methods of fermentation and the morphology and culture of yeast; also to provide for brewers and brewery superintendents all the facilities of a completely equipped laboratory for physical, chemical and bacteriological purposes. A small annual fee entitles subscribers to the Consulting Bureau, to all the privileges of this laboratory, and to the advice and assistance of its scientific staff. Examinations and analyses of all raw materials, and intermediate and finished products and yeasts are conducted with the greatest accuracy and promptitude. The special investigations undertaken by the department of research during the past seven years have included: The value of raw grain as malt substitute; modern methods of fermentation in- vacuo; the analyses and isolation of yeast species with special reference to the cultivation of pure beer ferments."

Dr. Wyatt, a valued contributor to many scientific journals, usually publishes his essays on brewing in "The Brewers' Journal."

Chicago.—Dr. R. Wahl and Dr. Max Henius established a Scientific Station for Brewing in 1887, and the American Brewing Academy in 1891.

The objects of the Scientific Station are to aid in the progress of the art of brewing by scientific and practical researches; to assist the brewer in detecting disturbing influences leading to the production of faulty beer, ridding himself of these disturbing influences and manufacturing beer as economically as possible, without detrimentally affecting the quality of the article produced in any way.

The course of study at the Academy embraces arithmetic; chemistry and physics (with demonstrations); microscopy and bacteriology; brewing materials; saccharometry and alcoholometry; theory of malting and brewing; machinery; brewing apparatus and brewing utensils, and routine of brewing. There is also a six weeks' course in pure-yeast-culture.

A model brewery with spacious cellars, a bottling establishment and a pure-yeast-laboratory are connected with the Academy. The organ of these two establishments is the *American Brewers' Review*.

In view of the fact that the educational work performed by scientists would bear but meagre fruit without the assistance of the press, nearly every institution has, as we have seen, established its own organ. The close connection between the two educational factors renders it desirable to end this chapter with an enumeration of these and other

BREWING TRADE PERIODICALS.

Germany.—*Allgemeine Brauer und Hopfen Zeitung*, published in Nürnberg, Bavaria, official organ of the German Brewers' Union, the Bavarian, Wurttemberg and Baden Brewers' Unions and the Thuringian Brewers' Association; also the official medium for the publication of communications of all sections of the Brewers and Maltsters' Trade Society and the Brewmasters and Foreman Maltsters' Association of Germany.

Zeitschrift für das Gesammte Brauwesen, published in Munich. Organ of the Scientific Station for brewing in Munich, and of the Brewmasters' and Foreman Maltsters' Associations of Germany. Published by Professor L. Aubry, Dr. G. Holzner, aulic councillor, Dr. C. Lintner, sen., and Dr. C. T. Lintner, jr.

Wochenschrift für Brauerei, Berlin. Property of the "Association of Experimental and Scientific Institutions for Brewing." Published by Dr. Delbrück and M. Hayduck, Berlin.

Der Bierbrauer, Halle a. d. S. Founded in 1859 by G. E. Habich, published by Dr. C. Schneider and printed by Wilhelm Knapp.

Der Deutsche Bierbrauer, Stuttgart. Organ of the Practical School of Brewing in Augsburg and of the experimental station at Augsburg-Meiningen. Edited by E. Leyser, Stuttgart.

Die Deutsche Brauerzeitung, Berlin. Edited by A. Scholz, of that city.

Die Norddeutsche Brauerzeitung, Zeitschrift für Bierbrauerei, Malzfabrikation und Hopfenbau, Berlin. Editor and Publisher, B. Johannessohn, Polytechnische Buchhandlung.

"*Die Rheinisch-Westfälische Brauerzeitung*," Dortmund. Organ of the Rhenish-Westphalian Brewers' Association. Publisher, Franz Jacob Sickenberger.

Der Schwäbische Bierbrauer, Waldsee. Official organ of the Wurttemberg Brewers' Union and the III Section of the Brewing and Malting Trades' Society. Editor, A. G. Teicka; published by Siebel, Waldsee.

Elsässische Hopfen-Brauer- und Gasthaus-Zeitung. Published at Hagenau, Alsace. Organ of the Hop-Growers' Association of Alsace-Lorraine.

Die " Vereinszeitung für die Brauer in Deutschland, Oesterreich, Russland, Holland, Belgien, etc. Published in Berlin. Official organ of the Universal Brewers' Union and its foreign branches.*

Allgemeiner Anzeiger für Brauereien, Mälzereien und Hopfenbau. Chief office in Mannheim; branch office in Vienna, Austria.

Brauer und Brenner, Hamburg. Journal for the interests of workmen in breweries, distilleries and cellars.

---

* Several international brewers' congresses have been held, and this Universal Union derives its name and a somewhat phantasmal existence from such gatherings.

Brauer und Mälzer Kalender für Deutschland und Oesterreich, Stuttgart.

Austria-Hungary.—*Gambrinus,* Vienna. Edited and published by Sigmund Spitz and Adolf Lichtblau. Vienna, Edw. Schmid.

Allgemeine Zeitschrift für Bierbrauerei und Malzfabrikation, Vienna. Technical and scientific trade journal.

Oesterreichsiche Brauer- und Hopfenzeitung, Prague, Bohemia.

Der Böhmische Bierbrauer and *Kvas,* both mentioned before.

Great Britain and Ireland.—" *Brewing Trade Review,*" London. Established 1886. The official organ of the Country Brewers' Society. Owned by brewers and published in their interest monthly. Editors, J. Danvers Powers and Dr. E. R. Moritz.

" *The Brewers' Journal,*" London. Established 1895. Published on the 15th of each month.

" *Brewers' Guardian,*" London. Established 1871. Published fornightly.

" *Country Brewers' Gazette,*" London. Established 1877. Published fortnightly.

" *Northern Brewers' and Victuallers' Journal,*" Liverpool. Established 1890. Published weekly.

France.—*Le Brasseur,* Sedan. M. G. Rahon, editor.
Revue des Bières, Lille. T. P. Roux-Mutignon, editor.
Journal des Brasseurs, Lille. Puvrez-Bougois, editor.
Revue Universelle de la Brasserie et de la Malterie, Paris. Jean Paul Roux, editor.

Belgium.—*Le Petit Journal du Brasseur,* Brussels.
Le Moniteur de la Brasserie, Brussels.

United States.—*The American Brewer* (Der Amerikanische Bierbrauer), New York. Founded in 1868. Published monthly in English and German. Organ of the First Scientific Station for Brewing in the United States. M. Schwarz, editor.

The Brewers' Journal, New York. Established 1876. Published monthly in English and German. A. E. J. Tovey, editor.

Western Brewer, Chicago. Established in 1876. Published on the 15th of each month. Publishers, H. S. Rich & Co.

American Brewers' Review, Chicago. Published in English and German on the 20th of each month by Drs. Robert Wahl and Max Henius.

Der Brauer und Mälzer, Chicago. E. A. Sittig, proprietor. Published monthly in German and English.

Miscellaneous. — *Zymotechnist Tidskrift*, Copenhagen, Denmark. Edited and published by Alfred Jörgensen.

Svenska Brygareföreningen Manadsblad. Monthly organ of the Swedish Brewers' Union, published in Stockholm.

Switzerland.—*Brauerzeitung*, Zurich. Official organ of the Swiss Brewers' Union.

Australian Brewers' Journal, Melbourne, Victoria, Australia. Published on the 20th of each month. Devoted to the interests of brewers, distillers, licensed victuallers and kindred trades in Australasia.

BREWERS IN PUBLIC LIFE.

BREWERS IN THE GERMAN REICHSTAG AND BELGIAN SENATE. STATUS OF TRADE IN GREAT BRITAIN. BREWERS IN PARLIAMENT. TITLED BREWERS. BEQUEST OF BREWER JACOBSEN, OF COPENHAGEN. MUNIFICENT GIFTS BY LORDS IVEAGH, BURTON, HINDLIP, SIR ANDREW WALKER, SIR WILLIAM GILSTRAP. ANNUAL EXPENDITURE BY AMERICAN BREWERS FOR WORKS OF MERCY. EDUCATIONAL, SOCIAL AND CHARITABLE INSTITUTIONS FOUNDED OR ENDOWED BY VASSAR, MASSEY, BERGDOLL, BALLANTINE, KRUEGER, TREFZ, VOIGT, BUSCH, BURKHARDT, BECHTEL, HORRMANN, FINLAY, PABST, UIHLEIN, SCHANDEIN, SCHLITZ, SEIPP, SCHOENHOFEN, WACKER, ETC.

In public life the brewers have, as a class, maintained that enviable reputation for good citizenship, public-spirited generosity and munificent philanthropy which characterized the trade ever since the days of craft-gilds. Absurd prejudices against the trade, artificially engendered by the agitation of self-constituted moral censors, have not had any appreciable effect upon the social status of the brewers anywhere, and there is but one country (our own, unfortunately) where these prejudices sometimes succeed in politically ostracizing a capable and deserving citizen on account of his belonging to the trade.

In Germany brewers occupy many important municipal offices; in the last published register of the *Reichstag* (the German Parliament), to which the writer had access, he found among the members twelve brewers and more than three times that number in the registers of the legislative assemblies of the countries composing the German Empire. In the Netherlands, in Austria, in Belgium, etc., representatives of the brewing industry are quite as numerous in the municipal and legislative branches of the government as those of any other vocation.

Whenever legislative measures injuriously affecting the trade are threatening, we find the people siding with the brewers and compelling the government to abandon the proposed law. The average reader of newspapers is apt to look for such occurrences in England only, where a number of cabinets have succumbed to the popular opposition aroused by such measures; but they are quite as frequent in other beer-producing countries. A striking illustration is brought to mind by the recent death of M. Willems, proprietor of the Artois breweries, in Louvain, Belgium. Favorably known to the electors as an advocate of popular rights, he was elected to several important offices, which he filled with great credit to himself. He finally obtained a seat in the Belgian Senate, where he at once won fame by his successful leadership of the opposition to a proposed duty on malt. The political prominence thus won by leading the Senate majority promised a long and successful political career which was cut short, however, by his untimely demise in the winter of 1895.

So far as political power and social influence are concerned, the brewers of Great Britain and Ireland occupy an exceptional position, both by reason of their unparalleled organization and the high standing, the intellectual superiority and educational accomplishments of many of their leaders. There are now twenty-five brewers holding seats in Parliament, not counting those who belong to the House of Lords. On any question affecting the trade these representatives of the brewing industry may, according to a recent calculation based upon actual test-votes, depend upon the support of 432 members out of a total of 670, of whom only 195 are opposed to the trade and 41 doubtful.

Among the titled British brewers there are many men of most excellent qualities, who would have made their mark in any country and under any circumstances. Those more generally known among them are Lord Tweedmouth (Sir Dudley C. Marjoribanks, Bart., M. P.), who was raised to the peerage in 1881; he was a partner in Meux's Brewery Co., London. In 1894 he was succeeded by the second baron, his son, the Rt. Hon. E. Majoribanks, who, in addition to being a partner in the brewery, was a Privy Councellor, Member of Parliament and an active government "whip." Lord Burton (Mr. Michael Thomas Bass), Member of Parliament, head of the great brewing firm of Bass, Ratcliffe & Gretton, was created a peer with this title in 1886. In 1891 Sir Edward Guinness, Bart., head of the famous brewing firm of A. Guinness, Sons & Co., Dublin, was created a peer, with the title of Lord Iveagh. Hon. Samuel C. Allsopp, Member of Parliament, succeeded as second baron to the title of Lord Hindlip, created in 1886. He is the head of the celebrated brewing firm of S. Allsopp & Sons, Burton-on-Trent. Besides these, there are the following titled brewers, viz: Sir Gilbert Greenall, Bart. (Greenall & Co., Warrington); Sir Peter C. Walker, Bart. (P. Walker & Co., Warrington and Burton-on-Trent); Sir Thomas Fowell Buxton, Bart. (Truman, Hanbury & Buxton, London); Sir Harry Bullard (Bullard & Sons, Norwich); Sir William Gilstrap, Bart., who died February 15th, 1896 (of Gilstrap, Earp & Co., maltsters); Sir John Austin, Sir Reginald Hanson, Sir F. Milner and several others.

In charitable work of a private character, as in public benefactions, the brewers compare favorably with any other industry; it is doubtful, indeed, whether, according to the number of men engaged in it, any other trade has produced so many genuine philanthropists. Such bequests, for example, as that of Jacob Christian Jacobsen, of Carlsberg, Denmark, who, in the interest of science, left the whole of his immense establishment to the people of his country, are rare indeed. This splendid man, who with marvelous energy increased his annual sales from 4,000 hectolitres, in 1847, to 300,000 hectolitres, in 1887, seemed to have no other thought but the welfare of his people and the advancement of science. By his will he created a fund for the national support of men of science, the encouragement of scientific progress, the improvement of the Museum of Natural History in Frederiksborg and the maintenance of the famous Carlsberg Laboratory, devoted to experiment and research in the science of brewing. Nothing could show more clearly the sterling character of this man than a passage in his will, which reads:

"In the operation of the Carlsberg brewery, the invariable object shall be to attain the greatest possible excellence of the product without regard to present profits, so that this brewery and its output may serve as a model and by its example maintain Denmark's brewing industry in a high and creditable position."

Lord Iveagh (head of the firm of A. Guinness, Sons & Co., Dublin, Ireland) founded the Guinness Trust of $1,200,000 for the erection of houses in Dublin and London for the deserving poor. He expended a fortune on the restoration of St. Patrick's Cathedral, in Dublin, and has always been a bountiful contributor to deserving charities.

Lord Burton, head of the firm of Bass, Ratcliffe & Gretton, Burton-on-Trent, has been a liberal donor to public charities and improvements in that city. With his father, the late M. T. Bass, he defrayed the cost of erecting for his native city a new town-hall, assembly-room and library, the total cost of the buildings alone being about $900,000.

Lord Hindlip and his father, the first Lord, have been liberal contributors to the improvement of Burton-on-Trent, some of its finest public buildings and institutions having been founded and endowed by these public-spirited brewers.

Sir Andrew Walker, deceased, a leading brewer of Liverpool, built and endowed a fine picture gallery, which, with a costly collection of works of art, he presented to that city.

Sir William Gilstrap, Bart., of Gilstrap & Earp, maltsters, Newark-on-Trent, endowed and presented to that town a fine public library.

These few instances, taken at random from a long list of similar benefactions, convey but a faint idea of the brewers' liberality, for the major part of their works of charity elude alike observation and computation. No other industry is more frequently called upon for help and none responds to such calls more liberally than the brewing trade. To assist in building schools and churches, endowing colleges, securing permanent homes for social organizations, erecting monuments to the great men of the nation, helping deserving students and struggling scientists and artists, caring for the physical welfare of their own workmen and providing for their widows and orphans—to do all these things and many others like them, seems to be regarded by the average brewer as a common-place duty brooking no evasion.

In our own country, evidences of such noble work abound in every city where brewing has gained a firm foothold, and it is not an exaggeration to say that a sum of over $1,000,000 is annually expended by brewers for charitable purposes. The writer determined to have an accurate basis for an estimate of such expenditures and, therefore, addressed pertinent inquiries to every brewer in the land. The replies received warrant the above statement as to the aggregate amount thus expended annually for educational, charitable and social purposes. This should be borne in mind when an attempt is to be made to compare public benefactions by American brewers with the bequests and donations of their European confrères. In addition to this, one ought not to lose sight of the fact that our brewing industry, although as old as American civilization, only began to develop within the past thirty-three years, and that a majority of the present prosperous establishments are still conducted by the very men who a few decades ago started out in life and trade with nothing more than a thorough knowledge of their calling, abundance of energy and an indomitable desire to conquer adverse circumstances. In 1862 the output of all the breweries operated in the United States amounted to less than the production of the London breweries two hundred years ago; even the very largest establishments produced not even half the quantity which is now rated as a moderate output for the average small brewery.

The rapid growth of the industry began about twenty-five years ago; another quarter-century will furnish more conspicuous evidences of the brewers' philanthropy than we have at present.

In surveying the work of American brewers in this line, attention is at once attracted to Vassar College, the very first collegiate institution based on the principle, now universally recognized, of the intellectual equality of both sexes. By founding this splendid college and endowing it with sufficient means to secure its unhampered development, Matthew Vassar, the simple brewer of Poughkeepsie, has done more for the cause of woman's intellectual emancipation than any combination of men and women could have accomplished by a century of mere platform-agitation. We saw it stated somewhere that, in establishing the college, Vassar was not guided by any special educational theory, but that "his motive was one of general philanthropy." Strangely enough, the same writer explicitely avers that Vassar's desire was to "found and perpetuate an institution which should accomplish for women what our colleges are accomplishing for young men." It would be difficult, most assuredly, to imagine a grander educational theory than the one here expressed.

Vassar belonged to that class of struggling brewers who at the beginning of our century carried on their trade in the smaller towns under great difficulties and in the most primitive manner, often combining in their own persons both manufacturer and peddler. P. H. Smith, the historian of Dutchess County, probably exaggerates matters very considerably when he claims that Vassar " brewed ale, *a barrel at a time,* and carried it through the streets himself to deliver to his customers;" but there can be no doubt, judging from several inventories of similar early brewing plants in the towns along the Hudson, that in 1810, when Vassar started in business, his brewery was small enough to be manipulated by one man. Fifty-one years later he devoted a very large proportion of his wealth to the founding of this college and added to the sum from time to time until his donations and bequests amounted to $800,000.

William Massey, of Philadelphia, another ale-brewer of the old school, gave $100,000 to the House of Refuge, a State institution then located in his city, but since removed to the adjoining county of Delaware. His contributions to other educational and charitable institutions amount to $150,000; while Louis Bergdoll, of the same city, donated in the aggregate about $200,000 for like purposes.

The splendid gymnasium of Rutgers College, at New Brunswick, owes its existence to the munificence of Robert F. Ballantine, the head of the brewing firm of P. Ballantine & Sons, of Newark, N. J. Gottfried Krueger, of the same city, founded a home for aged men and women; he is also one of the founders of the

German hospital, and has given nearly $200,000 to other charitable, educational and social institutions. Mrs. E. Trefz, also of Newark, founded a training school for hospital nurses. E. W. Voigt donated to the people of Detroit, Mich., a park comprising nine acres, located in what is rapidly becoming the finest residential part of that beautiful city. Adolphus Busch, of the Anheuser-Busch Brewing Company, created and maintains the German chair at the Washington University of St. Louis, contributed largely to this and other educational institutions and donated twenty acres of land for an asylum conducted by the Sisters of the Good Shepherd.

Brooks Farm, once the home of a distinguished company of intellectual giants—a tract of land made famous the world over by its association with such names as Hawthorne, Margaret Fuller, Dana, Ripley, etc.—could not have been given over to a nobler object than that to which the late Gottlieb F. Burkhardt, a brewer of Boston, devoted it, when he donated the whole of the land, about 180 acres, to the Evangelical Lutheran Church for works of mercy. The place has been converted into an orphans' home, in which the Burkhardt family continue to take the deepest interest. The late August Horrmann and George Bechtel, both of Stapleton, S. I., were co-founders of the Staten Island Academy. The widow of the latter founded the Bechtel Ward in Smith's Infirmary. Col. William J. Finlay, founder of the Finlay Brewing Co., of Toledo, O., one of the many patriotic brewers who served their country in a military capacity, erected and gave to his city a beautiful monument dedicated to the memory of his friend General J. B. Stedman, the hero of Chicamauga. At his death he bequeathed $180,000 to charitable and educational institutions of his city. Captain Pabst, of the Pabst Brewing

Company, Milwaukee, erected and helps to maintain a handsome German theatre; his late partner, E. Schandein, gave a beautiful park to his native city, and endowed several educational institutions. The Schlitz Brewing Company, of the same city, expended a large sum of money for a Conservatory of Music, and when adverse circumstances impeded the development of this artschool, they turned the property over to the Society for Ethical Culture, free of rent. Brewers Conrad Seipp, Peter Schoenhofen and Frederick Wacker, all of Chicago, gave to charitable institutions $180,000, $75,000 and $50,000, respectively.

Many other similar evidences of philanthropy might be cited, but as they are not of a public character it would be indiscreet and contrary to the explicit wishes of the donors to mention them in this place. It may suffice to say that in the older communities a disproportionately large share of the money required for maintaining charitable, social and educational institutions, other than those supported by public funds, is contributed by brewers; while in the younger communities where brewing has gained a foothold, particularly in those of the Northeast, there is not a church, asylum, hospital, music-hall, etc., to the erection of which brewers have not contributed large sums.

Concerning the attitude of American brewers in matters of public import and interest, we shall in the following chapters find ample opportunity to cite historical evidences of sufficient weight to convince even the most sceptical of the truth of the opening lines of this chapter.

HISTORY OF THE UNITED STATES BREWERS' ASSOCIATION.

Chapter I.

STATUS OF AMERICAN BREWING BEFORE 1862. THREE PERIODS OF DEVELOPMENT AND TWO PERIODS OF DECADENCE. BREWING ENCOURAGED AND EXTENSIVELY PRACTICED IN COLONIAL DAYS; ITS FLOURISHING CONDITION. UNFAVORABLE CONDITIONS AND VASCILLATING FISCAL POLICY CONSPIRE WITH GROWING RUM-HABIT TO STAY GROWTH OF BREWING. DECADENCE. REVIVAL OF BREWING UNDER FIRST FEDERAL EXCISE SYSTEM. THE ERA OF FREE-RUM; DECADENCE OF BREWING. INTRODUCTION OF LAGER-BEER. RAPID DEVELOPMENT OF BREWING FROM 1842 TO 1862; A FEW COMPARATIVE DATA AS TO ITS GROWTH. OUTBREAK OF THE REBELLION. REVENUE-QUESTION. PROPOSED INTERNAL REVENUE SYSTEM. REPORT OF COMMITTEE ON WAYS AND MEANS. BREWERS FEEL NEED OF ORGANIZING. JOHN N. KATZENMAYER'S AGITATION AND CONSEQUENT ORGANIZATION OF THE NEW YORK BREWERS. CALL FOR NATIONAL CONVENTION OF BREWERS. TEXT OF LAW OF 1862. FIRST CONVENTION OF UNITED STATES BREWERS' ASSOCIATION. PERMANENT ORGANIZATION. DISCUSSION ON REVENUE-QUESTIONS. CORRESPONDENCE WITH TREASURY DEPARTMENT AS TO SEVERAL IMPORTANT POINTS. APPOINTMENT OF COMMITTEES. RESOLUTIONS AND REMONSTRANCES AS TO PAYMENT OF CERTAIN TAXES AND REGARDING BONDS, ENTRIES, ETC. CHARACTER OF PERMANENT ORGANIZATION. ADJOURNMENT.

A brief sketch of the state of American brewing before the organization of the Brewers' Association will doubtless interest all those readers who are not familiar with the historical works on this subject.*

The history of the trade presents three distinct periods of development and two periods of decadence. In early Colonial days it received considerable attention and fostering care from law-makers and executive officers. It was then a highly-honored occupation, favored and encouraged by the best people and practiced by the most respectable citizens. Many

---

* "Colonial Liquor Laws" and "Liquor Laws of the United States," both by G. Thomann.

of the latter's present-day descendants, who often parade ensigns armorial born of a fictitious heraldry, may find it rather difficult to reconcile their ancestral pride and aristocratic pretensions with their contempt for a trade which gave bread to their forefathers.

Household brewing and commercial brewing progressed abreast in Colonial days, and the laws regulating both, conceived in the somewhat paternal spirit peculiar to that period and not altogether discarded in our own time, prove beyond a doubt that, while economic and fiscal requirements were not ignored, moral and hygienic considerations determined the nature and scope of all legislative measures favoring the production of beer and its constitutent raw-materials. Unfortunately, the lack of a consistent policy and the conflicting elements of experimental legislation frustrated in many instances the manifest purpose of the lawmakers; yet, in spite of all impediments, brewing flourished for a time in all the colonies north of Maryland, until it was fairly smothered, one might say, by an excess of well-meant, but very much misapplied protection. Thus, for instance, in some colonies prohibitive duties were imposed upon imported malt for the express purpose of promoting domestic malting. Imported malt could be obtained at a much lower price than the domestic article; yet the brewer, although now virtually compelled to use the more expensive commodity produced at home, was not allowed to raise the price of his beer accordingly, the law-makers prescribing a maximum price much below the actual cost of the product. The result could not but be a temporary cessation of commercial brewing, followed by more experimental legislation designed to correct the unintentional error. Colonial liquor laws offer abundant evidence of similar mistakes which countervailing advantages might probably have rendered harmless, if our trade with the West Indies, yielding rum or its raw-material, had not counteracted the law-makers' obvious object and the people's former predilection for malt-liquors. Subsequently, rich harvests of grain, for which a ready market could not always be found, led to rural distillation, and this added to the weight that effectually handicapped brewing. The industry, which under the influence of wise legislation and judicious encouragement had grown to a considerable extent, began to stagnate and had almost ceased to exist before the middle of the second century of Colonial rule. The most generous legislative encouragement, such, for instance, as an act of the General Court of Massachusetts* exempting beer, brewing-plants and brewery buildings and premises from any taxation whatsoever, could not change this state of affairs.

Brewing was again revived and flourished for a time toward the end of the eighteenth century through the effects of the Federal excise-system which placed a considerable fiscal restraint upon rural distilleries, but resulted in the Whiskey-Rebellion. During the Congressional discussion upon this subject—a detailed account of which is contained in our "Colonial Liquor Laws"—a large majority of the speakers strongly advocated the encouragement of the brewing industry. After a comparatively brief space of time, this indirectly restrictive system made room for what is known as the free-whiskey policy, and then brewing again relapsed into its former highly unsatisfactory condition.

The introduction of lager-beer, in 1842, changed the aspect of things very considerably. An enormous influx

---

* The following sentence of the preamble clearly demonstrates the spirit of this act, viz.: "Whereas, the wholesome qualities of malt-liquors greatly recommend them to general use, as an important means of preserving the health of the citizens of this commonwealth, and of preventing the pernicious effect of spirituous liquors."

of immigrants, almost exclusively accustomed to the use of fermented beverages, imparted to the trade a powerful impetus during the succeeding twenty years—a period also remarkable for the nature and extent of the prohibitory movement and a parallel temperance agitation favoring the use of malt-liquors and aimed especially against the excessive use of ardent spirits. At the outbreak of the war of the rebellion, prohibitory efforts ceased entirely. The stay-at-home advocates of prohibition were silenced by the patriotism of their most vigorous opponents, the German-Americans, who, regardless of former political affiliations, upheld as a body the principles of the Republican party; while two hundred thousand of them voluntarily joined the ranks of the Union army before the days of bounties and conscriptions.

Statistical information concerning the three periods of development, roughly outlined in the foregoing sketch, are difficult to obtain. In colonial days, brewing in households and by tapsters prevailed to a considerable extent, but accurate estimates as to the quantities of malt-liquors produced and consumed are not available; even the output of the "common brewers" is a matter of mere conjecture. What we do know, however, is that the people of all classes and conditions used malt-liquors. In the Colonies of New-Plymouth and Massachusetts-Bay, tavern-keepers were compelled to keep beer, and common brewers and maltsters, usually men of distinguished standing in the community, received special encouragement and economic protection. In Connecticut, "a brew-house was regarded as an essential part of a homestead," and public brewing was specially favored. Governor Kieft established a public brewery in New York, and at Albany the Patroons monopolized public brewing.

Penn encouraged the industry in Pennsylvania and himself erected a brewery. In Rhode Island, a brewhouse was erected and conducted by the Commonwealth. In the Swedish settlements on the Delaware, brewing had early gained a foothold and was fostered in some measure after the Dutch conquest. The proprietors of East and West Jersey, particularly Deputy-Governor Gowen Lowrie, took the initiative in introducing malting and brewing. Governor Oglethorpe erected several breweries in Georgia, to the end that his prohibition of the use of ardent spirits might be carried out all the more effectually. Thus fostered by the authorities, brewing flourished as we have stated, in the earlier colonial periods, and from approximate estimates based upon various available data (such as tapsters' licenses, &c.), we may safely draw the conclusion that the annual consumption of malt-liquors amounted to twenty gallons per capita. Between this time and the second revival of brewing, the production dwindled to an insignificant figure. The time during which Hamilton's excise-system remained in force was too short to afford sufficient opportunity for anything like the former development of the industry. It is true, one of the incidental objects of the revenue-law was, as Hamilton stated, the encouragement and protection of the manufacture of malt-liquors, but countervailing conditions and influences frustrated this object. As to this point, it may be admissible to quote the following from our history of the subject, viz.:—

"It was surely not anticipated, and could not reasonably be expected that such a change of habits and tastes, as seemed necessary to popularize the use of fermented liquors, could be effected within one or two decades; furthermore, it must have been foreseen, that the manufacture of these beverages would at first be confined to certain localities, and depend for its prosperity upon the character and composition of the population. That the brewing industry progressed

The State of Brewing Before 1862.

considerably in those localities where it was introduced, shortly before and after the Revolution, is evidenced by a number of circumstances. As early as 1807 the production of malt-liquors, according to Gallatin's statement, was nearly equal to the consumption, yet the importation of malt into Pennsylvania had already ceased in 1793, thus showing that the adjuncts of brewing in the large establishments were rapidly being perfected."

The statistical data as to production or consumption during this period are very meagre, and the only means of approximately determining the condition of brewing are contained in the Digest of Manufactures of 1810, from which we compiled for a former publication the following table :—

States and Territories.	Population.	Number of Breweries.	Beer, Ale and Porter in Barrels of 31¼ Gallons.	Value.
Massachusetts	700,745	....	22,400	$86,450
New York	959,049	42	66,896	340,766
New Jersey	245,562	6	2,170	17,229
Pennsylvania	810,091	48	71,273	376,072
Delaware	72,674	2	476	7,616
Maryland	380,546	7	9,330	69,380
Virginia	979,622	7	4,251	23,898
Ohio	230,760	13	1,116	5,712
Georgia	252,433	1	1,878	11,268
District of Columbia	24,023	3	2,900	17,400
	4,655,505	129	182,690	$955,791

As to the progress of brewing from the time of the introduction of lager-beer (1842) to the year 1862, inclusive, we may form an adequate idea from two data derived from two different sources, namely, the Census of 1850 and the first report of the Commissioner of Internal Revenue. According to the former document, the production of beer amounted to 750,500 barrels in 1850, an increase of 567,810 barrels as compared with the production of beer in 1810. Three-fourths of this quantity was produced in the States of New York and Pennsylvania. In 1863 the production of beer amounted to 2,596,803 barrels, an increase of 2,028,993 barrels as compared with the production of the year 1850. New York and Pennsylvania produced one-half of this quantity. In the meantime, brewing—practically confined to 7 States and Territories in 1810—had gained a foothold in 31 States and Territories, and in some of the Western States assumed very considerable proportions.

Between 1842 and 1863 brewing had developed so rapidly and became so firmly established that it could, doubtless, have held its own ground successfully, even without discriminating legislation; but, on the other hand, it is quite certain that without such legislation it would never have become a national beverage, nor would its progress during the past thirty-five years have been what it actually is. Hence, the introduction of the internal-revenue system really proved a blessing to the trade, not only on this account, but also because it called into existence the *United States Brewers' Association*.

The first revenue law passed after the outbreak of the war, although based upon a treasury-report (July, 1861) showing an estimated deficit for the ensuing year (1861–62) of about $280,000,000, did not include excise taxes of any kind. It was generally known, however, that the Secretary of the Treasury had recommended them and that Congress failed to act on this recommendation, supported by a favorable report from the proper committee, only because a just and practicable system could not be agreed upon in so short a time without detailed information as to the nature and extent of the various objects upon which it was contemplated to impose the new tax. To meet this requirement, the Committee on Ways and Means had been instructed to prepare a suitable scheme. A subsequent report of the Secretary of the Treasury (December, 1861), conceived in a spirit of sanguine hopefulness as to the speedy termination of the war, seemed to render the work of this Committee unnecessary, the Secretary believing that a loan to the amount of $200,000,000, and an increase of direct taxes upon incomes, lands and houses, together with increased import-duties, would fully cover the prospective revenue deficiency. Notwithstanding this seemingly favorable state of affairs, the Committee continued its investigations with commendable zeal, giving exhaustive hearings to representatives of the various industries and commercial interests included in the proposed tax system.

At this juncture the brewers throughout the country probably felt more than ever the necessity of organizing, and there are many evidences of several sporadic and desultory attempts in that direction made by brewers in various parts of the country. Fortunately for the trade, the great principle of furthering temperate drinking-habits by substituting malt-liquors for ardent-spirits found many advocates in Congress and outside of it, and they, with several brewers who were on terms of intimate friendship with members of Congress, succeeded in frustrating inimical schemes launched against brewing by people of prohibitory proclivities, whose openly-avowed purpose it was to tax the manufacture to death. The Congressional discussion on the subject revealed a strong desire on the part of the ablest and most influential legislators to stimulate and foster the brewing industry, and even many of those members who, because representing Prohibition States, were supposed to be utterly opposed to the entire traffic, showed a laudable willingness to establish a broad discrimination in favor of malt-liquors. The general conviction that for moral and hygienic reasons the manufacture of wine and beer should receive whatever protection a discriminating tax-system could possibly afford, was no doubt strengthened by an official report on the sanitary condition of the camps of the Union army, showing exceptional healthfulness of those troops who freely used malt-liquors.

When the Ways and Means Committee finally presented their report (March 3rd, 1862), embodying a complete system of internal revenue, the provisions relating to the tax on fermented liquors realized all reasonable expectations of the friends of the trade, so far as the discrimination before referred to was concerned. The mode of collection and the safeguards against possible evasions of the law appear to have received less attention, however, than the importance of these questions demanded. A great latitude of discretionary power was (perhaps, intentionally) left to the executive officers whose experiences in regulating the system were probably expected to point out defects and shortcomings.

Under such circumstances the co-operation of all brewers became an absolute necessity. The new law received executive sanction on the 1st of July, 1862; a few days later, John N. Katzenmayer, a political refugee, formerly a wealthy banker, whom the German revolution of 1848 had driven from his native city on the banks of Lake Constance, and who had found occupation in the brewing firm of A. Schmid & Co., addressed a strong appeal to the brewers of New York City and vicinity, urging them to consider the advisibility of

New York Brewers Organize.

federating all brewers and kindred trades into one great national combination for the purpose of protecting their common interests and ensuring a uniform, faithful and conscientious obedience to the new law throughout the whole land. He clearly foresaw and appreciated the difficulty of organizing a national association without having first established a local nucleus in one of the larger beer-producing centers of the country, and he therefore strove at the very beginning to bring about a close and strong union between the brewers of the sister-cities New York, Brooklyn and Williamsburg and the adjoining suburban communities. Questions of a purely local character greatly assisted him in this undertaking. The brewers, for instance, had for years been victimized by delinquent debtors and everyone recognized the impossibility of remedying this evil without co-operation; the system of collecting empty packages was utterly imperfect and nothing short of a general agreement by all brewers could guard against losses arising from this source. Many similar matters, demanding prompt action, formed the subjects of discussion at the informal meetings and consultations brought about by Katzenmayer's circular letter, and in one of them it was finally decided to call a general meeting of all brewers doing business in New York and vicinity and to submit then and there the draft of a constitution.

This meeting was held on the 21st of August, 1862, in Pythagoras Hall, 134 Canal Street, New York. James Speyers, of Speyers & Bernheimer, presided and John N. Katzenmayer acted as secretary. Thirty-seven brewing firms were represented. A permanent organization was at once effected, and the local questions before referred to received due attention. At the very next general meeting, held on the 4th of September, a general discussion on the subject of internal revenue and the want of reliable information as to the practical operation of the law and the regulations promulgated for its enforcement led the way to the adoption of a resolution appointing a committee for the purpose of securing legal aid and advice in regard to several doubtful points, and of conferring with the Commissioner of Internal Revenue as to his interpretation of certain clauses of the law. At the same time a motion prevailed, declaring it to be the sense of the meeting that the officers should consider and report upon the advisability of calling a national convention of brewers. At a meeting held on the 23rd of October (the officers having in the meantime ascertained by correspondence with brewers in other States that this proposition was favorably received in every part of the Union), the local association adopted a resolution, in German, of which the following is a literal translation, viz: "*Resolved that a national congress of all members of our trade, and of delegates of brewers' associations wherever such associations exist, be held in Pythagoras Hall, in the city of New York, on the 12th of November, 1862, at 2 o'clock, P. M.; and that a committee of fourteen be elected, who together with the president and secretary shall make suitable arrangements both for the holding of said congress and the proper entertainment of its members.*"

The first convention committee was composed as follows: O. Johns, J. F. Betz and Limburger for New York; Schnadderbeck and Seitz for Long Island; Geo. Brueckner and W. Nopper for Morrisania and Melrose; Schweitzer and Kohler for Unionhill; Boppe, Lorenz and Schalk for Newark; John Bechtel for Staten Island; Speyers and Katzenmayer ex-officio.

To the end that the work of this committee in connection with the transactions of the first convention may be fully understood and appreciated, it is necessary to present here those provisions of the Act of July 1st, 1862, which relate to malt-liquors.

SEC. 50. *And be it further enacted*, That on and after the first day of August, eighteen hundred and sixty-two, there shall be paid on all beer, lager beer, ale, porter, and other similar fermented liquors by whatever name such liquors may be called, a duty of one dollar for each and every barrel containing not more than thirty-one gallons, and at a like rate for any other quantity or for fractional parts of a barrel, which shall be brewed or manufactured and sold or removed for consumption or sale within the United States or the Territories thereof, or within the District of Columbia, after that day; which duty shall be paid by the owner, agent, or superintendent of the brewery or premises in which such fermented liquors shall be made, and shall be paid at the time of rendering the accounts of such fermented liquors as chargeable with duty, as required to be rendered by the following section of this act : *Provided*, That fractional parts of a barrel shall be halves, quarters, eighths, and sixteenths, and any fractional part containing less than one-sixteenth, shall be accounted one-sixteenth ; more than one-sixteenth, and not more than one-eighth shall be accounted one-eighth ; more than one-eighth, and not more than one-quarter, shall be accounted one-quarter ; more than one-quarter, and not more than one-half, shall be accounted one-half ; more than one-half, shall be accounted one barrel.

SEC. 51. *And be it further enacted*, That every person who, on said first day of August, eighteen hundred and sixty-two, shall be the owner or occupant of any brewery or premises used or intended to be used for the purpose of brewing or making such fermented liquors, or who shall have such premises under his control or superintendence, as agent for the owner or occupant, or shall have in his possession or custody any vessel or vessels intended to be used on said premises in the manufacture of beer, lager beer, ale, porter, or other similar fermented liquors, either as owner, agent, or otherwise, shall from day to day, enter or cause to be entered in a book to be kept by him for that purpose, and which shall be open at all times, except Sundays, between the rising and setting of the sun, for the inspection of said collector, who may take any minutes or memorandum or transcripts thereof, the quantities of grain, or other vegetable productions or other substances, put into the mash-tub, or otherwise used for the purpose of producing beer, or for any other purpose, and the quantity or number of barrels and fractional parts of barrels of fermented liquors made and sold, or removed for consumption or sale, keeping separate account of the several kinds and descriptions ; and shall render to said collector, on the first day of each month in each year, or within ten days thereafter, a general account, in writing, taken from his books, of the quantities of grain, or other vegetable productions or other substances, put into the mash-tub, or otherwise used, for the purpose of producing beer, or for any other purpose, and the quantity or number of barrels and fractional parts of barrels of each kind of fermented liquors made and sold, or removed for consumption or sale, for one month preceding said day; and shall verify or cause to be verified the said entries, reports, books, and general accounts, on oath or general affirmation, to be taken before the collector or some officer authorized by the laws of the State to administer the same according to the form required by this Act where the same is prescribed; and shall also pay to the said collector the duties which, by this Act, ought to be paid on the liquor made and sold, or removed for consumption or sale, and in the said accounts mentioned, at the time of rendering the account thereof, as aforesaid. But where the manufacturer of any beer, lager beer or ale, manufactures the same in one collection district, and owns or hires a depot or warehouse for the storage and sale of such beer, lager beer, or ale, in another collection district, he may, instead of paying to the collector of the district where the same was manufactured the duties chargeable thereon, present to such collector or his deputy an invoice of the quantity or number of barrels about to be removed for the purpose of storage and sale, specifying in such invoice, with reasonable certainty, the depot or warehouse in which he intends to place such beer, lager beer, or ale; and thereupon such collector or deputy shall indorse on such invoice his permission for such removal, and shall at the same time transmit to the collector of the district in which such depot or warehouse is situated a duplicate of such invoice; and thereafter the manufacturer of the beer, lager beer, or ale so removed shall render the same account, and pay the same duties, and be subject to the same liabilities and penalties as if the beer, lager beer, or ale so removed had been manufactured in the district. The Commissioner of Internal Revenue may prescribe such rules as he may deem necessary for the purpose of carrying the provisions of this section into effect.

SEC. 52. *And be it further enacted*, That the entries made in the books required to be kept by the foregoing section shall, on said first day of each and every month, or within ten days thereafter, be verified by the oath or affirmation, to be taken as aforesaid, of the person or persons by whom such entries shall have been made, which oath or affirmation shall be certified at the end of such entries by the collector or officer administering the same, and shall be, in substance, as follows: "I do swear (or affirm) that the foregoing entries were made by me on the respective days specified, and that they state, according to the best of my knowledge and belief, the whole quantity of fermented liquors either brewed or brewed and sold at the brewery owned by ———, in the county of ———, amounting to ——— barrels."

SEC. 53. *And be it further enacted*, That the owner, agent, or superintendent aforesaid shall, in case the original entries required to be made in his books shall not have been made by himself, subjoin to the oath or affirmation the following oath or affirmation, to be taken as aforesaid : "I do swear (or affirm) that, to the best of my knowledge and belief, the foregoing entries are just and true, and that I have taken all the means in my power to make them so."

SEC. 54. *And be it further enacted*, That the owner, agent, or superintendent of any vessel or vessels used in making fermented liquors, or of any still, boiler, or other vessel used in the distillation of spirits on which duty is payable, who shall neglect or refuse to make true and exact entry and report of the same, or to do, or cause to be done, any of the things by this act required to be done as aforesaid, shall forfeit for every such neglect or refusal all the liquors and spirits made by or for him, and all the vessels used in making the same, and the stills, boilers, and other vessels used in distillation, together with the sum of five hundred dollars, to be recovered with costs of suit; which said liquors or spirits, with the vessels containing the same, with all the vessels used in making the same, may be seized by any collector of internal duties, and held by him until a decision shall be had thereon according to law : *Provided*, That such seizure be made within thirty days after the cause for the same may have occurred, and that proceedings to enforce said forfeiture shall have been commenced by such collector within twenty days of the seizure thereof. And the proceedings to enforce said forfeiture of said property shall be in the nature of a proceeding *in rem*, in the circuit or district court of the United States for the district where such seizure is made, or in any other court of competent jurisdiction.

SEC. 55. *And be it further enacted*, That in all cases in which the duties aforesaid, payable on spirituous liquors distilled and sold, or removed for consumption or sale, or beer, lager beer, ale, porter, and other similar fermented liquors, shall not be paid at the time of rendering the account of the same, as herein required, the person or persons chargeable therewith shall pay, in addition, ten per centum on the amount thereof ; and, until such duties with such addition shall be paid, they shall be and remain a lien upon the distillery where such liquors have been distilled, or the brewery where such liquors have been brewed, and upon the stills, boilers, vats, and all other implements thereto belonging, until the same shall have been paid ; and in case of refusal or neglect to pay said duties, with the addition, within ten days after the same shall have become payable, the amount thereof may be recovered by distraint and sale of the goods, chattels, and effects of the delinquent ; and, in case of such distraint, it shall be the duty of the officer charged with the collection to make, or cause to be made, an account of the goods, chattels, or effects which may be distrained, a copy of which, signed by the officer making such distraint, shall be left with the owner or possessor of such goods, chattels, or effects, at his, her, or their dwelling, with a note of the sum demanded, and the time and place of sale; and said officer shall forthwith cause a notification to be published in some newspaper, if any there be, within the county, and publicly posted up at the post office nearest to the residence of the person whose property shall be distrained, or at the court-house of the same county, if not more than ten miles distant, which notice shall specify the articles distrained, and the time and place proposed for the sale thereof, which time shall not be less than ten days'from the date of such notification, and the place proposed for sale not more than five miles distant from the place of making such distraint: *Provided*, That in every case of distraint for the payment of the duties aforesaid, the goods, chattels, or effects so distrained may and shall be restored to the owner or possessor if, prior to the sale thereof, payment or tender thereof shall be made to the proper officer charged with the collection, of the full amount demanded, together with such fee for levying and advertising, and such sum for the necessary and reasonable expenses of removing and keeping the goods, chattels, and effects so distrained as may be allowed in like cases by the laws or practice of the State or Territory wherein the distraint shall have been made ; but in case of non-payment or neglect to tender as aforesaid, the said officer shall proceed to sell the said goods, chattels, and effects at public auction, after due notice of the time and place of sale, and may and shall retain from the proceeds of such sale the amount demandable for the use of the United States, with the said necessary and reasonable expenses of said distraint and sale, as aforesaid, and a commission of five per centum thereon for his own use; rendering the overplus, if any there be, to the person whose goods, chattels, and effects shall have been distrained.

SEC. 56. *And be it further enacted*, That every person licensed as aforesaid to distill spirituous liquors, or licensed as a brewer, shall, once in each month, upon the request of the assessor or assistant assessor for the district in which his business as a distiller or brewer may be carried on, respectively, furnish the said assessor or assistant assessor with an abstract of the entries upon his books, herein provided to be made, showing the amount of spirituous liquor distilled and sold, or removed for consumption or sale, or of beer, lager beer, ale, porter, or other fermented liquor made and sold, or removed for consumption or sale, during the preceding month, respectively; the truth and correctness of which abstract shall be verified by the oath of the party so furnishing the same. And the said assessor or assistant assessor shall have the right to examine the books of such person for the purpose of ascertaining the correctness of such abstract. And for any neglect to furnish such abstract when requested, or refusal to furnish an examination of the books as aforesaid, the person so neglecting shall forfeit the sum of five hundred dollars.

The first convention met, at the place and time designated in the call, under singularly auspicious circumstances. The labors of the New York Association had resulted more favorably than could have been expected. Stimulated by Katzenmayer's epistolary efforts, brewers in other cities had come together and adopted measures designed to facilitate the organization of local associations. Several brewers, destined to play a most distinguished part in the history of the association, among them Frederick Lauer of Reading, Pa., had visited Washington to consult with the Revenue Commissioner and ascertained that while in many respects the Federal authorities seemed determined to construe and execute the law with the utmost rigor and severity, there was a commendable disposition to consult with the tax-payers with a view to avoiding undue hardships. Correspondence had been opened with the Revenue Office, and the result of this, together with the labors of the attorneys appointed both by the New York and the Pennsylvania brewers, enabled the Convention Committee to present an order of business which, considering the difficulties that had to be overcome, reflects great credit upon the organizers of the meeting. In the absence of Mr. James Speyers, whom a severe illness confined to his room, the vice-president of the New York Association, Mr. A. Schmid, called the convention to order.

Although Katzenmayer's agitation encompassed the whole Union, exclusive of the rebellious States, it was found that no part of the great West was represented. The following are the names of the delegates, and the places represented by them, viz: Schinnerer and Weber, Albany; Seeger, Baltimore; Benz, Bridgeport; Limburger, Brooklyn; J. D. Baumann, Cypress Hill; Koehler, of Koehler and Fink, Guttenberg; Roemmelt, of Roemmelt and Leicht, Hudson City; Brueckner and M. Haffen, Melrose; Guandt, Nopper and Stueckle, Morrisania; Lorenz, of Lorenz and Hensler, and Schalk, of Schalk Bros., Newark; Ahles, Gillig, Guentzer, Huepfel, Johns, Katzenmayer and Schaefer, of F. & M. Schaefer, New York; Balz and Bergner, Philadelphia; Straub, Pittsburg; Lauer, Reading; Robinson, Scranton; Bechtel and A. Schmid, Staten Island; Licht, Liebmann, Seitz and Schnadderbeck, Williamsburg; Korb, East New York, and Zinsser representing the newly organized Brewers' Association of Rochester, N. Y.

In a written address, read by Secretary Katzenmayer, the absent President of the New York Association dwelt upon the considerations and motives which had prompted the New York Association to take the initiative and laid particular stress upon the difficulties which would necessarily confront the trade if harmonious co-operation on the part of *all* brewers in all matters relating to the subject of internal revenue could not at once be secured by means of a national organization such as his associates contemplated. The regular organization of the convention was effected by the election of these officers, viz.: President, Frederick Lauer of Reading; Secretaries,

John R. Katzenmayer and Otto Johns; Vice-Presidents, Schinnerer and Weber of Albany, Seeger of Baltimore, Benz of Bridgeport, Stueckle of Morrisania, Schalk of Newark, Schmid, Sommer and Speyers of New York, Balz and Bergner of Philadelphia, Straub of Pittsburg, Robinson of Scranton, Bechtel of Staten Island, Schweitzer of Union Hill, Liebmann and Schneider of Williamsburg.*

The functions of these officers pertained exclusively to, and expired with, the convention. When the question of a permanent national organization came up, being first in the order of business, it at once became evident that both the organizers and a majority of the delegates inclined strongly to the opinion that a federation of local associations, organized on a representative basis, would best answer the purposes and objects of the trade. From the very beginning, this idea seemed so pronounced and strong that a definite proposition embodying it evoked no discussion and was accepted almost unanimously.

This foregone conclusion proved to be premature and contrary to the actual state of affairs as it then existed and subsequently developed. As we shall presently see, the wisdom of depending entirely upon the representative system appeared questionable even at this first convention. As a matter of fact, the resolution in regard to this point was in a measure neutralized by another resolution adopted at the end of the second day's session. Be that as it may, in order to comprehend fully and clearly the further proceedings bearing upon this subject, it must be borne in mind that everything relating to the ultimate character of a national body was made contingent and dependent upon the work of

---

* Many of the cities named here have since then lost their autonomy and become merged in the greater communities adjoining them.

organizing local associations. With this aim in view, the convention resolved that, until otherwise ordered at a subsequent convention, New York should be the seat of the executive office, and that the president, vice-president, treasurer and secretary of the New York Association should, until otherwise ordered, constitute the Executive Board of the national body. The funds required for the maintenance of the association and the execution of the labors and duties assigned to it, were to be raised by regular contributions from the various affiliated local bodies. A special committee, to whom this matter was referred on the first day of the convention, reported on the following day in a somewhat vague manner that the sum of $500 should be placed at the disposal of the Executive Board, and that this sum be raised by an assessment to be levied upon the local associations in proportion to the number of brewers belonging to them as members. With the adoption of this proposition, the question of organization was disposed of for the time being, but, as we have intimated, came up again at the end of the session.

Having thus effected what may be styled a semi-permanent organization, the convention at once proceeded to a very thorough consideration of the tax-question. Several points of the law and certain regulations promulgated by the Revenue Office demanded immediate action. The bonds required from brewers for the faithful performance of their fiscal obligations seemed unwarranted; the almost unlimited power conferred upon minor officers of the tax-department in regard to searches, the examination of books, &c., inflicted unnecessary hardships upon the tax-payers; the intention of the Government to collect tax upon beer brewed during the winter of 1861–62, and virtually sold at the prices prevailing before imposition of said tax, was regarded as an injustice. The New York brewers had, as we have seen, engaged an attorney (John J. Freedman) to ascertain, and give an opinion on, the spirit and letter of the law as to the latter point, while Frederick Lauer had, through his counsel, addressed to the Commissioner of Internal Revenue a formal remonstrance against the collection of the tax upon such beers. In the regular course of the pre-arranged order of business, the opinion of Mr. Freedman and the correspondence of Lauer with Commissioner Boutwell were submitted to the convention as the basis of discussion. In Freedman's opinion, supported by the judgment of ex-Recorder Smith, the Government had no power to collect the tax on such beer; but, judging from the official reply to Lauer's remonstrance, the Government construed the law differently. The Lauer case, presented to Boutwell, embodied all the essential points of the brewers' contention and was in every way well-fitted to thorougly test the claims of our side. During the months of December, January, February and March, 1862, the stock of lager-beer for summer use had been brewed. In March and April, contracts with customers had been made and prices agreed upon for certain weekly quantities until the middle of October, when the newly brewed winter beer became fit for use. At the time the contracts were concluded, the tax-law was not in force, nor were the stipulated prices agreed upon with any reference to an anticipated revenue-measure. Naturally enough, the customers manifested a decided disinclination to permit any deviation from contract-prices and, hence, the whole burden would fall upon the manufacturer. All brewers were perfectly willing to pay the tax upon beer brewed and sold after the first of September, but a construction of the law which made them liable for tax upon beer manufactured before that date appeared to them unjust and unjustifiable. A very significant fact was brought to the surface by the Lauer remonstrance, namely, that some brewers operated small stills in connection with their brewery, merely as a kind of economic adjunct for the more profitable utilization of brewer's grains. Lauer was one of these brewers, and he believed, somewhat naïvely, that the Government might regard this still as part of his brewing establishment and would not compel him to obtain a distiller's license. We mention this fact, not only as an interesting illustration of brewers' practices in past times, but also because the reply which the Commissioner gave to Lauer's remonstrance refers to it. This reply reads as follows, viz. :—

TREASURY DEPARTMENT,
Office of Internal Revenue, Nov. 3d, 1862.

SIR :—Your letter of the 30th ulto., in regard to the payment of tax upon beer manufactured prior to the passage of the excise law, has been received, and in reply I have to say that,

If the vaults to which you refer, in which the beer is stored, are not upon the premises where the beer was manufactured, but entirely separate, distinct and at a distance therefrom, and the beer was removed from the premises to the said vaults previous to the first of September, then the beer is exempt.

If on the other hand the beer was not removed from the premises of the brewery prior to Setember first, the tax must be paid.

And if the said beer is sold in pursuance of the contracts bona fide made, before the passage of the Excise Act, viz.: July first, 1862, the manufacturer and seller would have claim upon the purchaser for the amount of tax paid, as per Section 69.

The collector must decide whether the person who has a small still in his brewery for distilling the refuse matter of the brewery is required to take out a distiller's license or not.

Very respectfully, your obedient servant,
(Signed.) C. F. ESTEE,
Acting Commissioner.

Although unfamiliar with parliamentary rules and usages, and totally unaccustomed to public business of any kind, with no sort of training other than that required for the successful conduct of their trade, the sturdy founders of the United States Brewers' Association at once grasped the situation and displayed an almost marvellous sagacity and aptitude in dealing with the difficult questions placed before them. Schalk and Lauer led the discussions, and the former submitted a resolution, couched in calm and dispassionate but exceedingly incisive language, protesting against the injustice of any attempt to collect tax upon malt-liquors manufactured in December, 1861, and January, February and March, 1862. To lend force to this manifesto it was resolved to appoint a special committee, with power to at once represent the association at Washington for the purpose of inducing Commissioner Boutwell to refrain from the proposed course. Failing in this, the committee was instructed to appeal to Congress for suitable remedial legislation. This committee was composed of Lauer of Reading, Balz of Philadelphia and Speyers of New York, Katzenmayer having declined to serve on account of other arduous duties.

The whole of the second day was taken up by further discussions on the other revenue questions before referred to. The intricate details of the process of brewing as affected by the law, and the varying modes of book-keeping in vogue in brewing establishments, seemed to preclude the possibility of reaching satisfactory conclusions as to such changes as might reasonably be asked for while Congress was in session. In order to be fully prepared in this respect, the convention referred the task of preparing a draft of amendments to a committee composed of Straub of Pittsburgh, Eichenlaub of Cincinnati, Urich of St. Louis, Melms of Milwaukee, Deverey of Chicago, Lauer of Reading, Psotta of Philadelphia, Schalk of Newark, and Katzenmayer of New York. It must be regarded as a striking evidence of the foresight and wisdom of the founders that this committee was so constituted as to embrace such important brewing centres as Cincinnati, St. Louis, Milwaukee and Chicago, although not a single representative of the brewers of these cities was present at the convention.

The financial question again received some attention when Liebmann asked in what manner it was proposed to defray the expenses likely to be incurred by the two committees just elected by the convention. The discussion on the subject was interrupted and ended by the offer of the New York Association to advance whatever sums might be needed until the next convention.

The provisions of the law requiring daily entries of materials used in brewing and of the number of barrels of beer brewed required an immediate agreement among the tax-paying brewers as to the mode and manner of estimating the number of barrels actually produced from day to day. The framers of the law evidently underrated, or did not know the difficulty of complying with this requirement, yet it was apprehended that revenue officials would insist upon the brewers' swearing to the absolute correctness of an entry which in the very nature of things could not but be a mere matter of guess-work. Uniformity of action on the part of all brewers appeared desirable in this respect, and it was therefore resolved that if sworn statements of the quantity of beer produced daily were really demanded, the brewers should base their calculations upon the assumption that two bushels of malt yielded one barrel of beer.

Jacob Pfaff, of Boston, anxious to become a member of the association, revived the discussion on the subject of the permanent organization. He pointed out that as yet a brewers' association had not been organized in Boston and that, unless the convention would permit him and others to join the association of New York, he failed to see how he ever could become a member. The convention immediately passed a resolution permitting brewers residing in cities where no associations existed to join the local association of the nearest city. This resolution was coupled with the expression of a desire that many brewers would embrace this indirect method of becoming members. By way of emphasizing the determination to adopt the representative system, the convention decided that the Executive Board should henceforth correspond only with local associations and that any information desired by individual brewers in any part of the country must be obtained through this channel. Evidently, the organizer firmly believed that this mildly coercive measure would facilitate and accelerate the formation of local bodies; but they seemed not to perceive that if their plan should fail they would effectually frustrate their own purposes, for they then would have neither local organizations nor individual members. Probably the organizers, who were also the leading minds of the New York brewers, judged of the general condition of things in the light of their local experiences and saw no good reason why brewers in Chicago, Boston, Philadelphia and all other brewing centres should have to encounter any difficulties in this direction.

An ovation to President Lauer and the adoption of a resolution designating Philadelphia as the place of the next meeting, formed the concluding acts of the *first brewers' convention.* It is well to bear in mind that no name or title for the association was officially adopted at this convention; up to the fourth meeting it was called the Lager-beer Brewers' Association, but more frequently it was mentioned as the National Brewers' Association or Brewers' Congress.

Chapter II.

CHARACTER OF FIRST CONVENTION'S WORK; ITS IMPRESSION UPON THE TRADE. ALE-BREWERS WILLING TO CO-OPERATE. WHY GERMAN WAS USED EXCLUSIVELY AT THE CONVENTION; THE ASSOCIATIONS' SUBSEQUENT ATTITUDE IN REGARD TO THE TWO LANGUAGES. SECOND CONVENTION MEETS AT PHILADELPHIA; ITS COMPOSITION. LOCAL ASSOCIATION OF PHILADELPHIA; ITS CHARACTER. PATRIOTIC APPEAL TO MEMBERS BY PRESIDENT. APPOINTMENT OF COMMITTEES. EFFORTS TO ORGANIZE LOCAL ASSOCIATIONS. DRAWBACKS OF REPRESENTATIVE SYSTEM AND COMPROMISE NECESSITATED BY IT. BIOGRAPHICAL SKETCH OF MEMBERS OF AGITATION COMMITTEE; THEIR SIGNIFICANT EXPERIENCES AND EFFICIENT WORK AT WASHINGTON; GREAT COURTESY SHOWN THEM BY EMINENT STATESMEN; GOVERNMENT APPRECIATES BREWERS' LOYALTY AND INTEGRITY. WHAT BREWERS ASKED FOR AND COMPLAINED OF. DELEGATION OF ALE-BREWERS OFFER ASSISTANCE AND ARE MADE HONORARY MEMBERS; EFFECT OF THIS MOVE.

The unexpected aptitude for public business evinced by the first congress, and evidenced by the work actually accomplished and the systematic and very thorough arrangement for proper agitations, could not fail to produce on the trade a deep and lasting impression. Hundreds of congratulatory letters were received from brewers throughout the country, and nearly every one contained offers of assistance. Although the entire proceedings, including debates, motions and resolutions, were conducted and printed exclusively in the German language, the English-speaking brewers readily perceived that the judicious course pursued by their German-American confrères was admirably adapted to the situation, and it redounds to their credit that, although as yet reluctant to become members, they immediately sought to assist the movement. It might be supposed that clannishness prompted the adoption of the German as the official language of the first convention, but such an assumption would be very far from the truth. Nothing could have been more natural or justifiable under the peculiar circumstances surrounding this first gathering. Lager-beer brewers had originated the movement, and between them and the ale-brewers commercial or social relations had not yet been established. The entire body of convention-delegates consisted of German-Americans, a majority of whom, although sufficiently familiar with the English language to fully understand it when spoken, were not capable of expressing themselves in that tongue with such fluency, correctness and accuracy as the occasion required; on the other hand, the order of business was submitted in German and it was in this language that the temporary chairman opened the convention. As there was not a single brewer present who could not understand and speak German, while only a few delegates spoke English fluently, the German was adopted as a matter of course and without any preliminary agreement to that effect, either expressed or implied. We dwell upon this peculiar feature, because in after-years, when the necessity for co-operation had become less imperative, the preponderance of the German element and the preference which by force of habit was given to the German language, had the very natural effect of causing a feeling of estrangement and discontent on the part of many ale-brewers. As soon as this became generally known, however, the association, true to the catholicity and cosmopolitan spirit that always distinguished it, cheerfully placed both languages on equal footing and finally, in recent years, gave precedence to the English language.

At the second convention the German language was still the only one used and the minutes were also printed exclusively in German. The reader will readily understand from what occurred at this convention and will presently be stated, why, at the very next meeting, a change was effected in this particular.

Second Convention. 119

When the second convention met at Philadelphia (No. 343 North Third Street), on the 4th of February, 1863, that part of the internal revenue system which relates to the tax upon malt-liquors was actually and fully in operation, and the brewers everywhere had, through their own personal experiences, been made aware of the necessity of co-operation. The number of delegates present and of the firms represented eloquently testified to the general prevalence of this conviction. We reproduce a list of the delegates, not only as a matter of record and historical interest, but more especially because, by a comparison with the attendance at the first convention, it will serve as a means of guaging the rapidity and extent of the association's development within less than three months—the period of time which lies between the first and the second meeting. There were present or represented the following firms, viz.:—

J. Pfaff, Boston; A. Ziegele, Buffalo; Huck, Chicago; Kleiner, Moerlein, Eichenlaub, Koehler and Constans, Cincinnati (these five delegates also represented Columbus, O.); H. C. Dreis, Davenport; H. Frisch, Harrisburg; J. J. Springer, Lancaster; Limburger, Long Island; Melms, Milwaukee; A. Schalk, Newark; Schaefer, A. Huepfel, Sommer and Katzenmayer, New York; Psotta (of Bergdoll & Psotta), Klump, Elsaesser, Vollmer, Born, L. Talmon, H. Gehring, C. Theis, Joerger, Loesch, Zickler, Orth and Rothacker, Hauser and Schemm, Presser and Lubbermann, G. Bergner, J. & P. Balz, M. Kreig, F. Haas, Lips and Kittmayer, Wolff and Grauch, Philadelphia; J. N. Straub, Pittsburg; Lauer, as the representative of his own firm and N. A. Felix and H. Seidel, Reading; W. Bertsche, Rondout; W. Fox, Sandusky; Robinson, Scranton; Thines, Trenton; Yuengling, Pottsville; Roemmelt and Leicht, Union Hill. O. Johns of New York represented several breweries of Sheboygan, Wis.

The brewers of Philadelphia were among the very first to organize a local association; but, in keeping with the precedent established by their New York colleagues, they had confined their organization to lager-beer brewers, nearly all of whom were also of German birth or descent. In all likelihood, only the lack of personal contact and intercourse succeeded in creating the fleeting impression on either side that a division of interests was desired or sought to be established. It is no less probable that here, as in New York, the adoption of German as the official language operated at first like a barrier or dividing line, more imaginary than real, between the two branches of the industry. Whatever may have been the reason, the fact remains that at the time of the second convention the Philadelphia association was composed exclusively of lager-beer brewers, and that only this part of the industry was represented by properly accredited delegates to the convention. The ale-brewers, however, were not willing to look on passively and let others bear the brunt of the labor. A generous spirit prompted them to a course which we shall presently have occasion to dwell upon.

Schemm, as president of the Philadelphia association, welcomed the delegates and opened the convention, whereupon Katzenmayer announced the resignation of President Speyers, who, since the last convention, had severed his connection with the trade. In a letter which took the place of the customary address, the retiring president emphasized the wisdom of firmly and unwaveringly pursuing the policy adopted at the first meeting. According to this policy and his own conviction, it was the duty of all brewers to maintain and defend the rights of the trade at all hazards, but at the same time to exert themselves to the utmost, to the end that the law be faithfully obeyed, according to its purport and intent, throughout the land. An allusion to Lincoln's heroic efforts for the preservation of the Union elicited a spontaneous outburst of patriotic en-

Second Convention. 121

thusiasm, quite characteristic of a class of manufacturers whose integrity and loyalty of purpose the Federal Treasury Department, a few years later, saw fit to single out, in a public document, as worthy of unstinted praise. The election of officers resulted as follows, viz.: President, F. Lauer; Vice-Presidents, Kern, Pfaff, Ziegele, Huck, Dries, Eichenlaub, Frisch, Springer, Limburger, Melms, Schalk, Sommer, Schemm, Straub, Bertsche, Fox, Robinson, Bechtel, Thines and Leicht; Secretaries, O. Johns and G. Bergner.

From the records, it is impossible to gather how many local associations, excepting those of New York and Philadelphia, were represented, nor have we any means of knowing whether (at that time) any others, not mentioned before, existed at all.* From certain very brief and meagre reports it may be inferred, however, that in all the larger cities, such as Cincinnati, Chicago, Milwaukee, Pittsburg and Buffalo, the brewers had organized themselves either permanently or for the purpose of suitable representation at the national convention. In connection with the question as to how and at what rate dues were to be collected, the subject of membership and local associations cropped out again, and both the discussions and the committee's reports on the three closely related matters again disclosed the fact that a purely representative-system would not answer the legitimate purposes of a national body which ought to have included every member of the industry, then widely and thinly scattered over an immense extent of territory. Individual membership of all—which, by the way, would not have precluded the organization of local bodies— should have been aimed at from the beginning, all the more so because local dissensions might bring about the

---

* Rochester had an association which does not appear to have been represented.

dissolution of local associations, thus weakening the national body in proportion to the numerical strength of the dissolved association. The organizers had not yet sufficiently tested their system in practical operation and still believed that missionary work would perfect it and do away with all shortcomings. Yet they could not ignore the disadvantage of propagating the opinion among brewers that the national association would almost rather have no members at all, than to have members not belonging to local associations.

This view evidently actuated a special committee, entrusted with the matter, to report for adoption a resolution fixing the initiation fee at $2 for every member, and the monthly dues at 20 cents for every 100 barrels of beer sold, making it the duty of the local association to collect both the dues and the fees. But the resolution (which was unanimously adopted) provided expressly that brewers not belonging to any local association might become members and would be entitled to the same privileges and benefits secured to members of such associations. The necessity for such a definition of rights and privileges clearly proves the anomaly of the plan of organization. As the reader may wonder why it should be deemed necessary and proper to criticise here the representative-system as applied to the association, it may as well be stated that this system, long since abrogated to the great benefit and advantage of the association, has of late found a few able advocates and was at one time actually re-proposed, but rejected. In a proper treatment of our subject, the lessons taught by the association's history ought, for the benefit of our successors, be placed in a clear and true light.

By far the most interesting part of the proceedings of this convention was the report of the special committee empowered to confer with the Revenue Office and, in the event of its failure to obtain relief at this source, to appeal to Congress for remedial legislation inhibiting the collection of the tax on beer brewed before the enactment of the tax-law. Here we have to deal with the first public step taken by American brewers, as a body, in a public matter.* Let us see how they bore and acquitted themselves, how they proceeded, what impression they made and what they accomplished. The Committee consisted of Lauer, Balz and Speyers. The latter, an able and well-educated man, manifested great interest in the affairs of the association and appeared willing enough to devote his time and energy to the common welfare. Illness and his subsequent retirement from business reduced his usefulness to a comparatively small measure. In Balz, unusual strength of character was wedded to an amiable and equable temperament, touching goodness of heart and a very generous spirit. As to Lauer's character and standing, the records of the association preserve a most eloquent oration delivered by H. H. Rueter at the unveiling of a Lauer statue in a public park of Reading, Pa. From this it appears that Lauer was eminently well qualified for the work entrusted to him. He had occupied prominent positions in the local government of Reading, was mainly instrumental in raising this place to the rank of a city, was a leader or helper of many industrial enterprises, an active member of every benevolent institution in his region, a

---

* This applies only to modern times. In Colonial days brewers frequently engaged in politics, and it is a source of pride and gratification to note that they were always on the side of popular rights. When in 1644, Kieft, Governor of New York, imposed an increased excise upon beer against the expressed wish of the "Eight Men," the brewers stoutly refused to pay the tax on constitutional grounds. True, their opposition could not prevail against Kieft's tyrannical use and abuse of power, and their beer was confiscated; but they were landed as champions of popular rights. O'Callaghan, the historian of New York, takes this view of the occurrence and adds, significantly enough, that "henceforth the impression became a conviction that neither justice nor the government was impartially administered." In post-Colonial times the brewers often appeared before Congress in matters relating to their trade.

patron and trustee of the Keystone State Normal School, a vestryman and trustee of Trinity Church of Reading; one of the most prominent and trusted men of his town and county and, more than all this, a man of enthusiastic patriotism and staunch loyalty. Concerning the latter traits his eulogist, on the occasion referred to, used these words:—

"His business interests forbidding the acceptance of political office, he declined offered Congressional nomination. As a delegate to the memorable National Convention at Charleston, S. C., in 1860, Frederick Lauer determinedly opposed the heresy of secession, and earnestly endeavored to secure the adoption of a platform and the nomination of a candidate for the presidency which would guarantee the preservation of the Union. True to his loyal principles, when the struggle for its maintenance came, he equipped, at his own expense, a full company of men, which served throughout the war in the 104th Pennsylvania Regiment."

For the contemplated object, a better or more judicious selection could not have been made than that of Lauer, a true man, an exemplary citizen and a sterling patriot. Meeting at Philadelphia for the purpose of agreeing upon a suitable plan of action, the Committee, faithful to its instructions, first sought the advice of a lawyer on the primary proposition of a visit to Washington for the purpose of inducing the Revenue Commissioner to rescind his order. With equal fidelity to the ethics of his calling, the lawyer advised against the journey on the ground that in all probability Commissioner Boutwell would peremptorily decline to accede to such a request without first obtaining legal advice from the Solicitor of the Treasury Department. This officer would probably desire to confer with the brewers' attorney, and thus an agreement might be reached. He proposed a considerable delay in order to enable him to seek out a proper mode of procedure. Such a course seemed altogether too indirect and dilatory to the aggressive and fiery spirit of Lauer, and he induced the Committee to proceed to Washington immediately, without entirely abandoning the idea of seeking the lawyer's help if their own resources should fail.

Their first experience at Washington ought to be blazoned in imperishable letters in every place where brewers meet to discuss their relations to and with the Government. The very first legislator whom they visited, Hon. J. W. Killinger, a Pennsylvania-German, representing the Lebanon and Dauphin District in the lower house of Congress, warned them most impressively against sending a lawyer or any outsider to Washington, not only because their interests had many warm friends and able advocates in both houses, but especially because if they themselves personally appeared before a Congressional committee, anything they might have to say would receive more respectful and deferential hearing, and anything they might deem it their right to ask for would be more readily granted. Forcibly impressed with the soundness of this advice, the Committee determined to proceed without legal aid. Senator Preston King of New York, Senator Sherman of Ohio, Representative H. T. Stevens (himself interested in brewing) and Morrill of Vermont, cheerfully listened to the brewers' remonstrance and promised to advocate the enactment of an adequate remedial law. Within the next two or three days such a bill was, indeed, introduced and rapidly progressed; it would undoubtedly have passed, had not the insertion of extraneous matter required its re-committment to the Committee on Ways and Means. Both from this Committee and the Finance

Committee of the Senate the brewers received exceedingly courteous treatment and the promise of speedy action. What must have struck the brewers' delegation as a singularly strong confirmation of Killinger's warning was the fact that Senator Cowen, of his own accord, also admonished them never to send a lawyer to represent their interests, but to come themselves whenever they desired and believed themselves entitled to legislative relief. These assurances of good will were not, as might be supposed, mere hollow phrases of diplomatic politicians. In those sombre days of the nation's profoundest distress and sorrow there was little room for petty artifices and tricks; public affairs of every kind had a deep tinge of sadness and earnestness; everybody was solemnly earnest and serious in words and deeds. What Sherman, King, Cowen, Stevens and Morrill told the Committee must have appeared to Lauer as the faint echo of the stirring and ringing words which these men had spoken in the halls of Congress when the beer-tax was under discussion and when every man of note had a good word for the brewing industry, both on economic and moral and hygienic grounds. But these general considerations were strengthened by the patriotic attitude of the whole trade. The example of Lauer, who organized a company of Union soldiers, was not an isolated one; everywhere, particularly in the border States, brewers stanchly upheld the cause of the Union, and where they did not organize troops and either send or lead them to the front, they manifested in other ways their willingness to serve their country. Now that the representatives of this trade appeared before Congressional committees, with unbounded confidence in the sense of justice of the Government, to ask for redress, the reception accorded to them could not well have been otherwise than cordial, considerate and kind. Although the proposed law had not yet been enacted, the encouraging report on the committee's work and experiences seemed to assure the delegates to the convention that their other propositions concerning the revenue-laws would receive due attention, if presented in proper form and suitable manner. Among these, we find a reduction of the tax together with a modification of the method of collection. The time for demanding a tax-reduction was certainly not well chosen, but the enormously increased prices of the raw-materials and of labor, coupled with the difficulty of uniformly increasing the price of beer, afforded sufficient warrant for an effort in this direction. Nevertheless, many members apprehended that this step would be regarded as premature and, as a consequence, the committee appointed for this purpose was not definitely instructed as to the extent of the reduction that should be asked for.

A new question had presented itself since the first convention. A brewing establishment at Cincinnati (Sandmann & Lackmann), who sold their product in the manner then in vogue, *i. e.*, by having their drivers call upon dealers so as to supply them with the necessary quantity of beer, had been notified by Collector Pullan that they must obtain a peddler's license. To their appeal from this ruling the Revenue Office replied as follows, viz. :—

TREASURY DEPARTMENT,
Office of Internal Revenue,
Washington, Jan. 2d, 1863.

The case of Sandmann & Lackman, manufacturers of beer, I return, because it does not seem sufficiently plain from their affidavit whether they are liable to license as peddlers or not. If they only deliver beer that has been previously sold or contracted for, then they are not peddlers. But if they run their wagons for the purpose of selling their beer from place to place, then (even though they are selling their own manufacture) they must be considered and licensed as peddlers.

Yours respectfully,
GEORGE T. BOUTWELL,
Commissioner.

This matter was also referred to the Committee on Federal Legislation. At this point an announcement was made for which we have endeavored to prepare the reader. A delegation of ale-brewers, consisting of Read of NewYork and Gaul, Leeds and Collins of Philadelphia, through one of the delegates, asked for the privilege of the floor which was cheerfully granted. Collins, destined to play an enviable part in the history of the association, addressed the convention, expressing his surprise and gratification at the numerous attendance, and declaring his and his constituents' willingness to cooperate with the national association. He freely confessed that their efforts to concentrate their forces had not been quite as successful as he had hoped and expected. The ale-brewers desired more particularly to assist the Committee on Federal Legislation, both financially and otherwise, and believed that frequent consultation and exchange of views could not but tend to render their common labors more effective. The convention conferred honorary membership on the four representatives of the ale-trade, thus handsomely acknowledging and reciprocating the friendly advances made by their fellow-manufacturers.

Close personal connection and official intercourse was thus established, apparently without any special effort on either side; the simple, straightforward course of the ale-brewers, together with its cordial appreciation on the part of the convention, marked the beginning of an era of harmonious and most successful co-operation. The results flowing from this occurrence affected the nature of subsequent meetings very favorably and had a direct bearing on the pending work.

Chapter III.

THIRD CONVENTION ; ITS COMPOSITION. WORK OF COMMITTEES. JUSTICE OF BREWERS' CLAIMS. CONGRESS PASSES SEVERAL AMENDMENTS ASKED FOR BY BREWERS. ALE-BREWERS' RECOGNIZED AS MEMBERS AND TAKE ACTIVE PART. A NEW COMMITTEE CREATED ; IMPORTANT LABORS ASSIGNED TO IT ; IS TO WORK FOR REDUCTION OF TAX ; INTERNAL TRADE AFFAIRS ; THE NEED OF A NEWSPAPER AND OF A SUBSTITUTE FOR PITCH. NEW COMMITTEE COMPOSED OF EXCELLENT MEN. FOURTH CONVENTION:; NEW DEPARTURE IN MANY RESPECTS: PARLIAMENTARY USAGES BEGIN TO BE OBSERVED ; FIRST NOMINATING COMMITTEE AND SPECIAL CONVENTION COMMITTEES; THE LATTERS' EXCELLENT REPORTS. JOINT EXECUTIVE COMMITTEE EMBRACING ALE-BREWERS. MEMBERSHIP AND FINANCIAL STATUS. PERMANENT AGITATION COMMITTEE. THE ASSOCIATION ADOPTS ITS PRESENT TITLE. AGITATION FOR TAX-REDUCTION ABANDONED FOR PATRIOTIC REASONS. MAGNIFICENT ARGUMENTS SUBMITTED TO CONGRESS PREVENT INCREASE OF TAX. TREASURY DEPARTMENT CONFERS WITH ASSOCIATION ; WELCOMES ITS OFFER OF ASSISTANCE IN COLLECTING TAX. PATRIOTIC SPEECH BY COLLINS. RESOLUTION EXPRESSING LOYAL SENTIMENTS AND PROVIDING FOR ACTION AGAINST DELINQUENT TAX-PAYERS. PRESENTATION OF HANDSOME GIFTS TO LAUER AND KATZENMAYER. ELECTION OF OFFICERS; ANOTHER NEW DEPARTURE.

A desire to avoid useless repetition and to present the more important and interesting matters in narrative form, without too close an observance of the chronological order of convention-proceedings, prompts the writer to combine the third and the fourth conventions. The third convention took place at Cincinnati (No. 400 Vine Street) on the 28th and 29th of October, 1863. It will be noticed that within less than a year three national meetings had been held. The proceedings at once assumed a bi-lingual character. The list of delegates*

---

* This is the list of delegates : Allegheny, G. Gant ; Alton, L. Wilhelm ; Buffalo, J. L. Haherstro ; Cincinnati, G. Bach, L. Bauer, M. Beck, C. Boss, G. A. Boss, G. F. Bnck, G. F. Eichenlanb, W. Fay, C. H. Gogreve, G. M. Herancourt, W. Hofmeister, J. Hochenleitner, J. Kaufmann, F. Kleiner, M. Kleiner, G. Kloetter, G. Koehler, T. Koehler, H. Lackmann, C. Moerlein, F. Mueller, S. Nichaus, R. Rheinhold, J. H. Sandmann, J. A. Schaefer, J. Schaller, L. Schneider, R. S. Schultz, A. Walker, Arch. Walker, J. Walker, W. Walker, P. Weyand, C. Windisch, D. Young ; Columbus, F. Anthony, L. Hoster ; Covington, F. Knoll, C. Lang, C. Geishauer ; Davenport, H. C. Dreis, for himself and fifty-five members of Belleview, British

Third Convention. 131

contains many new names, both of men and places, and among the former the reader will readily recognize quite a number who, in subsequent years, have won enduring fame in brewing circles by their eminent services to the common cause. The ale-brewers' associations of New York, Philadelphia and Cincinnati had sent delegates to this convention, among them Henry Clausen of New York, F. Collins and A. Hugel of Philadelphia, and Walker and Schultz of Cincinnati. New York was still the seat of the Executive Board, with John Bechtel as President and Katzenmayer as Secretary. Frederick Lauer again occupied the presidential chair, assisted by Secretaries C. H. Gogreve and J. L. Haberstoh, and fourteen vice-presidents, representing as many States and Territories. The representatives of the ale-brewers' associations were recognized, by virtue of a resolution to that effect, as regular members of the convention, entitled to seat and vote; yet the old stumbling-block, *i.e.*, the general question of membership, of the rights of individual members as compared with those of members representing local associations and of the manner of voting, gave rise to a lengthy discussion and the adoption of a resolution which again revealed the insufficiency of the plan of organization. We quote this resolution literally, as it appears in the English

Hollow, Burlington, Cedar Falls, Cedar Rapids, Davenport, Dubuque, Fort Madison, Fulton, Galena, Garnaville, Guttenberg, Independence, Iowa City, Koekuk, Lansing, Le Claire, Liberty Township, Mineral Point, Muscatine, Nauvoo, New Vienna, Potosi, Rock Island, Sheriff's Mount and Wausaw ; Dayton, A. Becherer, F. Eichenhofer, Sander, C. Schwind, J. Schwind ; Hamilton, J. Dingfelder, J. W. Sohn ; Hudson City, N. J., J. Roemmelt ; Ironton, Ohio, L. Ebert ; Louisville, P. Tompert, P. Zang ; Milwaukee, J. Obermann ; Newark, N. J., F. Kolb ; Newark, Ohio, M. Morath ; Newport, P. Constans ; New York, Bechtel, Katzenmayer, S. K. M. Kepner, F. Schaefer ; Philadelphia, G. Bergner, F. Collins, A. Hugel, P. Schemm, R. Vollmer ; Pittsburgh, J. Gangwish, M. Hechelmann, D. Lntz ; Portsmouth, Ohio, J. Layher ; Reading, F. Lauer, for himself and for A. Felix, L. J. Bartlett, P. Barbey, H. Flotow and J. Rhodes ; St. Louis, A. Fritz, C. G. Stifel, J. Winkelmeyer ; Washington, D. C., E. Loeffler ; Wheeling, A. Reymann ; Madison, Ind., W. F. Belser and M. Greiner.

minutes. Its German origin is easily traceable in the quaint construction of its sentences, its idiomatic peculiarity and marked Germanisms:—

> "1. Every brewer can become a member of the United States Brewers' Association, and can vote in the Convention, under the condition that he pays the same fee of two dollars a person for the membership, and twenty cents for every one hundred barrels of beer sold, as it is prescribed for every one of the local association, provided, that he is residing at any place where a local association could not yet be established, or where he cannot sell his beer within the reach of a local association. 2. The delegates of the local associations, assembled in convention, give their votes for as many members as they represent; therefore, also a proportion is granted to every one of them, in case a local association should send several delegates, which will be found by dividing the number of delegates in the total number of all members of the said local association. The President is hereby respectfully requested to give us the acquittal."

Since the second convention, the labors of the Committee on National Legislation (now consisting of Lauer for the Middle-States, Pfaff for the East and Kleiner for the West) had in some respects been crowned with unexpected success. Associating themselves with the ale-brewers Collins and Leeds of Philadelphia, and Reed, Price and Ferguson of New York, the Committee, scarcely a week after the second convention, proceeded to Washington and asked for and obtained another hearing before the Committee on Ways and Means. Their argument, a masterly array of pointed and incisive facts couched in excellent language, covered every point of the previous remonstrances and derived uncommon force from a comparison with the rate of taxes and the mode of taxation and collection prevailing in the principal beer-producing countries. The lawmakers appeared perfectly willing to concede three of the remedial measures asked for, and finally agreed to provide (1) for the refunding of taxes unlawfully collected, (2) for the proper rating of fractional parts of casks, and (3) for the revocation of the clause compelling brewers to keep an account of the quantity of malt put into the mash-tub. The proceedings of the Committee on Ways and Means seem to indicate that a majority of its members believed that the original law was not designed to tax old stock, and they were all the more firmly convinced of the justice of the brewers' side, because even the Revenue Office did not pursue a uniform policy in regard to the matter, but appeared to allow the collectors in the various districts to use their own judgment as to whether such taxes should or should not be collected. The House of Representatives accordingly passed a bill embodying a clause specifically providing for the refunding of such over-paid taxes, but the Senate failed to concur in it, and thus the amendatory bill ultimately became a law without it. The amendments, as passed, temporarily reduced the tax from one dollar to sixty cents per barrel, and provided for the proper rating of the fractional parts of barrels. The reduction of the tax was to remain in force only until the 1st of April, 1864; thereafter the original tax was to be collected. The brewers' proposition that the tax be *permanently* reduced to fifty cents per barrel encountered not only strenuous opposition, but a very decided counter-effort in the form of an agitation in favor of a considerable increase beyond the original rate. So menacing had this movement become during the time which elapsed between the concessions made to brewers and the date of the third convention, that immediate and prompt action appeared imperatively necessary. The convention fully understood those considerations which ought to prompt wise and thoughtful law-makers to protect a young and struggling industry producing a wholesome and mild stimulant, and they could not ignore either the growing popularity of their product or its effect upon the drinking-habits of a people formerly addicted almost exclusively to the copious use of ardent spirits. They made the best use of their opportunities.—Impartially distributing the offices and honors at his disposal, President Bechtel had appointed Frederick Collins, one of the representatives of the ale-brewers, as chairman of a Committee on Resolutions. On the second day of the convention, this gentleman reported the following resolutions, viz. :—

"Whereas, the Convention of the United States Brewers' Association, held in Cincinnati, October 28, 1863, embrace the present favorable opportunity of expressing their firm adherence to the government of the United States, and their readiness to contribute, by every means in their power, to the support of the constituted authorities in the suppression of this widespread and wicked rebellion; and whereas, the timely relief afforded by the Act of Congress, approved March 3, 1863, has enabled the brewers to continue to furnish a wholesome and nutritious beverage to the people of the United States, whereby the consumption of malt-liquors has largely increased, and our proportioned contribution to the support of the government been maintained; and whereas, the circumstances which induced the passage of the above Act, continue in greater force by the unprecedented high prices of barley and hops, and the largely increased expenses of brewing in high prices of labor, fuel and everything that appertains to our business; therefore, resolved, that in the opinion of this Convention, we are fully convinced, by an experience of fifteen months in the payment of the excise tax, that it is important that the tax should be fixed upon such a basis as shall be specific in its provisions, in order that we may be able to adapt our business to the increased popularity of malt-liquors. Resolved, that a memorial expressive of the sentiments contained in these resolutions, be issued by this Convention, praying Congress that at the expiration of the present amended Act, before referred to, the tax on malt-liquors be fixed at fifty cents a barrel, the other provisions remaining unchanged. Resolved, that the Central Committee are hereby directed to continue their efforts with the government to secure the passage of an Act by Congress, providing for the re-imbursement of taxes paid by brewers on beer brewed prior to September 1,

1862 ; it being obvious, from a misapprehension of the collectors in the several districts, who required the payment of said tax by some and not by others, that the enforcement of the law has been partial in its operation and unjust to those brewers who promptly responded to the demand of said collectors."

The Central or Executive Committee, repeatedly named in these resolutions, had not yet been organized, and the impression seemed to have prevailed that the Executive Board, *i. e.*, the board of officers of the New York Association, was meant. A subsequent motion to the effect that an Executive Committee be created, dispelled this erroneons impression and caused the first notable division among the delegates to the convention —one part of them advocating the creation of a committee to be composed of one representative from each State, the other claiming that, for the sake of quick and effective work, the committee should be as small as possible. The latter won, and a committee of three (F. Lauer, J. A. Sohn and J. Roemmelt) was appointed with power to add to their number at will and pleasure. The reader will doubtless note the singular division of labors and functions growing out of the original plan of organization. Bechtel was president of the association, but Lauer was president of the convention; the officers of the New York association formed the Executive Board of the national body, yet here was another Executive Committee virtually assuming all the more important functions usually pertaining to the former office. This state of affairs tended to confuse the members, and it is not at all surprising that at this, as at every preceding meeting, motions were made that presupposed a condition of things which did not exist. Many believed that any measure relating to trade-affairs adopted by one local association must necessarily be binding upon every other, and that it was the duty of the national association to enforce it. Years went by before the entire trade understood that the regulation of the traffic and intercourse with dealers are purely local matters, to be disposed of by local associations. At this (third) convention, the loss of kegs through the dishonesty of dealers formed the subject of a motion to the effect that all members should be compelled to charge the value of each keg to the customer, this sum to be re-imbursed upon the return of the empty package. Of course, the motion did not prevail, but in its stead a resolution was adopted strongly recommending such a course to all local associations—a precedent frequently followed in succeeding years.

Neither constitution and by-laws nor parliamentary rules had as yet been adopted; such rules as the emergencies of the hour demanded were promulgated from time to time in a somewhat crude and primitive, though quite effective manner. At this convention some members evidently talked too much, for Tomppert of Louisville proposed, and the convention decreed, that no member should have the right to speak longer than ten minutes upon any matter, nor be allowed to digress from the subject or speak a second time, unless all members desiring to speak had been heard.

It deserves to be mentioned that even thus early the members of the trade recognized the necessity of having a newspaper devoted to their interests. They felt that they must have some means whereby to enlighten the public upon their aims and objects and at the same time to defend their calling against unwarranted attacks. Besides this, a medium of communication in matters of commercial and industrial interest appeared desirable. Kleiner of Cincinnati gave expression to this sentiment in a resolution directing the officers of the association either to establish a journal or to secure the services of a newspaper already established. Although received with marked favor, the resolution was postponed for the reason that more important questions required the expenditure of all the money that could be raised.

Owing to the war, the cost of materials of all kinds rose rapidly and disproportionately, and some commodities, indispensable to brewers, became so scarce that the manufacturers demanded exorbitant prices for them. Brewers' pitch was one of these. In view of this fact the convention offered a premium of $500 for a cheap and good substitute * for pitch, authorizing the Executive Committee (not the Executive Board) to examine and test whatever substances may be offered and award the premium to the inventor of the cheapest and most useful.

The newly elected Executive Committee immediately sought and obtained the co-operation of a committee from each of the Pennsylvania and New York Brewers' Associations, the former consisting of F. Collins, R. Smith, J. T. Thomas, A. Hugel and F. Seitz; the latter, including New Jersey Brewers, of M. P. Read, A. A. Dunlap, W. Price, D. Jones, J. Flanagan and P. Ammermann.

During the succeeding year this splendid body of men attended to all legislative matters and laid the foundation for those systematic, thorough and accurate methods which have ever since then distinguished the associations' public agitations. Their work, a report of which was submitted to the *fourth* convention, elicited the admiration not only of their associates, but also of many members of Congress and all those officers of the Government with whom they had official dealings and

---

* In the minutes the word surrogate is used for substitute.

upon whose good-will and friendly diposition depended all their chances of success. A brief outline and summary of the composition and work of the fourth convention ought to precede a review of these matters, all the more so because this meeting marks a new departure in several very essential elements of the corporate life of the association. The attendance was exceedingly numerous and many new men came to the front. At the very beginning a marked improvement in the management of parliamentary affairs made itself felt; many things that had formerly been taken for granted or deemed unnecessary, now claimed and received serious attention and consideration. Thus the president (John Bechtel), in opening the convention, no longer contented himself with a simple call to order and a few words of greeting, but delivered a very impressive opening address, briefly reviewing past and outlining future work, and laying particular stress upon a pending proposition, placed upon the order of business, to bring about a closer union with the ale-brewers' associations. He extended a particularly cordial welcome to the delegates of these associations, who, as he expressed it, "are here with us that we may go hand in hand in all future consultations bearing upon the interests of all branches of our business." The details of organization were also more in harmony with parliamentary usuages than at any of the preceding meetings, inasmuch as the report of a regularly constituted nominating committee took the place of the former, rather irregular, method of nominations. F. Lauer was re-elected president; J. Schlitz, of Milwaukee and L. Haberstroh, of Buffalo, secretaries. As soon as Lauer had taken the chair, Katzenmayer announced the order of business and suggested the appointment of special committees, to whom should be referred the various matters requiring action.

No less than seven different committees were thus appointed, each entrusted with very important affairs. All reported on the second day, and their reports compare very favorably, both as to substance and form, with present-day documents of this nature.

It was at this convention that the association, by virtue of a resolution submitted by one of these committees, adopted the name and title of *United States Brewers' Association*. The adoption of this title formed part of an effort to establish a closer union with the ale-brewers. The committee recommended and the convention resolved that henceforth a Joint Executive Committee, to be composed of representatives of both branches of the trade, should co-operate in all matters affecting common interests, and that whatever expenses might be incurred in protecting these interests should be borne jointly. This arrangement, though only a temporary makeshift, worked admirably for the time being and proved to be the best that could have been adopted, in view of a manifest disinclination on the part of a majority of ale-brewers to become members, individually, of the national body; in fact, so long as this association continued to cling to the representative-system nothing else could reasonably be expected. Secretary Katzenmayer again reported at this convention that a vast majority of the brewers of the country were not members of local associations and, consequently, had not contributed a penny to the funds expended for their protection. Here again the attempt to overcome this indifference took the shape of an appeal to the members of the trade to establish or join local associations. The great difficulty which confronted the officers—a difficulty scarcely intelligible in our days—lay in the want of a trade-register or other similar source of information as to the names and addresses of the brewers throughout the country. The only available source of information was the Revenue Office and there the method of compiling the reports from the large number of collectors was just about being perfected so as to include the desired data. That the number of individual and corporate members must have still been exceedingly small at this time, cannot be doubted. Positive evidence as to actual membership cannot be derived from any preceding records; in fact, the only available figures of any kind were presented at this convention in the form of a financial statement covering the entire period of the national association's existence, *i. e.*, from November 12, 1862, to September 18, 1864. The amount of money received during these twenty-two months from all sources amounted, in the aggregate, to $9,270.29; the expenditures to $5,773.83, including the secretary's salary at $15 per month, the attorney's fees at $405, and printing and postage at $559.51. The remainder, exclusive of $341 expended in the attempt to secure a suitable substitute for pitch, covered every necessary expenditure growing out of the agitation described in the foregoing pages.

In connection with what has been shown as to the general progress and improvement in the management of association affairs, it remains to be stated that at this convention a permanent Agitation Committee was created, similar in composition, objects, duties and functions to the present Vigilance Committee. The first committee consisted of Lauer, chairman; J. Pfaff, Massachusetts; J. Bechtel, New York; H. Schalk, New Jersey; G. Bergner, Philadelphia; Jacob Seeger, Maryland; Juenemann, District of Columbia; Hechelmann, West Virginia; Kleiner and Eichenlaub, Ohio; W. F. Belser, Indiana; S. Geisbauer, Kentucky; J. A. Hack, Illinois; C. T. Melms, Wisconsin; A. Heeb, Iowa, and C. G. Stifel, Missouri.

The attempt to obtain a material answering the purpose of brewers' pitch failed, for the reason that the only available offer, made by J. Werner & Co. of Mannheim (Baden), would have necessitated the expenditure of $5,000 for the purchase of patent-rights, and of an enormous sum for the erection, equipment and operation of a factory in this country. Besides this, the examining committee doubted the usefulness of the article. It would certainly have been extremely unwise to engage in such an extensive and costly enterprise, in view of the probability that before the factory could be put into practical operation the price of brewers' pitch would sink to its former level. It must be of interest to present-day brewers to learn that the substitute offered by the German manufacturers consisted of a glazing substance, similar to the one exhibited at a recent convention and found to be quite as unsuitable for the purpose in question, as Werner's substitute was pronounced to be.

At the time when the Committee on Legislation, appointed at the Cincinnati convention, entered upon its extremely arduous, difficult and delicate mission (October, 1863), the Government, confronted with gigantic difficulties for which the history of our country offers no parallel, was straining every nerve to preserve the credit of the nation. True, the battle of Gettysburg had turned the tide of disasters which before had almost overwhelmed our armies, but the rebellion was far from being ended, and the necessary expenditures of the war exceeded all previous standards. To ask for a reduction of the tax on malt-liquors at such a time would have been more than injudicious and unwise, no matter how burdensome the existing tax may have been; it would have been highly unpatriotic to ask for relief under such circumstances, and the members of the committee, who fully appreciated this, deserve admiration and unmeasured praise for the courage and manhood they displayed in arbitrarily modifying their instructions and partially abandoning a policy which would have been barely less than suicidal. They observed the upward tendency of all taxes and felt that in the face of a strongly-urged proposition to increase the beer-tax, a request for its reduction should not be pressed. Guided by such considerations, the committee submitted to Congress one of the best arguments ever prepared on the subject. They had to meet the opposition of the distillers who had, from the beginning, become notorious for their extensive frauds upon the revenue and who, not content with their ill-gotten, enormous gains, sought to drive brewing to the wall—a policy to which they have been faithful to this day. The brewers' argument made a deep impression and attracted the attention of the Revenue Office, who perceived that the data contained in it might be made useful in perfecting the revenue-system. The principal features of the argument consisted of a comparison of the rates of taxes levied in European countries upon ardent spirits and malt-liquors, and of those inevitable conclusions with which we are now all perfectly familiar. Instead of striving for a reduction, the committee exerted itself to the utmost to prevent an increase of the tax, and in this they succeeded, thanks to their masterly exposition of the desirability of malt-liquors as a national beverage and the limits beyond which taxation cannot be carried without ruinously affecting the industry.

The committee's manly and patriotic bearing, the thoroughness of their argument and their intimate familiarity with this particular branch of the tax-system, prompted the Revenue Office to seek several interviews with them, at which the subject was fully discussed in connection with the general belief that the method of collection then practiced did not, for several reasons, yield the amount of money actually due to the government from the brewing industry. The brewers claimed, and the Revenue Commissioner conceded, that the alleged shortage was almost wholly due to the defective system, rather than to any fraudulent intent on the part of the tax-payers; the Commissioner certainly admitted, and the reports of his successors in office clearly prove, that wherever brewers' associations existed, efforts were being made by the brewers themselves to enforce the law, and that nowhere did there exist among brewers a combination like that of the distillers, called into existence for the sole purpose of evading the obligations to the government. The committee eagerly seized upon this opportunity of manifesting their constitutents' willingness to assist the government in collecting the tax and promised to urge their association to adopt proper means to this end. Accordingly, Collins, speaking for the committee, delivered at the fourth convention a ringing speech in favor of co-operating with the government in this matter. He pointed out the fact that the trade was not only menaced by an increase of tax, but also by a burdensome control rendered necessary by reason of evasions of the law. His appeal to the patriotism of brewers elicited unbounded enthusiasm, and when he stated that the government, in its efforts to suppress the existing unparalleled rebellion, should have the support and assistance of every honest brewer, tumultuous applause resounded through the hall, testifying to the deep impression made by his words. The convention then adopted these resolutions expressing, more eloquently than any comment upon them possibly could, the motives which prompted and the sentiments which inspired the association, viz.:—

"1. That in consideration of the great wants of the government and the continuance of our national struggle to maintain the Union, we cheerfully acquiesce in the present rate of tax of $1 per barrel, believing that at the expiration of the war it will be the pleasure of Congress to reduce it in accordance with our petition. 2. That the secretary of this convention be instructed to address a circular-letter to each local association of brewers throughout the United States, expressing fully the views of this Convention, of the paramount necessity of a faithful payment of the tax due by brewers to the government, and requesting the appointment by them of a committee of three of their members, whose duty it shall be to examine each and every month the records of the collectors of their districts; and when an evasion of the law is supposed to exist, it shall be the duty of said committee to call on the delinquent brewer, and, if their suspicions are well-grounded, to remonstrate with him and request the payment of the full amount of his taxes. In case of his failure to comply with the same, he shall be reported to the local association within the section of the country in which he resides for their further action. 3. That a committee, consisting of five members of this convention, be appointed to visit Washington and confer with the Commissioner of Internal Revenue on this subject, in accordance with the invitation extended by him, and contained in a letter addressed to Mr. F. Collins of Philadelphia, dated 30th of August (1864), and to obtain from him the necessary authority for the above committees to have access to the records of the collectors of the tax paid by each brewer within their section of the State."

In the further progress of our narrative, the reader will become aware that it was not an exaggeration to claim that this convention laid the foundation for some of the most valuable and enduring institutions of the association and promulgated, in unmistakable terms, the quintescence of what has since been, and must forever after be and remain, the policy of the trade. Even at the very next convention, as we shall presently see, the seed sown at Milwaukee bore precious fruit in profuse abundance.

Gratitude and keen appreciation of inestimably valuable services prompted the delegates to present a silver set to President Lauer and a gold watch and chain to Katzenmayer, the presentation in each case affording a welcome opportunity for well-deserved panegyrics and a description of the merits of these two men.

Contrary to former custom, and somewhat incongrously, the convention, in again designating New York as the seat of the association's Executive Board, elected J. Bechtel as president, Schaefer as treasurer and Katzenmayer as secretary. Formerly, the New York association elected their officers and the national convention simply resolved that the officers thus elected should constitute the Executive Board of the national body. The departure from this rule may be regarded as the first step in the direction of a more logical arrangement in regard to the regular officers of the association.*

---

* The delegates to the 4th Convention were as follows, viz : Baltimore, J. Seeger, E. Stifel, T. Beck; Buffalo, J. Haberstroh; Cincinnati, F. Kleiner, C. H. Gogreve, C. Moerlein, J. Kauffmann, P. Weyand; Columbus, Ohio, L. Hoster; Covington, C. Geisbauer; Davenport, P. Littig, M. Fraham; Dubuque, J. Schwendt, A. Heep; Galena, Ill., J. Haser, R. Speyer, M. Moeller, G. F. Voltz; Hudson City, N. J., J. Roemmelt; Iowa City, G. L. Ruppert; Kenosha, R. A. Brown; Louisville, J. Stein; Madison, W. F. Belser; Mequon River, Wis., A. Zimmermann; Milwaukee, T. Obermann, C. Bast, J. Enes, J. Beck, G. Schweickhart, V. Blatz, P. Best, H. Stoltz, J. B. Mayer, J. F. Hohl, C. T. Melms, J. Schlitz; New Albany, Ind., P. Reising; Newark, N. J., R. F. Ballantine, H. Schalk; Newark, O., M. Morath; New York City, F. Schaefer, J. N. Katzenmayer; Philadelphia, C. Psotta, F. Collins, G. Bergner, R. Gray, P. Guckes; Pittsburgh, X. Waltz, G. Siedle, G. Gerst, M. Hechelman, M. Schaefer, J. Rodes, C. Meiser, D. Lutz; Quincy, J. Dick; Reading, F. Lauer; Rochester, H. Will; Rock Island, J. Schmid, I. Huber; Staten Island, J. Bechtel; St. Louis, C. G. Stifel, J. Uhrig, H. Koehler; West Bend, Wis., S. Meyer; Wheeling, A. Reymann, and Zanesville, C. F. Achauer.

Chapter IV.

MODE OF TAX-COLLECTION DEFECTIVE. SECRETARY McCULLOCH SEEKS BREWERS' ADVICE; THEIR MOTIVES APPRECIATED, AND COMPLAINTS ATTENDED TO. PROPOSED REVISION OF REVENUE-LAW; SPECIAL COMMISSION APPOINTED. BREWERS' RESOLVE TO ASSIST GOVERNMENT AND APPOINT A COMMITTEE TO STUDY THE EXCISE-QUESTION IN EUROPE. SECRETARY OF THE TREASURY APPROVES THE PLAN. COMPOSITION OF THE COMMITTEE; ITS DEPARTURE FOR EUROPE. AGITATION COMMITTEE DEFEATS TAX-INCREASE; OLD TAX CHEERFULLY BORNE. FIFTH CONVENTION MEETS AT BALTIMORE; ITS COMPOSITION AND VITAL IMPORTANCE. RELATIONS TO REVENUE OFFICE. COURT DECIDES AGAINST TAXING BEER CONSUMED BY BREWERS. PROPOSITIONS RELATING TO SCIENTIFIC IMPROVEMENTS IN BREWING; DAWN OF PROGRESSIVE ERA. A WAR INCIDENT. SPECIAL REVENUE COMMISSIONER WELLS REPRESENTS GOVERNMENT AT CONVENTION; HIS RECEPTION AND HIS SPEECH. COLLINS READS REPORT OF EUROPEAN COMMISSION; THE SPECIAL COMMISSIONER'S OPINION OF IT. SPECIAL COMMITTEE CONFERS WITH GOVERNMENT'S REPRESENTATIVE AS TO CHANGE IN MODE OF TAXATION; RECOMMENDS ADOPTION OF REVENUE STAMPS. ANOTHER SPECIAL COMMITTEE APPOINTED TO AGREE WITH COMMISSIONER WELLS UPON DETAILS OF STAMP LAW. COMMISSIONER WELLS EMBODIES BREWERS' MEMORIAL IN HIS REPORT; EXTRACT FROM THE LATTER. EXTRACTS FROM BREWERS' MEMORIAL.

At a time when evasions of the tax-law were in common practice, the attitude of the brewers' associations throughout the country could not but produce a most favorable impression at Washington. The brewers claimed no credit whatever for this, nor did they believe themselves entitled to special favors on account of it; quite the contrary was the case. They believed, as a leading spirit of the fourth convention said many years afterward, that they had only done their duty to their country—a country they loved faithfully and well. Whatever may have been the brewers' view of it, the Government certainly interpreted their action as springing from a spirit of patriotism and an integrity of purpose which deserved recognition. Up to this time the brewers' negotiations at Washington had been with the Commissioner of Internal Revenue only, but after their aims became known by means of the resolutions quoted in the preceding chapter, the Secretary of the Treasury (McCulloch) himself invited the brewers' representatives to consult with him in regard to a more effective enforcement of the law, and such modifications in the mode of collection as their knowledge and experience might suggest. Their motives were now so well understood and appreciated that they encountered no difficulty in ridding the trade of petty annoyances which some collectors, construing the law too strictly and literally, had in many instances inflicted upon it. Thus, for instance, the brewers justly complained of a repeated attempt to meddle with the commercial conduct of the brewing business by compelling brewers in certain cases to take out peddlers' licenses; in some districts the collectors went so far as to require the payment of tax for beer removed from one part of the brewery to another for private consumption. All such minor complaints now received immediate attention and the causes of them were invariably removed with commendable promptness. The chief defects of the system—manifest in all its extensive ramifications embracing nearly every industry and calling—could not be so easily remedied. Many of its features, which in theory seemed feasible enough, proved to be utterly impracticable when put into operation, while some of the provisions of the law specially designed to prevent fraud had the effect of facilitating it.

Appreciating the danger and difficulty of again legislating upon the subject on purely theoretical and somewhat experimental lines, Congress, at the suggestion of the Secretary of the Treasury, enacted a law—approved March 3, 1865—creating a Special Revenue Commission, whose duty it was to investigate the entire system and the nature and extent of the principal sources of internal revenue, to the end that the law might be amended in accordance both with the requirements of the exchequer, and such considerations as all honest tax-payers had a right to expect from a just and impartial Government. The enactment of this law had scarcely become generally known when a number of local brewers' associations almost simultaneously discussed the advisability of assisting the newly created Commission in that part of their labors which related to the tax on malt-liquors. It is impossible to determine who first proposed such a course; there can be no doubt, however, that the credit for formulating a definite plan of action belonged to Collins of Philadelphia. The general proposition was so entirely in harmony and keeping with the association's policy that its simultaneous advocacy by several members and associations must have seemed perfectly natural; but the mode and manner of the proposed assistance remained a mooted question until Collins conceived the plan of sending a committee of brewers to Europe for the purpose of studying and reporting upon the different excise-systems and, particularly, upon the mode of taxation and method of collection. On the 7th of March, three days after the approval of the Act creating the Special Revenue Commission, he submitted his plan in the form of a resolution to the ale-brewers' and the lager-beer brewers' associations of Philadelphia, with the understanding that, in the event of its adoption, the concurrence and explicit sanction of the Executive Board of the national body and of all the local associations should at once be secured so as to make the movement a national one in every sense. Unanimously adopted by the Philadelphia brewers, the resolution was sent to New York, approved in a general meeting of the brewers of that city, and sanctioned by the

Executive Board of the United States Brewers' Association; other associations adopted similar resolutions. The committee chosen by the association consisted of F. Collins, of Philadelphia; M. P. Read, of New York, and F. Lauer.

Notified of this timely action, the Secretary of the Treasury forwarded an exceedingly flattering letter to the committee, fully approving the undertaking and plainly intimating that the Special Revenue Commissioners (for whom he was certainly authorized to speak, although he had not yet appointed them), would gladly accept and make use of the committee's report, and that he himself looked forward with great interest to the results of the contemplated enquiry. This imparted to their mission a quasi-official character that could not but facilitate their labors. Provided with special passports and strong letters of recommendation to a great number of prominent brewers, statesmen and scientists, the committee sailed on the 19th of April, and, landing at Queenstown, at once started out on their unique tour.

In the meantime, the Agitation Committee, specially instructed to watch Congressional legislation and to maintain the trade's satisfactory relations to the Treasury Department, succeeded in convincing the members of their association that all efforts in the direction of a tax-reduction should cease, and that the existing tax of $1.00 per barrel ought cheerfully and promptly to be paid by every brewer in the land. Their admonition derived particular force from the fact that, shortly before the enactment of the law for the revision of the revenue-system, a proposition to increase the tax upon malt-liquors to $1.50 per barrel was defeated by a majority of only four votes. The chairman of the brewers' committee, assisted by Bergner, Baltz, Gaul, Grey,

O'Neill and Vollmer, of Philadelphia ; Col. Price, of New York ; Schalk, of Newark ; Col. Gerst, of Pittsburgh ; Eichenlaub and Kleiner, of Cincinnati, argued against this increase before the Committee on Ways and Means and by their strong argument won over to their side several members who had originally intended to advocate the increase on the floor of the House, but now opposed it. By their correspondence with local associations and individual members, the committee succeeded in completely changing the views of those brewers who, at the fourth convention, strenuously advocated a reduction of the tax ; in fact, everybody now seemed to be perfectly satisfied, and the tax, formerly regarded as burdensome to an "infant industry," was now looked upon as a reasonable fiscal measure made necessary by the needs of the nation. In connection with this twofold agitation, the committee continued to urge upon all associations the necessity of an unrelenting war upon all dishonest practices, and particularly upon those designed to curtail the amount of money justly due to the Government.

This was the state of affairs when the fifth convention took place at Baltimore, on the 18th of October, 1865. At this distance, we have no means of knowing what considerations prompted the selection of Baltimore, in spite of the fact that an equally cordial invitation had been received, among many others, from the brewers of Washington. If ever prudential reasons pleaded for holding a brewers' meeting at the seat of the Federal Government, it certainly was at this time, when the association was about to consummate a work destined to play an important part in the legislative and executive efforts by which the revenue-system was finally placed upon a practicable, just and equitable basis. It is true, that when the resolution designating

Fifth Convention. 151

Baltimore as the place for holding the fifth convention was adopted, the brewers could have had no idea of this work and its far-reaching results, because the circumstances which led to it had not yet occurred; but even without this additional incentive, there was in the very nature of the other work undertaken by the fourth convention more than a sufficiency of reasons for selecting Washington. It will always remain a source of deep regret that this selection was not made.

Before proceeding to a consideration of that part of the great work by which the fifth convention won enduring fame and an enviable distinction, we may briefly summarize the general character of this meeting. It was less numerously attended than must have been expected in view of the paramount importance of pending questions;* the entire West was represented by only ten brewers—strong, influential, energetic and wise men, all of them, but not sufficiently familiar with the whole Western trade to represent it adequately and intelligently; with them came the first delegate from Colorado, then a Territory. Owing to a railroad accident, the Cincinnati delegates arrived too late to participate in the proceedings of the first day's session. The New England States had no representation whatever. Baltimore was represented by sixteen, and New

---

* This is a list of the delegates to this convention, viz.: Albany, C. W. Schindler; Baltimore, G. Bauernschmidt, J. Bauernschmidt, A. Beck, Th. Beck, J. Beier, J. G. Hoffmann, G. Reissendorfer, O. v. Johe, G. Papst, M. Pringsheim, G. Rossmark, G. Rost, J. Seeger, E. Stiefel, G. F. Wiessner, J. F. Wiessner; Colorado Territory, Albert Selack; Iowa City, M. Tschirgi; Lancaster, J. J. Springer; Lebanon, F. Laner, J. Hartmann, J. Yost; Milwaukee, P. Best, V. Blatz, Hohl; Newark, N. J., Ehehalt; New York, Bechtel, Clansen, Katzenmayer Kuntz, Sommer, Ammermann, Ballantine, Lewis, Marr, Milbank, Read, Schwartz; Philadelphia, Baltz, Benz, Bergner, Joerger, Orth, Schemm, Collins, Ganl, Grey, Guckes, Smith; Pittsburgh, Fuellback, Gerst, Heim, Nusser; Reading, F. Lauer; St. Louis, Fenerbacher, Rothweiler, C. Stifel; Washington, Abner, Dickson, Kaiser, Kozel, Maak, Richter; Wheeling, West Virginia, F. J. Rothacker; Wilkesbarre, Pa., Reichard; York, Pa., A. Webel.

York and Pennsylvania by thirty delegates, the total number of brewers in attendance being seventy-two. Bechtel still occupied the office of president of the association, Lauer was re-elected as president of the convention and with him, G. Bergner of Philadelphia and J. M. Lewis of New York, as secretaries, and the following vice-presidents: Read, New York; Ballantine, New Jersey; Heim, Pennsylvania; Beck, Maryland; Kleiner, Ohio; Huck, Illinois; Best, Wisconsin; Stifel, Missouri; Tschirgi, Iowa; Rothacker, West Virginia; Maak, District of Columbia; Selack, Colorado.

Several minor complaints concerning arbitrary rulings by revenue-collectors engaged the attention of the convention, but were not deemed of sufficient weight to warrant extraordinary measures, inasmuch as the Revenue Commissioner had previously signified his perfect willingness to remove the wrongs complained of. A similar course would probably have been adopted with regard to an attempt made by the collectors of Cincinnati and St. Louis to collect the tax upon beer consumed by brewery workmen, but the St. Louis brewers had already instituted legal proceedings against the Revenue Office, and, even while the convention was in session, a dispatch was received from St. Louis announcing the courts' decision in favor of the brewers. The Treasury Department immediately notified the association that an appeal from this decision was not contemplated, the Revenue Commissioner being convinced of the injustice of taxing beer given to journeymen-brewers free of charge.

If there were no other features to distinguish this convention, it would, indeed, be sufficiently remarkable and deserving of special attention and study for its labors bearing on the scientific progress of the art of brewing. As has been stated in a preceding chapter, the old-time brewer evinced a strong dislike for scientific processes, yet sometimes fell an easy prey to quacks who speculated upon their victims' lack of scientific training as well as upon their belief in so-called trade-secrets. A considerable portion of the old conservative element still clung to the industry thirty years ago; it was just then that an appreciation of the advantages of scientific methods began to dawn upon the members of the trade. At this (fifth) convention the delegates considered two propositions intended to improve the process of brewing, one emanating from a scientist, Prof. G. C. Habich, of Wiesbaden, the other from C. W. Schindler, a practical brewer of Albany. The fact that both persons presented their schemes with a view to selling it to the association does not diminish our interest in the matter, nor is the question as to whether the proposed processes possessed any real merit or not, of any particular importance to us; we are interested in the spirit which made possible the discussion of such matters by an organized body of old-time brewers. Prof. Habich's plan covered comprehensively all the chemical transformations and mechanical details incident to mashing, cooling and fermenting, and to steeping, couching, flooring, sweating and kiln-drying; his principal improvements included a saving of time, labor and material without any deterioration of the quality of the product. Schindler believed that he had discovered a method by which a brewer might save 10 per cent. of malt and 50 per cent. of fuel, and yet be able to produce and put upon the market, within twenty days, a clear, brilliant, effervescent lager-beer, very much like the Bavarian brews. Both Habich and Schindler claimed to have discovered a process of manufacturing dry yeast, capable of being preserved for a considerable length of time. Naturally enough, both offers were declined, but the discussion they elicited seems to have produced a salutary effect; for, thereafter it became a regular practice to bring before the conventions all matters touching upon this subject, and in this way a mass of useful information was disseminated throughout the trade. These discussions then took the place now so admirably filled by the technical committee of the association, the brewers' schools and the trade-journals.

An incident occurred at this convention which deserves to be preserved because it throws a strong light upon the spirit of the times. E. Richter, who, before the war had established a brewery at Richmond, Va., appealed to the association for the loan of a stated sum of money to enable him to re-establish himself in business. Like the vast majority of Germans, he was an ardent Unionist and a sincere lover of his adopted country, and, although fully aware of the persecutions to which Unionists were exposed even before the passage of the ordinance of secession, he took no pains whatever to conceal his unswerving fealty to the Union, thus rendering himself so obnoxious that he had to leave the city in order to save his life. Every attempt to recover possession of his property having failed, he appealed to his trade-associates for help—which the association could not give, but which was privately extended to him by the delegates in ample measure.

When Lauer called for the report of the Special Committee sent to Europe on the mission before described, Collins, its chairman, informed the convention that Special Revenue Commissioner A. D. Wells had been deputed by his Department to be present at the brewers' convention, in order to discuss with the delegates the subject-matter of the report and the conclusions that may be reached by the delegates as to the simplest, safest and most effective mode of taxation. Wells had sent his card to the committee and Collins now proposed that the Commissioner be invited to the floor. The suggestion was acted upon and Collins and Ballantine were instructed to escort Mr. Wells to the hall. As soon as the representative of the Government appeared upon the threshold, the delegates rose in a body and remained standing until the formal introduction had taken place, when Mr. Wells at once addressed them, thanking them for their courtesy and explaining the objects of his visit, as viewed by himself and his superiors. The chronicler of the association's life deplores the unusual meagreness of the minutes of this convention; only a single copy of the proceedings has been preserved and this, being printed in the German, does not present even the fragmentary quotations from Mr. Wells' speech in the original language. From what this officer subsequently stated in his official reports, we may infer, in part, what his speech was intended to convey to the minds of the delegates. He believed at the time, that at least 40 per cent. of the tax due from brewers had not been collected and he based this estimate upon the data contained in the Census of 1860, and a certain approximative ratio of increase at which he arrived by inferential reasoning and a calculation founded upon statements made by prominent brewers as to the increase of production in their establishments within a stated period of time. The revenue reports of later years, when the whole amount of the tax was unquestionably paid into the treasury, clearly show that his estimate was greatly exaggerated; yet the fact remained that a proportion of the tax was not paid, in spite of the association's strenuous efforts. He expressed the hope that a co-operation with the brewers would enable the Department to devise a more effective method of taxation.

Although the reading of the committee's voluminous report occupied fully three hours, the interest in its subject-matter never flagged or abated for a moment and when, amid vociferous applause, the end of it had been reached, the Special Revenue Commissioner at once attested his appreciation of the work by the assurance that he would embody it verbatim in his annual report to Congress and would call special attention to its astounding wealth of economic and statistical information. At his own suggestion, a sub-committee was appointed to confer with him, then and there, and to formulate, if possible, a statement embodying such suggestions concerning the modification of existing laws as might to them and to him appear reasonable and feasible. A committee of nineteen delegates, representing both branches of the trade and the principal beer-producing States, was immediately appointed, which, on the following day, in the presence of Commissioner Wells, submitted a report of which only a German translation has been preserved. The substance of it is to the effect that during the conference with the Commissioner three modes of taxation had been discussed, viz.: (1) a tax upon malt or barley; (2) a tax on the worts while in the fermentation vats; (3) a tax upon the finished product under an improved mode of collection. As to the tax on malt or barley the committee expressed the opinion, and Wells agreed with them, that in rural districts where the brewer can obtain his supply of raw material from the agricultural producer direct and can malt it in his own establishment, a proper supervision over the quantities used could not be exercised by the revenue-officers. The second mode of taxation appeared objectionable because it would require an army of additional revenue-inspectors and even then could not be effectually carried out in the rural districts, while it would necessitate irksome inspections, searches and other detrimental interferences with the business. Agreeing that the old tax upon the finished product should be retained, the committee proposed, and the convention adopted, a resolution to the effect *that this tax should be collected by means of a stamp to be affixed to every brewer's package sold and removed from the place of its manufacture.*

For the purpose of determining upon the details of this innovation, the convention appointed a special committee, consisting of Collins, Read, Lauer, Bergner, Kleiner, Ammermann and Katzenmayer, who organized in the presence of the Special Revenue Commissioner and received from him the assurance that he would from time to time consult with them and participate in their deliberations whenever a final agreement would be likely to be reached. He faithfully fulfilled his promises. Two months after the committee's first meeting (held in Philadelphia on the 8th of November) he submitted to Congress a report, from which we quote the following extract, viz. :—

"Upon the announcement of the appointment of this commission in the spring of 1865, the National Brewers' Association appointed a committee of three of their most prominent members, to visit Europe, and examine, carefnlly and in detail, the results of the working of the systems of taxation in regard to fermented liquors adopted in those countries of Europe, where the demand for such liquors is more general and extensive than in the United States. The report of that committee, comprising a great amount of information touching this industry, now so rapidly developing itself in the United States, has, by vote of the Brewers' Association, been placed in the hands of the commission, and is now at the disposal of Congress for publication if they deem it expedient. The commission believe that its publication would be of great benefit to the brewing interest of the country, and, indirectly, to the revenue; and they therefore recommend it.

As the present rate of tax imposed upon fermented liquors, viz.: one dollar per barrel of thirty-one gallons, is in excess of the rate imposed by any of the States of Europe (Austria excepted); and as the present rate, moreover, in the opinion of the commission, after full consideration, is believed to be fully up to the revenue standard; and as such is all but unanimously acquiesced in by the brewing interest of the country, they would, therefore, recommend that the existing rate be neither increased nor diminished.

The determination of the proper mode of collecting the tax on fermented liquors, and preventing the large amount of fraud which has heretofore, undoubtedly, been committed in regard to the same, has been to the commission a subject of no little difficulty. By reference to their Special Report (No. 6), it will be seen that a tax on malt in this country is not practicable; neither is the plan, also investigated by the commission, of gauging and assessing the liquors, either in the "coppers" during the process of manufacture, or subsequently, while in the fermenting vats. Abandoning both of these methods, therefore, they have, with the full concurrence and assistance of the leading brewers of the country, devised a plan for collecting the tax by means of a stamp, printed on insoluble parchment paper, to be affixed to each barrel sold and removed from the place of its manufacture, with a requirement that the same be cancelled by the retailer or consumer.

Specimens of the stamps assigned for this purpose have been prepared for submission to Congress, while the full details of the plan are given in the special report referred to. With the adoption of this system, and the retention of the present rate of excise, the commission estimate that the government may rely upon an immediate annual revenue from fermented liquors, of at least five millions of dollars."

The report of the Brewers' Commission covers thirty-nine closely printed pages, and treats not only of the modes of taxation and collection, the amount of taxes, production of beer, &c., but also of nearly every economic feature of the trade, of brewing-processes in vogue in the various countries, of the production and quality of raw-materials, of improvements in malting, refrigerating and bottling, the commercial practices of European manufacturers and many other details of the greatest interest to brewers. Besides this, it presents historical data bearing on the excise-system and many exceedingly valuable hints and conclusions as to the spirit of the laws relating to brewing. It would not be expedient to reproduce the entire report and we, therefore, place before the reader only an extract from it, leaving out everything not directly connected with the tax-question. Such an extract will be all the more useful, as it will enable the reader to compare the condition of the trade in 1865 with its status in 1895, as described in a preceding chapter. The extracts read as follows, viz. :—

BREWERS' MEMORIAL TO CONGRESS.

Great Britain.—The establishment of the excise in England was consummated in 1643, when the first tax was imposed on beer, at the rate of 1s. ber barrel. Increased at subsequent periods, it was finally repealed in 1830. The duty on malt was first imposed in 1679, at the rate of 6¼d. per bushel, and, after various changes and fluctuations, was placed at 2s. 7d. in 1821, at which rate, with the addition of 5 per cent., it was continued until the war with Russia. It was then advanced to 4s. per bushel, at which rate it continued for two years, 1854 and 1855, diminishing the consumption from 36,000,000 bushels in 1853 to 30,000,000 bushels in 1855. The result, as we were informed by one of the principal brewers in London, was "a miserable failure; it destroyed the profits of the brewers, who were unable to advance their prices to cover the increased cost of malt." The duty was reduced to the previous rate in 1856, viz.: 2s. 7d. and 5 per cent., equal to 2s. 8¼d. per bushel, or 21s. 8d. per quarter of eight bushels. The effect, so far as increased consumption is concerned, was immediate, the quantity charged with duty in 1856 being 34,439,475, and the yearly average for six years thereafter, including 1862, was 38,190,975 bushels.

As the debt of the nation influences its taxation, we herewith present the total amount of the national debt of Great Britain; and in reference to this and other statistical facts, we shall extract, where it is convenient to do so, from the able report of the Chancellor of the Exchequer, Mr. Gladstone, presented to the House of Commons on the 27th of April :—

On the 31st of March, 1865, the public debt of Great
Britain amounted to............................. £808,288,000
The revenue for the past year....................... 70,313,000
The actual expenditure............................ 66,462,000

Of this amount, £6,337,000 was received from the duty on malt, and £10,173,000 on British spirits.

The highly prosperous condition of the manufacturing and commercial interests of Great Britain, with the prospect of its continuance, induced the Chancellor to recommend a reduction of a portion of the taxes, corresponding nearly to the amount of the surplus revenue of the past year, and, although there was a large party in the House advocating a reduction or entire repeal of the duty on malt, he selected three other sources of revenue to which, in his judgment, the surplus should be applied, and recommended that the duty on tea be reduced from 1s. to 6d. per pound, the income tax from an average of 6d. per pound sterling to 4d., or a little more than 1½ per cent., and a considerable reduction on the fire insurance tax. In these measures he was sustained by Parliament. And we may here remark that, however desirable a reduction of the public debt may be, the people of Great Britain greatly prefer that the surplus revenue should be applied to a reduction of indirect taxation, the effect being more immediate in cheapening articles of consumption on which the duty is reduced, or from which it is withdrawn. It is believed that three-fourths, at least, of the national debt is permanently invested; executors, administrators, trustees of estates, guardians, courts of law, all invest in these Government securities. They offer undoubted security, while its distribution among all classes of capitalists tends to strengthen and secure the stability of the Government. It was from no feeling of hostility to the measure, as will be seen, that the Chancellor did not recommend a repeal or reduction of the malt duty. His argument was, that it was not taxed as high, proportionately, as tea. We have seen that the excise duty on malt is 2s. 8½d. per bushel, or 21s. 8d. per quarter of eight bushels, and that it has not exceeded this rate for the last forty-four years, except during the years 1854 and 1855. In addition to this, there is a license duty on beer of 3d. per barrel, imposed in lieu of the hop-duty, which was repealed in 1862. It will also be borne in mind that the English barley is much heavier than ours, and that the standard weight is 56 pounds per bushel, while ours is but 48, and that the malt is proportionately more productive. In order to compare the British excise duty with our own, theirs being based on the malt and ours on the beer, we have first to obtain the average produce of malt in Great Britain and then to assimilate their measure and our own. The result of our inquiry and observation proves that this product is equivalent, on an average, to four barrels of beer from the quarter of malt; this estimate is confirmed by the figures of the Chancellor of the Exchequer. The English barrel contains 36 imperial gallons, or 144 quarts. The duty on this quantity, then, is 21s. 8d. sterling and 3d. per barrel of beer. At this rate, estimating the pound sterling to be $4.84, the tax amounts to $1.31 per barrel of 36 imperial gallons of 277.2 inches, equal to 43.2 American gallons of 231 inches, and 94 cents for 31 gallons.

We could present the various rates of duty on beer from their first imposition, exhibiting their numerous fluctuations, their increase and decrease, and the corresponding increase and decrease of consumption, but our object has been to obtain the more matured experience of the governments of Europe, and to recommend to our own Government the adoption of that experience which it has taken them centuries to acquire. In striking proof of the disastrous effect of excessive taxation, we remind you of the well-known fact that in Scotland, when the tax of 2s. 3d. per barrel, imposed in 1707 on the favorite beverage of the people, termed "two-penny" beer, was increased to 3s. 4d. per barrel, the consumption, which before had averaged annually 450,000 barrels, was reduced to 100,000 barrels, and continued to decline till it ceased entirely. And at the present time, when the consumption of malt in the United Kingdom amounts to 43,848,050 bushels, only 1,906,190 bushels are used in Scotland. The result of this unwise measure was the substitution of whiskey as the common beverage of the people, which proved most unhappy in its effects.

The manufacture of malt-liquor is on the increase, not only in Great Britain, but also throughout all Europe, and the consumption is equal to the production. In reference to the consumption of beer in England, the Chancellor asks: "Has the Englishman changed his nature? Has he ceased to supply himself with a sufficient proportion of this excellent and truly national drink?" and then remarks: "On the contrary, the figures all tend upward. In 1841 the consumption of malt in Great Britain was 1.701 bushels per head of the population; in 1863 it was 1.793 per head. Now, that, I think, furnishes evidence of a very handsome growth. But how stands the case with spirits? During year after year, during the period to which I am referring, additional burdens have been laid. In 1841 the consumption per head of spirits in Great Britain was .763 gallons, while in 1863, to my great joy and satisfaction, it had sunk to .645." "The consumption of beer in England," he further remarks, "in 1720 was 6,000,000 barrels, or at the rate of a barrel per head, for the population at that time was only 6,000,000. In 1830 the consumption was 8,000,000 barrels, and in that year, I regret to say, it had sunk from one barrel to two-thirds of a barrel per head. In 1864, however, so powerful were the restorative processes which had been introduced, and so much had the consumption of beer been assisted by the legislation which took place in regard to spirits and otherwise, we go back, with a population of 20,000,000, to the good old scale, and consume 20,000,000 barrels, or exactly the same quantity per head as in 1722. Malt, we may say, lies half-way between the stronger liquors, such as wine and spirits, on the one hand, and tea on the other. I grant that beer ought to be taxed more lightly than the wines which compete with it, and more lightly than spirits."

From these remarks of Mr. Gladstone, the policy of the British Government is quite obvious, viz.: to derive the greatest revenue from the greatest consumption of beer, and the greatest revenue from the smallest consumption of spirits; to encourage the consumption of the one, and to discourage the consumption of the other.

Belgium.—The population of Belgium in 1863 was 4,894,071, of which 1,298,394 were residents of cities and towns, and 3,595,677 of the country. The Belgian debt at the end of 1864 was 609,236,133 francs, paying a yearly interest of 33,303,778 francs. The revenue of the Government for the present year is 159,512,770 francs. The general expenditure, including the interest on the public debt, 154,044,740 francs. The excise duty for beer is imposed on the malt at 4 francs per hectolitre, and is equivalent to 2 francs 5 centimes per hectolitre on the finished beer, or 49.6 cents for 31 American gallons. Before commencing his operations, the brewer notifies the excise officer, who gauges the quantity of malt, estimating the quantity of beer the malt will produce.

The importation of foreign beer in 1863 was 17,488 hectolitres, and the exportation for the same period 21,964. The consumption of beer per head in Belgium is largely on the increase, notwithstanding its indifferent quality; for the period from 1861 to 1863 it was 1.38 hectolitres, or 36.4 American gallons. The duty on spirits is small, and is charged at 2 francs 45 centimes per hectolitre (or 48 cents for 26.4 American gallons) on the contents of the vessel, and 35 francs per hectolitre on foreign spirits, equal to 25.8 cents per American gallon. The Government, however, charges a license duty for the sale of it by retailers, and this produces a revenue of 1,257,676 francs. The account of the revenue from beer appears to be kept with that of cider and vinegar, and we were unable to obtain the amount derived from beer alone. The following table shows the amount of revenue derived from spirits, and from beer and vinegar, from 1859 to 1863, inclusive:—

Year.	Spirits.	Beer and Vinegar.
1859	6,940,069 francs	7,880,751 francs
1860	8,673,106 "	8,701,216 "
1861	9,193,810 "	12,874,647 "
1862	10,762,664 "	12,946,925 "
1863	11,657,435 "	13,576,574 "

Wurttemberg.—The tax in this kingdom is imposed on the malt, and is 1 guilder 36 kreutzers, or 64 cents, on a centner (110 pounds). An eimer (77⅔ gallons of beer) is produced from 6 simri of malt, or 158 pounds. The tax being 64 cents on 110 pounds, is, therefore, equivalent to 36¾ cents per barrel of 31 gallons. The brewer receives from the excise officer a form or blank, on which is entered the quantity of malt to be ground for each brewing. The mill used for grinding the malt is under the control of the excise officer, who returns his certificate to the Department of Excise, and payment is demanded quarterly of the brewer for the amount of tax accrued during the three months. There is also a trade or license tax imposed of 3 kreutzers (2 cents) on an ohm (40 gallons), or 1¼ cents on 30 gallons. No change has taken place in the rate of taxation for the past thirty-eight years. No tax is imposed on wine when first manufactured, nor on the stock, nor on the sales of wholesale dealers, unless sold by them in less quantities than 25 bottles. The retail dealers pay an octroi, or municipal tax of 10 per cent. on their sales. The beer is pale, light and of excellent quality. It is sold by the brewers at a price equivalent to $4 per barrel of 31 gallons, and by the retailers at 12 kreutzers (9 cents) per maas (nearly half a gallon). The consumption is increasing to an extraordinary extent, when we consider the large quantity and excellent quality of wine produced in the kingdom. It is now three times greater than it was twenty years ago. This increase is the more surprising when we keep in view the decrease of the population during that period.

164 *History U. S. Brewers' Association—Chapter IV.*

According to the census of 1864, the population of Wurttemberg was 1,748,338 souls, having increased since 1861 27,620, and being no greater now than it was sixteen years ago, a decrease from 1,744,595 to 1,669,710 having taken place during the revolutionary periods in consequence of the vast immigration to the United States. The quality of malt is very similar to that produced in Great Britain, to whose ports it is frequently shipped. It is sold, on the average, for 6 guilders for 110 pounds, or $74\frac{8}{10}$ cents for an American bushel of 34 pounds. The hops used by the brewers are produced within the kingdom and sell for an average price of 28 to 40 cents per pound. The workmen employed in the breweries are paid 5 florins, or $2 per week, in addition to their board and lodging, furnished by the brewers. Spirits are distilled chiefly from the small fruits and the refuse of grapes, but little grain being used. They are principally used for manufacturing purposes, and only in rare instances drunk as a beverage. The tax on them is quite small. Before the brewing business had become so extensive, the beverages used by the people were cider and wine, made from grapes and small fruits. The public gardens are numerous in the cities, towns and villages, but nowhere does intemperance exist. The revenue derived from the tax on malt is 900,000 florins, or $360,000, about one-fifth of the amount raised by indirect taxation. The revenue from the tax on spirits is 150,000 florins, or $60,000. We take pleasure in acknowledging our obligations to Emil Klauprecht, Esq., United States Consul, for much valuable information in relation to this kingdom, as well as for his kind courtesies and attentions.

Bavaria.—Your Commissioners arrived in Munich, the capital of Bavaria, on the 30th of May, and prosecuted their inquiries with much interest. For several centuries, Bavaria has been celebrated for its peculiar system of brewing, the excellence of its beer, the extent of its manufacture and its general use among the people. The Bavarian Government first imposed a tax on malt liquors in 1290 of 7½ kreutzers for weak and 10 kreutzers for strong beer. Modifications of the tax were made in 1350, 1543, 1673 and 1750, increasing the rate, though lightly, and in 1811 the tax was fixed at its present rate. It is placed on the malt at the rate of 5 florins ($2) per scheffel, equivalent to 252 American pounds. A scheffel of malt produces 6½ eimers of beer. An eimer of beer is 18 gallons American measure. The tax, therefore, is equivalent to 53 cents per barrel of 31 gallons of beer. The tax is paid quarterly. The brewer is required by the Government to take out a permit before commencing his operations and the malt, before being ground, is measured and weighed by the excise officer. The brewer is also required to use only malt, hops, yeast and water in mannfacturing his beer. For any violation of the laws, for evading the payment of the tax, or using substitutes for the above-named materials, a penalty is imposed of $70 for the first, $140 for the second, and $210 for the third offence, the latter also involving the confiscation of the delinqnent's property.

The prices, wholesale and retail, at which beer is sold are fixed by the Government. By special act of the Legislature these restrictions, at the solicitation of the brewers, have been removed to take effect October 1st of this year. Beer is sold by the brewers, for present use, at 5¼ florins ($2.20) per eimer (18 gallons), and for stock or lager-beer 6¼ florins ($2.60). It is retailed at 6¼ kreutzers (4¼ cents) per maas, the retailer having but 1 florin per eimer. A retailer having entered into arrangements with the brewer for his supplies of beer for six months of one year, is prohibited by law from obtaining his beer from any other brewery during the term of his engagement, and in the event of his failing to make payment for his beer, a judgment and execution, taking precedence over other claims, are issued against him by the civil officers. An allowance of 5 per cent. on the tax rate is made by the Government to the brewers, as a special privilege over other manufacturers. The brewers are permitted to distil their refuse matters into spirits, without being compelled to pay an additional tax. Notwithstanding the protection extended by the Government to the brewers, the profits of the latter are but small. It was stated, by one of those most prominently engaged in the business, that his capital had not yielded, for 25 years past, more than 7½ per cent. annually. The Government has derived a revenue from the tax on malt in the

year 1811	1,000,000 florins	or	$400,000.00
" 1830	4,000,000 "	"	1,600,000.00
" 1860	7,000,000 "	"	2,800,000.00
" 1864	9,000,000 "	"	3,600,000.00

The population of Bavaria in 1864 was....................4,689,837
  " national debt................................$121,100,000.00
  "   "   income... .... 51,500,000.00
  "   "   expenditures 35,636,700.00

We estimate the consumption of beer in Bavaria at 6,792,452 eimers, which does not include the province on the Rhine. In the years 1816 and 1817, the barley crops having failed, the price of barley advanced to 23½ florins ($9.40) per scheffel, enhancing also the price of beer; as a consequence the consumption was materially reduced. In 1819, barley being abundant, the price declined to 5 florins ($2.00) per scheffel and continued low till 1844, never exceeding 10 florins or $4 per scheffel. From 1818 to 1843, the brewing business proving profitable, many new breweries were established, those in operation selling at from 500 to 800 per cent. in excess of their former value. In Munich, in 1848, 54 breweries were engaged in making beer, when the supply became so abundant in the market and the prices so reduced that the losses sustained by the brewers were very large, and many breweries were closed, only 24 continuing in operation. The consumption of malt-liquor throughout the kingdom is largely increasing, it being one hundred times greater than it was 20 years ago. It is truly a national beverage, used by the people at their meals, at their places of public amusement and at their festivals, and is largely substituted by the poorer classes for coffee. It is a novel sight, to an American, to see the people, early in the morning, drinking beer in the market places whilst eating their breakfast. Having accepted an invitation from Mr. Richard Connor, Acting Consul for the United States, we attended the celebration of the Annual Festival of the Artists, held near Munich on the 3rd of June. There were assembled nearly 10,000 people of both sexes, who passed the day and evening in the lively enjoyment of their games, music and various amusements, and drinking their wine, coffee and beer, but nowhere could be found any drunkenness or impropriety of conduct.

Previous to the year 1811 the brewing establishments belonged to the nobility and clergy, who were alone entitled to conduct them, the latter, not being permitted to vend beer, brewed only for their own use and that of the monastic institutions to which they were attached. In 1785 the people were permitted to brew for their own use, but prohibited from making sale of beer. The people, accustomed to purchasing beer at low prices, oppose any advance beyond the usual cost of their favorite beverage. When in the year 1847, in consequence of a partial failure of the barley harvests of the three preceding years, the price of beer advanced from $4\frac{1}{2}$ cents to 6 cents per quart, it caused a riot. The Government, apprehensive of serious consequences to the public peace, was compelled to order a reduction to the former prices.

Austria.—The tax is laid on the worts in the coolers. These, when reduced to a temperature of 14 degrees Reaumur, are weighed for their specific gravity by an officer of the excise, who is present at each brewing and gauges the quantity. It amounts to 79 kreutzers per eimer of 9 degrees gravity, and 7 kreutzers for every additional degree. In 1859 an additional rate was imposed of 20 per centum, termed a war-tax. The average strength of the best qualities of the beer is 13 degrees gravity. The saccharometer adopted by the Government shows 2 degrees where the English shows 3 degrees. The beer pays a tax of 128.4 kreutzers per eimer; a kreutzer is equal to ½ a cent; an eimer, to 14.95 gallons. To produce an eimer of beer it requires 28¾ pounds of malt. Compared with the average quality of malt required to make a barrel of 31 gallons, the tax would be equivalent to $1.12¼. The following figures, received from the National Bureau of Statistics, exhibit the receipts of the Government for beer and spirits for 1862:—

Population of Austria.	Taxes paid on beer.	Pop. of Hungary and Transylvania.	Tax paid on beer.	Pop. of the whole Empire.	Tax on beer.	Tax on Spirits.
18,760,142	$7,634,741	17,507,506	$558,725	36,267,648	$8,193,457	$6,933,695

The city of Vienna contains a population of 520,000 souls. From the Secretary of the Brewers' Association we obtained the following statement, showing the quantity of beer consumed in the city, viz.: In 1845, 715,280 barrels; in 1855, 683,050 barrels; in 1864, 1,203,810 barrels.

The increase in the consumption of beer, though gradual, is less than in most other States of Germany. Not only in Austria proper, but also in the provinces, the beer produced by the Bavarian fermentation is superseding that brewed by the English fermentation. In the year 1857 there were 3,388 breweries, and in 1863, 3,230. Those producing beer by top-fermentation numbered 1,384; the others, 712; whereas in 1863 the former were reduced to 740 and the latter increased to 1,285. Other brewers manufacture a portion of each description. The tax on spirits in Austria amounts to 6 kreutzers on each per cent. of a Vienna eimer, besides 20 per cent. war-tax; that is to say, an eimer of spirits of 50 per cent. alcoholic strength pays 3 florins tax, besides 20 per cent. war-tax, or $1.80 per eimer, 14.95 gallons. The United Empire of Austria derived the following revenue from beer, wine, cider, perry and spirits, from the year 1862 to 1864, inclusive:—

	Beer. Florins.	Wine, Cider and Perry. Florins.	Spirits. Florins.
1862	16,367,920	7,065,899	13,858,388
1863	16,471,141	6,331,732	15,764,690
1864	16,513,133	6,283,092	14,283,754

The total revenue from the three sources amounted to $18,539,989 in 1864. The production of spirits is on the decrease. No tax is paid on wine by the producer; if sold to the dealer, a tax is imposed as follows: On 1 eimer (15 gallons) of wine, sweet from the press, without regard to quality or strength, 1 florin 40 kreutzers, or 70 cents; on cider, before fermentation, 1 florin 28 kreutzers, equal to 64 cents. An additional war-tax has been imposed since 1859 of 20 per cent. Wines are largely produced in Austria proper, and in Hungaria and Transylvania.

Saxony.—The tax is imposed on the malt, and amounts to 1 guilder (50 cents) on 100 pounds. Two and a half eimers, or 45 gallons of beer, are produced from 110 pounds of malt. The tax, therefore, is equivalent to 34.4 cents per American barrel of 31 gallons. This tax has existed for a period of fifty years. In some of the larger breweries the tax is commuted by the payment of a sum determined by the revenue department of the Government. Most of the breweries are organized as stock-companies, and are in successful operation. The brewing of beer on a larger scale is of comparatively recent date; it was not until within a period of fifteen years that the Bavarian system was introduced, which imparted a strong impetus to the business. Since that time the consumption of beer has increased more than a hundred-fold, and is becoming the general drink of the people. The native wines are free from taxation. Foreign wines are charged with a duty of $2.80 per hundredweight when imported. In 1856 the production of beer amounted to one million and a half eimers, or 900,000 American barrels. In 1864 it had increased to 1,500,000 barrels. The population of the former year was about two million souls, and in the latter had increased to two and a third millions. The importation of beer from Bavaria during the same period increased from 60,000 barrels to 90,000 barrels, in addition to which large quantities are annually imported from Bohemia. The export from Saxony, according to the railroad statistics, amounted to 21,600 barrels in 1864. The barley is of superior quality, and sells for $1.87½ per scheffel (140 pounds), or 70.5 cents for 48 pounds. Beer is sold by the cask at from $2.80 to $3.15 per eimer (18 gallons), and by the retailer at 6⅜ cents per quart.

Prussia.—The tax is laid on the malt. The excise officer, being notified, visits the brewery and weighs, in his own scales (which in his absence is kept under lock and key), the malt intended for brewing. The certificate of weight is sent to the Collector of Taxes, who collects the amount of tax from the brewer. It amounts to 25 silver groschens per centner, or 110 pounds. It requires 65 pounds to make a tonne of beer (30.2 gallons). The tax on a tonne of beer is 34.4 cents, or 36.25 cents on an American barrel of 31 gallons. No change in the rate has taken place for 35 years. The beer in this kingdom is brewed on the Bavarian system. It is pale and of light gravity. But little hop is used, the beer being preserved by ice-covering and surrounding the vaults in which it is stored. It is sold at 7 thalers ($4.90) for 31 gallons, and per quart at 3 silver groschens, or 7 cents. Barley sells at 65 cents for 48 pounds. Hops ordinarily average about 40 cents per pound, and about 1½ pound is used per tonne. Malt sells for 30 to 40 cents higher per scheffel of 70 pounds than the price of barley. The quantity produced being inadequate to the want of the brewers, they have to import largely from the neighboring States. The consumption of Berlin, containing a population of 550,000, amounts to 600 tonnes of beer, or 587 barrels of 31 gallons, per diem. The consumption of malt-liquor is estimated to increase from 17 to 20 per cent. per annum, and it has increased at this rate for ten years past. One of the largest breweries in Berlin is the stock-company called The Tivoli Brewery Company, situated in the suburbs of the city. The capital amounts to 1,400,000 thalers, or $980,000. It covers an area of 13 acres. Large and commodious buildings of stone have been erected, under which are deep and extensive vaults for the storage of the beer. There is also attached to the establishment a large and ornamental saloon, capable of containing 3,000 persons, with adjoining gardens, tastefully arranged. The production amounts to 300,000 eimers, or about 175,000 American barrels, annually. There are now eleven large breweries in successful operation in and near the city. A former King of Prussia, at the instance of the Queen, who was a Bavarian princess and regarded the general use of malt-liquors by her subjects as essential to their contentment and good behavior, sent two young men to Bavaria to acquire a practical knowledge of the art of brewing in that country. On their return, a brewery was erected at the expense of the King at Potsdam, 18 miles from Berlin, and capital furnished to conduct the business, which was placed in charge of some of his favorites. The brewery was subsequently sold to them, and, under the patronage of the Government, they were successful in the business, and acquired large fortunes from the profits thereof. Since that time the Bavarian system of brewing has been adopted by all the brewers. A "weiss," or white beer, is brewed to a small extent, but is not popular with the masses of the people. We saw it only in use by the students of the University. Prof. Rau stated the tax on distilled spirits to be at the rate of 1 silver groschen per quart. A silver groschen is equal to 2.43 cents. The tax, therefore, amounts to 9¾ cents per gallon. The revenue derived from beer amounts to 1,200,000 Prussian thalers, or $840,000. The population of Prussia is 18,491,220.

German Tax-Union.—At the present time there are 19,234 breweries in the countries composing the German Zollverein, and 13,208 distilleries, whose products are chiefly used in the arts, or exported to other countries. Regarding beer as essential to the legitimate wants of the people, the rulers of Germany, from the earliest period, have contributed in many ways to its consumption. They have imposed but light burdens on its manufacture in the form of taxation, and have adopted such measures as have insured to the people its good quality at low prices. In thus directing the tastes of the public in the use of this wholesome beverage, they have made beer the national drink, and their subjects proverbial for their sobriety and industry. The revised tariff of the Zollverein went into operation on the first of July, 1865. The duties on barley and hops remain unchanged. On spirits it has been reduced, whether in casks or bottles, from 8 to 6 thalers, on wine from 8 to 4 thalers, and on beer from 8 to ⅔ thalers per hundredweight, which latter great reduction has been regarded by the people as a further encouragement to its consumption. It was deeply interesting to us, in passing from one city to another, to view the vast extent of territory employed in the cultivation of the grape, principally on the precipitious sides of the hills that could not be otherwise utilized. In the States of Prussia, Bavaria, Wurttemberg, Baden, Hesse-Darmstadt, Nassau, Thuringia and Hesse-Cassel, the vineyards cover an area of 389,124 Prussian acres, producing an average of 5,000,000 ohms of wine, or nearly 200,000,000 gallons.

France.—It is interesting to notice that, in this wine country, the consumption of beer is annually increasing and produces a revenue equal to one-sixth of that of wine. Within the past two years this increase has been more marked and rapid that at any previous period, and we are informed, from a source that should be quite reliable, that the consumption in the city of Paris, which in 1863 was 450,000 hectolitres, or 383,000 barrels, will this year reach 1,000,000 hectolitres, or 851,600 barrels. By the courtesy of Mr. Fould, the Minister of Finance, we were introduced to M. Amé, of the Finance Department, who furnished us with the following details: The Government tax on beer is 2 francs and 88 centimes per hectolitre

(26.41 gallons) and 60 centimes on small beer. The duty on spirits is 90 francs per hectolitre for 100 degrees of strength, equal to 66½ cents per gallon; at 50 degrees 45 francs, and in like proportion. On wine the duty is 60 centimes for consumption and, when sold, 1 franc and 20 centimes per hectolitre. The duty is paid on the twenty-fifth of each month for the month preceding. The following statement shows the revenue derived from wines, cider and perry, spirits and beer, for the years 1859, '60, '61, '62 and '63, inclusive:—

	1859.	1860.	1861.	1862.	1863.
	Francs.	Francs.	Francs.	Francs.	Francs.
Wine.....	92,982,085	85,966,297	86,730,261	93,581,101	98,302,319
Cider & Perry...	11,516,484	10,991,478	13,475,445	12,874,060	13,569,851
Spirits....	53,765,472	66,886,546	79,129,296	81,528,983	82,832,239
Beer......	15,685,854	15,251,374	15,864,099	16,204,450	16,419,072
	173,949,895	179,095,695	195,199,101	204,188,594	211,123,481

The mode of assessing the duty, we are informed, is precisely the same as at Hesse-Darmstadt. The Government duty on beer of 2 francs and 88 centimes per hectolitre amounts to 66 cents for 31 American gallons, and on small beer to 14 cents. The price of barley for the past year has averaged from 14.95 to 15 francs for 100 kilogrammes, or 220 pounds. This is equivalent to 63.8 cents per American bushel. The price of 30 francs for winter, and 33 francs for summer beer, is equal to $6.87 and $7.85 per American barrel, respectively. It is retailed from 35 to 40 centimes, or 6 to 8 cents per glass, one-third of a litre, or rather more than a pint. The small beer is retailed at 10 centimes, or 2 cents, for the same quantity. It will be seen that the entire revenue from these sources produces but little more than one-half of that of Great Britain, in a population one-fourth greater. Wine is the common drink of the French people, and they are proverbially temperate. A large quantity of spirits (eau de vie, or brandy) is produced but is mostly exported to other countries.

Russia.—It is stated by Prof. Rau that the tax in Russia is imposed on the malt, being 20 silver groschens, or 46¾ cents on 110 pounds.

The latter will produce 37½ gallons of beer of ordinary strength, hence, for 31 gallons the tax amounts to $38\frac{1}{10}$ cents. The tax on spirits amounts to 72 cents per gallon. Spirits are much more generally used by the people than wine or beer, and much intemperance prevails in that country.

Denmark, Sweden and Norway.—We are informed by Dr. Hebbe that there is no beer-tax in Denmark nor Sweden. In Norway there is a tax on malt equal to 50 cents on a barrel of beer.

In the recital of the foregoing facts and narrative of the travels of your Commissioners, we have endeavored to convey a correct statement of the excise laws pertaining to malt-liquors in Great Britain and the European States, the modes adopted for their collection and the policy pursued by their Governments in giving a practical encouragement to the manufacture and consumption of beer, recognized as an excellent beverage for the people, harmless in its effects and conducive to their health and good morals. We have also shown, briefly and, we fear, imperfectly, the magnitude of the business, the large amount of capital invested, the skill employed, the care bestowed, and the thorough organization and admirable system in use in the management of the brewing establishments.

Contingencies of the Brewing Business.—It may not be out of place to call your attention to the peculiar characteristics of the brewing business, and the circumstances which determine the marketable value of beer. To those practically acquainted with the manufacture of malt-liquors, whether ale, porter or lager-beer, we will be sustained in the opinion that, in scarcely any other branch of manufacturing are there so many obstacles to the production of a marketable article as in that of malt-liquors. Limited as the brewer is to the use of barley for the manufacture of his malt, and to hops, for which (as a pleasant and aromatic bitter and preserver of his perishable commodity) there is no substitute, though wet harvests may have rendered the former unsound and unpropitious seasons impaired the strength and value of the latter, he is compelled to use them. To unsoundness in the grain, and the blight of the hop (which has so alarmingly manifested itself, for the last few years, in the agricultural districts of this country, and the consequent difficulty of obtaining a sufficient quantity of the best qualities to insure the keeping of the beer for any length of time) are mainly attributable the losses of the brewer which, in this country, have been in some years so disastrous as to cause bankruptcy in many instances. An eminent and long experienced and established brewing firm of England, it was stated, had not less than 20,000 barrels of beer returned to them by their customers in one year as unsaleable. The sudden atmospheric changes ofttimes impair the quality of the beer. Unavoidable exposure, in transporting it from the brewery to a distant point of consumption, to severe cold destroying its briskness and rendering it vapid and unpalatable; or to the summer's sun, which may cause acidity and the bursting of the casks, contribute to the disappointments and heavy losses to which the business is liable. A speculative demand for beer is never known. It is not bought and sold in large quantities, and never appears in the published lists of prices current. Nor can it be advanced simultaneously with the increased cost of the raw materials. An increase in the price of the glass, or measure, to the consumer at once diminishes the sale, and it is plainly apparent that the large consumption in those countries we have visited is mainly attributable to the cheapness at which it is sold. It was remarked by one of the most celebrated and successful brewers of Great Britain that some years the profits of the business did not exceed five per cent. on the capital employed, and by one, equally intelligent and respectable, in Bavaria, that for the last twenty-five years his capital had not yielded a profit larger than $7\frac{1}{4}$ per cent. annually.

Importance of the Brewing Interest to Agriculturists.—The brewing interests are becoming of great importance to the agriculturists of this country. The estimated annual production of malt-liquors in the United States is 5,000,000 of barrels, in the manufacture of which 12,000,000 bushels of barley and 15,000,000 pounds of hops are required. To grow this large quantity of material, at an average yield of 30 bushels of barley and 1,000 pounds of hops per acre, there must be employed in the cultivation of the former say, 400,000 acres, and in the latter 15,000 acres of land, or 415,000 acres for both. Heretofore these have proved to be among the most profitable of the crops to the farmer, and, owing to the limited portion of the year during which the maltster and brewer can conduct their operations to advantage, they find a ready market, and generally before the navigation of our rivers and canals is closed by ice. If the policy of our Government, like the policy of Governments of Europe, be in the encouragement and not the restraint of the manufacture of malt-liquors, we predict that within a period of ten years from the present time their consumption will increase twofold beyond their present quantity, requiring a corresponding increase in the production of barley and hops.

Beneficial Effects of the Use of Malt-Liquors on Public Morals.—
Permit us, in conclusion, to refer to the effects of the general use of
malt-liquors on the habits and morals of the people, a subject of no
less interest to the statesman than to the philanthropist. The use of
stimulants appears to be general amongst the nations of the earth,
civilized and barbarous. The large consumption of distilled spirits,
wines, beer, tea, coffee and tobacco, shows this desire to be so
universal that it is scarcely inappropriate to call it a natural appetite.
But there is a wide difference between the use of these stimulants,
as beverages, upon national habits. While the free indulgence
of the first is the fruitful cause of domestic misery, pauperism,
disease and crime, in others the effects are so harmless that men,
women and children daily partake of them with impunity. The
fearful consequences of the excessive use of ardent spirits the most
florid declamation cannot too highly color. Its hideous statistics
have been collected from prisons, almshouses and hospitals; from
the dwellings of the rich, where domestic misery was mocked by the
luxury and splendor which surrounded it; from the dwellings of
the poor, where, alas! it imposes still heavier burdens upon the
gaunt shoulders of poverty. Statesmen, philosophers, warriors,
poets, have each contributed their quota to the dismal category.
Humanity has wept over it, but her efforts to arrest it have been but
partial and transient. Legislation prohibiting the sale of spirits and
fermented liquors and voluntary pledges of total abstinence from
their use have been tried in vain. Your Commissioners think they
can say, with confidence, yet with deep regret, that the efforts of
temperance societies thus far have failed to diminish, to any appreciable
extent, the use of spirits as a beverage. In aiming at too
much, they have accomplished too little; and this, we conceive, has
arisen chiefly from the unwise course of including fermented drinks
in the pledges required. Nor has the prohibitory legislation in some
of the New England States been more successful. It has succeeded
in placing a screen at the door of the bar-room, but not in arresting
the traffic at the bar. To make cold water the exclusive national
beverage has been found, and ever will be found, as we believe,
impracticable; and, if practicable, would not be permanent. The
same craving for some stimulant which made man abandon those
primitive habits when his beverage was "water from the spring,"
would induce him to do it again, as long as human nature remains
unchanged.

The remedy for national intemperance, we are persuaded, is not
in the abolition or disuse of every beverage but cold water, but in the
substitution for a harmful beverage one which is harmless. We

feel that the manufacturing and vending of malt-liquor is not injurious to our fellow-citizens, but that the more the manufacture and sale of it is extended, the more will temperance be promoted and the revenue of the Government increased. Malt-liquor has been pronounced by high medical authority "not only an innocent, but a wholesome beverage for those whose diet is not very nutritive." "Happy is that country," says an eminent English physician, "whose laboring classes prefer such a beverage to those mischievous potations of ardent spirits." Our own observation, and information derived from others, both attest the truth of this remark. We have seen, as we have stated above, thousands of persons—men, women and children—in the German States, assembled drinking their national beverage and enjoying their national games and sports with the greatest hilarity, and have failed to see a drunken one among them. The natives of these States, who emigrate to this country, bring with them their preference for the beverage, and the sports and amusements of their fatherland. No policemen are required to protect the public peace from any disturbance of it by a "Saengerfest" or "Turnverein." When the services of the police are required at these festivals, it is to guard their peaceful reunions and innocent enjoyments from the insolent and riotous intrusion of ruffians inspired by quite different potations. The consequence of an habitual indulgence, which leads so frequently to the excessive use of spirits, is that, when the stimulus is withdrawn, the nervous system is depressed below its normal tone. The result is that craving which we call the thirst for liquor. An artificial stimulus, then, is necessary to restore their normal condition, and the quantity required for this purpose constantly increases. But no such effects follow from the use of malt-liquors, which have nutriment in the malt, a tonic in the hop, and contain but a small percentage of alcohol. They are stimulants, it is true ; but, like tea and coffee, "they cheer, but do not inebriate." Hence, it is comparatively easy for a man to abandon the habit of using malt-liquor to excess, perhaps easier than to abandon the excessive use of tea and coffee ; while every man's observation will tell him how rare are the instances in which the deep drinkers of ardent spirits have been able to liberate themselves from the thraldom of a demon to whom they voluntarily became slaves. Our country has just passed through a gigantic civil war. Four millions of laborers have passed from a state of bondage and tutelage to that of freedom and self-dependence ; they have emerged from a condition unfriendly to the cultivation of strength of will and habits of self-control. Their habits and, consequently, the wealth which their industry will add to the country, will be influenced in some degree by the beverage of which they will habitually partake. What shall this be? Shall it be distilled spirits, whose habitual use induces that intemperance which statesmen and philanthropists alike deplore? Or shall it be a mild and harmless beverage, which the taste and policy of the most civilized communities approve, and whose beneficial effects on national habits their national character for temperance demonstrates? The future character of the whole laboring population of the Southern section of our country will be influenced by the response of the Government to these questions. It is true, the Government cannot, by direct legislation, prescribe what shall be the beverage of the people, or any part of them; but they can discriminate in their excise laws, as they have done in their tariff laws, between subjects of taxation, for reasons of public policy. As they have given incidental protection to manufactures in their duties on imports, they can, in the same way, in their excise laws, encourage any other object which concerns the welfare of the people.

END OF PART I.

Documentary History

⚜ OF THE ⚜

United States Brewers' Association.

With a Sketch of Ancient Brewers' Gilds, Modern Brewers' Associations, Scientific Stations, and Schools, Publications, Laws and Statistics Relating to Brewing Throughout the World, Brewers in Public Life, &c.

PART II.

NEW YORK:
UNITED STATES BREWERS' ASSOCIATION.
1898.

CONTENTS.

                                                                                                    PAGE.

CHAPTER V.—Effect of Brewers' Memorial. Revenue Commissioner and Brewers in conference; agree upon new system. Convention postponed. Cholera in St. Louis; observations regarding it. New Revenue law and regulations. Insufficiency of rebate. Wells on rebate. Sixth convention. Resolution against, and historical note on, prohibition. Patriotism of German-Americans. Patriotic brewers. Colonel Stifel's services. Appeal to trade. Brewers ask for increased rebate and reduction of malt-duty, also for abolition of bonds, etc. Lauer's singular proposition as to distilling by brewers. Should national association participate in local campaigns? Reasons for and against. First attempt at literary work. Enquiry into brewers' immunity from cholera; essay on disease of hop-plant. Financial status of association. Death of J. N. Katzenmayer; biographical notes; succeeded by his son Richard. President Clausen's splendid efforts for the association. Seventh convention. Discomfiture of Washington Committee. Congress deaf to brewers' appeal. Prohibitory agitation and counter-agitation. Massachusetts enquiry into prohibition, and its effect throughout the country. Governor Andrew's exposition of its errors. Gross on beer in New York Constitutional Convention. Proposed literary work. Dr. Baud and Prof. Koch on cholera. Washington Committee re-organized. Defects of, and data on, representative system. Lack of by-laws; Clausen moves to supply want of them. Bergner on hop-trade; joint action decided upon... 177-205

CHAPTER VI.—Hop-tare. Rigorous proceedings by revenue-officers; complaints by brewers; Commissioner grants relief. Adverse legislation proposed; malt-tax and abolition of rebate. Revenue status of Sternewirth defined. Wells opposed to increased taxation of trade; assists brewers by favorable reports. Brewers before Ways and Means Committee argue against malt-tax, the gauging of tanks, the ambiguous provisions relating to daily entries of beer brewed, and to branding of casks; also plead for more equitable process of seizure for violation of law. Submit memorial and draft. Vote of thanks to Lauer. Convention adopts manner of voting. Clausen proposes drafting of statutes. Financial status. Discussion and motive as to official language. Attitude of ale-brewers and praise-worthy exceptions. National Prohibition Party; its organization urged by Good Templars; resolutions hostile to brewers. Officers of eighth convention and list of delegates.. 206-220

CHAPTER VII.—Status of trade in 1868; its flourishing condition in spite of adverse conditions; increased production. Ninth convention. National Prohibition Convention called; resolution on subject. Know-

II   CONTENTS.—*Continued.*

PAGE.

Nothingism and Prohibition against German-American patriotism. Brewers' scathing review of craze. Washington Committee unsuccessful, re-iterate previous argument and submit amendments to old, and draft of new law; but propose neither reduction nor relaxation of safeguards. Brewers anxious to prevent fraud; object to bond, because the brewer is the creditor, not the debtor of treasury; hence bond and certain books unnecessary. Trade conveniences asked for; their singular character. Kindred trades join association. Officers and committees of convention. Settlement of brewers' claims; noteworthy reason for delay. Discussion on malt-duty; extent and nature of barley culture; reasons for superiority of Canada malt. Establishment of Brewers' Academy proposed; action of convention; personal note. Constitution submitted. *Personnel* of association; state of trade. Comparison between ale-trade and lager-trade; reminiscences. Diverging claims as to date of introduction of lager-beer. Brewing before and after 1852, with various personal notes and comparisons. List of delegates.. 221–238

CHAPTER VIII.—Prohibitory movement in Iowa; some of its more prominent opponents; Werthmueller and Dreis lead. Character of population. State of brewing in Iowa; brewers organized. Tenth convention. Interesting reminiscences and parallel as to feasts. Representative system in operation; how managed; its defects. Constitution and by-laws discussed and adopted; its main object; its merits and shortcomings. Name of association again changed. Status of president settled; also that of associate members. Brewers' journal subsidized. Brewers' Academy; necessity for it conceded; divergence of opinion as to means; some for, others against making it an association institute; plan of organization and course of study; matter postponed. German brewers to be organized nationally; Franco-Prussian war intervenes and frustrates effort; American brewers' premature greeting. Fiscal condition of association. President honored, secretary appreciated. Brewers' Fire Insurance Company established; is successful. Rebate and duty on malt; Schenck's opposition to, and Wells' support of, brewers. Schenck's methods; his speech on floor of House and Brooks' and Judd's reply. Discrimination between distilled and fermented drinks; slight concession in this particular. Metallic stamps rejected. Officers and list of delegates............. 239–260

CHAPTER IX.—Progress of trade. Novel aspect of eleventh convention; trade-exhibits show development of industry. Brewers' and distillers' journal in English; incongruity of dual character; distillers dropped. Brewers' associations founded in Baltimore, Brooklyn, New Orleans. Eastern brewers' insurance flourishing. Status of Pittsburg brewers, services of Gerst. Character of opening addresses changed; President Clausen's remarkable speech; he and Lauer plead for total abolition of tax, or substitution of capacity-tax for stamp-tax. What brewers hoped for, and why. Beer as a temperance drink should bear no war-tax. Revenue officers' arbitrary course produces discontent among brewers and opposition to system. Resolutions on this subject quoted. Canvass of Congress as to abolition of beer-tax; discouraging result; Representative Degener's view. Rebate again; brewers ask increase, Commissioner proposes decrease to 4 per cent.;

CONTENTS.—*Continued.* III

PAGE.

singular reasoning in support of latter rate; general characteristics of revenue subordinates; their dictatorial moods. The Commissioner sends Louis Schade to attend convention. Schade's antecedents; his study of revenue questions; his and Flintoff's address. Project of brewers' academy in *statu quo;* again postponed. Delegates to German Brewers' Congress. Death of Eichenlaub. Gift to Clausen. List of delegates.. 261-276

CHAPTER X.—State of trade in New York; production; flourishing condition of association; ale-brewers organized. Brewers' Association of Williamsburgh; its officers; personal notes. Associations organized in Boston; its officers and character; production of beer; personal notes. Brewers organized in Cleveland, New Haven, Hartford, Albany, Troy and Lucerne County, Pa.; personal notes. Political retrospect. Liberal Republican movement. Greeley, presidential candidate; his sumptuary record; attitude of German-Americans critically considered. The Raster plank; Raster's character and place in his party. Unwarranted attack on brewers on account of Republican plank; controversy regarding it; set at rest by Raster; historical summary. Brewers' position. Twelfth convention. Clausen's speech against Greeley; considered in conjunction with political situation. Bi-lingual proceedings. Significant speech by former revenue officer; praises for brewers. Brewers' committee meets with great success at Capitol; have friends in both Houses; their honesty contrasted with distillers' frauds; their bill passed, being Act of June, 1872. Discrimination in favor of beer established; its inestimable advantage and immediate effect. Synopsis of new law. Why brewers failed in some respects; remarkable speech of Commissioners' representative. Prohibition to be tested in court. Schade's and Flintoff's address. H. H. Rueter's maiden speech, a splendid effort. Drink question in Massachusetts. Brewers' Academy; interesting debate; project rejected. Assistance to individual brewers; precedent................. 277-310

CHAPTER XI.—Prohibition vote in 1872; comparison with German vote. Result of election; its cause not appreciated. Rueter's Republican counterpart to Clausen's declaration. Prohibitionists' efforts for Federal legislation and their change of base. Thirteenth convention in Cleveland. Personal notes. Clausen's address, a valuable historical essay. The status of the drink-question reviewed. Conflicting interests of brewers and distillers; the latter's inimical attitude. Efforts favoring malt-liquors; Worth's bill backed by popular movement. Prohibitionists change their tactics; they attack beer exclusively; claim it leads to whiskey-drinking, destroys physical and mental powers and produces pauperism and crime; they become allies of distillers; brewers' counter-argument submitted by Clausen; a masterly arraignment and refutation; brewers' unequivocal resolution in regard to it. Means of publication discussed; Obermann's plan adopted. $2,000 appropriated for establishing *Sentinel.* Finances of association. J. Liebmann's proposition to establish literary bureau laid upon table; reason for this action. Judicial decisions as to prohibition briefly reviewed. The Bartemeyer case. Rueter on Massachusetts test-case; association assumes defense. *Personnel* of convention and strength and prosperity of association. M. Kleiner's

CONTENTS.—*Continued.*

death; biographical notes and resolutions. First prohibitory bill in Congress. Internal revenue matters; Commissioner's favorable decisions. Schade on immigration. Pasteur's researches. Brewers' grains as feed for cows. List of delegates.................................. 311-336

CHAPTER XII.—New England Association; Frank Jones its president; personal note. Brewing and liquor laws in New Hampshire, Maine, Massachusetts, Rhode Island and Connecticut. The Woman's Crusade; its cause and place of origin; Mother Stewart; Dio Lewis organizes the women of Hillsboro; what they accomplished. Lewis' theory; his character; origin of Washingtonians. Fourteenth convention. Clausen's address; recommends an appeal to the people; quotes *Tribune* on crusade. Dr. Hammond against prohibition and on use and abuse of drink; wishes to see brewing encouraged. Bismarck's drinking habit. Minister Francis on sobriety of beer-drinkers; pertinent statistics. Prohibitionists' statement as to deaths caused by alcohol, disproved by statistics; amusing incident. Commission bill introduced in Congress; Schurz and Bayard oppose it; consistent attitude of brewers towards it. Internal affairs; new men; W. A. Miles. Convention officers. Finances. Schade's *Sentinel* eulogized; former appropriation donated. Usefulness of Flintoff, Schwarz and Lewis. Reymann; personal note. Attitude of press. Hop-duty; combination of interests favors it. Alleged discrepancy between brewers' estimated and actual output; discrepancy explained to Commissioner, who affords no relief; brewers must sue collector ; Commissioner suggests that brewers propose new methods; Bergner's proposition referred to local associations. The Bartemeyer case decided; nature of decision. Rueter's address. Brewers' appeal to the people of the United States... 337-371

CHAPTER XIII.—Fiscal policy of the Government; simultaneous reduction of debt and taxation. Panic of 1873 in the midst of prosperity; its effect and cause; brewers' address in relation to it. President Clausen, sick and over-worked, resigns; Rueter succeeds him; personal notes. Convention at Cincinnati; state of industry past and present; personal reminiscence; career of a Cincinnati brewer. President Rueter's address; review of association's work; eloquent promulgation of guiding principles; prohibitory agitation dissected. The Whiskey-Ring, considered historically and in relation to attitude of revenue office towards brewers. The 2½ bushel decision; arbitrary rulings and petty annoyances. Brewers sue revenue collectors. Appointment of a Washington attorney; his and committees' work. Congressional matters; fiscal policy changed; increase of beer-tax threatened; brewers oppose it successfully, acquiescing in increased hop-duty; new tariff and increased internal taxes. Brewers' success in relation to spigot-hole clause ; law amended ; its text. Special-tax decision; brewers object to it and seek Congressional remedy. Officers of association. Vote of thanks to Clausen, Schaefer and Amerman; personal notes. Scientific essays recommended; Schwarz on progress of brewing; his attitude concerning unmalted cereals. Charges of adulteration and Flintoff's reply. Lauer's speech on immigration; repels Curtis' attack. National Maltsters' Association organized; its composition and objects. Reduction of dues proposed. Death-roll. Decrease of breweries. List of delegates.. 372-403

CONTENTS.—*Continued.*   V

PAGE.

CHAPTER XIV.—Centennial Exhibition; attempt to exclude brewers; historical parallel; brewers proceed aggressively; appeal to brewing and kindred trades in favor of separate exhibit; enthusiastic responses enable Executive to begin work. Brewers' Exhibition committee create five departments and erect separate building; make use of educational opportunities; publish valuable pamphlet. Description of building and exhibit. Effect of exhibition. German brewers praise it; send delegate. Sixteenth convention. Bergner's salutatory and Rueter's reply reflecting spirit animating brewers. Rueter's review of the taxation and treatment of brewing in foreign countries compared with American laws. President quotes Bowditch and others in favor of beer; reviews internal affairs of association and makes valuable suggestions; pleads eloquently for harmony and devotion to common cause. Lauer's address incisive and to the point, replete with telling illustrations. The Association's work at Washington; Executive assumes greater part of labors with attorney. The Revenue office persecute brewers under 2½ bushel decision; brewers remonstrate, resort to courts and finally appeal to Congress. Kehr bill introduced; able argument by brewers; House passes bill, also Senate; Senator Dawes eulogizes brewers. Text of Act. Reprehensible attitude of new Revenue Commissioner; more persecutions and another appeal to Congress, followed by introduction of another bill. Commission bill again passes Senate; Senator Bayard's scathing criticism of it. Resolutions, their gist and character. Constitution and incorporation of Association. Discussion of maximum revenue and rate of dues; report of committees on subject; treasurer's bond not sanctioned; dues not increased. Reimbursement of local associations for expenses in general interest. Convention Committee and convention appropriation determined upon; cause and result of action. Membership statistics to be prepared; unsatisfactory condition of them. Membership and deaths. Literary bureau to be established. Maltsters propose fixing of uniform grades of barley. Minor matters. Elections. List of delegates.. 404–437

CHAPTER XV.—Attitude of prohibitionists towards trade; oppose brewers' exhibit and boycott Exhibition; their vote 1872 to 1876; analysis of their political weakness; their presidential vote; platform. Platform of Republican and Democratic parties. Tilden's opinion on prohibition. The drink-question in presidential campaign. Prohibitionists demand Federal prohibition. Blair offers prohibitory amendment to constitution. Seventeenth convention. Origin, development and status of brewing in Milwaukee and Wisconsin; personal notes. New departure; Obermann and the Mayor greet delegates at a "commers." Rueter's address; quotes Gov. Rice's veto message; extracts of message; comments thereon; valuable historical material; charge of adulteration exploded. Schade on unconstitutionality of prohibitory laws; thinks Section 8, Article I, covers point; defects of his opinion; what constitution requires and prohibitory laws aim at with regard to Federal taxation. Section 3,243 of Revenue Act to be amended, because incongruous, illogical and unjust to the taxed trades. Rueter's claim that taxation sanctions; Lauer on same subject, both referring to said section. Minor revenue matters promptly settled by new Commissioner G. B. Raum. Raum's record; his fairness and efficiency; allows 2½ bushel claims; brewers appreciate his course. Duty on

VI   CONTENTS.—*Continued.*

PAGE.

hops and malt; American hop-growers undersell foreign growers in foreign markets, yet insist on protective duty; introduction of hop-extract weakens their absolute control of market. Officers of convention. Changes effected by new constitution in nature of membership, functions of officers and committees, and the character of association; other features; its weak points. Liability of association for expenses incurred by members; claims of Milwaukee and Baltimore associations; discussion on subject; drift of opinions; dangerous precedents. Attempt in Michigan to impose extra tax on outside brewers; misunderstanding as to Michigan brewers cleared away. Appropriations, dues, membership, etc. Deaths. Adulteration. New journals. Officers and delegates. Text of constitution.................................. 438-477

ERROR.—On page 261, in twenty-sixth line of captions, read "Eichenlaub," instead of Kleiner.

Chapter V.

EFFECT OF BREWERS' MEMORIAL. REVENUE COMMISSIONER AND BREWERS IN CONFERENCE; AGREE UPON NEW SYSTEM. CONVENTION POSTPONED. CHOLERA IN ST. LOUIS; OBSERVATIONS REGARDING IT. NEW REVENUE LAW AND REGULATIONS. INSUFFICIENCY OF REBATE. WELLS ON REBATE. SIXTH CONVENTION. RESOLUTION AGAINST, AND HISTORICAL NOTE ON, PROHIBITION. PATRIOTISM OF GERMAN-AMERICANS. PATRIOTIC BREWERS. COLONEL STIFEL'S SERVICES. APPEAL TO TRADE. BREWERS ASK FOR INCREASED REBATE AND REDUCTION OF MALT-DUTY, ALSO FOR ABOLITION OF BONDS, ETC. LAUER'S SINGULAR PROPOSITION AS TO DISTILLING BY BREWERS. SHOULD NATIONAL ASSOCIATION PARTICIPATE IN LOCAL CAMPAIGNS? REASONS FOR AND AGAINST. FIRST ATTEMPT AT LITERARY WORK. ENQUIRY INTO BREWERS' IMMUNITY FROM CHOLERA; ESSAY ON DISEASE OF HOP-PLANT. FINANCIAL STATUS OF ASSOCIATION. DEATH OF J. N. KATZENMAYER; BIOGRAPHICAL NOTES; SUCCEEDED BY HIS SON RICHARD. PRESIDENT CLAUSEN'S SPLENDID EFFORTS FOR THE ASSOCIATION. SEVENTH CONVENTION. DISCOMFITURE OF WASHINGTON COMMITTEE. CONGRESS DEAF TO BREWERS' APPEAL. PROHIBITORY AGITATION AND COUNTER-AGITATION. MASSACHUSETTS ENQUIRY INTO PROHIBITION, AND ITS EFFECT THROUGHOUT THE COUNTRY. GOVERNOR ANDREW'S EXPOSITION OF ITS ERRORS. GROSS ON BEER IN NEW YORK CONSTITUTIONAL CONVENTION. PROPOSED LITERARY WORK. DR. BAUD AND PROF. KOCH ON CHOLERA. WASHINGTON COMMITTEE RE-ORGANIZED. DEFECTS OF, AND DATA ON, REPRESENTATIVE SYSTEM. LACK OF BY-LAWS; CLAUSEN MOVES TO SUPPLY WANT OF THEM. BERGNER ON HOP-TARE; JOINT ACTION DECIDED UPON.

The brewers' memorial, a synopsis of which is embodied in the preceding chapter, was generally regarded as a most meritorious work fully deserving careful study and consideration on the part of the Federal lawmakers and worthy of emulation by all other industries. Forming part of the report of the Special Revenue Commissioner, it was submitted to Congress in this spirit and resulted, as our readers are aware, in the introduction of the stamp-system which has been in force ever since then. As a manifestation of patriotism and of a strong desire to secure to the treasury the full amount of the tax, the attitude of the brewers in this matter impressed the public mind all the more strongly on account of a multiplicity of ingenious tax-evasions and flagrant frauds which clearly indicated a potent tendency towards an opposite course in some of the more important revenue-trades. The brewers' committee appointed at the Fifth Congress, for the purpose of discussing the regulative details of the proposed innovation met the Revenue Commissioners in the Custom House at Philadelphia on the 8th day of November, 1865, and an agreement was reached then and there covering every essential point of the new system. In fact, the representatives of the Government and those of the brewers' association encountered no difficulty or impediment in their labors; they were wholly at accord with each other and so thoroughly and rapidly did they dispose of their task that the new revenue-regulations necessitated by the change of system were in full force and effect even before the next Brewers' Congress assembled at St. Louis.

According to arrangements determined upon during the preceding year, this meeting—the sixth brewers' convention—should have been held at St. Louis in the month of September, 1866; but the prevalence of cholera in that city demanded the postponement of the meeting to the 18th of October of the same year. The advisability of selecting another city for the meeting—a city located outside of the infected belt—seems not even to have been considered or suggested; at least there is no record of any proposition of this kind. This indifference to danger which, superficially considered, appears almost inexplicable, may have been prompted by a very interesting medical observation which derives particular force from subsequent experiences of a similar character, notably those made during the terrible epidemic which in recent years depopulated some sections of the city of Hamburg. It was to the effect that the workmen employed in the St. Louis breweries who, as a rule, were addicted to the copious use of beer, enjoyed a very remarkable immunity from cholera infection during the entire duration of the epidemic, the relative proportion of deaths being infinitely smaller than either the general death-rate or the mortality in any other trade. The interpolation of this fact at the very beginning of a chapter should not be regarded as an unwarrantable digression from the main subject, for in narrating the history of the trade and association it should be the aim of a faithful chronicler to present a synchronical record of all events in any manner affecting the industry or throwing light upon any one of the many questions which have been and are being raised with regard to the consumption of malt-liquors and its effects considered from all points of view. In this particular instance there is all the more need and justification for this course, because in later years the matter referred to became the subject of methodical investigations on the part of scientific bodies and medical authorities, and because, naturally enough, in subsequent chapters of this history a review of the results of these researches cannot possibly be omitted. Hence, the reader will doubtless appreciate our endeavor to enable him to judge intelligently both of the origin, the development and the present status of this question.

It has already been stated that the new revenue regulations had been in force several months before the brewers' association again met in convention. These new regulations, issued by the Office of Internal Revenue under date of August 31st, 1866, recapitulate briefly the then existing requirements as to notice of intention to engage in brewing, brewers' bond, books of materials and monthly returns of quantities brewed and sold, and then go on to describe the practical operation of the stamp-system, which in all essential features was nearly the same as that existing to-day. Stamps denoting payment of tax on fermented liquors were to be sold by the collector to the brewers in his district only, but to the brewer was reserved the right to purchase stamps in any other district, if for any reason whatsoever the collector at his place of business should refuse or be unable to sell the required number of stamps. For affixing these stamps the regulations prescribed that a hole $2\frac{3}{4}$ inches in diameter and $\frac{1}{8}$ inch deep be countersunk in the head of the barrel in such a position as to bring the spigot at the lower edge of the stamp where the perforations were to be made; the stamp to be pasted on this countersunk hole with the perforated portion over the spigot hole and, if necessary, four tacks were to be used, in addition to the paste, for fastening the stamps; stamps to be cancelled at the time of being affixed by writing or imprinting thereon the name of the brewing firm and date of such cancellation.

A rebate of seven and one-half per centum of the value denoted by the stamps was even then allowed to the brewer, and in addition to this the law permitted the sale, for manufacturing purposes, of sour or damaged beer without payment of tax, provided such liquors, rendered unfit for use as beverages, were removed from the brewing premises in vessels unlike those ordinarily used for malt-liquors.

The removal of beer from the brewery *without affixing* the requisite stamps was absolutely forbidden except in cases where the place of storage was not directly connected with the brewery; and in such cases, whether the storage vaults were located within the same revenue district as the brewery or in any other district, the brewer was allowed, upon proper application, to affix the necessary stamps at the place of storage and at the time when the vessels containing the liquors left the warehouse. As a safeguard against fraudulent practices the brewer was required, as we have seen, to keep and render an account not only of all materials purchased, but also of the quantity of beer brewed and of all stamps bought by him. The collector, on his part, had to keep an account with *each* brewer in his district showing the denominations and entire value of all stamps sold each month. These precautionary measures, added to the almost unlimited power of the collector in the matter of inspecting brewing establishments and examining books, rendered frauds absolutely impossible; but very much less would have answered the same purpose without unduly harrassing the trade; and it was upon these very points that the Brewers' Committee, showing in every other respect a most commendable readiness to assist the Government's representatives in securing a wholly automatic system for the prevention of tax-evasions, believed to be entitled to less onerous terms.

They also seemed to think that a rebate of seven and one-half per centum was an entirely insufficient allowance; in fact, the Special Revenue Commission had agreed to recommend a rebate of ten per centum, while the Brewers' Committee emphasized the necessity of increasing even this higher rate of rebate so far as the tax upon ale and porter was concerned, being of the opinion that the losses arising from the bursting of casks and leakage of vessels containing these beverages were much larger than those incidental to the handling of lager-beer. Recent publications throw a singular light upon this question. Mr. D. A. Wells, who was then at the head of the Special Revenue Commission, evidently did not fully understand the brewers' position; nor does he appear to understand it even now, for, in an article published in the *Popular Science Monthly* for April, 1897, he asserts that the rebate allowed to the brewers is "assumed to represent the difference between the theoretical barrel unit of thirty-one gallons and the quantity contained in the commercial or trade-supply barrel, which, owing to re-driving of hoops and re-pitching, averages from twenty-eight to twenty-eight and one-half gallons." In 1865 the brewers surely never based their claim upon this ground, and if Mr. Wells really held the same opinion in 1865 which he expressed in 1897, he evidently succeeded in effectually concealing it.

The foregoing summary shows the exact status of the revenue question at the time when Mr. Charles G. Stifel, as president of the local association of St. Louis, called the sixth convention to order and invited Mr. Henry Clausen, Jr., of New York, to take the chair. The former president, Mr. John Bechtel, having retired from active business, the local association of New York had elected Mr. Clausen in his stead and, under the singular system of organization which still prevailed at that time, this gentlemen became, by virtue of his local office, president of the national association. But, as we have seen from previous reports, the function of this office did not necessarily include the duty of presiding at the conventions. The meeting after having been called to order and having listened to an address by the president, always proceeded to organize by the election of officers for the term of the meeting, and, as a rule, the officers so elected were not those of the executive of the national association. In this case G. Bergner, of Philadelphia, was elected presiding officer, with Frederick Lauer as honorary president, and the following vice-presidents, to wit: P. Ahles, New York; J. H. Ballantine, New Jersey; John Mueller and John Reichard, Pennsylvania; G. Klatter, Ohio; A. Reymann, West Virginia; P. Constans, Kentucky; J. A. Huck, Illinois;

C. G. Stifel, Missouri, and J. Schott, Iowa. W. J. Lemp, of St. Louis, and J. M. Lewis, of New York, acted as secretaries.

This convention is remarkable (among other things which will receive attention hereafter) for the fact that for the first time in the history of the association the question of prohibition as a political factor came up, if not for discussion, at least as one of the considerations which the delegates believed should have induced every brewer to join the organization. In spite of repeated efforts the number of individual members was still very small, and the local associations evinced such indifference to the national affairs that even such cities as Boston, Baltimore, Buffalo, Albany, Rochester and Louisville were not represented at the meeting. Mr. Baltz, of Philadelphia, voicing the sentiments of his association, therefore proposed the adoption by the convention of an appeal to the trade, which proposition was instantly acted upon to the exclusion of all other business, and resulted in the publishing of a stirring call. It is this document in which occurs the aforementioned reference to prohibition. We have it even on prohibitory authority that special efforts in favor of compulsory total abstinence ceased entirely from 1856 to 1865, the very period during which the brewing industry entered upon the era of its marvellous development and progress. Up to 1855 the agitation in favor of prohibitory legislation, though sporadic, ill-sustained and more or less halfhearted, was pretty general in nearly all the States north of the Ohio. From that time up to Lincoln's election it continued to lose its hold upon the minds of those people who had theretofore shown interest in it, and when the cannon of Fort Sumter announced the commencement of actual warfare it disappeared entirely. Prohibitionists admit this, as is shown in every history of the movement written by them, but they would have us believe that their own solicitude for the perpetuity of free institutions silenced within their hearts, for a time at least, their longing for the blissful state of universal sobriety. The fact is, however, that, although prohibitionists endeavored to maintain their agitation, the average politicians, who for selfish purposes had formerly countenanced their efforts, now ignored them in the face of the powerful support which the Republican party received from German-Americans. In a former publication* the chronicler stated the case in these words, viz.:

"The outbreak of the 'irrepressible conflict' put a stop to the prohibitory movement in spite of the alleged intimate connection between slavery and rum. Why was it thus? Because the party which fought slavery and rum (rum, of course, meaning all kinds of intoxicants) found a most powerful ally against slavery in the German element, which German element was and is just as earnestly opposed to prohibition as it was to slavery. It was this aid from so unexpected a quarter that obstructed the prohibitory movement for over twenty years. Up to the year 1857 prohibition had been voted on, and either adopted and enforced, or adopted and declared unconstitutional, in Maine, Delaware, Rhode Island, Massachusetts, Vermont, Michigan, Connecticut, Indiana, Iowa, New York, New Hampshire and Illinois. In all of the States named, in which the German votes were worth having, the prohibitory movement came to a halt as soon as the late unpleasantness began."

It is certainly worthy of note that the patriotic sentiments which actuated the mass of German-American citizens were enthusiastically shared by the brewers throughout the country, many of whom joined the army, gallantly fighting for the noble cause; while others, being too old to serve, raised troops at their own expense

---

* Real and Imaginary Effects of Intemperance, page 18.

and sent them to the field. In the very city and State in which the sixth convention was held the Union cause derived its principal strength from German-Americans to whose efforts is due in a great measure the saving of Missouri for the Union. Brewer C. G. Stifel organized and commanded the Fifth Regiment of the Missouri Reserve Corps. Before engaging in active operations the regiment was quartered in their colonel's brewery and malt-house. On the very first muster-day the regiment, to whom was subsequently assigned the task of protecting Western Missouri, had a serious encounter with a Know-Nothing mob which gave the raw troops and their gallant commander a welcome opportunity of testing their martial spirit and mettle. Jaeger, another St. Louis brewer, well known in the days before the war, died of wounds received on the field of battle. In the course of this narrative the reader will be made acquainted with similar examples of the brewers' patriotism and bravery.

Immediately after the termination of the Civil War the prohibitory movement was revived in several States, and this fact gave rise to its mention at the St. Louis convention. It is well to bear this in mind, for the prohibitionists availed themselves of this reference in the brewers' call and of a resolution adopted at the next succeeding convention as of a welcome pretext for organizing a national party, expressly created, as was frankly avowed, for the purpose of "wiping out the brewing trade." That part of the appeal to the trade, adopted by the sixth convention, which bears on this subject, reads as follows:

"Do not believe that our labors are ended and that the battle is over and victory won, but rather remember that just now a note of war is sounded against us by fanatics who, in pretending to support Sunday and temperance laws, are, in fact, trying to annihilate the self-respect and independence of mankind and the liberty of conscience and trade."

In their report to the convention the Washington Committee made no recommendations or suggestions concerning the new revenue system, the rebate excepted; and as to this they proposed an effort in favor of an increase from 7½ to 10 per centum.

Two other propositions of considerable importance emanated from this body, however, which deserve special mention. One was that the reciprocity treaty between Canada and the United States, which had been abrogated since the war, should be revived, as the Canadian barley was then supposed to have become indispensable to the brewing trade in the United States. It has always been held that the climate and soil of Canada particularly favored the cultivation of barley, and that consequently the Canadian product is superior to that raised in our country; but this could not have been the only consideration which prompted the proposition here referred to. The fact was that the proper cultivation of barley in the Union had not kept pace with the growth of the brewing industry, and in some years the available supply of *maltable* barley fell short of the demand. The reader need not be told that the vast tracts of fertile barley soil in the Northwestern States, which now produce immense quantities of excellent raw material, had not then been brought under the plow.

The other proposition will strike the brewers of the *fin de siècle* as somewhat singular, if not almost incomprehensible. The committee expressed the opinion that every brewer should be allowed, as a matter of right, to distill the offal derived from the process of brewing, *i. e.*, to transform brewers' grain into ardent spirits without payment of tax. They considered as oppressive and unjust the law prohibiting such distillation, and assigned these reasons for their opinion, viz.:

"Even in despotic countries breweries are allowed to distill the refuse accumulating without tax, as it is considered only good management to make use of all appertaining to brewing. In Europe that is all embraced in the brewers' tax on malt-liquors. The apparatus used for such distilling cannot be used for distilling grain, and, as a matter of course, no advantage can be taken by the brewer. It is hoped that the next Congress will repeal this clause."

It would be difficult to find in the whole history of the association so lame, illogical and untenable an argument; and small wonder it is that Congress failed to realize the somewhat naïve expectations of the committee. The law imposed a certain tax upon malt-liquors and another upon ardent spirits. Hence, if a brewer brewed beer and distilled spirits, the fact that he paid a beer-tax could not possibly entitle him to again use the grains for making spirits without paying the spirit-tax. The practice of utilizing brewers' grains in the manner indicated could not have been as general as might be inferred from the committee's report; in fact, diligent inquiry produced contrary evidence. True, some of the older brewers practiced both brewing and distilling, but neither in America nor in Europe has this custom ever prevailed to any considerable extent.

The Special Committee, to whom this report was referred, evidently took this view of the matter, for in their recommendations they ignore it entirely, suggesting in a general way that the Washington Committee be given discretionary power, and only be instructed to endeavor to secure the revocation of the clauses relating to the keeping of material-books and the rendering of monthly accounts of sales—it being generally held that under the stamp-system these onerous requirements, entailing much labor and expense, could safely be dispensed with. The Washington Committee, appointed subsequently and consisting of F. Lauer, J. H. Ballantine, Edward Stiefel, P. Baltz, H. Clausen, Jr., Eichenlaub and Gerst, organized immediately and succeeded in having the following programme adopted: 1. That a blank space for cancellation be provided on the tax-stamps. 2. That F. Lauer be given plenary power in regard to the refunding of taxes paid on beer brewed prior to September 1st, 1862. 3. That the committee should use their own judgment and discretion as to the advisability of petitioning Congress for the right to distill brewers' grains without payment of tax. 4. That Congress be petitioned to reduce the duty upon barley from fifteen to five cents per bushel, the standard bushel to be fixed at fifty pounds. 5. That, if deemed advisable, Congress should be petitioned for a reduction of the tax on "common beer," as distinguished from "lager beer."

Two questions of great importance and of the most far-reaching significance, each involving one of the fundamental conditions upon which depended the usefulness and vitality of the association, were first broached at this convention, namely, (1) the question as to whether the parent body should financially and otherwise assist local associations in furthering or opposing State excise laws, pure and simple, having no bearing on the subject of prohibition or on the brewing business as such; and (2) to what extent the national association should engage in literary work to the end that prejudices, errors, preconceived notions and wilful misrepresentations concerning the use of malt-liquors might be corrected.

The former question assumed tangible shape in a proposition, submitted by H. Clausen, Jr., to the effect that a national reserve fund be created for defensive purposes, to be used in the various States whenever the trade should be threatened by unfavorable legislation. As an example and case in point, the originator of this plan cited the wholly unexpected passage in the preceding year, of an Act amending the excise laws of the State of New York. Nothing contained in this law entailed unusual hardships upon the brewers, nor were its provisions calculated in any way to interfere with the brewing industry beyond what was then and is now deemed inevitable in any attempt to regulate the traffic. Clearly then the local association alone could possibly be effected by the enactment, and it would have been more than unwise to admit that it was the duty of the national association to assist in whatever defensive or other measures may have been necessary under the circumstances. Discussion upon the subject seems to have been limited to a few remarks by Mr. Baltz, of Philadelphia; whatever he may have said (the minutes are silent upon this point) his words appear to have sufficed to shift the basis of the proposition and to secure assent to a motion, made in its stead, that the local associations be urged to create such funds locally, leaving open for future deliberation the question as to the practicability and desirability of merging these local funds into one general fund.

As to a literary agitation two distinct propositions served to bring it prominently into the foreground; one was made by F. Lauer, the other by M. Kleiner, and both were adopted, thus establishing a precedent which must be regarded as the starting point of the association's enduring work in this direction. By the text of the resolution based upon the former proposition the Executive was instructed to republish, in the English and German languages, a pamphlet on the cause, effect and cure of a disease of the hop-plant; while the other aimed at the preparation and publication of a pamphlet on the effects of cholera upon people accustomed to the use of malt-liquors. M. Kleiner prefaced his motion by a statement that, contrary to a popular belief, beer-drinkers had enjoyed remarkable immunity from infection during the prevalence of the epidemic in St. Louis. He therefore desired to place into the hands of the secretary, for the purpose indicated, reliable statistics as to the number of men employed in breweries, the number who became infected by the disease and the number of those who died from cholera.

Internal and financial affairs of the association were not in a very flourishing condition at that time; the total receipts from regular dues amounted to but $1,365.53; the contribution towards defraying the expenses of the European Commission to $1,980.60; initiation fees to $20.00, and the unexpended balance of the preceding year to $1,669.12, making a total of $5,035.25, of which $2,612.92 had been expended in 1865. The regular dues were fixed at 20 cents for each 100 barrels sold.

As usual, the officers of the New York association were also elected to the executive offices of the national association, *i. e.*, Henry Clausen, Jr., president; Frederick Schaefer, treasurer, and J. N. Katzenmayer, secretary. The latter, having severed his connection with the trade, at first declined re-election, but finally yielded to the committee's entreaties and very many flattering remarks by members who, from the floor of the convention, expressed the conviction that it would be difficult to find for the office a man possessing his experience and knowledge of the needs and wants of the trade.*

---

*The following is a list of delegates present at the sixth convention:—George Gerst, Allegheny, Pa.; J. A. Huck, Chicago, Ill.; G. Klotter, G. F. Eichenlaub, M. Kleiner, J. Kaufmann, H. Lackmann, P. Weyand, Cincinnati, O.; C. Schott, Highland, Ill.; Fred. Lauer, Reading, Pa.; John Schott, Muscatine, Ia.; J. H. Ballantine, Newark, N. J.; P. Constans, Newport, Ky.; P. Ables, H. Clausen, Jr., F. Schaefer, J. N. Katzenmayer, J. M. Lewis, New York, N. Y.; P. Baltz, G. Bergner, Philadelphia, Pa.; John Mueller, Pittsburg, Pa., Ch. G. Stifel, W. Lemp, Anheuser & Co., Brinkwirth & Griessedich, Ekerle & Simon, F. Ferie, Feuerbacher & Schlossstein, Fritz & Wainwright, Grone & Co., Hamm & Langstrass, Huber & Appel, L. Koch, Kuntz & Hoffmeister, Koehler & Bro., G. Rothweiler Sohnsider & Breidenbach, C. Sohnerr, W. Stumpf, J. Uhrig, M. Weiss, A. Wettkamp, St. Louis, Mo.; A. Reymann, Wheeling, W. Va.; J. Reichard, Wilkesbarre, Pa.

At the very next convention (the seventh), which was held at Chicago on the 5th of June, 1867, the Executive Committee announced the death of John N. Katzenmayer, and on the second convention-day the association caused to be placed upon record these words:—

"With feelings of profound sorrow we have received information of the death of our brother John N. Katzenmayer, late secretary of the principal association. The deceased was an industrious member and one of the founders of the association. His example of industry, manliness and righteousness deserves to be imitated by every brewer. In him we lose a strong support and his family a faithful husband and loving father. Such noble souls return to their Almighty Creator. Peace be to his ashes."

To John N. Katzenmayer belongs, indeed, as has already been shown, the enviable distinction of having taken the first step towards organizing the brewers of this country, and to his aptitude as an organizer and his energy as the propagator of a new idea must in a considerable measure be ascribed the strength of the young organization. During the Revolution of 1848 he had probably acquired a knowledge of popular agitations and some experience in regard to deliberative bodies. His participation in the revolutionary movement was mainly confined to his own native city of Constance where, at first, he threw his influence upon the side of those who upheld the principles which the majority of the Frankfort Parliament advocated and adhered to. The part assigned to him by his ability and his political and social standing was not such as to make him a very prominent figure for the historian, but it is safe to say that within his sphere he exercised very marked influence. In his whole career one fact stands out in bold relief, namely, that he had the courage of his convictions. A proof of this may be found in Blum's recent work on the Revolution, in which is reproduced a printed pronunciamento dated April 13th, 1848, and signed by Zogelmann, Dr.

Vanotti, Katzenmayer and Kayser, denouncing Hecker's courageous, although totally premature, operations in the lake-district. Katzenmayer commanded a batallion of "Freischärler." General Franz Sigel, in a letter addressed to the chronicler, speaks very highly of Katzenmayer and his efforts in organizing the Constance contingent.

With the sagacity, quick determination and clear-sightedness that characterized the whole of his subsequent career, President Henry Clausen, Jr., thus suddenly deprived of his able assistant, himself as yet unfamiliar with the internal affairs of the association and having none of the necessary books and documents in his possession, at once entered into negotiations with Mr. Richard Katzenmayer, a son of the deceased secretary, and finding him well posted in his father's labors, succeeded in securing his services for the association. Clausen, as was his habit and practice, promptly assumed the initiative in all matters pertaining to the executive, and so thoroughly did he grasp his mission that when the seventh convention opened at Chicago he and his equally apt adjutors were fully masters of the situation, prepared to continue the good work and to add very materially to the effectiveness and usefulness of the association.

The convention was called to order by J. A. Huck, of Chicago; then listened to an excellent address by H. Clausen, Jr., and at once elected C. G. Stifel, of St. Louis, chairman, with F. Lauer as honorary president, G. Bergner, of Philadelphia, and H. Gottfried, of Chicago, secretaries, and the following vice-presidents, viz.: D. Wilkens, New York; C. Geisele, New Jersey; J. Robinson, Pennsylvania; C. Boss, Ohio; A. Reymann, West Virginia; P. Constans, Kentucky; J. Brand, Illinois; W. J. Lemp, Missouri; T. Schmid, Iowa; J. Klinghammer, Indiana, and V. Blatz, Wisconsin.

Untoward combinations had prevented the Washington Committee from accomplishing any one of the special tasks assigned to them. The protective policy of the ruling party, stimulated by interested parties, frustrated the attempt to lower the duty upon barley; in fact, the Congressional Committee even recommended an increase from 15 to 20 cents per bushel; but the new tariff-measure failed at this session. Misjudging the actual motive of the lawmakers the Washington Committee expressed the belief that a more numerous and more representative body of brewers should have presented the association's wishes to Congress, and that such a body would have met with better success. Following this reasoning, they recommended the appointment of a Legislative Committee of twenty-five, to be composed of representatives from all States in which the brewing industry had gained a foothold. No mention was made of the supposed right of the brewer to distill offal; in fact no other matter was reported upon by this committee, except the question of prohibition.

In his opening address, the president had already dwelt upon this subject and foreshadowed a proposition to take a decided stand upon the side of liberal views as against that fanaticism which derided the well-established fact that in any effort to change the drinking habits of the people the encouragement of the use of malt-liquors must be the paramount consideration. The committee in concluding their report used these words: "Moral reformers are running wild with unsound notions. Their ignorance of human nature led them into secret combinations to prejudice the minds of the American people against a trade that, if not interfered with, would bring about a great moral reform of the excessive use of alcoholic liquors." Unfortunately the meagre reports of discussions, which is one of the serious obstacles confronting the chronicler, affords no clue as to the particular combinations referred to or the text of the proposed laws to which the indignant protest applied. What little information there is indicates that the prohibitory agitation in Iowa, and the attempts made in several States to place malt-liquors in one and the same category with ardent spirits, led to this declaration. As to the State of New York there can be no doubt that the sporadic efforts which were then being made to rigidly enforce the Sunday laws induced the action taken at this convention. A special committee consisting of Eichenlaub, Robinson, Dreis, Clausen, Stifel, Schalk, Miller and Blatz reported resolutions, setting forth that inasmuch as the action and influence of the temperance party is in direct opposition to the principles of individual freedom and political equity upon which the American Union is founded, the association determined to use all legitimate means to oppose the tide of fanaticism and to protect their rights as citizens, supporting only such parties and candidates as were known to favor liberal laws. Brewers should be organized throughout the land and induced to make common cause with all societies opposed to fanaticism. Particular stress was laid upon the necessity of making known to the people the nature of social life and the character of recreation and amusement among German-Americans, the object evidently being to convince fair-minded citizens and lawmakers that genuine piety and strictest morality are not at all incompatible with liberal views concerning the sanctity of the Sabbath.

A careful perusal of the newspaper files covering the period here in question shows that a strong popular movement in favor of tolerant laws was then in progress in the State of New York, and that the societies, who had engaged in the work, looked to the brewers for material support and assistance. The Metropolitan Excise Law which, rigidly executed, effectually prevented any amusements on Sunday, had aroused great discontent among the people and an organization had been effected for the purpose of securing relief. On the 4th of June, 1866, an imposing mass-meeting was held at Union Square, in the city of New York, in which resolutions were adopted denouncing the puritanical spirit of the law. Judge John J. Freedman, subsequently the attorney for the brewers' association, delivered a very able address, and Mayor Hoffman and other prominent men in letters addressed to the chairman expressed their sympathy with, and approval of, the movement. This and the other matters before-mentioned probably gave rise to the convention's action.

The execution of the plan outlined in the resolution was entrusted to a committee consisting of two delegates from each of the States represented at the convention, to wit: Clausen and Kuntz, New York; Bergner and Nusser, Pennsylvania; Baltz and Melms, Wisconsin; Schmitt and Tschirgi, Iowa; Schalk and Geisele, New Jersey; Huck and Dick, Illinois; Feuerbach and Stifel, Missouri; Reymann, West Virginia, and Belzer and Schmitt, Indiana.

It may as well be stated right here that the subsequent activity of this committee was confined during the next two years to the States of Iowa and New York. To one familiar with the course of prohibitory legislation and matters relating thereto, it must appear rather singular that neither at this nor the preceding brewers' convention was there any mention made of the remarkable status of this question in Massachusetts, where Prohibition had just then (1867) been made the subject of a most thorough investigation, resulting in a complete negation of every presumption in its favor, and ultimately bringing about the enactment of a license-law. Neither the brewers of Massachusetts nor those of any other New England State were represented at this brewers' convention, and this regrettable fact probably accounts for the absence of any mention of the Massachusetts agitation. Considered from the point of view of the brewer, this investigation is by far the most important event of that or, in fact, of any period; the report upon it and upon the enquiry conducted subsequently by the Board of Health of that State must be regarded as the first methodical attempt to controvert by literary and scientific means the untenable notions propagated by prohibitionists. Many years after the event the brewers' association republished extracts from these reports* which in the lapse of so many years have not forfeited a particle of their convincing force and potent effect, and are all the more valuable and useful because they emanated not from parties directly interested, but from eminent lawmakers and statesmen whose wisdom, patriotism and rectitude have become household-words throughout the land. A history of the brewers' association lacking proper mention of these enquiries and more especially of Governor John A. Andrew's magnificent argument entitled "The Errors of Prohibition," published in the very year of the seventh brewers' convention, would be sadly deficient in essentials. Even to this day Andrew's argument, though necessarily less comprehensive and exhaustive than many subsequent publications, stands unparalleled as a masterly exposition of the errors of Prohibition from every conceivable point of view, not only the social, the moral, the religious, the medical, but more especially the philosophical and political;—and as a plea in behalf of personal liberty,

---

* See "Intemperance in the Light of Cosmic Laws" and Governor J. A. Andrew's masterly argument.

supported by telling utterances of the master-minds of all civilized nations, it is irresistible in its thrilling eloquence. Quoting the opinions of the ablest and wisest men in Massachusetts and fortifying their utterances with the views of such eminent statesmen and thinkers as Milton, Cromwell, Burke, Humboldt, Mills, Talleyrand, etc., he denied the right of government to pass into the domestic and private sphere of life and characterized as imminently perilous to both political and personal liberty every argument justifying interference in such matters. His most effective quotation was probably the one from an address delivered in 1842 by John Quincy Adams before the Temperance Society of Norfolk County (Mass.).

"Forget not the rights of personal freedom. Self-government is the foundation of all our political and social institutions, and it is by self-government alone that the law of temperance can be enforced. Seek not to enforce upon your brother, by legislative enactment, that virtue which he can possess only by the dictate of his own conscience and the energy of his own will."

What a pity that the seventh brewers' convention had not been informed of the work that had just then been completed in Massachusetts! How much more incisive and forcible could the delegates have made their protests and appeals, had Andrew's superb oration been placed before them! It will presently be shown that throughout the country the Massachusetts agitation exercised a most potent influence upon both sides of the question, strengthening the ranks of the friends of personal liberty, and exasperating to an almost incredible degree the advocates of compulsory abstinence. The arguments here referred to undoubtedly influenced the discussion and helped to shape the course of events in the Constitutional Convention of the State of New York, held in 1867–68, when the proposition to incorporate a prohibitory clause into the constitution came up for consideration. It called forth another most valuable contribution to the literature upon this subject, —a contribution of which, also, incredible as it may seem, no mention is made in any proceedings of brewers' conventions. We refer to the address delivered by Magnus Gross, a member of said convention, who had studied the economic, hygienic and physiological sides of the question, and who to his thorough knowledge of the subject joined a peculiar fitness for its scientific treatment by reason of his professional training as a chemist. It may not be amiss to quote here the conclusion of his peroration:—

"There is not now a European government that does not more or less encourage the manufacture of malt-liquors as one of the surest means of benefiting alike the State and the people. As to the States of the Union, there is none in which at one place or another the brewing industry could not be permanently established. The State of New York, however, if alive to her own interest, will hold a foremost rank in this respect, because her climate is best adapted to the manufacture and consumption of malt-liquors, and its soil can produce barley as well as hops in abundance. I presume, Sir, to have presented sufficient reasons and facts to induce every well-wisher of the commonwealth, and every earnest friend of the cause of true temperance and good morals in particular, to lend his voice to the encouragement of the lager-beer industry, and to assist in nationalizing a beverage which combined science and experience recommend as best adapted and most conducive to the system and condition of men in the middle zone, as well as a successful and lasting effort toward the abatement of intemperance. If to what I have said on this subject is added the unanswerable argument on the "Errors of Prohibition," left us as a legacy by a truly great and patriotic man, the honored son of a neighboring State, who has but recently departed from life—the information on this vexed and much-perverted question will be deemed satisfactory, if not complete, by all those who seek the truth rather than have their prejudices, notions and idiosyncrasies gratified. To avoid a repetition in less felicitous and convincing language than that used by the late Governor Andrew of Massachusetts, I have confined my discourse to the chemico-physiological and economical part of the subject, referring as to its moral, philosophical and legal aspects to the argument of this master-mind, whose premature demise has been a severe loss to his State and to the country. Sir, I leave this subject in the hands of a body of wise, discriminating and experienced men with the recommendation that in some suitable form and manner a clause should be inserted in the Constitution, which favors the manufacture and consumption of domestic wines and malt-liquors as a national beverage, and as the surest means of promoting the cause of true temperance."

Owing to the death of Secretary Katzenmayer the enquiry into beer-drinkers' manifest immunity from cholera infection, suffered an interruption which proved fatal to the whole scheme. Personal experiences and observations submitted by members from St. Louis, Cincinnati and Chicago confirmed the assertion that the use of beer acted as a preventive of the infection, but in the absence of a comparative statistical statement such as the original resolution contemplated, the data thus presented could not possibly serve the purpose. Stifel, of St. Louis, Kleiner, of Cincinnati, and Huck, of Chicago, gave interesting information upon the subject, but with this general discussion, unavailable for purposes of an educational campaign, the proposed work reached its premature end, and its object remained in abeyance for many subsequent years. In the very next year (1868), by the way, Dr Baud, chief physician for epidemic diseases for the Department of the Seine, published a pamphlet in which he recommended the use of malt-liquors by cholera patients. Prof. Koch's later researches showed, as is well known, that the cholera bacillus cannot live in beer. The publication of the other pamphlet, determined upon at the preceding Congress, *i. e.*, an essay on the cause, effect and cure of a certain hop-disease was not mentioned at this meeting, and as among the records of the association a copy of such a work is not to be found, it appears doubtful whether the convention's instruction upon this point has been carried out. Perhaps the death of the secretary also frustrated this object.

Pursuant to Lauer's suggestion, the Washington Committee was re-organized and its membership increased to twenty-seven; it now consisted of F. Lauer, S. Huston, G. Bergner and G. Gerst for Pennsylvania; Ballantine and Schalck for New Jersey, C. Belzer and C. Schmitt for Indiana; G. Coste and C. G. Stifel for Missouri; Grund for Kansas; J. Dick and H. B. Miller for Illinois; H. Clausen, Jr., D. Jones, J. Scheu, F. Greenway for New York; G. F. Eichenlaub and M. Kleiner for Ohio; C. Wolf and P. Constans for Kentucky; Dr. Dreis for Iowa; Eldredge, C. F. Melms and V. Blatz for Wisconsin.

As has been seen, the original object of the re-organization was to make the committee more effective by giving each State a proper representation; but countervailing circumstances militated against this endeavor, and the actual condition of affairs again proved that the strict adherence to a purely representative system upon a geographical and numerical basis could not work well. The working forces of the organization had to be recruited from the ranks of those brewers who demonstrated their ability and evinced their willingness to labor for the common good, and the question as to what State or what proportion of the country's beer-production they represented deserved no more consideration than the question as to whether all the beer-producing States, or even a majority of them, were properly considered in the matter of appointments. The State which furnished the greatest number of workers, necessarily secured the most numerous representation. Pennsylvania had four representatives on the committee, and New York an equal number, although the latter State produced more than twice the quantity of beer brewed in the former; the production of New York being 1,824,764, that of Pennsylvania only 831,886 barrels. Massachusetts, with a production of 274,834 barrels, had no representative at all; while Indiana, with a production of only 127,495 barrels, had two. The latter disparity has already been explained by reference to the fact that the brewers of Massachusetts, who in later years gave the association some of its most capable officers, betrayed great indifference and even failed to send a single delegate to the convention. If the representative system had been adopted and rigidly adhered to in the beginning the organization could not have lived. As it was, those who attended the conventions actually performed all necessary work for the trade.

Some method should doubtless have been devised, at the very outset, by which the wish of a majority of those who belonged to the association could have been ascertained, but as this was not the case much confusion arose. In this particular, as in all matters relating to parliamentary usage, every meeting created its own rules and practices according to the circumstances and conditions surrounding it. Henry Clausen, Jr., who by reason of his inclination towards political activity had acquired a considerable knowledge of such things, at once perceived the crudeness of the entire scheme of organization, but being a novice in his office, and withal rather a modest man, hesitated to definitely propose a radical departure from the old usage, although he spoke very pointedly of these shortcomings. We shall presently see that he soon overcame his diffidence in this respect, becoming both the projector and to a great extent the author of a constitution and by-laws. At this meeting he confined his reformatory efforts to regulating the manner of voting, which in the absence of fixed rules had been managed differently at every convention. This proposition, unanimously adopted, read as follows, viz. :—

"That the secretary of the executive is hereby directed to call upon the societies to instruct their representatives whether they prefer to have delegates vote by the whole number of members, or whether the action of the majority of delegates present shall be binding upon the entire association."

In conjunction with the foregoing review of this question we present as a means of comparison a statistical table showing the production of malt-liquors by States and Territories from 1863 to 1867 inclusive.

The total quantities of tax-paid malt-liquors published annually in an appendix to the associations' convention report, will, in some instances, be found to differ slightly from the figures stated in this table, for the reason that nearly all data obtainable from the Revenue Office at the usual time for holding the annual conventions are subject more or less to corrections upon final revision at the end of each fiscal year. The accompanying table was prepared entirely from corrected abstracts, due allowance having been made for the varying heads under which collection reports were rendered at different times. As is stated in the note appended to the table, statistical exhibits of quantities are not prepared by the Revenue Office, cognizance being taken only of the various sources of revenue provided for under the internal revenue system. It will readily be understood that under such circumstances absolute accuracy and correctness of the periodical tables published in convention reports is well-nigh impossible; yet, for all practical purposes of the hour these tables ordinarily suffice. In a history of the association, however, a defective exhibit of this character would scarcely be excusable, hence the chronicler undertook a thorough revision of the data bearing on subject.

STATEMENT BY STATES AND TERRITORIES OF THE PRODUCTION OF FERMENTED LIQUORS DURING THE YEARS ENDING JUNE 30TH, FROM 1863 TO 1867, INCLUSIVE.

STATES AND TERRITORIES.	1863. Barrels. 60 cents.	1864. Barrels. 60 cents.	1865. Barrels. $1.00.	1866. Barrels. $1.00.	1867. Barrels. $1.00.	REMARKS.
Alabama				377	687	
Arkansas				511	105	
California	81,412	80,561	79,688	89,455	149,049	NOTE.
Colorado	1,178	1,552	1,535	1,656	2,495	
Connecticut	13,035	18,792	24,381	26,168	88,954	This statement has been made up from the recapitulation of *collections* from each specific source of revenue, there being no tables of quantities. For 1863 and 1864, the collections were reported under the heads of "Ale," "Beer," "Lager Beer" and "Porter," at the rate of 60 cents per barrel. For 1865, 1866 and 1867, the collections were reported under the head of "Fermented Liquors," at the rate of $1.00 per barrel. Fractions have been disregarded—⅛ and over being considered a whole; less than ⅛, nothing. The statement has been proved, and has been found absolutely correct.
Delaware	712	1,103	1,254	1,293	2,494	
Georgia				1,851	2,689	
Idaho				1,679	1,840	
Illinois	156,645	259,284	271,343	419,870	487,559	
Indiana	53,843	75,914	102,818	124,992	137,405	
Iowa	21,026	32,458	40,615	69,907	99,666	
Kansas	4,138	6,498	8,656	13,180	17,528	
Kentucky	52,111	48,177	62,956	90,612	86,189	
Louisiana		41,777	24,417	31,642	27,763	
Maine	2,207	2,463	1,933	4,676	5,277	
Maryland	64,864	106,948	97,011	114,729	128,079	
Massachusetts	119,000	163,052	148,662	388,665	274,834	
Michigan	29,654	60,919	88,889	106,331	198,935	
Minnesota	7,766	12,253	14,325	27,929	39,682	
Mississippi					406	
Missouri	138,631	187,380	218,301	268,263	266,615	
Montana			574	1,781	1,858	
Nebraska	868	1,880	2,403	3,161	4,956	
Nevada	2,518	7,884	5,683	8,750	6,307	
New Hampshire	25,945	36,797	35,846	43,630	72,495	
New Jersey	183,830	221,102	217,718	303,908	387,112	
New York	969,094	1,300,496	1,148,391	1,564,948	1,324,764	
North Carolina				35	26	
Ohio	240,781	349,477	354,752	516,040	519,295	
Oregon	1,547	2,494	1,933	4,948	5,518	
Pennsylvania	348,862	517,147	527,327	607,460	581,896	
Rhode Island	7,029	10,471	8,628	10,887	11,514	
South Carolina					746	
Tennessee		3,594	23,683	21,811	13,781	
Texas				5,709	9,101	
Utah	84	159	423	463	715	
Vermont	1,371	1,783	2,050	2,165	3,080	
Virginia	9,071	3,807	3,335	3,717	6,645	
West Virginia		24,796	15,487	24,447	22,524	
Wisconsin	62,048	102,564	97,946	136,610	193,105	
Washington Territory	812	1,008	1,484	1,417	2,303	
Arizona Territory					64	
District of Columbia	3,580	15,360	18,741	20,175	19,760	
New Mexico	321	833	361	259	651	
	2,596,803	3,706,198	3,657,183	5,115,140	5,519,332	

Discouraged by so many recent failures, the Washington Committee had become less sanguine in their hopes and expectations and somewhat distrustful of their ability to secure what was deemed needful legislation. Hence, they modestly recommended, in the briefest possible terms, that nothing beyond an increase of the rebate from 7½ to 10 per cent. upon purchases of stamps, and a reduction of the duty upon barley to five cents per bushel should be sought to be obtained.

A purely commercial question, the first of its nature, was brought before this meeting by G. Bergner of Philadelphia. Up to that time and, in fact, for many years thereafter, the hop-growers insisted upon payment for the gross-weight of bales or sacks of hops, including the packing-material, at the rate of the price charged for hops. The unexpectedly sudden development of brewing having created a demand for hops exceeding the supply, the market value of the product rose very rapidly, until it reached an unprecedented figure. Naturally enough, the cost of the packing-material, entirely useless to the buyer, but bought at high hop-prices, became quite an important item in the profit and loss account of the brewer. Individual protests could not prevail against the tyranny of an established custom, unless all brewers were not only in a position to threaten the discontinuance of commercial relations with their hop-dealers, but also had it in their power to carry out this threat. With an abundant supply and vigorous competition this might possibly have been comparatively easy; but under the circumstances before related nothing short of concerted action and a very determined stand could bring about the desired result.

Of a very practical turn of mind and endowed with an unusually clear perception, Mr. Bergner fully understood the situation and, therefore, proposed that every member should pledge himself not to buy any hops unless every bale and sack be marked with both the gross and the net weight; nor to pay for any quantity exceeding the actual weight of the hops, exclusive of the packing material. Dealers refusing to comply with this requirement and condition were to be informed that members could not and would not deal with them. This proposition met with unanimous approbation and to the end that it might be put into execution in the ensuing autumn—the time when the new hop-crop would be placed into the market—brewers and hop-dealers were to be notified of the agreement by circular letter in addition to the notice to be published in the principal newspapers throughout the country.

Although introduced thus early in the history of the association, the object of this agreement was very far from its realization; it loomed up from time to time, receiving more or less thorough consideration, and leading to many emphatic declarations; but it was not, as we shall presently see, until many years after the seventh convention that a binding arrangement, universally acceded to and respected, was effected by the trade.*

---

* The following is a list of the delegates present at the seventh convention, viz. :

George Gerst, Allegheny, Pa.; A. Ziegele, Jacob Scheu, Hugh Boyle, Buffalo, N. Y.; Ph. Neu, Belleville, Ill.; J. M. Hughes, Cleveland, O.; A. Baierle, Busch & Brand, Binz & Lassarle, Downer & Bemis, Ellel & Co., Gottfried & Schoenhofen, J. A. Huck, George Hiller, Haas & Powell, Chas. Keller, H. B. Miller & Son, Mueller & Bros., G. Metz, Moser Bros., Rehm & Bartholomae, Seipp & Lehmann, Schmid, Katz & Lorenz, K. G. Schmitt, E. Steege, W. Saladin, John Stutz, Mich. Lieben, Schmitt & Bender, Stupp & Co., Fr. Wacker, Chas. Woelffer, Luke Wagner, Chicago, Ill.; C. Boss, G. F. Eichenlaub, M. Kleiner, John Kauffmann, H. Lackmann, C. Moerlein, U. Windisch, Cincinnati, O.; L. P. Hoster, J. Schlee, Columbus, O.; H. C. Dreis, F. C. Knepper, M. Frahm, Davenport, Ia.; F. Kempf, M. Tschirgi, T. Schmid, Dubuque, Ia.; A. Leicht, Jr., Hudson City, N. J.; A. Geiger, George Holz, Iowa City, Ia.; F. Laner, Reading, Pe.; V. Blatz, F. Pabst, J. Hohl, K. T. Melms, Milwaukee, Wis.; John Eichler, Morrisenia, N. Y.; H. Schalk, Chas. Geisele, Newark, N. J.; M. Mohrath, Newark, O.; Jacob Ahles, H. Clausen, Jr.; Anth. Hnepfel, M. Kuntz, David Jones, Fr. Schaefer, J. Schmid, D. Wilkens, New York, N. Y.; P. Constans, Newport, Ky.; G. Gergner, Ph. Guckes, Henry Rothacker, J. Orth, Philadelphia, Pe.; E. Huhn, Peoria, Ill.; J. Klinghammer, Plymouth, Ind.; John Nusser, Pittsburg, Pa.; H. Appel, Theo. Eckerle, M. Feuerbacher, Robt. Jacobs, Henry Hoehler, W. J. Lemp, C. G. Stifel, C. Spitzfeden, T. Uhrig, St. Louis, Mo.; J. Robinson, Scranton, Pa.; John Dick, Quincy, Ill.; George Baer, Wilkesberre, Pe.; A. Reymann, Wheeling, W. Va.

Chapter VI.

HOP-TARE. RIGOROUS PROCEEDINGS BY REVENUE-OFFICERS; COMPLAINTS BY BREWERS; COMMISSIONER GRANTS RELIEF. ADVERSE LEGISLATION PROPOSED; MALT-TAX AND ABOLITION OF REBATE. REVENUE STATUS OF STERNEWIRTH DEFINED. WELLS OPPOSED TO INCREASED TAXATION OF TRADE; ASSISTS BREWERS BY FAVORABLE REPORTS. BREWERS BEFORE WAYS AND MEANS COMMITTEE ARGUE AGAINST MALT-TAX, THE GAUGING OF TANKS, THE AMBIGUOUS PROVISIONS RELATING TO DAILY ENTRIES OF BEER BREWED, AND TO BRANDING OF CASKS; ALSO PLEAD FOR MORE EQUITABLE PROCESS OF SEIZURE FOR VIOLATION OF LAW. SUBMIT MEMORIAL AND DRAFT. VOTE OF THANKS TO LAUER. CONVENTION ADOPTS MANNER OF VOTING. CLAUSEN PROPOSES DRAFTING OF STATUTES. FINANCIAL STATUS. DISCUSSION AND MOTIVE AS TO OFFICIAL LANGUAGE. ATTITUDE OF ALE-BREWERS AND PRAISE-WORTHY EXCEPTIONS. NATIONAL PROHIBITION PARTY; ITS ORGANIZATION URGED BY GOOD TEMPLARS; RESOLUTIONS HOSTILE TO BREWERS. OFFICERS OF EIGHTH CONVENTION AND LIST OF DELEGATES.

At the very next convention—the eighth, held at Buffalo, N. Y., on the 8th and 9th of July, 1868, it transpired that no less on account of the vigorous opposition of the hop-dealers than owing to a lack of determination on the part of the brewers, the attempt to regulate the question of hop-tare failed ignominiously, and President Clausen in his opening address expressed the opinion that the brewers' resolution could never be carried out unless the legislatures of the hop-growing States could be induced to enact a law embodying the reasonable demands of the trade. Business of greater importance prevented further action at this convention, which for various reasons proved to be one of the most interesting gatherings.

The brewers' association of Buffalo, said to have been on the verge of dissolution in the preceding year, had made special efforts to do honor to their guests, and in this attempt also succeeded in again binding together more firmly the members of the local trade. Their president, Joseph L. Haberstroh, a well-known and much respected citizen, one of the early settlers, and at one time sheriff of Erie County, dwelt with particular emphasis upon this point, and dilated upon the beneficient effects produced upon the trade generally by the work of the parent association.

It is more than probable that the same causes tended to impress upon the minds of the brewers not only of Buffalo, but of every other brewing centre, the imperative necessity of co-operation. Affairs at Washington had assumed a threatening aspect for the industry. The fiscal policy of the Government was far from being definitely settled, and in endeavoring to secure a permanent basis for tax-legislation, the Federal lawmakers were but too prone to heed the demands of local interests and partisan considerations. The enemies of the brewing industry, particularly the representatives of Prohibition States, seized upon every opportunity of further burdening the hated vocation. Many new burdens had been proposed in Congress, among them the discontinuance of the rebate, a tax upon malt, and several stringent provisions concerning the mode of manufacture. In addition to this, many collectors, either from an excess of official zeal or from motives still less commendable, had harrassed the brewers and in some instances gone so far in their unreasonably and unlawfully rigorous execution of the law as to peremptorily close several breweries in various parts of the country. Thanks to the prompt intervention of the Washington Committee, and the favorable disposition of both the Commissioner of Internal Revenue, E. A. Rollins, and his associate, the Special Revenue Commissioner D. A. Wells, relief was speedily obtained in all these cases.

In order to prevent a recurrence of such deplorable practices the Washington Committee, assisted by John J. Freedman, submitted to Secretary McCulloch of the

Treasury Department a very able memorial describing in detail and explaining minutely the process of brewing, the cellar system, and the mercantile usage in vogue in breweries; and showing that under existing laws many practices of revenue officers could not but be regarded as an unlawful, arbitrary and needlessly harsh exercise of official power.

One of the many arbitrary rulings of some collectors was to the effect that beer consumed upon brewery premises by brewery employees should be taxed at the rate of $1.00 per barrel. Commissioner Rollins, after hearing the remonstrances of the Washington Committee, at once reversed this absurd ruling and definitely decided for all time to come the status of the *Sternewirth*. He ruled that "beer drunk by men regularly employed in a brewery during their work, when the same is drunk by them in the cellars or vaults connected with the brewery, but has not been removed therefrom, is not subject to tax, and the vessels containing the same need not be stamped *unless the brewer receives a consideration for the same.* If the beer is given to the men as part of their wages, or as an inducement to work for less wages than they would otherwise demand, it amounts to a sale, and the beer is liable to a tax."

The custom of furnishing beer to the journeymen brewers, free of charge, evidently impressed some collectors as being so entirely contrary to ordinary business methods that they naturally suspected some sort of wrongdoing, or, at least, presumed that the beer thus liberally given away in copious quantities must necessarily represent a part of the workman's compensation. They could not understand the liberality of the manufacturer who allowed his helpers to consume at will and pleasure any quantity of the drink they produced. The custom has doubtless been transmitted to us from the mediæval age when the monastic brewery dispensed its bountiful hospitality to thirsty and weary wayfarers.

As to the proposed amendments to the revenue law, before referred to, it appears that Special Revenue Commissioner Wells, who in those days, whatever may be said of him now, entertained a most favorable opinion of the great utility of brewing, both from an economic and a moral point of view, did not approve of increased tax burdens nor of more rigorous measures of surveillance, as is evident from his reports for the years 1867 and 1868.* In all of his reports he maintained that the industry was already sufficiently taxed, and that those engaged in it had on all occasions evinced such a degree of integrity and honesty as to render further precautionary provisions unnecessary. When on this occasion, F. Lauer, Wm. Massey, G. Bergner, M. Kleiner, Col. G. Gerst and S. Huston, accompanied by Congressman J. L. Getz, called upon him at Washington, he promised to assist and subsequently did give his aid to the committee. Robert L. Schenk was at that time the chairman of the Committee on Ways and Means of the House of Representatives, and through his courtesy Lauer and his associates had obtained an opportunity of personally laying the trade's wishes and grievances before the lawmakers. Both Schenk and Wells suggested the wisdom of printing and distributing the brewers' argument as to rebate, barley-duty, malt-tax and all kindred matters. During the oral argument it became manifest that not a single member of the Ways and Means Committee had an adequate idea of the losses which the allowance of a rebate

---

* The latter report is out of print and it is difficult, if not impossible, to obtain a copy. Even the Treasury Department has bnt a single one. The chronicler, by a singular stroke of good luck, came into the possession of the very copy nsed by Robert L. Schenk, then Chairman of the Committee on Ways and Means. It bears his antograph both on the fly-leaf and the title-page, and shows signs of diligent perusal.

of 7½ per cent. was intended to cover. From incidental allusions it is to be inferred that much of the inimical spirit with which some lawmakers treated the brewing industry arose from a total misconception of the matter, produced, no doubt, by the underhand machinations of the distillers, unwittingly aided by the prohibitionists. So far as additional safeguards against possible frauds were concerned Chairman Schenk himself, in his address to the Committee of the Whole on the state of the Union in favor of revenue amendments (June 1st, 1868), demonstrated very pointedly, though, of course, not directly, that more rigorous surveillance was unnecessary, when he said that the actual revenues from the tax on malt-liquors exceeded very considerably the estimated income from this source.

The brewers presented a second memorial to Congress at this session, and re-inforced this by a general petition praying for a revision of the law upon certain lines and within the scope, purport and intent of a bill which they had drawn and appended to said petition; but Congress adjourned without passing any law, before the date of the Buffalo convention, and matters were held in abeyance until the succeeding session in the winter of 1868.

The full text of *all* these arguments, remonstrances and petitions has not been preserved; yet, as to their intrinsic merit, from a literary and economic point of view, one can readily form an accurate opinion from the influence they undoubtedly exercised upon the pertinent recommendations by the proper Federal officers. The brewers' objections to the proposed tax-bill may be summed up as follows, viz.: The annual tax of fifty dollars upon all sales of malt not exceeding twenty-five thousand dollars, and of two dollars for every additional thousand dollars in excess of this sum, would virtually have amounted to an additional beer-tax of seven to eight cents upon every barrel of beer which could not have been added to the price of beer. Even according to Commissioner Wells' opinion, the brewing industry was amply taxed and the brewers were undoubtedly justified in pointing out the fact that while nearly all other and many older and more flourishing industries had borne and were still bearing so slight a burden of taxation, their trade, still in its infancy and doubly hampered by State and local restrictions, should not be singled out as a fit subject for additional restraint. The bill also provided that every vat, tank or other vessel having a capacity of more than one hogshead, whether used in the brew-house or the cellar, should be accurately gauged and measured, and that such measurement, together with the name of the gauger, should conspicuously and permanently be painted or branded upon every such vessel in figures and letters not less than three inches in length. The obvious object of this provision again demonstrated the lawmakers' unfamiliarity with brewing. The object evidently was to enable the inspector to determine at a glance the quantity of beer on hand; but that, of course, was in reality impossible, as the fermenting vats, for instance, can never be filled to the utmost limit of their capacity, while storage vats must be re-filled from time to time from other casks. Hence the department could not have derived any advantage from this arrangement, while the brewer would have been put to unnecessary expense, labor and inconvenience.

There was another provision equally unwarranted by the actual mode of manufacture. It would have required the brewer, before selling sour beer for manufacturing purposes, to cause the spoiled product to be inspected by a revenue officer, and to secure from him a proper certificate and inventory both of which he must deliver to the purchaser. Under the then existing law damaged beer, unfit for use as a beverage, could be sold for manufacturing purposes without payment of tax, provided it was removed from the brewery in vessels totally different from those used for marketable beer. This was considered a sufficient safeguard against fraud, and the brewers very justly argued that they would let the whole stuff go to waste, rather than expose themselves to the endless worry and inconvenience of notifying an inspector and awaiting his pleasure whenever, by reason of leakage or other cause, any quantity of beer turned sour,—a not infrequent occurrence during the summer months.

One of the principal complaints of brewers was the inconsiderate procedure of revenue officers in regard to those sections of the law which required the manufacturer to make daily entries of the exact quantity of beer brewed by them. The *modus operandi* was not prescribed and the revenue commissioner declined to establish a rule, thus leaving each one of his subordinates at liberty to subject the brewers to endless annoyances. Possibly that part of the proposed bill which required the gauging of vats, tuns and other vessels, was intended to obviate the difficulty. We have seen that the association protested against this innovation, and there the matter rested for the time being.

While the records relative to these remonstrances are incomplete, they, fortunately, present the full text of the brewers' memorial suggesting a revision of several sections of the existing law. It reads as follows, viz.:

To the Honorable,
 The Senate and House of Representatives of the
  United States of America:

The undersigned, on behalf of the brewers of the United States, respectfully represent:

That they cordially approve of the suggestions and recommendations in relation to fermented liquors, contained in the last report of the Hon. David A. Wells, Special Commissioner of the Revenue, and they most respectfully and urgently request, in addition thereto, that for the reasons set forth in the memorial presented by the Associated Brewers' Society of New York and vicinity, to the Hon. Hugh McCullough, Secretary of the Treasury, and the Hon. Edward A. Rollins, Commissioner of Internal Revenue, in the month of September, 1867, the following features should be incorporated into the Internal Revenue Law:

(1.) That no brewery shall hereafter be seized and closed, except after an examination duly had before some competent and responsible officer, upon notice to the owner thereof, at which examination he shall have the right to meet his accusers, to cross-examine them, and to examine witnesses and adduce evidence on his own behalf, at which examination, the facts justifying a seizure shall be clearly proven; that no re-assessment or assessment for any alleged deficiency, under section 9 of the Act of July 13th, 1866, shall hereafter be made, except after a like examination, duly had upon a like notice, at which examination the facts justifying the assessment shall be clearly proven ; and that in said proceedings a mere technical violation of law or excusable omission to comply with any provision of law, or an alleged surplus or deficiency of beer on hand, shall not constitute a sufficient ground of seizure or assessment, as long as no actual damage has been sustained by the United States, in consequence thereof.

Upon pp. 12 and 13 of the printed memorial herein-before referred to, it is shown that the adoption of these provisions will not enable a brewer to cover up a fraud.

(2.) The requirement of section 49 of Act of July 13th, 1866, that the brewer should enter from day to day, in the book required to be kept by him, "the description of packages and number of barrels and fractional parts of barrels of fermented liquors made," should be abolished, because compliance with this requirement is impossible. If it be deemed essential that a brewer should keep an account of beer made, in addition to the account of beer sold, or removed for consumption or sale, and in addition to the account of materials purchased, the law should be made to require him to make entry of each brewing, together with an estimate of the number of barrels which each brewing is expected to yield ; or else an entry of each brewing, and the number of barrels of water used for the same, from which quantity of water a deduction of 35 per cent. should be made, as provided by the laws of France, Baden, Hesse Darmstadt, Nassau, etc., etc., for evaporation, waste and other losses.

(3.) The words "or to do, or cause to be done, any of the things by law required to be done by him as aforesaid," should be stricken out of section 51 of the Act of July 13th, 1866, as too indefinite. If that section is not stringent enough without these words, it could be made more stringent by adding an enumeration and clear definition of the offences for which punishment is to be prescribed. As it now stands, every oppressive act of a revenue officer can readily be justified under its indefinite language. In the same manner the section should specify what acts on the part of a brewer amount to or should be considered as an attempt to evade the payment of the tax. As it reads at present, every collector may construe the sentence, "who shall evade or attempt to evade the payment of the tax thereon," to suit himself.

(4.) Section 55 of the Act of July 13th, 1866, leaves it discretionary with the Commissioner of Internal Revenue to prescribe the *manner* in which the name of the brewer, or firm, and the place of the brewery shall be *marked* upon the hogshead, barrel or other vessels. As a shipment of beer from St. Louis to New Orleans has been seized because the beer was shipped in packages furnished by the buyers to the brewer, with the name of another brewer *branded* thereon, which brand the St. Louis brewer declined to efface therefrom, although he nailed a printed card bearing his name and place of his brewery *over* the same, this section should be so amended as to strike out therefrom the words, "in such a manner as shall be prescribed by the Commissioner of Internal Revenue," and to insert in place thereof the words, "in a conspicuous manner." And at the end of said section the following should be added: "But brewers may remove fermented liquors of their own manufacture from their breweries, or other places of manufacture, in packages or vessels furnished for that purpose by the buyer or buyers, and having the name of the buyer, or firm name of the buyers, marked or branded thereon; provided the name of the person, firm, or corporation by whom such fermented liquor was manufactured, and the place where the same has been made, is also in a conspicuous manner marked on, or affixed to, every hogshead, barrel, keg, or other vessel containing the fermented liquor so proposed to be removed."

(5.) The deduction of 7½ per cent. allowed by section 52 of the Act of July 13th, 1866, upon the sale of stamps being an insufficient compensation for all losses intended to be covered thereby, the same should be increased to 15 per cent., especially as the losses under the new stamp system, proposed to be substituted for the present one, will be more numerous, in consequence of the very nature of the new stamp.

(6.) In conclusion, the undersigned most earnestly urge a reduction of the duty on Canada barley to the same figure as before the expiration of the reciprocity treaty, namely, five cents per bushel, for the reason that the quantity of barley grown in the United States is insufficient to supply the demands of the trade. In fact, the farmers of the United States find it more profitable to raise wheat and corn, than barley, while on the other hand the light soil of Canada is more adapted for the raising of barley.

The Washington Committee certainly had done magnificent work and its chairman fully deserved the praise and recognition expressed in this resolution adopted by the eighth convention:

> The eighth Brewers' Congress of the United States of America, by acclamation, have resolved to express their heartfelt thanks to the Honorable Frederick Lauer, Chairman of the Committee on Agitation for the protection of the brewing industry in the United States, which thanks Mr. Lauer has richly deserved by his indefatigable activity, great prudence, correct discernment, rare sagacity and energy, which qualities he has so eminently brought to bear on the difficult and wearying transactions in Washington. The Congress hope that Mr. Lauer will continue to devote his excellent talents to the interests of brewing, and that he will never tire to fight as a champion for free industry, especially in the interest of the brewing business, and oppose as heretofore the unjust fanaticism of those who fight against the civilizing influence of beverages produced from hops and malt.
>
> JOHN EICHLER,
> CHRISTIAN MOERLEIN, } Committee.
> L. J. KADISCH,
>
> ED. KISTNER, President.
>
> ALBERT ZIEGELE, } Secretaries.
> GUSTAVUS BERGNER,

Through President Clausen's efforts a re-organization of the local association of New York had been effected and to his uncommon administrative ability must be attributed the flourishing condition of that body at the time of the convention. The haphazard method of conducting deliberations had been superceded by a well-digested parliamentary code, and the rights and privileges of members as well as the duties, functions and prerogatives of officers and committees were fully and clearly established in a constitution and by-laws. In all these particulars this local body excelled the parent association, and President Clausen naturally desired to remedy these shortcomings and imperfections. His proposition to allow local associations to determine as to whether the work of the convention should be decided by a vote of a majority of delegates present or by a proxy vote to be cast by the delegates for the whole number of members constituting their respective organizations, did not result as he, doubtless, had expected. Only New York and Milwaukee voted in favor of the majority-plan; while Davenport, Columbus, Chicago, Cincinnati, Philadelphia, St. Louis, Newark and Pittsburg declared in favor of the latter method. The anomaly of such a makeshift, especially in view of the utter impossibility of applying the representative-system in a logical manner to all internal affairs, must have convinced Henry Clausen, Jr., still more strongly of the necessity of a re-organization and the adoption of a constitution and by-laws. He accordingly proposed that the Executive be instructed to "draft and report to the next convention proper statutes for the guidance of the principal association defining the aims and objects to be pursued." This motion was adopted and forms the first of a series of similar efforts by which the energetic leader succeeded in placing the society upon a firm and enduring basis.

At a preceding meeting the dues had been fixed at twenty cents on each 100 barrels of beer sold, with the understanding that the total amount due from the associations should be collected by their respective secretaries, and paid to the treasurer. This plan was now retained, although it did not seem to work very well. The dues collected throughout the year (1867–68) amounted in the aggregate to but $2,955.00; the balance of the preceding year amounted to $4,765.00, hence the association had an available fund of $7,720.00. The expenditures did not exceed $3,200.00; of which $1,000.00 was paid to the secretary as his annual salary, and $1,130.00 to the Washington Committee for traveling and other expenses; the remainder covered all other expenditures including those for printing and postage.

From various indications it must be inferred that in spite of the amicable advances related in a preceding chapter, the ale-brewers, as a body, still kept aloof from the association, most likely because the German language still dominated almost exclusively at the conventions. President Clausen, born in America, but descended from a sturdy stock of North-German immigrants, spoke both languages with equal ease and fluency. He clearly perceived the lingual obstacle which prevented a closer union—so essential and necessary to the success of the trade at this critical period—and was animated by a sincere desire to remove it in what seemed to him the most effective way. He proposed that at every succeeding convention the English language only should be used, as all those who attended the meeting were fully conversant with it and would not, therefore, experience any inconvenience; while the change would undoubtedly bring into the association every ale-brewer in the land. The delegates rose almost *en masse* against this move, and a very decided opposition, to which Stifel, Dreis, Boss, Rocke, and Schemm gave utterance, showed that the trade was not yet ripe for such a proposition. Clausen would have failed even if he had proposed to conduct the proceedings in English and German, as occasion might require. This was shown when Schemm made such a motion for bi-lingual proceedings and met with an equally strong resistance. Finally, the convention adopted this resolution, viz. :

"*Resolved*, that if in future Congresses proceedings of importance should make it desirable to translate and communicate the same in English, each delegate shall on motion to that effect, duly adopted, be entitled to have said proceedings stated and explained in the said language."

Great credit justly belongs to those ale-brewers, like William Massey of Philadelphia, John P. Ballantine of Newark, and others, who, although totally unfamiliar with the German language, nevertheless devoted their time, energy and means to the interests of the association. At this very convention, which adopted the foregoing resolution, W. Massey demonstrated his zeal and eagerness to serve the association by proposing that the maltsters and hop-dealers be invited to become associate members. Assailed upon every side, exposed to an unreasonable and unreasoning antagonism and laboring under the disadvantage of brutal prejudices, the trade had need, indeed, of the advice and aid of every man in any way connected with or dependent upon it. The convention could not fail to realize this. Massey's motion was adopted and thus was taken the first step towards unifying kindred trades in all matters affecting the brewing industry.

In another part of this book, it has been stated that the resolution relative to prohibition, adopted at the seventh brewers' convention, served the enemies of the trade as a welcome pretext for an agitation in favor of organizing a national party. Here is the proof. The chief court of the Good Templars at its session in 1868, referring to the brewers' resolution, recommended "the organization of a national political party which shall embrace in its platform of principles prohibition of the manufacture, importation and sale of intoxicating liquors to be used as a beverage." At the Sixth National Temperance convention, held at Cleveland, Ohio, July 29th and 30th, 1868, the following resolution, which its author characterized as "antagonistic of the action of the Brewers' Congress," was adopted without a dissenting voice, viz.:

"*Whereas*, The liquor dealers of our country have declared the traffic in intoxicating drinks to be a legitimate part of commerce, and deny the right to prohibit or restrict the same, and through their leagues and Congress have repeatedly avowed their purpose to vote for no man in favor of total abstinence, and have constantly used their political power for the continuance of their trade, and have, in the past, received the countenance of political parties in support of the positions thus assumed; therefore,

"*Resolved*, That, in behalf of the public peace and welfare we accept the issue, and will meet them at the polls in resistance of these iniquitous demands;

"*Resolved*, That temperance, having its political as well as moral aspects and duties, demands the persistent use of the ballot for its promotion; and the convention urge the friends of the cause to refuse to vote for any candidate who denies the application of the just powers of the civil government to the suppression of the liquor traffic, and exhort the friends of temperance, by every practical method in their several localities, to secure righteous political action for the advancement of the cause."

As to the minor details of this important convention, mention deserves to be made of the fact that towards the close of the meeting there was a spirited competition for the honor of entertaining the association at the ninth convention. Six cities vied with each other for this distinction and the strife was particularly lively between New York and Newark. It was not allayed until G. Bergner pointed out that as no convention had yet been held in New Jersey, the Newark brewers were entitled to an acceptance of their invitation.

The following is a list of the officers of the eighth convention, to wit: **President, Edward Kistner, Cincinnati; Honorary President,**

F. Lauer; Vice-Presidents : A. Huepfel, New York; J. P. Ballantine and G. Wiedemeyer, Newark; P. Schemm, and William Massey, Philadelphia; C. Moerlein, Cincinnati; A. Reymann, West Virginia; C. Seipp, Chicago; J. Uhrig, St. Louis; H. C. Dreis, Davenport; J. J. Obermann, Milwaukee, and P. Constans, Newport. Secretaries : G. Bergner, Philadelphia, and Albert Ziegele, Buffalo. Sergt.-at-Arms, Jacob Scheu, Buffalo. The Executive, consisting of President H. Clausen, Jr., Treasurer F. Schaefer, and Secretary R. Katzenmayer, was unanimously re-elected.*

---

* The following is a list of delegates present at the eighth convention:—

George Gerst, Allegheny, Pa.; Baumgarten, by Ch. Wette, Attorney, M. Beck, John Bickel, Charles Gerber, David Haas, Joseph L. Haberstroh, A. Hafner, Heiser & Holser, Joseph Jost, Xavier Kaltenbach, Gerhard Lang, Lang & Gottmann, Frederick Loersch, Messmer & Schamel, A. Muschal, George Rochevot, George Roos, Alois Schaefer, J. F. Schaentaleim, Jacob Scheu, Schleicher & Jaeger, John Schuessler, Julius Schwartz, Voetsch & Co., Mrs. G. Weber, Weyand & Schoetter, Albert Ziegele, Charles Zilch, Buffalo N. Y.; L. C. Huck, L. I. Kadisch, C. Seipp, Chicago, Ill.; Christian Boss, John Hauck, John Kauffmann, Edward Kistner, George Klotter, Fred. Knoll, C. Moerlein, Cincinnati, O.; Conrad Born, Louis P. Hoster, Columbus, O.; M. B. Angell, Cooperstown, N. Y.; H. C. Dreis, Davenport, Ia.; George Dottenweich, Dunkirk, N. Y.; Fred. Lauer, Lebanon, Pa.; Demangeot & Schmidt, Hilbert & Seeman, Lancaster, N. Y.; D. Knab, Jr., J. J. Obermann, Milwaukee, Wis.; John Eichler, Morrisania, N. Y.; Chas. Kolb, Gustav E. Wiedenmayer, Newark, N. J.; Jacob Ahles, John Brown, Henry Clausen, Jr., S. B. Butcher, Peter Doelger, John J. Freedman, Anton Haepfel, Michael Kuntz, J. M. Lewis, C. Moser, Hermann Rocke, Fred. Schaefer, C. Schmitt, Robert B. Young, New York, N. Y.; Gustevus Bergner, Frederick Blackburne, Jr., William Massey, Peter Schemm, Philadelphia, Pa.; George Gerst, Pittsburg, Pa.; F. Lauer, Pottsville, Pa.; F. Lauer, Reading, Pa.; E. Einheuser, Charles G. Stifel, Joseph Uhrig, St. Louis, Mo.; George Bechtel, Staten Island, N. Y.; George Zent, Tonawanda, N. Y.; A. Reymann, Wheeling, W. Va.; Joseph Liebmann, Williamsburgh .I., N. Y.

Chapter VII.

STATUS OF TRADE IN 1868; ITS FLOURISHING CONDITION IN SPITE OF ADVERSE CONDITIONS; INCREASED PRODUCTION. NINTH CONVENTION. NATIONAL PROHIBITION CONVENTION CALLED; RESOLUTION ON SUBJECT. KNOW-NOTHINGISM AND PROHIBITION AGAINST GERMAN-AMERICAN PATRIOTISM. BREWERS SCATHING REVIEW OF CRAZE. WASHINGTON COMMITTEE UNSUCCESSFUL, RE-ITERATE PREVIOUS ARGUMENT AND SUBMIT AMENDMENTS TO OLD, AND DRAFT OF NEW LAW; BUT PROPOSE NEITHER REDUCTION, NOR RELAXATION OF SAFEGUARDS. BREWERS ANXIOUS TO PREVENT FRAUD; OBJECT TO BOND BECAUSE THE BREWER IS THE CREDITOR NOT THE DEBTOR OF TREASURY; HENCE BOND AND CERTAIN BOOKS UNNECESSARY. TRADE CONVENIENCES ASKED FOR; THEIR SINGULAR CHARACTER. KINDRED TRADES JOIN ASSOCIATION. OFFICERS AND COMMITTEES OF CONVENTION. SETTLEMENT OF BREWERS' CLAIMS; NOTEWORTHY REASON FOR DELAY. DISCUSSION ON MALT-DUTY; EXTENT AND NATURE OF BARLEY CULTURE; REASONS FOR SUPERIORITY OF CANADA MALT. ESTABLISHMENT OF BREWERS' ACADEMY PROPOSED; ACTION OF CONVENTION; PERSONAL NOTE. CONSTITUTION SUBMITTED. *PERSONNEL* OF ASSOCIATION; STATE OF TRADE. COMPARISON BETWEEN ALE-TRADE AND LAGER-TRADE; REMINISCENCES. DIVERGING CLAIMS AS TO DATE OF INTRODUCTION OF LAGER-BREWING BEFORE AND AFTER 1852, WITH VARIOUS PERSONAL NOTES AND COMPARISONS. LIST OF DELEGATES.

With the foregoing pen-picture of the complex and important labors of the eighth convention before him, the reader may form an approximately correct idea of the status of the trade in the year 1868. Brewing had gained a foothold in nearly every Western, Eastern and Middle State, and the total production of the young industry amounted to 5,685,663 barrels. Local associations, more or less firmly organized, existed in New York, Pennsylvania, New Jersey, Missouri, Wisconsin, Illinois, Ohio and Iowa, the latter body having been re-formed in that year. *The American Brewer*, a semi-monthly journal devoted entirely to the interests of the trade, had been established in January of that year by A. Meckert, of New York, and responded so ably to the wants of the brewers that upon Clausen's recommendation it was made the organ of the association.

All this indicates a measure of progress and success that must have surprised even those who were mainly instrumental in bringing it about. The industry thus early manifested its potentiality and its almost illimitable possibilities. The progress achieved had to be won against innumerable drawbacks and impediments, and it is well-nigh impossible to surmise what proportions the development of American brewing would have reached, if the trade had received that fostering care and paternal protection which Congress bestowed upon other much older domestic industries.

Large as the production of the year 1868 must appear in comparison with the production of 1863 or 1864, it nevertheless indicates an appreciable retrograde movement as compared with the preceding year. There was, in fact, a decrease of 123,682 barrels, caused, as was generally assumed, by the high prices of brewing materials, especially malt, which had driven many smaller brewers out of the business. Almost 90 per cent. of this loss was sustained by the brewers of New York and Pennsylvania. In the next year lost ground was recovered, however, and from that time onward, excepting a few critical years, the production continued to increase steadily, until within very recent years, when a downward tendency again set in.

While the ninth convention assembled at Newark, N. J., on the 2d of June, 1869, welcomed by the veteran brewer, Adolph Schalk, then president of the local Brewers' Association, the call for a national convention of prohibitionists had already been issued (May 25th, 1869), and although the proceedings of the brewers' convention make no mention of it, we may safely assume that President Clausen, ever on the alert, knew and fully understood its purport, for in his address, an admirable document, he dwelt at length and with strong emphasis upon the dangers which threatened the trade, and made it the imperative duty of every brewer to take an active part in politics for the protection of his business and the defense of his rights as a citizen and tax-payer. The prohibitionists' call, addressed to the "friends of temperance, law and order," inaugurated an entirely new departure in the prohibitory movement; it ushered in what may be styled the culminating period of the craze and thus marks an epochal turning-point in the history of this agitation. Viewed from the standpoint of the brewers' association its historical importance is so obvious, that the reproduction of the literal text of its principal part requires neither explanation nor apology. It reads as follows, viz.:

"The moral, social and political evils of intemperance and the non-enforcement of the liquor laws are so fearful and prominent, and the causes thereof are so intrenched and protected by governmental authority and party interest, that the suppression of these evils calls upon the friends of temperance; and the duties connected with home, religion and public peace demand that old political ties and associations shall be sundered, and a distinct political party, with prohibition of the traffic in intoxicating drinks as the most prominent feature, should be organized.

"The distinctive political issues that have for years past interested the American people are now comparatively unimportant, or fully settled, and in this aspect the time is auspicious for a decided and practical effort to overcome the dread power of the liquor-trade."

During the discussion upon this call nearly every speaker asserted that the brewers had organized "to take temperance into politics," and that therefore a political counter-movement had become necessary. It is a well-known fact, however, that for almost a quarter of a century before the organization of the brewers these same self-constituted guardians of public morality had invaded the domain of politics and sought by all sorts of means to annihilate the trade through legislative enactments. Below the surface of this agitation there always has been a strong under-current of nativism which could easily be traced even at this time. Lamenting the palpable decline of their political influence, many writers and speakers openly declared that the German-American vote prevented the success of their cause, and one of their historians (James Black) explained that "the unity of language, customs and interests is so strong a bond that it sways supreme, and hence it is understood that to secure the German vote is to secure an election." The truth of the matter is that in those days the ruling party, appreciating the patriotism of the German-Americans, of whom a disproportionately large number (about 200,000) served in the Union Army from the beginning to the end of the war, could not well afford to ignore the just claims of that part of the voting population, particularly in view of the fact that in many Western and some Eastern States the party pledged to the grand task of preserving the Union derived an essential part of its strength from this very source. The officers of the brewers' association fully understood this feature of the antagonism and enmity which confronted them, and none perceived its significance more clearly than the chairman of the Agitation Committee, in whose report occurs the following statement, worthy, indeed, of being preserved in an enduring form for the benefit of coming generations of brewers: " The Germans of the United States and their descendants have encountered no small opposition and no inconsiderable degree of obloquy and injustice in their attempt to introduce into this country their national festivals and the health-giving beverages, beer and wine. The opposition emanates from a Puritanical element which endeavors to enforce as its rule of action, in law and morals, the false idea that the abuse of the things of this life can only be cured by the total prohibition of their use. But many eminent men, lawmakers and philanthropists, are beginning to show a disposition to accept the truth, which has been exemplified for centuries in the social habits and customs, physical conditions and national characteristics of the Teutonic race, that the surest protection against habitual drunkenness and the train of evils that follow intemperance is to be found in encouraging the use of wines and malt-liquors, at once nutritious and stimulating, and invigorating and strengthening mind and body."

Congressional work, so far as the revenue law relating to malt-liquors was concerned, had remained in *statu quo*, and the Washington Committee had little material to report upon beyond the suggestions and recommendations contained in their last-quoted petition. The revised tax bill, prepared by the Committee on Ways and Means of the Fortieth Congress, was pending when the latter body adjourned, and little doubt existed that it would form the basis of whatever measures the same committee was likely to submit to the next Congress.

The ninth convention, therefore, wisely concluded to again petition Congress for a modification of the law of 1866, re-iterating in substance the points of the previous memorials. But this was not all. The petition, drafted by Counsellors Joseph J. Lewis and Charles T. Bonsall, but signed by the entire Committee on Agitation, had, in fact, a two-fold purpose, *i. e.*, (1) to suggest necessary amendments to the law of 1866, and (2) to submit the draft of an act designed to supercede the entire statute then in force. True, the latter had the sanction of the trade at the time of its introduction into Congress, but in the light of subsequent experiences many provisions, which in theory seemed just, fair and useful, proved to be the very opposite in practice. This applies principally to details of the system which nothing short of actual practice could have tested. Not a single proposition advanced by the association had the slightest tendency to diminish the revenue from this source. The brewers recognized the fact that the interests of the Government were identical with those of the honest producer and dealer, and that the prosperity of their business depended, in a very large measure, upon the efficiency of the law compelling payment of the tax and preventing and punishing fraudulent evasions. They understood that a competition between tax-paying and non-tax-paying manufacturers must inevitably prove ruinous to the former. They were and are to-day as much interested as the Government in a rigorous enforcement of the law; and in reality one of the principal objects of the founders of the association *was* to prevent the perpetration of fraudulent attempts upon the revenue and to ensure the strictest honesty and integrity in the conduct of the brewing business.

The amendments to the Act of 1866, proposed by the association, rested upon a solid foundation of justice and equity. That section which required every brewer to execute yearly a bond in double the amount of the tax for which he might become liable during any one month, conditioned that he will pay such tax and keep certain books relating to sales, was clearly an unwarrantable and totally unnecessary hardship. Under the original revenue-method, when the brewer paid his tax only once in each month and not until after the sale of his product or its removal for consumption, there was ample justification for exacting a bond; but after the introduction of the stamp-system, when the brewer paid his tax in advance by affixing a stamp upon every barrel of beer before it left his possession, the case was reversed; and the brewer, instead of being a debtor, became the creditor of the Government. The main object of the bond having been to secure the payment of tax, the requirement became useless as soon as the brewer had to make payment in advance. The keeping of books showing these transactions was merely a secondary requirement growing out of the main and essential condition of the bond.

The privilege of removing malt-liquors manufactured in one collection-district to a place of storage located in another was confined, under section 54 of the Act of 1866, to brewers of ale and porter; evidently an unintentional discrimination against lager-beer brewers. The association asked that this obvious injustice to the latter class of manufacturers be eliminated from the law.

Among the more noteworthy provisions embodied in the brewers' draft there was one which throws a strong light upon a very interesting practice in vogue among brewers in the early days of the association—a practice revealing the exceedingly friendly relations which must have existed even then among the pioneers of the modern trade. The object of the clause was to allow a brewer to remove from a brewery belonging to another person malt-liquors purchased for the purpose of supplying the customers of the purchaser in his own vessels, branded with his own name and place of manufacture as prescribed by law. It frequently happened, it seems, that a brewer received more orders for beer than he could himself fill from the product of his establishment, and in that case he obtained the required quantity from a neighboring brewery. Willing to help each other, without taking their customers into their confidence in a matter which was purely one of trade-convenience, the brewers now asked the lawmakers to permit the removal of "tax-paid" beer from one brewery in barrels belonging to another. The permission sought to be obtained would have been simply a trade-convenience, not involving any loss to the Government, nor weakening the safeguards against frauds.

Another provision, both new and perhaps also somewhat novel,—the necessity or utility of which the present-day brewer may not so readily perceive—was to the effect that all malt-liquor or tun-liquor in the first stages of fermentation, known as unfermented wort, sold by one brewer to another for the purpose of producing fermentation or enlivening old beer, should not be liable to payment of tax on the part of the seller, but on the part of the buyer. Aside from the merely regulatory details of the projected measure there is but one more point deserving notice, namely, that clause which provided that whenever a licensed brewer, by reason of an accident by fire or flood, or by reason of repairs, or other circumstances, should be compelled to carry on his business, wholly or in part, at some other place within the same or an adjoining district, he should be permitted to do so without obtaining a new license or paying another special tax.

For the sake of preserving a certain measure of continuity, as far as compatible with the chronological order of things, we have in the foregoing virtually forestalled the course of events, for it is clear that this petition was not drafted until some time after the adjournment of the ninth convention.

Of this gathering much remains to be said which stands in close relation to the work of the succeeding convention, and it may not, therefore, be amiss to summarize, before proceeding to these matters, the more important deliberations and those personal items which a conscientious chronicler cannot with propriety omit. Worthy of mention, above all things, is the fact that the appeal to the kindred trades, mentioned in the preceding chapter, had the effect of swelling the ranks of the delegates by the accession of nineteen representatives of the hop and malt trade, some of whom, like Neidlinger, Schmidt & Co., Chr. Trefz, Pier Bros. and others, have remained stanch and loyal supporters of the association up to the present day. In the general list of delegates occur for the *first* time the names of some brewers, who in subsequent years rose to eminence in the trade and organization, and to enviable distinction in both public and private life. The mere reference to this list, appended to this chapter, and a perusal of it by the reader would suffice to show to what extent this is true; but we shall presently endeavor to give a cursory description of the "Then and Now."

Edward Kistner, of Cincinnati, was again elected presiding officer, with F. Lauer as honorary president, and the following vice-presidents: New York, Joseph Schmidt; New Jersey, Gottfried Krueger and Peter Ballantine; Pennsylvania, Charles Engel and Robert Gray; Ohio, Conrad Windisch; Illinois, George Schmitt; Missouri, Charles G. Stifel; Iowa, A. Werthmueller; Wisconsin, Joseph Schlitz; Kentucky, Charles Geissbauer; West Virginia, A. Reymann; Massachusetts, J. Pfaff; Indiana, W. Baelzer; Maryland, Jacob Seeger. Secretaries: Henry Lawson, of Pennsylvania, and Otto Lademan, of Missouri. Sergeant-at-Arms: John Laible, of New Jersey.

In the lists of the special committees occur the names of Joseph Liebmann (Brooklyn), Jacob Ahles (New York), G. Bergner (Philadelphia), Herman Schalk (Newark), Christian Boss (Cincinnati), George Gerst (Philadelphia), A. Werthmueller (Dubuque), George Bechtel (Staten Island), Gustav Weidemayer (Newark), Conrad Windisch (Cincinnati), and Peter Schemm (Philadelphia). The entire Committee on Agitation was re-elected with but the one exception, that upon Joseph Schlitz, of

Milwaukee, fell the task of filling the vacancy created by the demise of his colleague C. F. Melms, of the same city.

Among the matters of special interest we note the final settlement of the brewers' claims arising out of the unlawful collection of taxes on malt-liquors brewed prior to September 1st, 1862. Introduced at the very first national gathering of brewers, the subject-matter constituted one of the determining motives for co-operation; less on account of its intrinsic importance than as an illustration of the many ways in which, under the Federal excise-system, the interests of the trade may be jeopardized by imperfect laws, or unwise or arbitrary interpretations of law on the part of revenue officers. An exhaustive argument covering every point of the claim had immediately been submitted by the association to the court of claims, but instead of harmoniously co-operating with the committee, many of the principal claimants commenced independent actions and thus, instead of obtaining a speedy refunding of the amounts erroneously collected, caused confusion and delay which almost frustrated the entire object. This incident, by the way, conveys a lesson that present-day brewers might do well to bear in mind. The same tendency to break away from plans of action thoroughly matured and advantageously launched by competent committees of the association, has of late years been exhibited in some quarters, and in a number of instances has helped to defeat judicious endeavors. In the case under consideration fortuitous circumstances neutralized the ill-advised course of independent claimants, and in 1869, the last claim (that of Roemelt & Leicht, of Hudson City, N. J., amounting to $1,650) having been paid, the committee was finally relieved from its responsibility in the premises.

The presence, before noted, of quite a number of maltsters led to an instructive discussion upon the duty upon malt and barley. Friendly and well-disposed as the Committee on Ways and Means had been to the trade from the beginning, no argument, however convincing, could incline them to a favorable consideration of the petition praying for a reduction of this duty ; in fact, as will be shown presently, Schenk, taking umbrage at what he deemed an undue insistence on the part of the brewers, became rather bitter in his treatment of the matter, and on the floor of the House of Representatives indulged in a passionate diatribe against the trade. The duty of fifteen cents upon every bushel of barley really amounted to very much more than the nominal sum, because the duty had to be paid in gold which was then at a very high premium. From the point of view of the protective system the levying of a duty upon a raw-material, constituting one of the two essential necessaries of an American industry, could not possibly be justified, and as a means of stimulating the domestic production of barley the measure seemed unnecessary, as there was no scarcity of the commodity. According to official reports, published by the Department of Agriculture, the production of barley in the United States amounted, in 1868, to 26,000,000 bushels; the importation of foreign, principally Canadian, barley to but 3,500,000 bushels. Not a lack of quantity, but of quality formed the basis of the brewers' claim, it being generally assumed (whether rightly or wrongly, it is unnecessary to discuss) that the maltable portion of the domestic production would not cover the demand unless a very much lower quality-standard than had theretofore prevailed were adopted. Whatever difference climate and the relative character of the soil in its pristine state may have produced—the chronicler confesses that he is rather sceptical as to these

232 *History U. S. Brewers' Association—Chapter VII.*

claims—there can be no doubt that in Canada, where the raising of barley was much older than in the United States, very much greater care had been bestowed upon the cultivation of the soil and by the judicious selection and transplantation of suitable English seeds, such as the Chevalier, uncommonly favorable results had been obtained. The merits of the brewers' case, considered in this light and under the general aspect of the American protective system, could not fail to impress fair-minded lawmakers, but, unfortunately, whenever at that time or in subsequent years the interests of this industry clashed with those of the husbandmen, the discomfiture of the former seemed inevitable; it was virtually a foregone conclusion.

Brewers familiar with the present status of American brewing academies and scientific stations, and interested in these valuable institutions of learning and research, would be far from satisfied with such mention of the earliest beginning of these efforts as can be gleaned from the report of the ninth convention. From it one could but learn that Adolph Schalk "moved to consider whether it be expedient to direct the Executive Committee to submit plans for a brewers' school connected with a small brewery." The record shows only this and the statement that the motion was adopted with the understanding that such plans should be submitted to the local associations two months before the next meeting. The reader will desire to know more. Well, since the eighth convention the semi-monthly journal known as *Der Amerikanische Bierbrauer* had passed out of the hands of Meckert into those of Anton Schwarz, who in July, 1868, had superceded Mr. Ruschhaupt as editor, and before the end of the year secured the ownership of the periodical. Familiar with the theory and practice of brewing and particularly well-posted in all modern achievements of mechanical invention and scientific research, he at once perceived a wide field of usefulness before him, more especially in view of the fact that the exclusively practical training of the early brewers served to favor the schemes of unprincipled impostors who posed as inventors and scientists. The idea of establishing a school under the auspices and with the means of the association grew out of this knowledge, and its promulgation was the first step in this all-important matter; although, as the reader knows, subsequent events led to the adoption of a course wholly different from that proposed by Schwarz, leaving the field entirely to his personal energy and spirit of enterprise, until in after-years his success created a wholesome and very competent competition.

The constitution and by-laws, drafted by the Executive Committee pursuant to instructions before referred to, were submitted at this meeting and ordered to be printed to the end that the delegates to the next convention be enabled to discuss and intelligently vote upon the subject-matter in the light of whatever instructions their associations might give them. These and other matters, mentioned before, were finally disposed of at the next convention and will, therefore, be treated of in the succeeding chapter.

Various minor notes, insignificant in themselves, which one finds interlarded, so to speak, between the main topics of the records, afford interesting glimpses of the *personnel* of the trade in those days, as compared with the present time. Thus, for instance, the two breweries which to-day produce the largest quantities of beer were not personally represented, but of their fealty and loyal adherence to the association we have documentary evidence in the shape of a congratulatory telegram from P. H. Best & Co., of Milwaukee, and a letter by Adolphus Busch, who, as secretary of the St. Louis Brewers' Association, states that their representative in Congress, G. A. Finckelnburg, had voluntarily offered his services to the trade, such a course being in harmony with what the people would naturally expect of a German-American congressman. In the year when Secretary Busch wrote this letter and Best sent his telegram, the whole State of Missouri produced little over 235,000 barrels, while Wisconsin's total production did not exceed 188,000 barrels of malt-liquors of all kinds. Iowa produced but 111,000 barrels, yet A. Werthmueller, one of the ablest men in the trade, who has since then rendered inestimable service to the cause, reported at the ninth convention that within the current year three brewers' associations had been organized in his State, *i. e.*, one each at Dubuque, Burlington and Davenport. By virtue of its producing of 412,000 barrels, New Jersey ranked fifth among the beer-producing States; New York being first, with 1,896,119; Pennsylvania, second, with 755,447; Ohio, third, with 551,623, and Illinois, fourth, with 457,407 barrels. Newark, the convention-city, produced 75 per cent. of this quantity and, of course, much the greater part of that was lager-beer. Throughout the State small breweries were in successful operation, but all upon what to-day would be considered a very insignificant scale. All the older establishments had been started on a small basis. The Schalks, of Newark, for instance, who were then among the most prosperous brewers, had begun their operations by weekly brews of *ten* barrels. William Peter, now of Union Hill, N. J., first brewed beer in 1860, upon rented premises, the kettle capacity of his establishment being 2¾ barrels, and his total output for that year amounting to but seventy-five barrels. Judge Gottfried Krueger, who afterwards became one of the leaders of his party, the guiding spirit of many successful enterprises and a benefactor to his city and State, also began business on a limited scale. He and Gottlieb Hill succeeded the firm of Laible & Adam, as owners in 1865. The brewery, it is true, had been established by Adam & Braun in 1852, ten years after Wagner had introduced the brewing of lager-beer into America, but the production had remained at a low figure, not exceeding 2,000 barrels in 1865. In 1867 the production amounted to 4,000, and in the year of the ninth convention to 18,000 barrels. P. Ballantine Sons were then classed as large brewers, but we must not lose sight of the fact that the founder of the house, who in 1840 had removed to Newark from Albany, after having built up a considerable business in the latter city, brewed ale and porter for which there was a much greater demand in the middle of the century than for lager-beer. Even in 1869 the relative proportion of ales and lager-beer was as 6 to 1 in some cities of the State of New York. Thus Albany, in 1869 produced 216,028 barrels, of which fully 200,000 barrels were ale and porter. As early as 1824 Albany had five extensive brewing establishments of which that of Fiddler & Taylor was supposed to be the largest in the United States, having a capacity of 250 barrels per day. In other cities of a larger German population the proportion was reversed, of course; as, for example, in Buffalo, where of 141,645 barrels produced in 1869, only 11,678 barrels were ale and porter. In the city of New York the disparity was still greater; but in Boston, and in fact throughout New England, ale preponderated very considerably even then, and the ale breweries, as compared with the lager-beer trade, had there as elsewhere the advantages of age. Some of these establishments—not very many, however—had been in operation ever since the beginning of the century, and of these a few remained in the hands of the same family for from three to five generations, as, for instance, the Miles Brewery in New York, the Evans Brewery in Hudson, etc. In Philadelphia, where the ale-trade had acquired an international reputation even before the Revolution, the ale brewers held their own ground very successfully, and some of the men who loyally responded to the associations' calls, like William Massey, Robert Gray, Huston and others, even forged ahead steadily for a time. Here also the advantage of age must be taken into consideration. For instance, the brewery owned by William Massey was originally established in the year 1822 by a company of farmers for the purpose of profitably utilizing their own barley. Robert Gray owned the brewery built in 1830 by Richard Taylor. Examples might be multiplied, but these must suffice for the present.

Philadelphia, as has already been stated elsewhere, is generally regarded as the birth-place of the lager-beer trade. In the absence of authentic information to the contrary we may accept this statement by which both the exact date of the first introduction of lager-beer and the name of the first American lager-beer brewer have been definitely established. It is upon the authority of Lauer, who brewed lager as early as 1844, that trade-historiographers hold that Wagner, a Bavarian brewer, established in business at Philadelphia, first brewed lager-beer in 1842. This claim is controverted by local historians of the city of Buffalo, who assert that as early as 1838 Jacob Roos brewed lager-beer in his establishment upon the site of the present Iroquois Brewery. Without going back quite so far, the same authorities present a still stronger case against the Wagner claim in the statement that Schanzlin & Hoffmann brewed "lager" in 1840, and both Joseph Friedmann and

Magnus Beck, previous to the year 1842. The earliest German brewers of the city of New York certainly do not claim priority in this respect. In Sommer's brewery, for instance, which in 1840 was located on Broadway, near 18th Street, only small-beer was brewed. And when the Schaefers, Fritz and Max, two venerable pioneers of the trade, bought this brewery in 1842, this mode of brewing was retained and continued for several years, probably as late as 1849. Fritz Schaefer is the gentleman whose name occurs in nearly every chapter of this history in connection with the financial status of the association, as he held the treasurership for many years. It would be an unprofitable and useless task to scrutinize the testimony presented for and against Lauer's assumption, or to enter into a methodical discussion of the matter. There is this to be said however. If the Buffalonian claim rests upon a solid foundation concerning the dates and the brewers named, a closer enquiry, if it were at all possible, would probably reveal the fact that the malt-liquor brewed prior to 1842 was not lager-beer, but of a kind generally known as "Schenkbier." If it were really Bavarian lager-beer, then Lauer's version as to the date of its introduction becomes clearly untenable; but right here we are confronted by certain facts as to brewing in the city of New York, which justify a strong presumption in favor of our explanation as to the nature of the beer in question. It is known that Gillig, the founder of several "dynasties of brewers," when beginning his business, in 1840, upon the very spot where now stand the Vanderbilt palaces, did not brew lager-beer. He continued to brew an ordinary Schenkbier until 1846, when, after removing his establishment to Third Street, he obtained from Philadelphia the necessary yeast for brewing lager-beer, and thenceforth manufactured this beverage. In like manner every available bit of information obtained by the writer in this and other cities seems but to confirm the Philadelphia claim to the effect that "lager" was introduced in 1842. Before the end of the decade—German immigration having in the meantime assumed unprecedented proportions—a considerable number of lager-beer breweries were established there as in every city having large German populations. Charles Engel, C. W. and Gustavus Bergner, C. C. Wolf, L. Bergdoll, C. Psotta, John Klumpp were among the more prominent pioneers. In the city of New York we have in addition to Gillig, the forty-eighter A. Schmidt, founder of the Lion Brewery; the two Rupperts, Franz and Valentine, A. Huepfel, John Bechtel, John Kress, Traudtmann, Rosenstein, Greunewald, Kirchhoff and a few others, whose names are not as familiar to the present generation.

In the succeeding decade (1852–1862) were established at least 60 per cent. of the breweries which furnished to the association much of its intellectual force, business energy and social strength. We shall again revert to this subject; but before leaving it, just one more interesting item. At the time of the ninth convention (1869), George Ehret was still a beginner, selling probably not more than 10,000 barrels. Two years before, he had established his own brewery with the generous assistance of his friend and former employer, Anton Huepfel, a man of exceeding goodness of heart and loftiness of mind.*

---

* The following is a list of delegates present at the ninth convention:

F. Hinckel, Jos. Vogelaeutner, Albany, N. Y.; Jos. L. Haberstroh, Albert Ziegele, Buffalo, N. Y.; Alfred Werthmueller, Burlington, Ia.; Cincinnati Delegation, Columbus, O.; George Schmidt, Chicago, Ill.; C. Boss, Fr. Eichenlaub, Henry Foss, Edward Kistner, Conrad Windsch, Cincinnati, O.; Charles Getsbaner, Covington, Ky.; A. Meckert, Guttenberg, N. J.; Fr. Laner, Lebanon, Pa.; Joseph Schlitz, F. Pabst, Milwaukee, Wis.; Henry Zeltner, Charles Rivinins, John Eichler, Morrisania, N. Y.; Anernhammer & Schelling, Peter Ballantine & Sons, John Baier, John A. Boppe, Gelssele & Woehr, Gruber, Kerr & Co., F. Hass, F. Haeusler, Joseph Hensler, John Helnikel, Hill & Krueger, F. J. Kastner, Knecht & Co., Chas. Kolb, John Laible, Morton & Bro., Joseph Nen, Newark Brewing Co., Schalk Bros., F. Stegmueller, Jos.

CHAPTER VIII.

PROHIBITORY MOVEMENT IN IOWA; SOME OF ITS MORE PROMINENT OPPONENTS; WERTHMUELLER AND DREIS LEAD. CHARACTER OF POPULATION. STATE OF BREWING IN IOWA; BREWERS ORGANIZED. TENTH CONVENTION. INTERESTING REMINISCENCES AND PARALLEL AS TO FEASTS. REPRESENTATIVE SYSTEM IN OPERATION; HOW MANAGED; ITS DEFECTS. CONSTITUTION AND BY-LAWS DISCUSSED AND ADOPTED; ITS MAIN OBJECT; ITS MERITS AND SHORTCOMINGS. NAME OF ASSOCIATION AGAIN CHANGED. STATUS OF PRESIDENT SETTLED; ALSO THAT OF ASSOCIATE MEMBERS. BREWERS' JOURNAL SUBSIDIZED. BREWERS' ACADEMY; NECESSITY FOR IT CONCEDED; DIVERGENCE OF OPINION AS TO MEANS; SOME FOR, OTHERS AGAINST MAKING IT AN ASSOCIATION INSTITUTE; PLAN OF ORGANIZATION AND COURSE OF STUDY; MATTER POSTPONED. GERMAN BREWERS' TO BE ORGANIZED NATIONALLY; FRANCO-PRUSSIAN WAR INTERVENES AND FRUSTRATES EFFORT; AMERICAN BREWERS' PREMATURE GREETING. FISCAL CONDITION OF ASSOCIATION. PRESIDENT HONORED, SECRETARY APPRECIATED. BREWERS' FIRE INSURANCE COMPANY ESTABLISHED AND SUCCESSFUL. REBATE AND DUTY ON MALT; SCHENCK'S OPPOSITION TO, AND WELLS' SUPPORT OF, BREWERS. SCHENCK'S METHODS; HIS SPEECH ON FLOOR OF HOUSE AND BROOKS' AND JUDDS' REPLY. DISCRIMINATION BETWEEN DISTILLED AND FERMENTED DRINKS; SLIGHT CONCESSION IN THIS PARTICULAR. METALLIC STAMPS REJECTED. OFFICERS AND LIST OF DELEGATES.

In inviting the association to hold its tenth convention at Davenport, Mr. A. Werthmueller, a highly educated and uncommonly intelligent gentleman, emphasized the fact that his adopted State had for years been the scene of a very virulent prohibitory campaign supported by a large number of newspapers. Excepting the German-

---

Seidel, George Tauwald, Wakenhut, Adam & Co., C. Wiedenmayer & Sons, Newark, N. J.; F. Kaufmann, Albert Schabel, Harrison, N. J.; Jacob Tanner, Eller & Bayer, Elizabeth, N. J.; Jacob Ahles, Peter Ahles, Armbruster, H. Clausen, Jr., Peter Doelger, Anton Doelger, Wm. Eckert, Anton Huepfel, H. Koehler, Michael Kuntz, J. J. Mentges, Jos. Schmid, F. Schaefer, F. Sommer, Jr., C. Stein, George Winter, New York, N. Y.; John Baltz, Gustavus Bergner, C. Engel, Robert Grey, Hall (of the firm of Massey, Huston & Co.), H. Lawser, C. Psotta, Peter Schemm, Charles Smith, Henry Walter, Philadelphia, Pa.; William Eberhardt, George Gerst, John Ober, Heinrich Wilhelm, Pittsburg, Pa.; F. Lauer, Pottsville, Pa.; F. Lauer, Reading, Pa.; Chas. Bischoff, George Bechtel, L. Rosenbaud, Joseph Ruebsam, Staten Island, N. Y.; Otto Lademann, Chas. G. Stifel, St. Louis, Mo.; Louis Ruscher, Troy, N. Y.; George Baer, Wilkesbarre, Pa.; Joseph Burger, Gaiser & Steinhaeuser, Jos. Liehmann, H. H. Linnemann, John Schuelder, Williamsburgh, L. I., N. Y.

Also the following representatives of the Hop and Malt trade:

E. D. Brenner, Baltimore, Md.; Eberhardt Kammerer, Cincinnati, O.; Louis Soehgen, Henry Schlosser, Ph. Hartmann, Hamilton, O.; Neidlinger, Schmid & Co., Akin & Ferry, Pier Bros., Alfred Flostroy, W. Knapp, Wm. Marr, John H. Ziudel, J. A. Marzen, J. L. W. Brown, J. D. Wheeler, Chr. Trefz, New York, N. Y.; F. Blackburne, Jr., Colfangh, W. W. Hughes, Philadelphia, Pa.

American Press, there was but one newspaper in the State, viz.: *The True Radical,* that seemed to appreciate the dangers of the movement. There were, however, very many influential forty-eighters, fully masters of the English language, who for years had carried on an educational campaign and succeeded in liberalizing public sentiment. Among these was the brewer Dr. H. C. Dreis, whose splendid advocacy of liberal views had gained for him the title of champion of the brewers' rights. His connection with the trade made his services all the more valuable. Of other equally prominent men who during many years wrote and spoke against the craze, we may mention T. Guelich, author of a very instructive pamphlet on Prohibition; J. S. Sibolt, Joseph Eiboeck and H. C. Bechtold, three editors of uncommon ability; the well-known poet Caspar Butz; F. W. Lehmann, and the brewers Werthmueller, C. Magnus, Rudolph and Heinrich Koehler.

The State of Iowa, like many of the agricultural States of the Northwest, was opened to civilization principally by New England farmers and a very numerous and most useful class of German and Scandinavian husbandmen, many of whom, fairly well-to-do freeholders at home, "came over the sea," at the urgent solicitation, one might say, of those officers of the State Government who had charge of what may be called the Immigration Department. The original prohibitory law of 1855 exempted native cider and wine. In 1858, for the very purpose of attracting immigration, a law was enacted permitting both the manufacture and sale (at wholesale and retail) of malt-liquors. In rapid succession other laws were passed which in their joint effect amounted to the establishment of an ordinary license-system; and the inevitable result was—as the lawmakers contemplated and expected—that the brewing industry began gradually to develop, the total production in the entire State amounting to 104,000 barrels in 1870—the year of the tenth convention. It was believed that the holding of the annual brewers' gathering in the principal city of this State would tend to dispel many of the prejudices to which prohibitionists usually appeal in their efforts to strengthen their cause.

The brewers of Iowa, very well organized in the principal cities of the State, having local associations in Burlington, Davenport and Dubuque, had also succeeded in bringing together and uniting into one body the brewers of the entire State; and it was this organization which, through its chairman, J. Huber, and its secretary, George E. Schlapp, welcomed the delegates to the tenth convention. An incident of the reception may present food for thought to present-day brewers. In their address of welcome these officers apologized for their inability to offer their guests sumptuous feasts and grand entertainments, and Secretary Schlapp expressed the fear that the delegates " would miss the luxuries they had found in larger cities "—luxuries which could not be had in the young city of Davenport, and even if they could have been obtained would have been beyond the means of the struggling local association. The inference must be that other cities had provided luxurious feasts for the delegates. If, however, we look a little more critically into this statement and its inference we shall find that compared with present-day affairs, even the larger cities offered exceedingly simple and modest feasts and entertainments in those days. By way of illustration the chronicler may be allowed to cite but one example. In 1870, the very year of the Davenport convention, the local association of New York City and vicinity gave a banquet for the avowed purpose of strengthening and extending the personal relations

between brewers. The banquet took place at M. Kuntz's
brewery, 77 Essex Street. Every guest was entitled, as
the invitation stated, to a meal and a bottle of wine
costing in all $1.50, which sum was paid out of the
general funds of the association. Happily, times and
conditions have changed; yet it is well to look back,
from time to time, to the end that we may realize the
conditions under which our fathers have labored and
struggled, and may remain gratefully mindful of the
duty we owe them. President Clausen in replying to
the apologetic address of Secretary Schlapp very properly stated that less luxury and more earnest work would
fully meet the wants of the trade;—and with this resolute
utterance, so characteristic of the man, he at once proceeded to business.

By far the most important work of this convention—
held on the 2d and 3d days of June, 1870, was the
adoption of the constitution referred to in the preceding chapter. It was at this meeting, too, that the
representative system, entitling one delegate to vote for
the entire number of members of his local association,
first went into effect. Before the vote upon the constitution, it had been ascertained that eleven associations
were represented; and, hence, eleven delegates were
formally designated by name to cast the corporate vote
of these bodies; they represented in all two hundred
and thirty-eight brewing firms, distributed as follows:
St. Louis (Stifel) 24 votes; Cincinnati (Foss) 23; Milwaukee (J. Obermann) 11; Philadelphia (Lawser) 23;
Dubuque, Iowa (Tschirgi) 3; Quincy, Ill. (Dick) 2;
Chicago (Schmidt) 12; Pittsburg (Gerst) 14; Newark,
N. J. (Bayer) 26; New York (Clausen) 69, and Iowa
(Anschuetz) 31. These delegates represented eight
States and ten cities, but there were represented at the
convention by one or more delegates, all members in

good standing, ten States and fourteen cities in addition to the fifteen cities of the State of Iowa, included, probably, in the body for whom Mr. Anschuetz acted as spokesman. From the proceedings no opinion can be formed as to the status of the delegates not included in the above apportionment; all that can be gleaned from the minutes is that the gentlemen representing the aforementioned associations constituted the voting power of the convention. Possibly the other delegates (see list of attending members at end of chapter), arrived later, that is, after the apportionment had been made; or they may have been permitted to cast individual votes. Whatever the mode may have been it is clear, even without more light upon the subject than is now available, that the anomaly of the system could not but be felt and appreciated even at that early stage of its practical application. Even those who favored it must have entertained doubts as to its equity and efficacy, for the proposition—ultimately adopted—to apply this manner of voting only in matters of the utmost importance, emanated from the advocates of what the proceedings style the "repartition system." The constitution of 1870, drafted, as we have seen, by the Executive Committee, differs very essentially from the fundamental law which at the present time governs the association; a simple comparison of the two documents would in itself suffice to illustrate the incessant upward and onward movement of the trade, and its unwearying efforts to attain higher levels in every respect. For this reason alone the reproduction of this first constitution would appear indispensable, even if its general value from a historical point of view did not secure for it a prominent place in a *documentary* history of the association. Leaving out the prefatory statement as to the general objects of the organization, this constitution reads as follows, viz.:

I.—ORGANIZATION.

SEC. 1. The association consists of the combined Brewers' Associations of the United States, and is known as the Principal Association of the Brewers of the United States.

SEC. 2. The communication between the Principal Association and the members of the different local associations is effected through the local associations, and with non-members the Principal Association will communicate directly.

SEC. 3. The association is under the care and direction of an executive, consisting of : (*a*) a president, (*b*) a vice-president (chairman of the Agitation Committee); (*c*) a treasurer, (*d*) a secretary, and an Agitation Committee composed of members from the different States.

SEC. 4. The Agitation Committee is provided with a chairman, who has unlimited power in urgent cases regarding the agitation. The committee shall watch over the entire interests of the brewers, and guard and defend them against outside influences in all trade matters, and report to each Congress the result of its activity.

SEC. 5. The Executive and Agitation Committees are only the executive power of the association, while to the regular annual convention or Congress of the brewers is left the legislative and directing power.

II.—ANNUAL CONGRESS OF THE BREWERS.

SEC. 1. The time of holding the same is always determined by the last previous Congress.

SEC. 2. The action of the Congress is binding on all associations and members, provided a majority of the delegates present have given their votes in favor of any measure.

SEC. 3. The voting shall be conducted on the repartition system.

SEC. 4. Each association shall elect its delegates, and these shall be entitled to cast the whole ballot of their associations.

SEC. 5. The number of delegates is unlimited.

PRELIMINARY PROCEEDINGS.
EXAMINATION OF CREDENTIALS.

SEC. 6. The credentials issued by the local associations must contain the number and names of the members to be represented, and must be signed by all the officers, and contain the correct address of the secretary.

PREPARATION OF THE FINANCIAL REPORT.

SEC. 7. For the purpose of facilitating a thorough revision of the principal account, every local association is requested to supply its delegates with a certificate, showing fully the amount of dues actually paid in and to be paid in. Arrears must be paid on this occasion.

OPENING OF THE PROCEEDINGS OF CONGRESS.
ORGANIZATION OF THE MEETING.

SEC. 8. Opening by the president. Election of several vice-presidents and two secretaries to officiate during the term of the Congress. Report concerning the presented and examined credentials. The president of the Principal Association will preside.

ORDER OF BUSINESS.

SEC. 9. The Congress will restrict its activity to the following points: On association business principally. The tax question, and all encroachments on the trade. The menacing attitude of the temperance party towards our trade. All special motions in the interest of the association. Deliberation as to the means of further extending the Brewers' Association. Appointment of location of future Executive Committee. Election of officers for the ensuing year. Appointment of place of meeting of the next annual Congress. Adjustment of accounts.

DUTIES OF OFFICERS.

SEC. 10. The president shall preside at all meetings, preserve order, and decide points of order raised. In case of an appeal to the meeting from the decision of the president, such question shall be brought to a division without debate. The president may, however, state the ground for his decision and the appealing member the cause of his appeal.

The president will appoint all standing and special committees unless special action otherwise is taken by the meeting. He is also a member *ex-officio* of all committees.

In the absence of the president one of the vice-presidents shall assume the duties of chairman.

It shall be the duty of the secretary to keep accurate minutes of the proceedings and to execute all necessary writings during the session of the Congress.

The Finance Committee appointed by the chairman shall endorse all bills of the Principal Association, if found correct, examine the accounts of the secretary and treasurer, and make a detailed report of the state of the finances to the meeting.

A sergeant-at-arms shall also be elected, who shall maintain order in the meeting.

III.—THE EXECUTIVE OF THE PRINCIPAL ASSOCIATION.

SEC. 1. The executive of the Principal Association is responsible for the immediate execution of the enactments of the Congress.

It shall represent the association in all outside matters, endeavor to make connections with similar societies, enter into correspondence, execute powers of attorney, examine claims against the association and order their payment, promote applications for admission, and keep well posted on all affairs touching the interest of the association or its members.

DUTIES OF THE MEMBERS OF THE EXECUTIVE.

SEC. 2. The president shall represent the association on all occasions.

SEC. 3. The treasurer is responsible for the faithful and punctual management of the association's funds, and must give bonds for the security of the association. He shall receive all initiation fees, periodical dues, and incidental receipts, keep accurate account of the same, and make an exact detailed report, accompanied with vouchers, to the Congress.

SEC. 4. The secretary shall execute and sign all documents of the executive, receive and open letters and submit them to the president, execute and sign orders for payment after their approval by the executive, issue invitations to regular and special conventions and to the meetings of the executive, and shall in every manner assist the president in keeping the affairs of the association in running order. He shall also correctly transcribe the proceedings of the Congress, and distribute printed copies to the members.

SEC. 5. The secretary shall be remunerated for his services, and the Congress shall fix the amount of his salary.

SEC. 6. The members of the Executive and the chairman of the Agitation Committee shall have the amount of their travelling expenses in attending the Congress re-imbursed from the principal treasury.

SEC. 7. Should extraordinary conditions or dangers menace the trade, the executive, after having obtained the consent of a majority of the associations, upon their being informed of the exact state of the case, shall have power to convene a Special Congress.

SEC. 8. The officers are elected for one year, and when a direct election by the Congress shall not seem desirable, the local association which has been designated as the seat of the executive shall, in their next session, ballot for a president, secretary and treasurer for the executive. The officers shall be re-eligible at the expiration of their term of office.

IV.—DUTIES OF THE MEMBERS OF THE ASSOCIATION.

SEC. 1. The rights and duties of the members of the association are perfectly equal. Every member shall enjoy the complete protection of the association so far as its activity extends. In return, each member binds himself to carry out faithfully all the enactments of the association, and especially to meet all demands promptly and effectively that may be made by the Agitation Committee for the protection of the trade.

SEC. 2. Each member also binds himself for the prompt payment of an assessment of twenty cents per 100 barrels of beer brewed and sold.

Payments are to be made semi-annually, and it is the duty of the officers of every local association to promptly collect the dues of the members and to transmit them to the treasurer of the Principal Association.

SEC. 3. In case extraordinary occurrences should render it necessary to obtain more funds than the amount of the regular dues, an extra assessment shall be laid on all members by resolution of the Congress.

SEC. 4. Members not belonging to any association will send their dues directly to the treasurer.

SEC. 5. In case any one of the confederate associations, through its attorney, renders direct service in the interest of the entire association, the Congress shall, upon application of the proper association, fix the amount of indemnity, and the same shall be deducted from its dues.

V.—ADMISSION TO THE ASSOCIATION.

SEC. 1. Everyone of unblemished character and carrying on a brewery on his own account is admissible to the association.

The initiation fee is fixed at $2.00 per member, payable when application is made.

Application for membership from parts where no local association exists may be made directly to the executive.

VI.—ALTERING THE CONSTITUTION.

Sec. 1. A motion to alter this constitution shall be made in writing and communicated to the executive three months before the meeting of Congress.

Two-thirds of all the members present must vote for the proposed alteration.

Sec. 2. The association shall continue to exist so long as 100 members vote against its dissolution.

The first paragraph betrays some indifference and a little inconsistency as to the name of the association. During the first years of its existence the loosely organized body of affiliated brewers' societies changed its name quite frequently; but at the fourth convention the title United States Brewers' Association had been formally adopted, a resolution to that effect having been incorporated into the minutes. Nevertheless, nearly every committee and many officers used the older terms in their official reports and communications, and now the framers of the constitution, discarding the resolution before-mentioned, selected the cumbersome designation "Principal Association of the Brewers of the United States." Considered as a whole, this first constitution reflects clearly the aims of the association at the time. Questions relating to the Internal Revenue still overshadowed every other consideration, so much so that neither the necessity of literary agitation nor the expediency of co-operation in matters touching upon the technical and scientific development of the art found expression in this statute, although both subjects had been seriously discussed at previous gatherings and again received considerable attention at the tenth convention and subsequent meetings.

The Executive and Agitation Committees constituted the only permanent working bodies, and their duties were confined within rather narrow limits, as compared with the present state of affairs. The somewhat anomalous condition of things which had hitherto prevailed with regard to the functions of the president of the association at conventions was finally done away with, the constitution imposing upon this officer the duty of presiding at all meetings of the whole body, as, in fact, by virtue of his knowledge and experience he alone was capable of doing to the best interests of the association. This very proper and logical arrangement should also have applied to the vice-president and secretary; but for some unaccountable reason the constitution provided for the election of several vice-presidents and secretaries who were to hold office only during the sessions of the conventions, assisting the president in conducting the proceedings. Purely ornamental in every respect, these offices were probably retained by sheer force of habit; or in deference, perhaps, to the wishes of the local associations who desired to see their representatives thus honored. In every other respect, excepting one, the constitution conformed pretty closely to the resolutions which had, from time to time, been adopted in regard to the conduct of business during and after the annual meetings, and consequently the discussion on the whole question was necessarily very brief, and the entire proceedings regarding it were confined to the reading of each article and section, followed by a separate vote upon each, and a general vote upon the whole measure. The exception here referred to concerned the admission of associate members.

At a preceding convention it had been decided to urge hop-growers, hop-dealers and maltsters to join the association, and a resolution to that effect had been responded to by a considerable number of "supply-men." The logical presumption must have been that the framers of the constitution would embody into this instrument an article admitting associate members and defining their rights and duties. The omission does not appear to have been intentional; but there is evidence that opinions differed as to the wisdom of the innovation; for when G. Bergner, of Philadelphia, called attention to this shortcoming and moved to amend Article II in such a way as to admit hop-dealers and maltsters, a very determined opposition arose against the motion. A lively debate took place, in which President Clausen finally participated, throwing the weight of the executive's influence into the scales in favor of the motion. By virtue of Bergner's amendment all persons of unblemished character connected with the trade became eligible to membership upon payment of an initiation fee of $2, and annual dues to the amount of $30. Bergner also moved that a committee be appointed to determine whether Article IV should not be so amended as "to transfer to *Der Amerikanische Bierbrauer* the printing of the convention proceedings and other official publications." Clausen and others strenuously opposed this, and Bergner thereupon withdrew his motion. The reader will probably recollect a resolution designating this journal for the publication of official communications, and expressly constituting it the official organ. President Clausen opposed Bergner's motion solely on the ground that he doubted the propriety of embodying such a measure into the constitution. Although he did not say so, he probably had in his mind the resolution here referred to and considered it amply sufficient for the purpose. The object of Mr. Bergner seemed to have been, however, to secure to the publisher of *Der Amerikanische Bierbrauer* a suitable compensation for this work, and he accordingly proposed that "a committee of three be appointed to ascertain the remuneration demanded for publishing the reports," etc. Upon the adoption of this motion the president appointed Gustavus Bergner, Adolphus Busch and John Kress as such committee. This committee at once reported favorably, submitting a resolution setting forth that in view of the large number of circulars and reports made necessary by the business of the association, it was desirable to have an official organ and that *Der Amerikanische Bierbrauer*, a journal eminently fitted for the purpose, be recognized as such for one year; that during that time the publisher shall publish all official communications and deliver fifty copies of each number of the journal to the secretary, for which he shall receive the sum of four hundred dollars out of the funds of the association.

The proposition to establish a Brewers' Academy under the control of the association, to be maintained by contributions from members of the trade, evoked a comprehensive discussion disclosing deep interest in the matter, but revealing at the same time a great diversity of opinions as to the most suitable means of accomplishing the desired object. Under instructions from the ninth convention the Executive Committee had inquired into the subject, consulted with the originator of the plan, Anton Schwarz, and availed themselves of all accessible information concerning similar institutions in European countries. As to the necessity of theoretical instruction, combined with the actual practice of the art, there could be no doubt, and so far as this question was concerned, it may be taken for granted that complete harmony and unanimity of opinion prevailed throughout the trade. The difficulty confronting the committee arose from a different quarter. While some of the more wealthy brewers seemed willing enough to contribute comparatively large sums for the establishment and maintenance of a school, the majority evidently believed that this part of the work should be left to private enterprise, their presumption being—as the chronicler assumes—that if the trade at large really felt the want of such an institution, if, in other words, the Brewers' Academy had really become a necessity, private enterprise would be amply rewarded for its efforts, and the school would then be maintained by those who reaped its benefits and enjoyed its educational advantages. That the committee reasoned differently is evident from their report; but neither the minutes nor any other material now available afford any clue as to their views upon this particular point. Probably their principal consideration was that such a school should be under the control of the association, and this would not have been possible unless the members consented to furnish the means for its establishment and maintenance. In every other respect their report left no room for doubt or conjecture. The institution was to have been located in New York City. In connection with it should have been established a model-brewery and chemical laboratory; the latter to be used for the benefit of all members, free of charge, for analyses of all kinds and the dissemination of scientific and technical knowledge concerning new inventions, improved methods of brewing and malting, and all kindred matters. The course of study, roughly outlined, was to have embraced chemistry, fermentation, natural philosophy, botany, agriculture, mechanics, mathematics, drawing, book-keeping, practical exercises in chemistry and the use of the microscope and sachrometer. To this theoretical course were to have been joined practical manipulations in the brewery, embracing all known methods and kinds of brewing, together with the malting processes as practiced in the various countries. In order to accomplish all this the committee proposed (we shall now quote their own words) that the institution be under the control of the Principal Association, which should issue a circular calling for voluntary subscriptions; all members paying $100, or more at once, to be life members and enjoy all privileges and participate in the property. Every local association should pledge itself to pay a stated sum annually until the college shall become self-supporting.

In the discussion on the subject, A. Werthmüeller opposed the clause pledging the pecuniary support of local associations; Adolphus Busch favored a more central location than New York; Obermann desired to refer the whole plan to the local associations; C. G. Stifel deemed it necessary to ascertain, above all things, whether the prospective voluntary contributions would cover the cost of establishing the school, which cost he estimated at $20,000; J. Huck believed that it would be better to entrust the whole scheme to private hands; Katzenmayer read a letter from Henry Bartholomay, offering a subscription of $100, and, finally, Clausen, leaving the Chair, declared himself in favor of Stifel's idea. When every objection had been heard, the convention adopted a motion by Stifel, amended by George Bechtel, to the effect that a committee of nine, including the executive, be appointed for the purpose of ascertaining the cost of such an institution, the amount of money that could be raised by subscription, and the number of pupils that would probably attend the school during the first year; all this to be accomplished by the usual mode of inquiry at a cost not to exceed five hundred dollars. The committee appointed under this resolution consisted of C. G. Stifel, Jacob Obermann, A. Schalk, G. Bergner, J. Hauck, A. Werthmueller, M. Kleinert, M. Kuntz and Adolphus Busch.

In that part of this book which treats of and is entitled "Modern Brewers' Association," it is shown that, with the exception of the Country Brewers' Society at London, established in 1822, there is no organized body of brewers older than the United States Brewers' Association. Singularly enough, even the brewers' organizations of the German States, including Bavaria, are very much younger, and the German National Association is even of more recent date than some of the latter. It was at the tenth convention that the American brewers were first notified that it was intended to hold a preliminary meeting of German brewers in the city of Dresden with a view to organizing a national association. The tenth convention at once caused to be drafted and forwarded to their German colleagues the following letter of brotherly greeting and congratulation, viz.:

"The brewers of the United States of America, assembled on the occasion of the Tenth Annual Brewers' Congress, in the city of Davenport, Ia., have heard, with great satisfaction, that the effort for a concentration of all available power in favor of a protective and defensive alliance for the advancement of the interests of the brewers' craft, has likewise broken ground in their native country. The recognition of the irrefutable truth 'that only through united action and co-operation can great results be obtained,' has also made patent in this country the necessity of closer alliance, and we can always look upon the highly successful results of our mutual efforts with great pride and satisfaction.

"May the greeting of your colleagues of the Western hemisphere find a hearty echo in all German hearts beyond the wide ocean, and let us hope that the German Brewers' Union, created under the most favorable auspices, will at all times vindicate their right, strengthen mutual esteem, and be of fruitful efficiency.

"In this spirit we request you to favorably accept our fraternal sentiments."

This congratulatory epistle proved to be somewhat premature. The declaration of war by Napoleon and the invasion of German territory by French troops interfered with the German brewers' plan; the Dresden meeting had to be postponed, and was not held until the 27th of July of the succeeding year.

The condition of the association presented an encouraging aspect in this year; strenuous efforts had been made to increase the membership, and an unlooked for measure of success crowned these endeavors. In many parts of the country, especially in Western Pennsylvania where George Gerst, of Pittsburg, had performed uncommonly successful missionary work for which the convention tendered him a vote of thanks. As a result of these efforts and the prompt payment of dues, the total fund amounted to nearly nine thousand dollars. The expenditures rose to a little over three thousand dollars, one-half of which had been used by the Washington Committee. It was this favorable state of affairs that probably prompted A. Busch to propose an increase of the secretary's salary to $1,200, and to appropriate the sum of $500 for a suitable gift to the president in recognition and due appreciation of his truly magnificent services. In the latter motion Busch was ably seconded by his townsman, C. G. Stifel. This episode was arranged and managed in a way that must have painfully embarrassed the prospective recipient of the gift. He was requested to retire from the hall for a moment, and when he had done so, yielding the Chair to John Kress, the motion was made, put to a vote and carried. So far all would have been well; but when the Secretary, gratified and elated at the distinction intended for his honored chief, rose in exultant eagerness to greet the returning president and to inform him "of the intention of the convention to honor Mr. Clausen with a present on the occasion of the next Brewers' Congress," he probably realized himself (in fact in afteryears he readily admitted) that there must be other ways less embarrassing to accomplish the same end.

The historian of the association would be unfaithful to his duty were he to omit mention of this fact; nor would it be justifiable in him to ignore another fact, namely, that on this occasion the Secretary again declined, as he had done before and many times thereafter, to accept an increase of salary.

An undertaking frequently attempted of late years, but never successfully consummated, had been launched at Milwaukee and seemed to promise success; it was a Brewers' Fire Insurance Company, designed, it appears, to apply the co-operative principle for the purpose of greater safety and economy. Jacob Obermann and J. Huck championed this enterprise at the convention stating that the company had made such progress that its capital was about to be increased to half a million dollars. By the establishment of agencies throughout the country the brewers, it was believed, could join this concern and thus become independent of other insurance companies who ordinarily placed breweries in the category of unsafe risks.

The resolutions adopted at this convention re-iterate the objections against certain provisions of the tariff and revenue laws, urged in the petition of which the preceding chapter contains a synopsis. The Washington Committee had not succeeded in impressing the Committee on Ways and Means with the justice of their demands; but, on the other hand, there seemed to be no very great prospect of passing the law proposed by this committee. Even while the convention was in session, Congressman Finkelnburg telegraphed to the president that the report of the Ways and Means Committee would not be acted upon in that session, and if it were "he would do his best to have the objectionable sections amended." Finkelnburg was not mistaken, as subsequent events showed, for the House of Representatives, although it at first sustained the Schenck Tariff, by which the duty upon barley would have been increased from

15 to 25 cents per bushel, and that upon malt from 20 to 30 per cent. ad valorem, did not ultimately adopt this measure; nor did any of the proposed changes of the revenue law meet with a better fate. In their principal contention concerning the exorbitant duty upon malt and barley, the brewers had the full and vigorous support of Special Revenue Commissioner Wells who again embodied the Washington Committee's argument into his report. But all this availed them nothing, nor did it prevail against Schenck's settled conviction that the brewing industry could easily bear any burden that the Ways and Means Committee might impose upon it. In defending his own and assailing the brewers' attitude he sometimes resorted to the unworthy trick of suppressing facts or of misstating them, and not infrequently he even made an absolutely false statement. An extract from his speech on the floor of the House when the duty on malt and barley was under consideration, very clearly demonstrated this regrettable disposition on his part. He said: "Now, Sir, these brewers have not had much to complain of, yet they have and do still complain. They have always advanced their own product beyond any burden we have laid upon it, always beyond any tax we have levied. They have formed combinations for the purpose of adding now a dollar and then another dollar on every cask of beer. I know it is usual in this country to pay great deference to the lager-beer producer. I have all that deference; but I believe they can afford to bear the burdens of the country as well as other citizens. It does not make any difference to the brewers, what burden we impose, for they do not bear it; but it comes last upon the consumer." An argument so flimsy and untrue could easily be refuted and Congressman James Brooks of New York and Judd of Chicago performed this task in splendid style. Naturally, with the

Chairman of the Ways and Means Committee in such an unfavorable frame of mind, there was little prospect of securing an increase of the rebate, in fact a decrease seemed more likely to receive Schenck's sanction and support; nor could it be expected that all the other incongruities of the revenue law, pointed out in the preceding chapter, would be dispassionately considered. Nevertheless, so judiciously persistent did the Brewers' Committee proceed after their discomfiture that they finally succeeded in convincing the committee of one of their claims, *i. e.*, the reduction to one-half of the former rate of the license for retailers selling only malt-liquors and wines. This discrimination in favor of the milder beverages had been, as we have repeatedly shown, the subject of lengthy discussions in Congress and the preponderance of opinion, as expressed in both houses, favored the brewers' claim. It found expression in the original act fixing the taxes upon malt-liquors and wines on the one hand and upon ardent spirits on the other; but it had not until then been applied to rates of retail dealers; nor was there any discrimination in the classification of the two kinds of drinks as sources of revenue. The brewers very wisely insisted upon this discrimination at every convention, embodying a suitable paragraph into the set of resolutions usually submitted by the Agitation Committee. As it has thus far been the rule of the chronicler to omit these resolutions, it may not be amiss in this connection to reproduce here that part of the convention resolutions which relates to the subject. It reads:

"*Resolved*, That while we recognize the fact, that in every system of taxation the highest duties are properly imposed on articles of mere luxury, and especially on those of a hurtful character, we are decidedly of the opinion that malt-liquors do not belong to any class of luxuries justly so denominated; for such liquors are not only harmless, but nutritious; and as long as beverages of any kind are within the reach of the poorer and laboring classes of the people, it is expedient that these liquors shall be accessible to such classes at the cheapest rates, in preference to those that are of a more stimulating and noxious nature. Through these means they became the national beverage, and a discrimination ought to be distinctly and broadly made in the imposition of the special tax laid on dealers, between dealers in malt-liquors and dealers in spirituous liquors, so as to favor the consumption of the most healthful and wholesome beverage."

The readers are aware that even as regards the tax on ardent spirits the discrimination did not last very long, for repeated reductions of rate finally lowered the tax until the discrimination was actually reversed, for a time at least. Another victory achieved by the committee in another quarter frustrated the attempt of an enterprising manufacturer to induce the revenue commissioner to adopt metallic revenue stamps, on the sophistical ground that in using paper stamps the brewers were needlessly exposed to prosecution for violations of the revenue act in case such stamps became detached by reason of moisture or careless fastening. The brewers promptly declined to avail themselves of the paternal care which the inventor intended to bestow upon them, and demonstrated to the satisfaction of the proper authorities that the change would require the labor of three men to attach the stamps where one man could easily do the work with paper stamps, and that the use of metallic stamps, which would have to be fastened with nails, would inevitably ruin the casks in a short time.

The old executive, consisting of President Clausen, Treasurer Schaefer and Secretary Katzenmayer, were re-elected; also the Agitation Committee, with few exceptions. This body now consisted of F. Lauer, William Massey, Gustavus Bergner, George Gerst, P. Ballantine, Charles Kolb, H. Clausen, Jr., David Jones, M. Kleiner, Chr. Boss, Jacob Scheu, F. Greenway, J. M. Hughes,

William Belzer, C. G. Stifel, J. Huck, P. Constans, Dr. H. C. Dreis, C. Eldredge, J. Schlitz, C. Born and L. Wolf.

Gerst of Pittsburg and Kuntz of New York entered into a spirited competition for the honor of entertaining the eleventh convention; neither would yield to the other, each insisted upon his right to test the sense of the meeting by a vote; and when this vote was finally taken, Pittsburg carried off the palm.*

---

* The following is a list of delegates present at the tenth convention:

Alfred Werthmueller (representing G. Bosch & Co.), A. Bosch, Bauer & Schaefer, William Metzger, Burlington, Ia.; Hoffbauer, J. Barthberger, Buffalo, Ia.; Gaiser & Schaefer, Chariton, Ia.; John Huck, George Schmidt, Peter Schoenhofen, Conrad Seipp, U. Busch, G. Gottfried, A. Magnus, Chicago, Ill.; H. Lackmann, H. Foss, Cincinnati, O.; J. H. Herzog, Covington, Ky.; Hail & Matthes, Des Moines, Ia.; M. Frahm, Knepper & Schlapp, Lehrkind & Bros., P. Littig, Noth & Son, Davenport, Ia.; V. Yegge, Dewitt, Ia.; F. Kempf, M. Tschirgi & Schwind (representing A. Heeb), I. Seeger, Duhnque, Ia.; J. Irrer, Fairfield, Ia.; Hotz & Geiger, G. L. Rupert, Iowa City, Ia.; J. W. Anschuetz (representing J. Kurz), Leiss & Bros., Pachstein & Nagel, Keokuk, Ia.; Schricker & Bros., Leclaire, Ia.; V. Blatz, F. Falk, Jacob Obermann, Albert Blatz, Jacob Felder, Milwaukee, Wis.; J. M. Herrmann, Montana, Ia.; J. Dold, J. Dorn, Muscatine, Ia.; John Baier, Newark, N. J.; F. Hausmann, G. T. Schenk, Nauvoo, Ill.; George Bechtel, Joseph Burger, Henry Clausen, Jr., John Kress, Michael Kuntz, Fr. Schaefer, A. Neidlinger, A. Schwarz, John Weber, Richard Katzenmayer, New York, N. Y.; Schaefer & Bauer, Ottumwa, Ia.; Charles Blattner & Co., Oscaloosa, Ia.; Gustavus Bergner, L. Bergdoll, Jacob Hohenadel, H. Lawser, G. Gindeley, William Hughes, Philadelphia, Pa.; G. Gerst, Pittsburg, Pa.; M. Dick, Quincy, Ill.; J. Huber, G. Wagner, Rock Island, Ill.; A. Busch, H. Koehler, Charles Stifel, St. Louis, Mo.; Schott & Bros., Warsaw, Ill.; A. Reymann, Wheeling, W. Va.

Chapter IX.

PROGRESS OF TRADE. NOVEL ASPECT OF ELEVENTH CONVENTION; TRADE-EXHIBITS SHOW DEVELOPMENT OF INDUSTRY. BREWERS' AND DISTILLERS' JOURNAL IN ENGLISH; INCONGRUITY OF DUAL CHARACTER; DISTILLERS DROPPED. BREWERS' ASSOCIATIONS FOUNDED IN BALTIMORE, BROOKLYN, NEW ORLEANS. EASTERN BREWERS' INSURANCE FLOURISHING. STATUS OF PITTSBURG BREWERS, SERVICES OF GERST. CHARACTER OF OPENING ADDRESSES CHANGED; PRESIDENT CLAUSEN'S REMARKABLE SPEECH; HE AND LAUER PLEAD FOR TOTAL ABOLITION OF TAX OR SUBSTITUTION OF CAPACITY-TAX FOR STAMP-TAX. WHAT BREWERS HOPED FOR AND WHY. BEER AS A TEMPERANCE DRINK SHOULD BEAR NO WAR-TAX. REVENUE OFFICERS' ARBITRARY COURSE PRODUCES DISCONTENT AMONG BREWERS AND OPPOSITION TO SYSTEM. RESOLUTIONS ON THIS SUBJECT QUOTED. CANVASS OF CONGRESS AS TO ABOLITION OF BEER-TAX; DISCOURAGING RESULT; REPRESENTATIVE DEGENER'S VIEW. REBATE AGAIN; BREWERS ASK INCREASE, COMMISSIONER PROPOSES DECREASE TO 4 PER CENT.; SINGULAR REASONING IN SUPPORT OF LATTER RATE; GENERAL CHARACTERISTICS OF REVENUE SUBORDINATES; THEIR DICTATORIAL MOODS. THE COMMISSIONER SENDS LOUIS SCHADE TO ATTEND CONVENTION. SCHADE'S ANTECEDENTS; HIS STUDY OF REVENUE QUESTIONS; HIS AND FLINTOFF'S ADDRESS. PROJECT OF BREWERS' ACADEMY IN *STATU QUO;* AGAIN POSTPONED. DELEGATES TO GERMAN BREWERS' CONGRESS. DEATH OF KLEINER. GIFT TO CLAUSEN. LIST OF DELEGATES.

In every respect both the brewing industry and the kindred trades advanced very rapidly within the twelve months that elapsed between the tenth and the eleventh conventions. The increase of production within this year exceeded one million barrels, or to be more exact, the actual output increased from 6,081,517 barrels in 1870 to 7,159,742 barrels in 1871, computing each quantity upon the basis of the fiscal year. These data could not, of course, be known at the time of the Pittsburg convention (June 7th and 8th), but sufficient statistical material was even then available to show what the total increase, at the rate officially quoted for three-quarters of the fiscal year, would amount to. Evidences of a different character indicated an almost equal rate of progress in other directions; in fact, the whole aspect of the Pittsburg convention—differing very essentially from that of all preceding meetings—seemed specially designed to afford an insight into this general advancement. This fact is mainly attributable to Bergner's suggestion, made and adopted at the tenth convention, that all industries related to or dependent upon brewing be invited to exhibit in the convention-building all modern appliances, recent inventions, improved implements, utensils and machineries, applicable to brewing and malting. As a result of this invitation the corridors and rooms of the Turner Hall (where the Pittsburg convention was held) were thronged with interesting exhibits of all kinds, presenting the aspect of a veritable bazaar, a sort of *impromptu* industrial exhibition. A review of the exhibits, among which the reader would recognize many articles still in use, would be out of place; it must suffice to say that the exhibition in its entirety presented an excellent gauge by which to measure the progress of the brewing industry and kindred trades.

During the year another brewers' journal, printed in the English language, had been established by Curson & Mundy, under the editorship of John Flintoff, a gentleman who, in later years, became officially connected with the association, both in an executive and a literary capacity. Singularly enough, the publishers of this journal at first intended to represent both the brewers' and distillers' interests, and indicated this intention in the selection of a title for their paper; it was called at first *The American Brewers' Gazette and Distillers' Journal*. It did not require much experience, it seems, to convince them of the incongruity of this dualism, for in their fifth number, published two weeks after the tenth convention, they dropped the sub-title, explaining editorially that they had become aware "that the interests of the brewers and distillers were not only *not* identical, but, on the contrary, decidedly inimical." Another evidence of the general progress achieved within this remarkable year lies in the fact that brewers' associations were organized in Baltimore, Md., Brooklyn, N. Y., and New Orleans, La.; and the Brewers' Insurance Company, upon which J. Obermann and Huck reported at the tenth convention, had found favor in the East to such an extent that an eastern branch had been organized, comprising as stockholders seventy-three of the best New York brewing firms, whose stock in the concern amounted in the aggregate to 178,900.

The Pittsburg convention is remarkable, by the way, for some other features which will claim the reader's attention in the further course of this narrative. The local association, organized, as has been stated, in the preceding year, included the brewers of the two sister cities, Pittsburg and Allegheny, and their president, George Gerst, took the deepest interest in the affairs of the parent association and the trade. To his zeal and energy must be attributed the fact that through all changes and vicissitudes the Pittsburg and Allegheny brewers always remained firm and loyal supporters of the national body, and preserved their local unions more successfully than many other associations. For so young an association the local brewers certainly made a splendid success of the eleventh convention, so far as their efforts could contribute to that end.

Of course this convention was governed entirely by the new constitution and in accordance with it the nominating committee, consisting of P. Doelger, R. Jacob, Chr. Moerlein, Jacob Ruppert and G. C. Webner, proposed the following gentlemen: Vice-Presidents for New York, Jos. Kuntz and P. Merkel; New Jersey, F. Volz and G. C. Webner; Pennsylvania, Peter Balz and George Gerst; Ohio, R. Reinbold and H. Voss;

Illinois, J. Huck; Iowa, Ignatz Huber; Missouri, R. Jacob; Wisconsin, J. Obermann; West Virginia, A. Reymann; Maryland, George Rost. Secretaries, Gustavus Bergner and William Eberhardt.

As a rule, the chronicler has hitherto refrained from reproducing the literal texts of the addresses with which the presiding officers opened the conventions; because ordinarily these addresses, except in so far as they summarized the more detailed reports of the committees, were merely of a salutatory character and contained a comparatively small measure of historical material. A partial departure from this rule now becomes necessary; for, beginning with this convention, the opening addresses assumed a totally different character, frequently embodying in the most concise form the policy of the association and interpreting and reflecting for the information of the Government and the public the aims, wishes, and complaints of the trade. President Clausen's opening address on this occasion derived its uncommon significance and importance from the fact that its author, in common with the chairman of the Agitation Committee, advocated a repeal of the law imposing an internal tax upon malt-liquors, or, as an alternative proposition, the abolition of the stamp-system and substitution of a tax based on the capacity of the plants. He said literally: "Malt-liquors are recognized as a temperance beverage, are wholesome and nutritious, and by the repeal, or at least a considerable reduction, of the tax rate on malt-liquors the Government could enable the people to obtain a cheap, excellent and nutritive beverage." One might be inclined to regard this as part of a purely academic exposition, were it not for the fact that F. Lauer supplemented these utterances by a statement which leaves no doubt that in those days the brewers actually believed, hoped and trusted that, as all other industries were being gradually relieved from the burden of war-taxes, the brewing trade would also sooner or later be thus exempted. This statement of the Agitation Committee reads as follows, viz:

"When the Internal Revenue law was first proposed and passed (August, 1862,) it was expressly stated, and so understood by the American people, that it was for war purposes, and that as soon as the war ceased the oppressive taxes would cease with it. Six years have elapsed since the war ended, and yet both the producer and consumer of the healthful and nutritious malt beverages, which are not a luxury, but a necessary part of diet to a large proportion of the people, are still compelled to pay the high war-taxes; and, judging from the course of the last Congress, we are to be taxed on indefinitely, not to contribute to the necessaries of Government, but to support the army of assessors and collectors for mere political purposes. Is it not time that this nation, claiming to be the freest on earth, should be released from the shackles of a despotic internal tax system? Let it no longer be liable to such a rebuke as was administered by President Dubbs, of the Swiss Confederacy, six years ago, to our Brewers' Tax Commissioners, of which I had the honor to be one: 'Are you not ashamed,' said he, 'to come here from that great American Republic to examine into the old, rotten, despotic European revenue laws? Switzerland has no such laws, neither would her people tolerate them. Her Republican form of government costs very little, and all her public revenues are derived from an economical system of import duties.'

"If we must continue to be taxed, let it be done in a simple way. I would propose a license on the capacity of the brewery, to be collected either quarterly or monthly, and security to be given for the payment. If the same were collected by the regularly chosen county and State assessors and collectors, millions of dollars would be saved per annum, honesty would be re-established, and we would be rid of an abominable system of espionage and depredation, which is all the more odious because practiced under color of laws."

From all we can learn, the revenue officers often abused their official functions and power, needlessly harassing the brewers by arbitrary interpretations of the regulations and by an utter disregard of the part which unavoidable accidents and mishaps played in the management of the trade. It happened sometimes that the most careful and honest brewer was criminally prosecuted for a mere technical violation of a minor provision, even where the absence of criminal intent was so manifest that even a child could have appreciated it. This naturally embittered the brewers and incensed them against the whole system. The chief trouble arose, it seems, from the difficulty of so affixing the revenue-stamps that neither the moisture of the casks, nor the water pouring down upon the loaded brewery wagons in rainy weather could rub it off. The revenue officers were fully aware of this difficulty, for from their cognizance of it arose many propositions to change the nature of the stamp; hence they should doubtless have made due allowance for all accidents and mishaps, when absence of criminal intent was manifest. Instead of that, they in many instances prosecuted brewers even when the stamps thus rubbed off were found upon the wagons. These and other annoyances had created a very bitter spirit among the trade, which found a rather vigorous expression in the resolutions adopted by the eleventh convention. In its entirety this is so remarkable and important a document, considered from a historical point of view, that a reproduction of that part which relates to internal revenue appears indispensable. It reads:

"*Resolved*, That the interests of the Government, justly considered, are identical with, and in no one respect diverse from their own, and that, therefore, they denounce tax-frauds as inconsistent with fidelity to the obligations of the members of this association. *Resolved*, That the prosperity of all honest brewers depends, in considerable measure, on the efficiency of the law under which the revenue is collected, and that, therefore, this association is directly interested that the provisions for taxing their manufactures shall be so framed as to be impossible to be evaded. *Resolved*, That while it is the duty of the brewers, as of all other citizens, to yield obedience to the Government, it is equally the duty of the Government to foster, encourage and protect the interests of brewers—the products of their industry being a beverage at once nutritious and wholesome and calculated to promote rational temperance—and to elevate the moral tone of society by superseding the use of more stimulating drinks. *Resolved*, That the laws of the United States relating to fermented liquors need revision in such a way that without relaxing in any respect their necessary rigor as to the due collection of the tax, they may impose no useless restrictions, create no needless obstructions to the freedom of trade, and require no vexatious and annoying interruptions to business that can be safely avoided, and also that they may be accommodated as nearly as possible to the ordinary modes of traffic as pursued by the wholesale and retail dealer. *Resolved*, That in an application which the representatives of this body made to the last United States Congress, they suggested various alterations concerning the various objects stated in the last resolution, and set them forth in a printed petition in a plain, succinct and intelligible form, and that they accompanied that petition with the draft of a bill which, if passed into an act, would not have impaired the efficiency of the law for the collection of the revenue, but would, in various particulars, have afforded important relief. *Resolved*, That the efforts thus made to procure a needed revision of the law did not receive the consideration its importance deserved, but, on the contrary, it was unjustly slighted, particularly by a majority of the Committee of Ways and Means, who, after long and unreasonable delays, suffered the Congress to expire without acting on the subject. *Resolved*, That this association will persevere in their efforts to obtain such a revision of the laws, affecting their business, as will accomplish the objects in these resolutions expressed, and will make application to the present Congress early in the session with the hope and expectation not only of an attentive hearing but of a successful result."

The committee who drafted these resolutions consisted of George Gerst, F. Haltnorth, A. Busch, F. Volz, J. Eichler, D. Yuengling, Jr., and P. Balz.

It seems that before the assembling of the eleventh Congress letters had been addressed to those members of Congress who had evinced, or were supposed to be actuated by, a friendly disposition towards the trade, requesting them to give their opinion as to the feasibility of repealing or reducing the beer-tax. The result of the enquiry could not have been very encouraging, judging from the only reply mentioned in the proceedings, namely, that of Degener, a German by birth, representative in Congress from Texas, a man of very liberal views and a strong champion of personal liberty. He wrote that "in the matter of the tax on beer he could do absolutely nothing," but expressed the opinion "that being the most eloquent temperance missionary, beer would soon do away with restrictive legislation." It may as well be stated at once that upon calm reflection the leaders of the association perceived the uselessness of any attempt to either repeal or reduce the tax, or to abolish the stamp-system; and, consequently, in spite of the contrary determination expressed in the resolutions before quoted, they in their petition to Congress only asked for the amendments outlined in their previous petition, adding, however, the request that the special tax required of brewers and retailers of malt-liquors be repealed. In this petition a singular reason is also urged for an increase of the rebate from $7\frac{1}{2}$ to 10 per cent. All other industries, it was stated, were then allowed a rebate of $2\frac{1}{2}$ per cent. on stamps purchased, the only reason for this allowance being that payment of tax was made in advance, that is to say, before the taxed article was placed upon the market.* As the same rule applied to the brewing industry, it was perfectly logical and reasonable to claim that this rebate should also be allowed to brewers, in addition to the amount intended to re-imburse them for losses of revenue stamps arising from leakage and other causes. Under the circumstances existing at that time the attempt to have the rebate increased to 10 per cent. must have appeared to be a very wise move, for although it was not at all likely that Congress would grant the brewers' petition, the strong reasons given for it undoubtedly had a tendency to act as a deterrent upon those Congressmen who intended to reduce the rebate to 4 per cent. as had been

---

* The Committee labored under an erroneous impression on this point

proposed by General Pleasanton, then commissioner of Internal Revenue. In advocating this reduction the commissioner resorted to a rather singular mode of reasoning. He held that the fraction rendered the keeping of true accounts difficult; he failed to explain however, why, if this reason were really good and tenable from a fiscal point of view, the elimination of the fraction, that is to say, the reduction of the rate to 7 per cent. or its increase to 8 per cent., would not have removed this alleged difficulty.

This singular proposition probably emanated originally from a subordinate officer of the department, not from General Pleasanton himself. Previous and subsequent experiences have taught the brewers to expect the smallest measure of favor or justice from these subordinate officers, who during many years of official routine acquire a habit of clinging to technicalities and construing any law in the strictest literal sense, regardless of its spirit or the manifest intention of its framer. The frequent changes in the chiefship of the office, bringing new and inexperienced men from totally different fields of activity to the head of the Revenue Office, gave these subordinates a peculiar advantage, inasmuch as every new commissioner, himself unfamiliar with the office-work, felt constrained to defer to their judgment. In this way these wholly irresponsible officials naturally got a taste for power which grew by indulgence. Some of them became veritable tyrants, brooking no objection and viewing every remonstrance very much in the light of an affront to their personal dignity, or to the majesty of the law embodied in their august persons. The ground upon which the proposition to reduce the rebate was based, savors very much of the book-keepers' narrow views, and there is all the less reason for assuming that Commissioner Pleasanton conceived this unjust and unreasonable scheme, because this brave war-veteran and admirable citizen at all times evinced a most friendly disposition towards the trade and great willingness to deal fairly and equitably with all tax-payers.

Of this disposition he gave a striking evidence just at this time by delegating Louis Schade of Washington, D. C., to represent the Revenue Office at the eleventh convention and to report the proceedings of this meeting for the information of the commissioner.

Schade's connection with the Revenue Office was confined to this mission; he did not then hold any Federal office, but, having of his own accord undertaken an investigation into the status of brewing, he came in personal contact with General Pleasanton, who himself appreciated the wisdom of gathering more statistical information than his office possessed at that time, and thus obtained from the chief of the internal tax-system authority to act for and in behalf of the Government. The motives which actuated him in this course were clearly stated by him in his speech to the brewers at the eleventh convention in these words: "My duty to the Government is merely to report your proceedings. My feelings and convictions are with you and all I can do for you will be done." Schade had formerly been employed in the State Department and was favorably known then as the author of an interesting statistical essay on immigration, and by his connection with the German-American Press in Chicago and other cities, as well as by his participation in several political campaigns before the war. Introduced by President Clausen to the eleventh convention, he delivered an address replete with historical facts, political allusions and valuable statistical information compiled from the reports of the revenue collectors. Of the latter data we reproduce the following, to wit:

STATES.	Under 500 bbls.	Over 500 bbls.	Total.
New York	140	247	387
Pennsylvania	171	182	353
Ohio	137	133	270
Wisconsin	146	83	229
Illinois	100	102	202
California	136	36	172
Michigan	94	54	148
Indiana	86	58	144
Missouri	70	56	126
Minnesota	82	41	123
Iowa	61	60	121
New Jersey	28	48	76
Maryland	32	36	68
Kentucky	21	22	43
Oregon	31	3	34
Nevada	29	5	34
Massachusetts	5	28	33
Texas	30	2	32

Kansas.......... 26	Maine............ 3	Colorado.........
Montana 24	Mississippi 3	Connecticut 20
Nebraska........ 21	New Hampshire.. 5	Delaware........ 5
New Mexico..... 9	North Carolina... 2	Georgia 4
Utah............ 10	Rhode Island.... 5	Louisiana........ 13
Arizona 6	Washington Ter. 8	South Carolina... 4
Dakota.......... 4	Wyoming........ 9	Tennessee....... 11
Idaho 3	District of Columbia............ 13	Vermont......... 3
Alabama......... 14		Virginia.......... 10
Arkansas........ 3	West Virginia... 15	

The only State where there was no brewery in 1870 was Florida. However, there has been one established during the present year, thus extending the realm of malt beverages over every State and Territory of the Union.

There were brewed during the year ending June 30th, 1870, 6,081,520 barrels of beer, or to every 6 $^{33}/_{100}$ persons one barrel.

In this production participated chiefly the following States:

	Number of barrels.	Inhabitants.	For every barrel, persons.
1. New York	1,992,958	4,374,499	2
2. Pennsylvania	788,034	3,519,601	4
3. Ohio	570,921	2,665,002	5
4. Illinois	432,278	2,538,400	6
5. New Jersey	432,088	906,096	2
6. Massachusetts	313,950	1,457,351	5
7. Missouri	259,111	1,721,295	7
8. California	190,368	560,223	3
9. Wisconsin	189,664	1,055,133	5
10. Michigan	129,626	1,184,059	9
11. Maryland	128,432	780,894	6
12. Indiana	124,302	1,680,637	13
13. Iowa	103,637	1,191,725	10
14. New Hampshire	77,036	318,300	4
15. Kentucky	66,640	1,321,011	19
16. Minnesota	56,720	439,706	8
17. Louisiana	48,636	726,915	15
18. Connecticut	43,706	537,454	12

In the same address Schade also reviewed the prohibitory movement of which he spoke in the most scathing terms. The same theme was again taken up on this occasion by John Flintoff of the *Brewers' Gazette*, who availed himself of this favorable opportunity of demonstrating his familiarity with the subject, and his fitness and ability to represent the trade's interest in his capacity as an editor.

Owing to the absence of C. G. Stifel, chairman of the Academy Committee, the plan to establish a brewers' school could not be considered in its regular order, but at the suggestion of President Clausen the matter was taken up informally with a view to testing the sense of the meeting. Joseph Kuntz, of New York, spoke very eloquently in favor of immediate action, and proposed the opening of a subscription-list. A. Werthmueller wrote, and M. Dick and P. Balz also spoke in favor of the scheme. C Moerlein, J. Ahles, and M. Hobelmann favored postponement; and Obermann and Kleiner desired to have more definite plans before action was taken. From all that can be learned the replies to the circular-letter of enquiry were neither very numerous nor very encouraging, so that even if Stifel has been present, the discussion would not have had a more solid basis than the opinions of individual members. As a sort of makeshift the convention finally adopted a motion to recommit the whole matter to the old committee with instructions to renew the enquiry and report at the next convention.

This disappointment to A. Schwarz was counterbalanced in a measure by a flattering resolution again designating his journal, *Der Amerikanische Bierbrauer*, as the official organ and appropriating the sum of $400, as compensation for services to be rendered in this capacity. The report embodying this resolution was signed by J. Kuntz, F. Lauer, R. Jacob, M. Dick and F. Kauffmann.

In a letter dated at Nuremberg, Germany, May 7th, 1871, it was announced that the first German Brewers' Congress, postponed, as has already been stated, owing to the outbreak of the Franco-Prussian war,* would be held at Dresden on the 27th of July, 1871. A delegation of American brewers representing the association was invited to attend the Congress. The convention at once accepted the invitation and appointed Valentine Blatz, Adolphus Schalk, Max Schaefer and Charles Fritz, all of whom were then sojourning in the Old Fatherland, to represent the United States Brewers' Association at this first national convention of German brewers.

---

* Although this designation is a misnomer, the war having been waged between the whole of Germany and France, we retain it, because it has been generally accepted by English-speaking people.

As compared with the preceding year the financial condition of the association showed so decided an improvement that the Finance Committee, consisting of J. Obermann, G. Klotter and H. Lawser felt justified in recommending, and the association in ordering, the investment of four thousand dollars in Government bonds, this amount being regarded as a permanent surplus over and above the sum annually required for the maintenance of the organization, unless unforeseen occurrences should upset this calculation. The total receipts, including the balance of the preceding year, amounted to $10,041.16, while the expenditures fell to considerably below $3,000.

The death of G. T. Eichenlaub, which had occurred during the early part of the year, called forth expressions of sincere regret from many delegates; for Eichenlaub, in addition to having been one of the founders and most active and intelligent supporters of the national association, was also instrumental in organizing the brewers of the State of Ohio, among whom he occupied the enviable position of a trusted friend and adviser. A pioneer of the art of brewing, he possessed unusual opportunities for knowing both the needs and the possibilities of the trade in his adopted State, to which German immigration had early directed its course in broad and steadily increasing currents.

The association's gift to President Clausen consisted of a tea-set of solid silver, which G. Bergner presented in a very neat address of which the following is an extract, viz.:

* * * "The agreeable duty falls to my lot to present and deliver to you, Mr. President, in the name of the Association of the Brewers of the United States this testimonial designed to express to you their highest, most heartfelt and well-merited regard. Receive it as such with the assurance that we all know how to appreciate and honor with feelings of deep gratitude that eager work for the good cause which, at the sacrifice of your own personal affairs, you have so unceasingly manifested, and this testimonial will be a blessing to you and to ourselves, when in the future your children may point to it with pride and exclaim, this is a memorial from the Brewers of the United States. May God so will it."

From President Clausen's reply we copy these sentences, viz. :

"I have often been placed in an embarrassing position, but I assure you candidly that on no former occasion have I felt so weak to clothe my sentiments and thoughts in words than to-day. I knew it already, that in pursuance of a resolution of the Davenport Congress a present was to be delivered to me to-day; during the past year it was utterly impossible for me to give it even a moment's thought, in what manner I should express my thanks. To-day I am in the same predicament. I know my situation and position as well as any one. In St. Louis you have elected me for the first time your president, and to-day I have the honor to preside at your Congress for the fifth time. You have not elected me on account of my ability, and I know my faults and weaknesses well; where is the man who has none? But I have devoted all my poor abilities to our common interests, and I nourished the purpose to retain this office only so long until from our mighty branch of industry which possesses dormant strength and ability in abundance, a man should arise, to fill my place more ably and more worthily. My success is based upon the fact that all my thoughts were concentrated upon the common welfare of the brewers, that on all occasions, and as ably as I could, I strove to advance the best interests of our association, and that neither from ambition nor personal interests did I devote all my limited powers to all and to each of our community. * * *"

Kuntz finally succeeded, though not without a spirited struggle, in securing for New York City the honor of entertaining the association at the next convent

---

* The following is a list of delegates present at the eleventh convention :—
C. Baeuerlein & Bro., Eberhard & Ober, P. Gerst, Gast Sons & Co., Hechelmann & Co., H. Herdt, H. Hoehl, George Lang, Lutz & Walz, Chas. Meyer, M. Metzger, John Miller, George Ober, G. Siedle, Stephan & Schmitt, Smith & Co., J. N. Straub & Co., T. Tschudy, Wacker & Steuernagel, Allegheny, Pa.; Robert Portner, Alexandria, Va.; F. Oberholz, Akron, O.; Louis Muth, G. Rost, Baltimore, Md.; H. Friedel, Hogl & Hoehrl, E. Hauch, John N. Nusser, J. M. Schaefer, H. Wilhelm, Birmingham, Pa.; H. Foss, M. Kleiner, George Klotter, Jr., C. Moerlein, R. Reinhold, G. Reiff, P. Weyand, Cincinnati, O.; C. Seipp, Peter Schoenhofen, Chicago, Ill.; Delegation of Cincinnati, Columbus, O.; J. Baehr, F. Haltnorth, J. Koestle, L. Schlater, Carl Sutter, Cleveland, O.; Jacob Obermann, A. Blatz, W. Coleman, Milwaukee, Wis.; Charles F. Geissele, F. Kaufmann, F. Volz, Gust. Wiedenmayer, G. Wehner, Newark, N. J.; Jacob Ahles, P. Ahles, Henry Clausen, Peter Doelger, John Eichler, Ph. Ebling, Chr. Huepfel, Jos. Kuntz, Ph. Merkel, Jacob Ruppert, Fr. Schaefer, Jos. Schmid, Richard Katzenmayer, New York, N. Y.; Gustavus Bergner, Peter Baltz, Jos. Fielmayer, Henry Lawser, Philadelphia, Pa.; H. Darlington, Frauenheim & Vilsack, John Gangwisch, Pier, Dannals & Co., Spencer, McKay & Co., G. Wainwright, Pittsburg, Pa.; George Lauer, D. G. Yuengling, Potteville, Pa.; Math. Dick, Quincy, Ill.; Ignatz Huber, Rock Island, Ill.; F. Lauer, Reading, Pa.; D. G. Yuengling, Jr., Richmond, Va.; A. Busch, R. Jacob, William Anhauser, St. Louis, Mo.; Henry Reinhardt, Staten Island, N. Y.; William Kaiser, Mich. Seitz, Williamsburgh, L. I.; A. Reymann, Wheeling, W. Va.; George Lauer, Wilkesbarre, Pa.

CHAPTER X.

STATE OF TRADE IN NEW YORK; PRODUCTION; FLOURISHING CONDITION OF ASSOCIATION; ALE-BREWERS ORGANIZED. BREWERS' ASSOCIATION OF WILLIAMSBURGH; ITS OFFICERS; PERSONAL NOTES. ASSOCIATIONS ORGANIZED IN BOSTON; ITS OFFICERS AND CHARACTER; PRODUCTION OF BEER; PERSONAL NOTES. BREWERS ORGANIZED IN CLEVELAND, NEW HAVEN, HARTFORD, ALBANY, TROY AND LUCERNE COUNTY, PA.; PERSONAL NOTES. POLITICAL RETROSPECT. LIBERAL REPUBLICAN MOVEMENT. GREELEY, PRESIDENTIAL CANDIDATE; HIS SUMPTUARY RECORD; ATTITUDE OF GERMAN-AMERICANS CRITICALLY CONSIDERED. THE RASTER-PLANK; RASTER'S CHARACTER AND PLACE IN HIS PARTY. UNWARRANTED ATTACK ON BREWERS ON ACCOUNT OF REPUBLICAN PLANK; CONTROVERSY REGARDING IT; SET AT REST BY RASTER; HISTORICAL SUMMARY. BREWERS' POSITION. TWELFTH CONVENTION. CLAUSEN'S SPEECH AGAINST GREELEY; CONSIDERED IN CONJUNCTION WITH POLITICAL SITUATION. BI-LINGUAL PROCEEDINGS. SIGNIFICANT SPEECH BY FORMER REVENUE OFFICER; PRAISES FOR BREWERS. BREWERS' COMMITTEE MEETS WITH GREAT SUCCESS AT CAPITOL; HAVE FRIENDS IN BOTH HOUSES; THEIR HONESTY CONTRASTED WITH DISTILLERS' FRAUDS; THEIR BILL PASSED, BEING ACT OF JUNE, 1872. DISCRIMINATION IN FAVOR OF BEER ESTABLISHED; ITS INESTIMABLE ADVANTAGE AND IMMEDIATE EFFECT. SYNOPSIS OF NEW LAW. WHY BREWERS FAILED IN SOME RESPECTS; REMARKABLE SPEECH OF COMMISSIONERS' REPRESENTATIVE. PROHIBITION TO BE TESTED IN COURT. SCHADE'S AND FLINTOFF'S ADDRESS. H. H. RUETER'S MAIDEN SPEECH, A SPLENDID EFFORT. DRINK QUESTION IN MASSACHUSETTS. BREWERS' ACADEMY; INTERESTING DEBATE; PROJECT REJECTED. ASSISTANCE TO INDIVIDUAL BREWERS; PRECEDENT.

During all the years reviewed in the foregoing chapters, the city of New York, then, as now, the foremost beer-producing centre of the Union, gave, as we have seen, to the association its entire executive, consisting of president, treasurer and secretary. Notwithstanding the well-understood fact that under the new constitution the selection of men from other cities and States was clearly and explicitly provided for, the old officers (Clausen, Schaefer and Katzenmayer) had been re-elected at the eleventh convention—a distinction as marked as it was well-deserved. There was, however, a special fitness in this oft-repeated choice at that particular time on account of the selection of New York as the place for holding the twelfth convention in 1872. The state of the industry in New York at that time must have been exceedingly gratifying to every man engaged in brewing. The production of malt-liquors in the entire State amounted to 2,602,505 barrels, representing nearly one-third of the total quantity produced in the United States. In the city and its immediate vicinity, including the nearest cities of the adjoining State of New Jersey, the principle of co-operation flourished to a remarkable extent. In addition to the New York Association of Lager-beer Brewers, there existed an ale-brewers' association, known as the Brewers' Association of New York and New Jersey (still existing at the present time), with David Jones as president, P. Amerman as vice-president, J. H. Ballantine, treasurer, and J. M. Lewis, secretary. Of the *personnel* of the trade in New York City the chronicler gave occasional details in several preceding chapters. The brewers of Brooklyn, or rather of Williamsburgh, were also organized; Joseph Liebmann being president of the association, H. B. Scharmann, secretary, and Joseph Burger, treasurer; three gentlemen who in after years attained unusual prominence in the parent association and the trade. Burger belonged to that class of brewers whose patriotism did not shrink from the dangers and hardships of war. He served during the Rebellion as lieutenant in a volunteer regiment, and subsequently rose to the colonelcy of the 28th N. Y. S. M. J. Liebmanu, like his father one of the founders of the association, and H. B. Scharmann always exercised considerable influence in local affairs. The former's firm then stood at the head of Brooklyn brewers in point of production, their output amounting to 60,000 barrels, while the average for the entire city did not probably exceed thirty-five thousand barrels per brewery. This firm, like so many ale-brewers before adverted to, had the incalculable advantage of age, their brewery having been established by Samuel Liebmann in 1854. Excepting the ale-breweries, there were few establishments in Williamsburgh or Brooklyn older than this one. Huber, Muench, Distler, Eppig, Fries, Fischer, Glueck, Illig, Melzer, Obermeyer, Seitz, etc., engaged in the business at a later period. Of the older breweries in the city of New York we have already given a cursory description in Chapter VII. The names of the firms who were in business and participated in the association's work in 1872 will be found in the list of delegates appended to this chapter.

A perusal of it will show that many cities not represented in former years had sent delegates, many of whom, like H. H. Rueter, for example, subsequently rose to eminence and distinction. The fact is that during the preceding year new local associations had been organized in Massachusetts (Boston), in Connecticut (Hartford and New Haven), in New York (Albany and Troy), in Ohio (Cleveland), in Illinois (Galena), and in Pennsylvania (Luzerne County). Of these the Boston association was by far the most numerous and important. A proposed bill prohibiting the sale of fermented liquors gave rise to the organization of this body which, by the way, was intended as a State organization admitting to membership any brewer doing business in Massachusetts. It was organized in March, 1872, its first officers being A. Richardson, president; Jacob Pfaff, vice-president; James McCormick, treasurer; Henry H. Rueter, secretary—the list of founders included these names in addition to those already given: W. F. Tufts, James M. Smith, J. K. Souther, G. F. Burkhardt, J. C. Nichols, Thomas Carberry, J. O. Kent, J. R. Alley, M. M. Hutchinson and William H. Nichols. Of the state of brewing in New England, and especially of the preponderance of the ale-trade, we have already given a brief outline. In 1872 the total production in Massachusetts amounted to 570,432, in Connecticut to 57,416, in New Hampshire to 101,311, and in Rhode Island to 17,808 barrels. As to the production in each brewery in the city of Boston figures are not accessible for every year; those nearest to the period here in question are the data for 1869–70, from which it appears that Boston's output amounted to 382,325 barrels; Rueter and Alley leading with 67,363, and A. Richardson, next in order, with an output of 64,917 barrels. By far the greatest part of this output consisted, as has been stated, of ale and porter. Hon. W. T. Van Nostrand, distinguished among his fellow-manufacturers by his career as legislator, ex-member of both houses of the State's legislative body, had just entered into the trade by purchasing the old Swan brewery, established in 1820. To John Roessle is due the distinction of being the first lager-brewer in Boston; he began to brew in the latter forties, and was soon followed by G. F. Burkhardt (of whose bounteous benevolence in founding an asylum on the famous Brooks Farm we have spoken elsewhere), by G. Habich, H. & J. Pfaff, Hechinger and others. In 1869–70 Roessle only produced 4,525 barrels, while Pfaff Bros. brewed 27,979 and G. F. Burkhardt 23,965 barrels. From the very names of a majority of the gentlemen who composed the Boston association the reader will have inferred that the official language of this body was not the German but the English, and we shall presently see that their representative, although himself a German by birth and a German scholar too, made his maiden speech at the twelfth convention in the English language, and thus helped to reconcile the delegates to the bi-lingual character of the proceedings, made imperatively necessary by various occurrences at this convention.

The Cleveland association embraced almost the entire trade of that city; C. Gehring was its president, and among the other officers and committees were men whose names became familiar to every brewer from their subsequent connection with the parent association's affairs—such men as Schlather, Baehr, Barkhardt, Braun, Schneider, Griebel, Haltnorth, Hughes, Rogers, Oppmann, Akley, Jahraus, Koestle, Muth, Hoffmann, Sutter, Heinz, Mueller, etc. Of the new association of Luzerne County, Pa., little is known at the present time except that it was organized by Ruckard, Baer and Hughes, who held the offices of president, secretary and treasurer, respectively. In Albany and Troy, of whose brewing-trade we give a brief account in another part of this book, the affairs of the local association were in a prosperous condition. At the head of the progressive movement we find the Amsdells, Colemans, Dobler, Taylor, Schrodt, Quinn & Nolan, Schneider, Dickson, Walker, Stoll, Pratt, Coolidge, Hinckel, Weinbender and others.

Before proceeding to summarize internal affairs of the association, as reflected by the convention reports, the chronicler feels it incumbent upon him to familiarize the reader with, or rather to revive in his memory, a number of half-forgotten historical incidents of the period here under consideration. Without this and a brief review of the political status of prohibition, the reader will scarcely be able to understand fully and estimate at their true worth and value a number of exceedingly favorable occurrences dwelt upon in the reports of the association's committees. As we have seen, the mass of German-American voters stood almost solidly upon the side of the Republican party at the outbreak of the War of the Rebellion; their affiliation with the grandest movement recorded in the country's history since the adoption of the constitution began to assume a very decided character as early as the time of Fremont's nomination (1856), and continued to grow in ponderous proportions up to Lincoln's first and second and Grant's first election. The causes which led to the Greeley movement at the close of Grant's first term of office are too well known to require more than casual mention. To what extent the German-American electors may have become disaffected by the incidents which aroused the magnificent opposition of Sumner and Schurz, it would be difficult to state accurately; but there can be no doubt of the widespread dissatisfaction caused among this part of our population by the undeniable fact that the prohibitory craze flourished most luxuriantly in some of the States in which the Republican party had full control; while in others, leading Republican politicians manifestly vacillated between the fear of offending the prohibitionists and the desire to retain the German-American vote, the former sentiment usually preponderating. When, in spite of this fact, the prohibitionists organized a national party, determined to sever their connection with their old political friends, and to nominate their own presidential candidate, political sagacity should have dictated an open declaration in favor of personal liberty on the part of the Republican party. It is true that there appeared to be less reason and justification for such a course, considered from the purely utilitarian point of view of the average politician, on account of the nomination of Horace Greeley, who was known throughout the country as a lifelong, ardent and devoted adherent of total abstinence and prohibition,—a fact warranting the presumption that German Republicans who naturally would not vote for the Democratic candidate, *could* not vote for Greeley, and that, therefore, they would exercise their right of franchise on the side of the regular Republicans. Nevertheless, the influence wielded by prominent German-Americans in the councils of the Republican party succeeded in repressing such unworthy considerations, and in having incorporated into the party's platform, adopted at Philadelphia, June 6th, 1872, the now famous Raster-plank, destined to become the subject of acrimonious contentions.

This plank received the sanction of the Republican convention on the very day on which the twelfth brewers' convention assembled at New York; hence, it could not and did not exercise any direct effect upon the proceedings of this gathering, and we shall presently show that the brewers had nothing whatsoever to do either with its framing, its introduction or its adoption. Its author, Hermann Raster, was unquestionably one of the ablest editors of the country, a man of profound erudition, equipped with all the inestimable accomplishments resulting from a thorough academic education acquired in one of the best German universities, and inspired by an overmastering love of liberty which had impelled him to sink all his hopes and aspirations in the German Revolution, and to become in the end one of the thousands of exiles, whose cultural work in their adopted country will never, we apprehend, be fully appreciated until such a man as Professor Learned, of the Pennsylvania University, shall have completed that self-imposed historical task of which his recent lectures afford us occasional hints and glimpses. As editor-in-chief of the Illinois *Staats-Zeitung*, Raster had uncommon opportunity of knowing the sentiments of German-American voters as reflected by the entire Press; he spoke neither for the brewers nor the liquor-dealers, but for the entire German-American population, pleading for a principle as noble and grand as any then formulated and embodied in the Republican platform. His attitude was simply typical of that of the entire German-American population, an attitude of which so eminent an historical authority as Professor von Holst wrote in terms of highest praise when he reviewed in Sybel's *Historische Zeitschrift* the work of Brice on the American Commonwealth.

The plank reads: "The Republican party propose to respect the rights reserved by the people to themselves as carefully as the powers delegated by them to the State and to the Federal Government. It disapproves of a resort to unconstitutional laws for the purpose of removing evils by interference with rights not surrendered by the people to either State or national governments." Although somewhat vague, certainly not as clear, incisive and pregnant as Raster should have preferred to make it, the plank could not well be misunderstood or misconstrued so far as its manifest aim and object was concerned. Nevertheless neither side accepted it unquestioningly as an unequivocal protest against prohibition, and the contention arising from the ambiguity of its phraseology was not set at rest until Raster himself, in a reply to a prohibitionist's enquiry, published a statement to the effect, that the Platform Committee adopted his draft with the full and explicit understanding that its purpose was the discountenancing of all so-called temperance (prohibitory) and Sunday laws; and that this purpose was meant to be expressed by reference to those rights of the people which had not been delegated to either national or State governments, it being assumed that the right to drink what one pleases (being responsible for his acts committed under the influence of strong drink) was among the rights not delegated by the people, but reserved to themselves.

Whether by reason of an obliquity of vision distorted by fanaticism, or whether yielding to a preference for the perversion of truth, which with some prohibitionists seems to be constitutional, the literary defenders of prohibition at once placed the responsibility for the adoption of the Raster-plank upon the shoulders of the brewers, and historians of the cause maintain to this day* "that the brewers brought the pressure of their numbers, wealth and organization to bear upon the leaders of the Republican and Democratic parties, and demanded as a price of their support not only unconditional submission to their dictum, but also party platform declaration and action against prohibitive legislation." The mendacity and absurdity of this charge so far as the Republican party is concerned, needs no further elucidation; and regarding the Democratic party no student of history, however obtuse he may be, need be told how utterly nonsensical the quoted words must appear. It requires an intellect of almost puerile calibre to suppose that a straddle policy such as Black imputes to the brewers could for a single moment have been misunderstood by, or have misled, the least astute politician.

In the light of history it is easy enough to summarize the situation. In 1872 a majority of German-American voters still adhered to the Republican party, and the same applies to a majority of brewers, who to-day are about equally divided between the two parties. Great disaffection existed among the German-Americans, and the Republican party clearly perceived the wisdom of removing its cause. Whatever this party undertook in order to recover lost ground and to retain that German-American support which it still possessed, naturally redounded to the benefit of the brewers, who accordingly shaped their course so as to maintain whatever coigne of

---

* See James Black's Brief History of Prohibition, pages 43 and 44.

vantage they, on their part, may thus have gained.
Weighed in the balance against their patriotism, their
industrial interests were exceedingly light whenever
they saw the welfare of the country emperilled—as it
was, for instance, during the war; but when later on,
no great issues being at stake, they became convinced
that their interests, equally with their rights as citizens,
were to be trampled under foot by an organized body
of fanatics, they resorted to the only legitimate means
of defense accorded to them under the constitution, *i. e.*,
that of their franchise, for the protection of both their
rights and their interests. That the attitude of the
German-American voters of both parties with regard to
sumptuary laws greatly assisted them in this endeavor
cannot be denied; but that they used their numbers
(there were about 2,500 brewers in the whole land!) and
their wealth to force the acceptance of the Raster-plank
is an assertion as absurd as it is false.

There can be no doubt that before the adoption of the
plank, leading Republicans had begun to appreciate the
drift of the prohibitory movement, and the wisdom of
conciliating liberal-minded citizens, and a result of this
clearer perception of the political requirements of the
hour, we find both the Congress of the United States
and the Administration more readily inclined to heed
the brewers' just demands concerning the internal
revenue law, as will presently be shown.

Thus matters stood when the twelfth convention
opened at New York. As the meeting was held in their
own city the officers of the national association, being
also officers of the local association, were both hosts and
guests, and in order to avoid embarrassing complications
which this dualism might possibly have caused, Vice-
President George Winter of the local association acted
for Clausen in the former capacity by greeting the

delegates in a very appropriate address; to which Clausen at once responded, delivering what the chronicler regards as one of the finest matter-of-fact speeches that had ever been heard in a brewers' convention up to that time. It was in the nature of a review of the attempts at restrictive and prohibitory legislation in the various States. From it we obtain a comprehensive view of the status of the drink-question at the time. Local option, usually considered a stepping-stone to constitutional prohibition, and restrictive laws of various nature had been advocated during the year in the legislatures of Pennsylvania, Iowa, Missouri, Massachusetts, Wisconsin, New Jersey, New York and Illinois. They were enacted and obtained full force of law only in Pennsylvania and Illinois; in the other States the Democratic opposition, aided by liberal Republicans, defeated them. Quoting the text of the platform adopted by a temperance convention held in Steinway Hall in the city of New York, Clausen exhorted his colleagues to imitate the example of their opponents by supporting at the polls those candidates only whose liberal views coincided with their own.

That an exhortation of this kind was at all needed illustrates very forcibly the falsity of the assertion that the "brewers had taken temperance into politics." The platform to which Clausen referred is typical of all similar utterances by prohibitionists; it contained the invariable injunction "that the suffrages of the temperance voters should in no case be cast for any candidate or party, national or State, not pledged to total abstinence for the individual and to prohibition as a legislative policy." This plank took temperance into politics, and if those opposed to these views, including the brewers, adopted the policy more tersely than elegantly expressed in the maxim that one must fight the devil with fire, they simply acted in self-defence, and on a line the legitimacy and efficacy of which the example of their adversaries had demonstrated. Unfortunately, the liberal voters did not everywhere emulate this example soon enough; hence Clausen's reproachful allusion to the indifference to politics evinced by so many brewers, in common with the average German-Americans, who were always willing enough to die for their country, but loath to "mix in politics," except when vital questions stirred their political conscience. The reader, who followed our introductory retrospect concerning the political situation at that time, will run no risk of misunderstanding the closing sentences of President Clausen's peroration, in which he gave utterances to this sentiment:

"At the Cincinnati convention they have placed at the head of their ticket a man (Horace Greeley) whose antecedents will warrant him a pliable tool in the hands of the temperance party, and none of you, gentlemen, can support him. It is necessary for you to make an issue at this election throughout the entire country, and *although I have belonged to the Democratic party ever since I have had a vote, I would sooner vote the Republican ticket than cast my ballot for such a candidate.*" That this sentiment was enthusiastically applauded by a body of men, four-fifths of whom still adhered at that time to the Republican party, shows plainly enough, how the brewers regarded the issue. The italicised part of the quotation subsequently led to a controversy which demonstrated the effect of the sentiment expressed in it upon the politicians. The *Tribune*, Horace Greeley's excellent newspaper, unfortunately tainted with the prohibitory vagary, but otherwise a powerful exponent of many of the principles for which three-fourths of the German-American citizens would have sacrificed all they valued most highly, published a letter from a Texan by name of O. F. Zink, who endeavored to prove that the Greeley Republicans deemed it beneath their dignity to make political capital out of the temperance question, while the Grant Republicans had in several State legislatures passed local option bills. To this letter, ostensibly addressed, but never directed or delivered, to the *Brewers' Gazette*, President Clausen replied in a dispassionate epistle in which, while expressing sincere respect for the great editor, he characterized Greeley's attitude and antecedents relative to the so-called temperance question as evidence of a regrettable eccentricity which should prevent every liberal citizen from voting for him.

The impression made by Clausen's speech upon the twelfth convention must have been a profound one, if we may judge from the unusual motion made then and there by H. B. Scharmann, one of the oldest and stanchest Republicans, to the effect that the thanks of the association and trade were due and should be tendered to Clausen for his speech—a motion which was carried unanimously and amidst vociferous applause. Among the many valuable services which Clausen rendered to the association this appeal ranks foremost, as it came just at the time when an open, fearless declaration and an effective rallying-cry was most sorely needed by the members of the trade, a majority of whom still clung to their old party with all the unswerving tenacity of conservative and loyal men.

The usual resolution of organization, so utterly useless, yet so conscientiously and punctiliously offered and carried out, resulted in the election of Lauer as honorary president, and the following officers, viz.: Vice-presidents: P. Amerman and Andrew Fink, New York; H. Schalk and J. H. Ballantine, New Jersey; William

Massey and George Gerst, Pennsylvania; M. Kleiner and Charles Gehring, Ohio; Conrad Seipp, Illinois; R. Lange, Iowa; R. Jacob and C. G. Stifel, Missouri; F. Pabst and Valentine Blatz, Wisconsin; E. J. Encker and Robert Portner, Virginia; F. Reymann, West Virginia; J. Seeger and L. Muth, Maryland; H. H. Rueter and J. C. Nichols, Massachusetts; Charles Geisbauer, Kentucky; and George Bassermann, Connecticut. Secretaries: G. Bergner, James M. Lewis and Joseph Schlitz. The committee who reported these nominations consisted of J. Kuntz, F. Pabst, P. Schemm, R. Lange and Joseph Hensler.

1872 is the year in which the contention concerning the official language was disposed of by the adoption of both the English and German. The causes which led to this action are very clear. In addition to L. Schade, Revenue Commissioner J. W. Douglass, successor to General Pleasanton, had delegated C. A. Bates, an officer of the Revenue Division, to represent him at the brewers' convention. Col. Josiah Gibbons, District Attorney for Iowa, formerly employed in the Internal Revenue Department, was also present for a purpose which it is difficult at the present time to ascertain. It was known that he desired to address the convention, and the courtesy of the floor was extended to him. The proportion of English-speaking brewers was larger than at any other previous convention. Under these circumstances it would have been both unwise and discourteous not to place the two languages upon an equal footing. G. Bergner, however, proposed that the proceedings be conducted in the English language exclusively, a proposition, which, if adopted, would have excluded some of the ablest members from participating in the deliberations, for although they could read and write and easily understand the language, and speak it sufficiently well for ordinary purposes, they did not master it to such an extent as to enable them to take part in public discussions. P. Blatz, H. B. Scharmann and Hermann Rocke spoke against, and C. Miller (of Tiffin, O.) for Bergner's motion. It was finally voted down, and in its stead the convention passed a resolution for bi-lingual proceedings. But towards the end of the convention the subject was again revived by a motion of M. Kleiner to the effect that in the future the proceedings of the conventions should be conducted in German one year and in English the next. He appealed to the German members to throw aside prejudice and to consider that among the men who had performed most valuable services at Washington many could not understand a word of German. The old discussion was thus renewed, and Schemm, Rocke, Massey, Baltz, Lauer and Joseph Burger took part in it. The latter finally secured a majority vote upon his bi-lingual resolution, which definitely settled the question.

The presence of C. A. Bates as an official representative of the Federal Government, indicative in itself of a desire on the part of the administration to heed the brewers' just representations, derived uncommon significance from the political conditions described in this chapter; it became an event of the highest importance by reason of the remarkable speech delivered by this gentleman at the convention. His speech had been prepared beforehand and there can be no doubt that before its delivery it had been read by Commissioner Douglass and most likely by Federal officers in still higher stations; at all events, Bates unhesitatingly asserted that he spoke for the Government. To the end that this historical document may be appreciated at its true value, we must review the work of the Brewers' Committee in Congress and the Department during the year 1871-72. Before doing so it may not be amiss to point out another noteworthy coincidence. It has already been stated that the Republican National Convention and the Twelfth Brewers' Congress convened on the same day, June 6th, 1872. Well, on the very same day the new revenue law (Act of June 6th, 1872), embodying many of the provisions asked for by the brewers, went into effect; in truth, the Act was the identical draft submitted by the brewers, but amended by Congress in several particulars, which will appear later. Lauer admitted his surprise and gratification at the cheerful readiness of the Committee on Ways and Means, of which H. L. Dawes was then chairman, to consider favorably the draft of a bill drawn by Lewis and agreed upon by the brewers at previous meetings. Almost without solicitation a large number of Congressmen assisted the brewers' committee with their influence, advice and vote. Surely this commendable attitude did not arise solely from political considerations. The reputation of the men who occupied it forbids such an assumption; but it is more than likely that a comparison of the practices of the Whiskey Ring with the undisputed honesty and rectitude of the brewers as tax-payers determined the course of such men as John H. Ketchum, Frederick T. Frelinghuysen, Reuben F. Fenton, E. H. Roberts, J. Lawrence Getz, George A. Halsey, G. A. Finkelnburg, H. L. Dawes and others—all members of the House of Representatives to whom the twelfth convention tendered votes of thanks. We shall presently see that Bates, the Government's representative, dwelt with particular emphasis upon such a comparison, and Col. Josiah Gibbons, whose presence at the convention has already been mentioned, also referred to it when, on being introduced to the convention, he said: "I am an old servant of the Government and while in the Internal Revenue Department was brought in contact with your trade and then formed a high estimate of brewers as a class, from the sensible, honorable and straightforward manner in which they conduct their business. During the time I was head of that section of the department of Internal Revenue which deals with the brewers, *there never came to my personal knowledge one single case of fraud by a brewer.*" Commissioner Douglass shared these opinions and sentiments, and in his intercourse with the brewers' representatives gave many evidences of a friendly disposition. Concerning the monthly accounts, for instance, which afforded ill-disposed special agents an opportunity and pretext to annoy and worry the brewers, sometimes for an ulterior purpose of a reprehensible character, he readily consented to a modification in the enforcement of the law to the extent of allowing the brewers, in rendering their monthly statements of malt-liquors brewed, sold and on hand, to swear to an estimated amount and account. He also promised not to countenance the projects of some speculators who wished to foist on the trade, through the Government, a new stamp and stamp-cancelling device. Concerning the draft of a new revenue law proposed by the brewers, he evinced readiness to assent in some, and reluctance to give his approval in other respects; but throughout his connection with these matters he displayed great fairness.

The Agitation Committee had two hearings before the Committee on Ways and Means, both being attended by Amerman, Howard, Lauer, Schaefer, Bergner, Massey, Betz, Hughes, Clausen, Lewis and Gardiner, accompanied by the association's attorney, J. M. Lewis. Revenue Commissioner Douglass and his law-officer Bates were present at each hearing. We need not recapitulate the claims of the brewers nor all the provisions of the law-draft they submitted, as the reader is already familiar with them. In one respect their attitude presented a new and striking feature. It was their determined effort to draw a broad line of demarcation between fermented beverages and spirituous liquors. They insisted that the manufacturers of, and dealers in, the two kinds of beverages should have separate classifications under the revenue-system, not only on account of the difference between these drinks, but more especially because under the laws of 1868, in which both beverages are indiscriminately classified under one and the same head, the revenue office in some instances made rulings totally inapplicable to fermented beverages, but manifestly designed by the lawmakers to be applied to distilled liquors.

Commissioner Douglass made no attempt at the hearings to refute any of the arguments urged by the Agitation Committee in favor of the proposed modifications, but he evidently objected to some of them none the less energetically after the committee had left Washington. Yet the Ways and Means Committee did not blindly adopt or follow his recommendation, as was shown by a rather characteristic incident which occurred in the committee when Lauer made his appearance there for the third time in order to ascertain what Dawes intended to do. He was greeted with these words: " Mr. Lauer, the Committee on Ways and Means are ready to report your bill any day, but you must convince the Internal Revenue office that you are right, for they oppose some sections of it." Such an intimation could not fail to have its effect. Douglass was immediately reasoned with, but could not be convinced that an increase of rebate would be just. Like all fiscal officers he wanted all the money he could get; his official conscience revolted against any attempt to attenuate the flow of revenue, and these scruples militated against any other considerations, however strongly supported by the ethical code of ordinary mortals.

When the bill, after having been dissected and discussed by a Committee of Conference, finally emerged from the committee room it did not contain all the provisions asked for by the brewers, but it did contain, besides many essential modifications, a clause broadly discriminating between malt-beverages and spirituous liquors, thus affording to the association a legal basis and sanction for the missionary work which they were about to inaugurate upon a larger scale than had hitherto been the case. Counsellor Lewis, to whom the association tendered a vote of thanks for drafting the bill now become a law, probably expressed the general opinion and sentiment in regard to this innovation when he said: "This convention will be memorable for drawing the line between malt and spirituous liquors, and separating one interest from the other. The time is now come when brewers can take the position and maintain it, that they are the temperance party of the country, and that the use of malt-liquors is beneficial and healthful to the people, tending to make them temperate and industrious." In other words, the Act of June 6th, 1872, treats fermented liquors as a separate source of revenue, totally distinct from any other; whereas formerly no such discrimination existed. No greater victory has ever been won by the association. The discrimination thus secured, also applied, of course, to retailers and therefore could not but prove of great value in another respect; because in some States malt-liquors were allowed to be sold where distilled spirits were prohibited. In such instances retailers had been deterred from engaging in the traffic on account of the large amount of the special tax required by the Federal Government from the retailer under the old indiscriminate classification.

This is the proper place to state that the advantage thus gained was at once followed up by a determined effort to secure for the principle of discrimination general recognition throughout the country. The Committee on Resolutions of the twelfth convention, consisting of Lauer, Amerman, Schlitz, Kleiner, Massey, Seipp, Pfaff, Jacobs and Bassermann submitted, among others, a resolution to the effect that the brewers throughout the United States be called upon to exert their influence in all political assemblies to the end that in the platforms of these bodies a plank may be incorporated according to malt-liquor its true position as a temperance beverage and a necessary article of consumption. Joseph Liebmann of Williamsburgh, N. Y., held that this resolution was neither broad nor comprehensive enough; he therefore offered a substitute declaring that the brewers are opposed to a union with those who represent exclusively the trade in spirituous liquors, and calling upon local associations to use their influence for the purpose of securing the exemption of malt-liquors from the operations of prohibitory laws. Perfectly correct in principle, the Liebmann resolution labored under the disadvantage of amounting in effect to a declaration of war upon the retailers, and was therefore strenuously opposed —particularly by Schemm of Philadelphia—and finally rejected in favor of the original resolution.

Now as to the modification of the old revenue acts, the careful reader, whose memory serves him moderately well, will readily perceive from the following synopsis that the Agitation Committee secured at least three-fourths of the amendments discussed in preceding chapters. Under previous acts the sale of sour or damaged beer had been made exceedingly difficult by the irksome and unreasonable precautionary measures before described. In the new law the original clause of the Act of 1866 took the place of the obnoxious section. It now read: "That when fermented liquor has become sour or damaged so as to be incapable for use as such, brewers may sell the same for manufacturing purposes, and may remove the same to places where it may be used for such purposes, in casks or other vessels unlike those ordinarily used for fermented liquors, containing, respectively, not less than one barrel each, and having the nature of their contents marked upon them, without affixing thereon the permit-stamp or stamps required."

The law also gave one brewer the right to fill with his own product casks belonging to another brewer—a trade convenience repeatedly asked for by the association. The section relating to this point reads as follows, viz.:

"That every brewer shall by branding mark, or caused to be marked, upon every hogshead, barrel, keg, or other vessel containing the fermented liquor made by him, before it is sold or removed from the brewery, or brewery-warehouse, or other place of manufacture, the name of the person, firm, or corporation by whom such liquor was manufactured, and the place where the same shall have been made. And any person, other than the owner thereof, or his agent, authorized so to do, who shall intentionally remove or deface such marks therefrom, shall be liable to a penalty of fifty dollars for each cask or vessel from which the mark is so removed or defaced: *Provided, however*, That when a brewer shall purchase fermented liquor finished and ready for sale from another brewer, in order to supply the customers of such purchaser, such purchaser may, upon written notice to the collector of his intention so to do, and under such regulations as the Commissioner of Internal Revenue may prescribe, furnish his own vessels, branded with his name and the place where his brewery is located, to be filled with the fermented liquor so purchased, and to be so removed; the proper stamp or stamps to be affixed and canceled as aforesaid, by the manufacturer, before removal."

Besides the improvement already noted, this section secured a further benefit to the brewer, inasmuch as in the part relating to the branding of packages, the former wording "in such manner as the Commissioner of Internal Revenue shall prescribe" was eliminated, thus removing the cause of what, as we have seen, proved an annoyance to the trade. The unequivocal provision for the branding of casks also safeguarded the proprietary rights of the brewer. Under the law of 1868, with no discrimination between the two kinds of beverages, the Internal Revenue Office imposed a wholesale liquor-dealers' tax on brewers who sold their own product at their warehouses or from their trucks. Under this construction of the law the revenue collectors in Pennsylvania had, in 1872, subjected the brewers to a tax of $100 for each beer wagon. In the law of 1872 the words malt-liquor and brewer were eliminated from that section under which this special tax was levied, thus making its provisions inapplicable to brewers; and to make the discrimination still more marked, the law provided that:

"Every person who sells or offers for sale malt-liquors in larger quantities than five gallons at one time, but who does not deal in spirituous liquors, shall be regarded as a wholesale dealer in malt-liquors and not a wholesale liquor-dealer, and shall pay a special tax of fifty dollars. Every person who sells or offers for sale malt-liquors in quantities of five gallons or less at one time, but who does not deal in spirituous liquors, shall be regarded as a retail dealer in malt-liquors and not a retail liquor-dealer, and shall pay a special tax of twenty dollars."

In the matter of daily entries and monthly returns of quantities produced the old law was so modified as to require an oath not as to the actual quantity in barrels and fractional barrels produced, but only as to the "*estimated* quantity produced in barrels." Another section of the new law afforded the relief so often asked for by the association in case of fire, flood or accident.

As to the removal, without payment of tax, of unfermented worts and of malt-liquors from breweries to warehouses, we quote the following from the Act of June 6th, 1872:

"That where malt-liquor or tun-liquor, in the first stages of fermentation, known as unfermented worts, of whatever kind, is sold by one brewer to another for the purpose of producing fermentation or enlivening old or stale ale, porter, lager-beer, or other fermented liquors, it shall not be liable to a tax to be paid by the seller thereof, but the tax on the same shall be paid by the purchaser thereof, when the same, having been mixed with the old or stale beer, is sold by him as provided by law, and such sale or transfer shall be subject to such restrictions and regulations as the Commissioner of Internal Revenue may prescribe."

"Brewers may remove or transport, or cause to be removed or transported, malt-liquor of their own manufacture, known as lager-beer, in quantities of not less than six barrels in one vessel, and may also remove or transport, or cause to be removed or transported, malt-liquors known as ale or porter, or any other malt-liquor not heretofore mentioned, in quantities not less than fifty barrels at a time, from their breweries or other places of manufacture to a depot, warehouse, or other place used exclusively for storage or sale in bulk, and occupied by them, from one part of one collection district to another part of the same collection district, or from one collection district to another collection district, without affixing the proper stamp on said vessels of lager-beer, ale, porter, and other malt-liquor at the brewery or place of manufacture, under a permit to be obtained from the collector of the district, (who is to grant the same upon application), wherein said malt-liquor is manufactured, to said depot or warehouse, but to no other place, under such rules and regulations as the Commissioner of Internal Revenue may prescribe, and thereafter the manufacturer of the malt-liquor so removed shall stamp the same when it leaves such depot or warehouse, in the same manner and under the same penalties and liabilities as when stamped at the brewery as herein provided; and the collector of the district in which such depot or warehouse is situated shall furnish the manufacturer with the stamps for stamping the same, as if the said malt-liquor had been manufactured in his district."

The foregoing synopsis of the Act of June 6th, 1872, shows how eminently effective must have been the arguments of the Agitation Committee. The reader now knows what the committee accomplished; we will let the Government's representative state wherein they failed and *why* they failed. No better authority could be cited upon this point, for the chairman of the Committee on Ways and Means frankly admitted, as we have seen, that the brewers' petition would be denied only in so far as it conflicted with the wishes of the Revenue Commissioner. After a few preliminary remarks the representative of the Federal Government spoke as follows:

"I am here in pursuance of your invitation, and by order of the Commissioner of Internal Revenue, to whose office I have been attached during the last eight years, for the purpose of learning your wants and views concerning that branch of the public service; also to give information to inquirers, as far as lies in my power, of the official construction placed upon Internal Revenue laws affecting the brewing interest. The opportunity here presents itself for a friendly interchange of views, and for taking the proper initiatory steps towards securing the action which shall result in perfect harmony between an office of the Government and the great national interest which you represent; and it must not be neglected.

"I recently enjoyed the peculiar honor of being present with the Commissioner of Internal Revenue before the Hon. Committee of Ways and Means of the House of Representatives, and there heard the arguments of your committee in favor of certain amendments to the Internal Revenue laws relative to brewing. Heard the replies of the Commissioner. You know the result. Your committee failed in obtaining one of the principal modifications asked for—that which provides for doing away with the brewers' bond. This is not their fault. They said all in favor of the measure that conscientious gentlemen could say. It is not the Commissioner's fault. He said no more than it was his duty as a conservator of the law to say. It is not the fault of our national legislators. It is simply because it does not appear reasonable at this time to grant this request. But I will say more on this point before I conclude.

"Congress has given you an Internal Revenue law milder in its provisions, less burdensome, than any law affecting any equally great interest. But you say, don't let us have these comparisons. *Let every class of tax-payers stand upon its own merits. Because distillers or tobacco manufacturers have defrauded the revenue is no reason why we should be subject to bonds. I believe in this argument, but I introduce this comparison for another purpose.* I wish to show you that in seeking to be relieved of some of the requirements of the Internal Revenue laws you may be doing what is not best for your own interest, even though you succeed. Let me illustrate. On the 13th of July, 1866, Congress passed a law providing for the transportation of distilled spirits, without payment of the tax, from one portion of the country to another, and for exportation of distilled spirits without payment of the tax. The frauds which were perpetrated under this law are something fearful to contemplate. The consequence was, that on the 20th of July, 1868, Congress passed another law prohibiting the transportation of spirits without payment of the tax, and virtually prohibiting its exportation. Nor were these the only retaliatory measures taken. No distiller at the present day, for this law is yet in force, can perform a single act as such except in the presence of an Internal Revenue officer, whom he is compelled to pay for watching him. All the grain or other material used in distilling must be received in the presence of the store-keeper, who keeps an account of it; everything that goes into the mash-tub is weighed by the store-keeper. He sees the mash conveyed to the fermenting tubs. There he watches it while it ferments, be the time 48 or 72 hours. And after the fluid gets into the still it may be said to pass out of the distiller's control altogether. The product of distillation is made to run into cisterns, which are locked up from the distiller and the key given to the gauger, and when the spirits are moved out of that room into another lock-up the act is accomplished in the presence of the store-keeper *and* the gauger. But I have not said a half or a quarter that might be said of the oppressive nature of this law. There are about sixty sections in it, and they generally wind up in this way : ' any person who shall violate any of the provisions of this section, shall be fined for every such offence not less than five hundred dollars, nor more than five thousand dollars, and imprisonment not less than six months, nor more than two years.' And every distiller is required to give thirty-seven bonds each year.

"But I will not dwell on this disagreeable picture. This was a bad disease, and a violent remedy was necessary. That apparently harsh law was fully indorsed by the people. It owes its existence to a party who chose General Grant as its standard bearer, and that very fall General Grant was chosen President of these United States.

"But your own case is so different. The law providing the mode of collecting the revenue of brewers was enacted July 13th, 1866, the same day that gave birth to the liberal provisions of law to distillers, and conceived in the same spirit. *But how widely different has been your course? Your moderation has won the esteem of the law-makers.* There was no change made in your law by the Act of

July 20th, 1868, nor any reference made therein, except in such words as these: 'provided that nothing in this section shall be construed to apply to fermented liquors.' And what was in that section? Why, fines, forfeitures and imprisonment as usual.

"*Yes, you have begun well. Let us take no backward step. I say us, for I am with you. The Commissioner of Internal Revenue is with you. The President is with you. Every patriotic citizen is with you, if you will hold to your course.*"

Following close upon this remarkable speech, which is but one of many official evidences of the brewers' absolute honesty, came L. Schade's statistical address and review of the prohibitory movement from which we quote the following interesting passage, viz.:

"It is your duty to protect yourselves and your profession. Do it in a firm, argumentative manner that will convince those opposed to you of their error. Bitter recriminations will do no good. There are, no doubt, honest men in the so-called temperance party, who are really actuated by philanthropical feelings. Tell them, by pointing at those States where the Maine Liquor Law has been in force, that under that law drunkenness has been increasing instead of decreasing, and more than all that, that those restrictive laws have introduced that terrible Asiatic vice of opium-eating. Already, judging from the last report of the Massachusetts Board of Health, the pæans of the so-called temperance men over the apparent success of their temperance laws, which are even now being enforced with fanatical zeal, are turned into lamentations at the unexpected discovery that the New Englanders, like the Turks, are using enormous quantities of opium as a stimulant and as a substitute for alcoholic drinks. Returns from twenty-four cities and towns of Massachusetts, show that the consumption of that drug is practiced to an alarming extent. In one town the reason given for its use is, that opium is 'more genteel' than alcohol, and in another, because the consumers are not willing to 'risk their reputation for temperance by taking alcoholic beverages.' In Boston, opium-eating is general, one man consuming one ounce every secular day and two ounces on Sunday. A regular customer of one druggist there is a noted and well-known *temperance lecturer*. The report of the board evidences, that in nearly all those places opium 'is in general use as a stimulant.' A physician in Worcester positively affirms that the alarming use of the drug in that town is 'in consequence of the restricted use of alcoholic liquors.'"

During the preceding year the Agitation Committee's sphere of activity had been considerably enlarged. Local associations requested assistance in the adoption of defensive measures against prohibitory attacks, and in at least two instances the proposition had been made to test the constitutionality of prohibition. One of these emanated from Iowa whence a suit had been carried to the Supreme Court of the United States to test the question as to whether or not the sale of intoxicating beverages in that State was legal. In the succeeding year Lauer proposed of his own accord to test the constitutionality of the Massachusetts law forbidding the salè of beer, an Act passed after the twelfth convention. A definite policy relative to these questions had not yet been formulated, as we shall presently show when returning to this and kindred subjects.

As to the Massachusetts law and the status of the whole question in that State in June, 1872, the reader can have no better, no more lucid or comprehensive presentation than that which Henry H. Rueter of Boston, gave in his maiden speech upon the floor of the convention. He had evidently come prepared to violate the language-rule, for he spoke in English and explained by way of apology that if he used any other tongue his fellow delegates from Boston would not understand him. True, the language resolution just passed made the apology appear in the light of a mere courtesy to those who were opposed to bi-lingual proceedings, but even so it helped to settle the conviction that the new departure must be adhered to in the interests of all.

The twelfth was the first brewers' convention at which the local association of Massachusetts, recently admitted to membership in the parent body, was represented, and their eloquent spokesman, when speaking of benefits bestowed upon the trade by the efforts of the association referred to this fact in these words, viz.:

"In expressing our feelings of gratitude to you, gentlemen, we have also to acknowledge, to our own mortification, that in the past we have been enjoying these advantages without any struggles on our part to obtain them; till now we have never put the shoulders to the wheel. But, gentlemen, I feel safe in promising for the future that henceforth the East will unite with the West in the struggle to obtain for our glorious trade that position, legally, morally and socially, which is accorded to it in other countries where its importance and true bearings are fully understood." This promise was made good in a splendid manner by the New England brewers, who have ever since been in the foremost rank of the defenders and supporters of our industry, and among them none more conspicuous than the bearer of this encouraging message to the twelfth convention. It was excessive modesty, by the way, that prompted the speaker to imply that his colleagues of New England had not up to that time taken part in the struggle for a just recognition of the brewers' rights. They had performed splendid work through the Boston newspapers, making most judicious use of the famous report of the Board of Health of Massachusetts, for which the twelfth convention tendered to its author, Dr. Bowditch, a vote of thanks. But a few weeks before the twelfth convention the *Boston Herald, Commercial Bulletin, Daily Advertiser* and *Evening Transcript* published separate series of instructive articles on the subject of malt-liquors written for the Brewers' Association of Massachusetts by John Flintoff.

So far as Rueter's address contains a survey of the situation in Massachusetts, it must be regarded as a valuable historical document, supplementing, as it does, by the observations of an eye-witness those vaguer impressions which the reader ordinarily derives from a history written by one far removed by time and space from the events which he describes. We quote this part of Rueter's speech:

"Till within a few years our law-makers recognized no distinction between fermented and distilled liquors. Lager-beer venders and rum sellers were synonymous terms. It made no difference whether a drink contained 4 or 50 per cent. of alcohol. During the last two or three years a distinction, however, has been made. Our legislatures found themselves placed between Scylla and Charibdis, between the pressure brought to bear upon them by temperance fanatics on one side, and the strong undercurrent of sound common sense of the people on the other side, which latter would not tolerate the enactment or at least enforcement of too stringent measures, which, besides, might endanger the stability of the dominant party of the State.

"To extract themselves from this dilemma they exempted fermented liquors from the list of proscribed drinks, while the law remained absolutely prohibitory as regards distilled liquors.

"For lack of moral courage, perhaps, this exemption for the past two years was not made outright, but conditional on a vote from each city and town in the commonwealth, on the first Tuesday of May, on the following question, 'Shall the manufacture or sale of ale, porter, lager-beer or wines be allowed in this city or town?' I would suggest to some legal mind among us to consider whether this proceeding is constitutional. Our legislators, chosen to frame our laws, re-delegate this power to their constituents, and instead of deciding themselves what is best, leave this decision in many places to that numerous class which will not reason, to fanatics.

"Two years ago this vote was left optional with cities and towns—the law read 'may vote,' leaving those places not voting free to sell. A year ago our enemies stole a march upon us, by changing this little word 'may' into 'shall,' thus depriving all places not voting of their privilege to manufacture and sell fermented liquors. By inattention to this change several important places were lost, which, however, were nearly all redeemed by our last vote, so that we stand better this year than last.

"Let me consider, in a few words, one of the reasons. Only last year the beer law was defeated in some places. It is a reason which ought to bring conviction to the minds of our opponents if they were open to conviction at all. The liquor trade sees in the brewing interest a powerful ally, from which they do not wish to be severed. The increased consumption of malt-liquors is also diminishing the sale and consumption of distilled liquors, and the dealers in these consequently suffer in their pockets, which, as is well known, are intimately related to a man's judgment. As a consequence, such voted against the sale of ale and beer. These unwilling witnesses bear testimony, that ale and beer are steadily and surely conquering the fiery spirit of distilled drinks, and, if ultimately the true objects of temperance shall have been accomplished, no thanks to our intemperate temperance fanatics, but to the brewers of this country.

"A distinct and special constabulary force is provided to enforce the law. Is it enforced? Let us see. If the occasional seizure of some gallons, sometimes only pints, of whiskey or rum from some poor Irish woman who is endeavoring to eke out a precarious existence by the sale of a glass of whiskey now and then, if her fining or possible imprisonment—while her rich and influential neighbor pursues his trade openly, and keeps a stock of hundreds of thousands—if this, I repeat, if this is enforcement, the law is enforced. If enforcement means an impartial application of the law to all parties offending, without distinction of station and influence, monetary or political, if it means that, then the enforcement most decidedly fails.

"Occasionally a spasmodic stringent application is made to a wider circle of dealers, always excepting largest offenders, and then the beauties of the law become apparent from some other point of view. Where, for instance, the sale formerly was openly transacted over the bar, all seems done away with. 'No liquor sold over this bar' is advertised in conspicuous notices.

But hold, there enters a woman followed by a large trunk, which, on being opened, apparently contains clothing or linens. I say apparently, for underneath lurks the gleam of the well-known black bottles in large numbers. They are slyly taken out, as slyly filled, and as slyly replaced, carried home into families, subjecting all their members to the temptation and influence of the demon within.

"Another illustration. When during any of these stringent but spasmodic enforcements of the law no drinks could be sold on the premises, as the law reads, the liquor was in some places doled out in medicine bottles, containing at least twice the quantity usually imbibed at one drink. The bottles were handed to the customer, taken just outside the house, poured into tumblers and drank. That was one way of evading the law.

"Let us now consider the general result of our prohibitory law. Taken as a whole, without distinction between fermented and distilled liquors, the law has been a decided failure, in its application and its results as regards the promotion of temperance. It has been a positive injury to the best interests of true temperance in the same ratio, as it has hindered or impeded the sale and consumption of malt-liquor. Besides, it has fostered vice in the shape of perjury, bribery and general corruption. It has been even attempted to make it subservient to money making by a sort of blackmailing process, namely, by parties bringing suit against liquor dealers and brewers for the recovery of all money paid by them for liquors or beer during the continuation of the laws. I am glad to say the scheme failed of success, but it well illustrates the extreme danger of the enactment of such arbitrary law."

Both the somewhat vague text of the second resolution concerning the establishment of a Brewers' Academy, re-committing the whole matter to the committee, and the indecisive and rather half-hearted discussion on the subject, as recorded in the preceding chapter, had foreshadowed the fate of this proposition. The renewed epistolary enquiry failed to create any new interest in the matter, and as those who favored and earnestly advocated the founding of such an educational institution differed materially as to the ways and means by which the desired end should be attained, unable to agree upon a common basis adapted alike to the requirements of the scheme and the needs and interests of the association, there was no possibility of acting favorably on Schwarz's project. Stifel, the chairman of the committee, was again unavoidably prevented from attending the convention, but he sent a letter enumerating the difficulties he encountered in the undertaking and recommending the postponement of the matter for five years. Had this recommendation been adopted, A. Schwarz would in all probability have awaited the end of this term; but, as matters stood, the members of the association undoubtedly perceived that they owed it to themselves and to Schwarz, as well as the trade, to decide the matter definitely in one way or another. Being themselves unwilling or unable to accomplish the object, they were in justice bound to give full sway to private enterprise by withdrawing entirely. Scarcely any discussion took place after Stifel's letter had been read; in fact, the proceedings only record the words of Kleiner, who appeared to be thoroughly convinced of the impossibility of establishing and maintaining the school; believing, as he plainly intimated, that even if the necessary capital could be raised among members, which was more than doubtful, the school would not be patronized because it would be much cheaper and more advantageous to have the sons of brewers educated in the old established institutions of Germany. Unfortunately, Kleiner did not live to see the error of his judgment and the fallacy of his reasoning, so far as the latter part of his objection was concerned. For once this astute, clear-sighted business man was mistaken, as much mistaken as any man, not endowed with prophetic vision, might have been in those days when the latent potentiality of the industry had just begun in some measure to be realized. In regard to the difficulty and, in fact, the injudiciousness of founding a school otherwise than as a private enterprise there could be but one opinion, and it was no more than could be expected that the convention would relegate the scheme to its originator; as in fact it did upon motion of Bergner, joined to that of Moerlein, "to discharge the committee with the thanks of the convention." In view of the further development of this matter, Schwarz certainly had no cause to regret, nor the association to repent, the course adopted in 1872.

At two successive conventions the association elected a committee on petitions, the necessity for creating this new body having arisen from the requests of the publishers of the two trade journals for pecuniary assistance. At the twelfth convention this committee, consisting of G. Baer, D. G. Yuengling, L. Schlather, A. F. Dobler and George Bassermann, also considered the petition of Oscar Rocke of Springfield, Mass., one of the victims of the Massachusetts law, who, in dire distress on account of the threatened destruction of his business, solicited his fellow-manufacturers' aid and support. This petition deserves mention, because in favorably reporting upon it, the committee formulated a principle which has been adhered to and maintained ever since that time. Although recommending that the petition be granted, the committee emphasized the propriety of specifically disclaiming the intention of establishing a precedent which might possibly be construed as the right of a member to ask, or the moral obligation of the association to grant, such aid. In the course of thirty-five years thousands of dollars have been generously donated to members visited by misfortune, but with the understanding in every instance that the principle formulated in 1872 must still be upheld.

After the re-election of the old executive and of a majority of the old members of the Agitation Committee, to whom were added H. H. Rueter and H. Pfaff as representatives of the newly created association of Massachusetts, this most remarkable and memorable convention came to an end.*

---

* The following is a list of delegates to the twelfth convention:

F. Dohler, Joseph Hochleitner, Albany, N. Y.; Robert Portner, Alexandria, Va.; J. Banernschmid, J. C. Rossmark, G. Bauernschmid, John G. Hoffman, Louis Muth, Jacob Seeger, Joseph Schreier, J. H. Vonder Horst, John F. Wisner, S. Strauss, J. Stromberg, H. Ellenbrook, Baltimore, Md.; H. H. Rueter, Henry Pfaff, John A. Kohl, John C. Nichols, Charles Dolen, Boston, Mass.; A. Ziegele, Georga Roehevot, C. Ziegele, Jr., S. Scheo, Buffalo, N. Y.; Henry Claus, Bridgeport, Conn.; M. Kleiner, George Klotter, Jr., H. Klinckhammer, C. Moerlein, R. Reimbold, L. Burger, Jac. Geier, H. Kreis, Cincinnati, O.; Charles Geisbaner, Covington, Ky.; Cincinnati Delegation, Columbus, O.; Conrad Seipp, Chicago, Ill.; Aug. Burkhardt, Charles Gehring, L. Schlather, Cleveland, O.; J. Marsh, R. Quaff, A. Shaw, Cooperstown, N. Y.; Col. Gibbin, R. Lange, Davenport, Ia.; A. J. Leetch, Ypsilanti, Mich.; M. Fischer, Lawrence, Mass.; Henry Frank, E. G. Hatsfeld, Lawrence Knapp, Lancaster, Pa.; V. Blatz, F. Falk, Fred. Pabst, J. Schlitz, Milwaukee, Wis.; George Bassermann, New Haven, Conn.; J. R. Vernam, Newburg, N. Y.; P. Ballantine & Sons, J. A. Boppe, P. Brook, Baier & Hill, Hill & Krueger, Joseph Heneler, F. Haas, Jos. Hartb, F. J. Kastner, Kaufmann & Hauck, Lius, Geyer & Co., John Laible, Newark Brewing Co., Schalk Bros., Schiener & Hartmann, C. Trefz, C. Wiedenmaier Sons, C. G. Woehr, Wackenhoth & Co., P. Wilhelm, Newark, N. J.; Peter Amerman, Jacob Ahles, Peter Ahles, John J. Betz & Co., Bernheimer & Schmid, S. Bernbeimer, Jr., Henry Clausen, F. Clauseu, Clausen & Bauer, Peter Doelger, Jos. Doelger & Sons, George Ehret, Eckert & Winter, H. Elias & Co., A. Finck, M. Groh, Anton Huepfel, C. Hoepfel, A. Huepfel, Hoffmann & Merkel, David Jones, John Kress, H. Koehler, J. J. Mentges, F. A. Neumann, Chas. Neumann, Ryerson & Yuengling, Jac. Robinson, C. Robinson, H. Roeke, J. Ruppert, Francis Ruppert, F. & M. Schaefer, F. Schaefer, Jr., Schwaner & Amend, August Schmid, Sebastian Sommer, Seb. Sommer, Jr., Conrad Stein, P. Schaefer, Schmitt & Koehne, Dan. Winkens, Neidlinger, Schmidt & Co., J. Koenigsberg, Robert Schroeder, David Stevenson, F. G. & J. N. Van Vliet, Tweddle & Pulling, G. E. & G. D. Kitching, S. & F. Uhlmann, A. & E. Schweyer, S. H. Jessup & Son, Wm. Zinsser & Co., Sebastian & Snal, E. Wattenberg, Schlesinger & Steinkampf, Theo. Apfe, Pier Bros., John Weber, Walther G. I. Wheeler, J. Schwarzwaelder, H. Steublog, J. H. Zindel, E. L. Ferry, W. H. Atkin & Son, J. S. & W. Brown, A. & F. Brown, Marx & Rawolle, Weilbacher & Loewi, J. Willes, August Roos, Cook & Radley, H. Keller & Schiffer, G. Blacke & Co., J. Flintoff, A. Schwarz, H. Thalmann, C. Heymann, F. Spies, F. Oliver, S. P. Kuap, J. Trageaer, F. Bender, Parker & Co., G. Wagner, C. Vix, New York City and vicinity; George Brueckner, J. Diehl, John Elchler, P. & W. Ebling, J. Groh, J. & M. Haffen, Jos. & L. F. Knntz, Peter Kirschhoff, Chas. Rivinius, G. Strauss, H. Zeltner, Morrisania and Melrose, N. Y.; Georga Bechtel, Chas. Bischoff, Rubsam & Horrmann, Reinhardt & Mueller, Setz & Diem, Staten Island, N. Y.; D. Bermes, Koehler & Kamena, L. Linnewerth, Peter & Hexamer, Union Hill and Guttenberg, N. J.; P. M. Blegen, Dohka Ferry, N. Y.; A. Luckhardt & Co., New Rochelle, N. Y.; Long Island Brewers' Association, J. Burger, George Distler, Eppig & Fischer, Barbara Fries, Glueck & Scharmann, H. Huguesa & Grass, Goetz & Muench, C. Illig, Charles Illig, S. Liebmann's Sons, H. H. Linnemann, Meltzer Bros., J. Marquardt, Obermeyer & Liebmann, John Schneider, N. Seitz, Sous, R. Selg, P. Schoenwald, Scharnagel & Reitzner, Weiz & Gaiser, Williamsburgh and Brooklyn, N. Y.; Gustavua Bergner, Peter Baltz, J. F. Betz, Georga Enser, J. Gardiner, L. Gross, Christ. Halsch, H. Lawser, William Massey, F. Orth, C. Psotta, G. F. Rothacker, P. Schemm, Christ. Schmidt, John Schlehel, A. Wolf, George H. Becker, W. W. Hughas, William H. Hughes, Philadelphia, Pa.; E. Franenheim, J. Gangwisch, George Gerst, Martin Hechelmann, Henry Heerdt, Gaorge Ober, Gottfried Siedle, G. Wacker, Pittsburg, Pa.; Oliver H. Booth, Poughkeepsie, N. Y.; H. R. Hughes, A. D. King, Pittston, Pa.; D. G. Yuengling, Pottsville, Pa.; Henry Bartholomay, Rochester, N. Y.; Fred. Lauer, P. Barhy, F. Lauer, Jr., Reading, Pa.; E. J. Eacker, D. G. Yuengling, Richmond, Va.; R. Jacobs, St. Louis, Mo.; J. Pfohl, B. Haeberle, Syracuse, N. Y.; Oscar Rocke, Springfield, Mass.; Christ. Mueller, Tiffin, O.; A. L. Ruscher, Troy, N. Y.; C. A. Bates and Louis Schade, official representatives U. S. Government, Washington, D. C.; A. Reymann, Wheeling, W. Va.; George Baer, J. Reichard, Wilkesbarre, Pa.

Chapter XI.

PROHIBITION VOTE IN 1872; COMPARISON WITH GERMAN VOTE. RESULT OF ELECTION; ITS CAUSE NOT APPRECIATED. RUETER'S REPUBLICAN COUNTERPART TO CLAUSEN'S DECLARATION. PROHIBITIONISTS' EFFORTS FOR FEDERAL LEGISLATION AND THEIR CHANGE OF BASE. THIRTEENTH CONVENTION IN CLEVELAND. PERSONAL NOTES. CLAUSEN'S ADDRESS, A VALUABLE HISTORICAL ESSAY. THE STATUS OF THE DRINK-QUESTION REVIEWED. CONFLICTING INTERESTS OF BREWERS AND DISTILLERS; THE LATTER'S INIMICAL ATTITUDE. EFFORTS FAVORING MALT-LIQUORS; WORTH'S BILL BACKED BY POPULAR MOVEMENT. PROHIBITIONISTS CHANGE THEIR TACTICS; THEY ATTACK BEER EXCLUSIVELY; CLAIM IT LEADS TO WHISKEY-DRINKING, DESTROYS PHYSICAL AND MENTAL POWERS AND PRODUCES PAUPERISM AND CRIME; THEY BECOME ALLIES OF DISTILLERS; BREWERS' COUNTER-ARGUMENT SUBMITTED BY CLAUSEN; A MASTERLY ARRAIGNMENT AND REFUTATION; BREWERS' UNEQUIVOCAL RESOLUTION IN REGARD TO IT. MEANS OF PUBLICATION DISCUSSED; OBERMANN'S PLAN ADOPTED. $2,000 APPROPRIATED FOR ESTABLISHING *SENTINEL*. FINANCES OF ASSOCIATION. J. LIEBMANN'S PROPOSITION TO ESTABLISH LITERARY BUREAU LAID UPON TABLE; REASON FOR THIS ACTION. JUDICIAL DECISIONS AS TO PROHIBITION BRIEFLY REVIEWED. THE BARTEMEYER CASE. RUETER ON MASSACHUSETTS TEST CASE; ASSOCIATION ASSUMES DEFENSE. *PERSONNEL* OF CONVENTION AND STRENGTH AND PROSPERITY OF ASSOCIATION. M. KLEINER'S DEATH; BIOGRAPHICAL NOTES AND RESOLUTIONS. FIRST PROHIBITORY BILL IN CONGRESS. INTERNAL REVENUE MATTERS; COMMISSIONER'S FAVORABLE DECISIONS. SCHADE ON IMMIGRATION. PASTEUR'S RESEARCHES. BREWERS' GRAINS AS FEED FOR COWS. LIST OF DELEGATES.

As a demonstration of either moral or numerical strength the independent political action of the Prohibition party in the presidential campaign of 1872 was an utter failure. It would be unduly dignifying its result to compare it to any of the minor revolts by which German Republicans, in various States, sought to convince their party that fealty to the organization could not induce them to vote for nominees of sumptuary proclivities.

The total strength of the prohibitionists, as manifested at the polls, amounted to just 5,508 votes, cast for their presidential candidate, James Black, of Lancaster, Pa.; and to this powerful array of ballots neither Maine nor Vermont contributed a single vote. Nothing was accomplished by this demonstration except, perhaps, to show the weakness of the organization and the folly of liberal voters in allowing these self-constituted reformers to dictate to parties. In every instance a firm course would have defeated them. Thus, to cite but one example, in the year preceding the presidential election, the Republicans of New Jersey had nominated for the gubernatorial chair a well-known friend of sumptuary legislation. The German Republicans, ignoring party affiliations in this particular instance, voted as a body for his Democratic opponent, Joel Parker, but sustained the rest of the Republican ticket. The result was that Parker was elected by a majority of over 6,000 votes, while the rest of the Democratic State ticket was defeated.

Clausen's declaration that he, a lifelong Democrat, would rather vote for Grant than for Greeley, was probably fully appreciated at the time (June 6th, 1872), although the Democratic convention, which ratified Greeley's nomination, did not meet until the succeeding month (July 9th). It was understood that the Democrats, although disappointed that a more moderate Republican had not been nominated at Cincinnati, would, nevertheless, also nominate Greeley, and Clausen's words really foreshadowed what would be and actually was the attitude of both the liberal Republicans and Democrats of German extraction. The whole situation was so exceedingly complicated by a number of conflicting political issues, aside from the principal questions which formed the main lines of demarcation, that it would be impossible to say what particular element of incongruity caused most havoc in the liberal Republican and the Democratic ranks; but there can be no doubt that next to the Democrats' sense of humiliation at being constrained to uphold a man who in every living question was their antipode, the revolt of the mass of liberal Republicans and Democrats, opposed to Greeley's prohibitory predilections, contributed most to Grant's victory. Measured by the standard of popular votes Grant's majority stood almost unparalleled; no greater or more decisive victory had been won by any presidential candidate since 1820. He received unprecedented majorities in every State having a large German-American population, and this fact alone suffices to demonstrate beyond a doubt that, like Clausen, many lifelong Democrats refused to support Greeley on account of his notorious inclination towards prohibitory measures.

The success of the Republican party did not, however, have the effect one might have expected under these circumstances. The victory was too sweeping and complete to induce a calm consideration of the causes which brought it about, and thus it happened that the Republican party in several States again favored the demands of prohibitionists. This applied especially to Massachusetts at the period here in question, and from this State emanated through the mouth of H. H. Rueter (at the thirteenth convention) the Republican counterpart to Clausen's Democratic declaration. In submitting a review of the situation, to which a more extended reference will be made elsewhere, he used these significant words:

"Our citizens of German extraction have almost as a body identified themselves with the Republican party, and have reason to point with pride to many results achieved with their assistance. It is not my purpose to make a futile attempt to wean them from long-cherished political associations and convictions. But it is my purpose to arouse my countrymen to a proper sense of their importance, power and influence within the Republican party, and to call upon them to assert the same and to change from a negative to a positive element of its construction." And if, the speaker argued in the further course of his address, these efforts prove abortive, it becomes the duty of every liberal citizen to sever his connection with the old party.

These two utterances emanating from two leading brewers holding totally different political views and convictions, indicate the drift of sentiments within the association at the time, and in their broader application they virtually reflect the disposition of the mass of voters opposed to prohibition. This period marks, in fact, the real beginning of the prohibitory agitation on national lines, with a trend towards redoubled efforts for constitutional inhibition within the States. And another new feature became manifest at about this time. While formerly all intoxicants were anathematized by prohibitionists with equal vehemence, malt-liquors were now singled out as being especially obnoxious and dangerous.

Of this change of base in the operations of the brewers' opponents the thirteenth convention affords many evidences. This gathering was held on the 4th and 5th days of June, 1873, at Cleveland, then, as now, the second city of the State of Ohio, and a considerable brewing centre even at that time. There is little to be added to what has already been stated relative to the young association of this city. The major part of the trade was in the hands of men who, though immigrated from abroad, had grown up, in an industrial sense, with the community. Among those who took active part in association affairs, a considerable proportion established their breweries in the fourth decade of the century; but the real development of the industry did not begin before the succeeding decade, when Hoffmann (1852),

Schlather (1857), Gehring (1857), and others embarked in the business. The latter, as president of the Cleveland association, opened the thirteenth convention.

Clausen's address on this occasion assumed the character of an historical essay dealing with liquor legislation from the day of the first introduction of the Maine law up to the time of the thirteenth convention. It was probably the very first attempt to summarize in so comprehensive a manner the legal aspect of the temperance movement, and as such, still possesses great value; because, aside from the data which have since been embodied in works of a more permanent character, and which it would, therefore, be useless to recapitulate here, they afford an insight into the gradual development of the laws at present existing in the States embraced within the scope of the review. Maine, it appears, was then, as now, piling amendment upon amendment in order to make the law enforceable; the legislature being compelled to act because official reports showed a frightful prevalence of intemperance and a most flourishing condition of the illicit traffic. New Hampshire fared no better in that year, yet the legislature rejected a Constabulary Bill. In Massachusetts the law permitting the sale of malt-liquors was abrogated. Connecticut had just adopted a stringent license-system in place of the old prohibitory law. The legislature of New York had during the Winter session of 1873 revived the former local-option law, but Governor Dix vetoed it. The Attorney-General of New Jersey in a masterly argument declared that the local-option law was unconstitutional. In Pennsylvania the first elections under local-option, introduced in the previous year, showed a strong public sentiment in favor of licensing the traffic. In Ohio, were the traffic was and is prohibited by constitutional injunction, the Adair-Act, being in effect a civil-damage law, was being tested as to its constitutionality. Illinois had also just adopted a civil-damage law, and prohibitionists endeavored to secure their favorite enactment. In these efforts they encountered the determined opposition of Governor Palmer and Bishop Foley, who both characterized compulsory measures of this nature as unreasonable, unjust and tyrannical. In Iowa the prohibitory law had been qualified by the requirement of a bond of $3,000, from every person selling liquors, and the limitation of the profits from such sale to 33 per cent. The Indiana license-law forbade selling on Sunday and restricted the traffic on week days to sales of liquors not to be drunk upon the sellers' premises.

The brewers fully understood that all restrictive laws had the invariable effect of curtailing the consumption of malt-liquors; while, by favoring a surreptitious traffic not amenable to any restraint whatever, they really tended to increase the consumption of ardent spirits. The distillers certainly appreciated this result, and this may explain their seeming indifference to the prohibitory agitation. In more recent years they have covertly assisted and sometimes openly favored such legislation. The manifest intention of very many of the most eminent statesmen to encourage the use of malt-liquors—a desire as old as the temperance movement itself, having been formulated in our country by Benjamin Rush and Alexander Hamilton—seems to have exasperated the distillers all the more, because in establishing a broad discrimination in the classification of the two kinds of drinks (referred to in the preceding chapter) Congress recognized the justice of the brewers' claim and imparted a strong impetus to the movement just then inaugurated in favor of State legislation encouraging the brewing industry. From the newspapers of the period it appears that very strong efforts were being made in that direction in several States, notably in New York, where Assemblyman Jacob Worth submitted a bill exempting lager-beer from the operation of all excise-laws. A mass-meeting of citizens of Kings County at once endorsed this bill and in a very exhaustive argument presented a powerful array of reasons why it should be passed. They asserted that owing to its small percentage of alcohol, the refreshing properties of its carbonic acid gas, the tonic properties of hops, and the nutritive quality of the extract of malt, beer is a wholesome and necessary beverage, grateful to the appetite and beneficial to the human constitution; that as a national beverage it is consistent with habits of sobriety and temperance; that in countries where its sale and consumption are protected and fostered by the government, crime as the result of intemperance is unknown; that it is the habitual beverage of that large proportion of citizens of the United States who are noted alike for their social geniality, their love of law and order, and their thrift and industry; that if protected and encouraged by wise laws, the use of beer will diminish the consumption of that class of beverages which, if indulged in to excess, are an incentive to crime. Worth, representing a large German-American constituency, surely required no urging on the part of the brewers to induce him to offer this bill. In his own argument he showed clearly that he was familiar with the various scientific investigations, chief among them that of Dr. Bowditch of Massachusetts, which gave to the ideas he advocated the character of irrefutable maxims.

No sooner had this agitation assumed definite shape, than the prohibitionists completely changed their base of operation, propounding, in the face of inconvertible testimony to the contrary, the theory that beer-drinking leads to whiskey-drinking, destroys the physical constitution, impairs the mental powers, vitiates the human stock, promotes pauperism and crime, demoralizes people and renders them insensible to the finer mental processes and moral emotions. The war between the brewers and prohibitionists now fairly began on these well-defined lines and has ever since been carried on with increasing vehemence, the antagonism of the total-abstainers growing in virulence and blind fanaticism in proportion to the countless discomfitures which they sustained at the ballot-box whenever the people had an opportunity of voting upon prohibition pure and simple, disentangled from political and partisan considerations. Virtually these prohibitionists now became the allies of the distillers. When the thirteenth convention met, their absurd assertions had just become generally known, and Clausen then and there presented the first counter-argument, written by an author whose name, unfortunately, is not preserved in our records. It could not have been either Flintoff or Lewis. Judging from the style and certain palpable indications of a scientific (probably medical) training, one might be inclined to attribute the essay to a gentleman who as poet, author, lecturer, and statesman has acquired a national reputation, and who, several years after the thirteenth convention, became one of the most formidable opponents of prohibition. The author proceeded in a thoroughly methodical way. The claim that beer-drinking leads to whiskey-drinking, was disposed of by a statistical exhibit showing that whereas the consumption of malt-liquors in the United States was steadily increasing, the consumption of whiskey, instead of increasing in proportionate ratio and in accordance with our rapidly growing population, actually showed a comparative decrease. The experience of other countries, in which malt-liquors are the popular beverage, and in which the consumption of beer has practically driven ardent spirits out of the market as a common drink, was also cited in refutation of this argument.

That beer-drinking destroys the physical constitution and impairs the mental powers and so vitiates the human stock, was still easier to disprove, the author simply comparing the sturdy Teutonic races with their notable physical endurance and strength, as displayed in their capacity for hard work and their bearing in many a hard-fought campaign, with the more volatile Latin races; the sturdy German immigrants and dwellers in States in which a goodly allowance of wholesome malt-liquor is consumed, to the lean, lank residents of Prohibition States; and showing by statistics that the physical stamina of the latter is steadily deteriorating. In the same manner, the mental capacity of the two classes was also compared, and it was easy to prove that the beer-drinking nations could claim their full share of the world's great intellects.

The assertion that beer-drinking promotes pauperism and crime was disposed of with the aid of statistics collected in the prohibition, the beer-drinking and the whiskey-drinking States and for the whole country, the resulting comparison showing that pauperism and the number of convictions for crime invariably decrease as the consumption of malt-liquor increases.

The effect of the consumption of beer on the finer mental processes and moral emotions of a people was revealed in the statistics concerning education and church-work collected in the different States. Maine and New Jersey were especially contrasted by the author. Taking the census of 1870 as the basis of his parallel, he showed how in Maine the population as compared with that of New Jersey was as 628 to 906, or over two-thirds; the value of church property, in

1870, was $5,200,853; it had 1,102 churches, capable of seating 376,038 people, and 1,079 Sunday-school libraries, with 277,742 volumes. In New Jersey, the same year, the church property was worth $18,347,150, with 1,384 churches, capable of seating 573,303 people, and 1,619 Sunday-school libraries, with 423,224 volumes. Maine issued 65 newspapers, with an aggregate circulation of 9,687,680 copies; New Jersey, 122 newspapers, with a circulation of 18,625,740 copies. Maine appropriated for public schools $841,526; New Jersey, $1,441,550. The wealth of the latter beer-drinking State, the value of her factories, her farms, her shipping, etc., exceeded that of prohibitory Maine in such a large measure as to render a comparison fairly ludicrous.

The theory that beer must necessarily injure the health of the consumer because it contains alcohol, and because alcohol, even if diluted, is a poison and must, if taken in certain quantities, destroy life, was met by comparing alcohol, as one of the constituents of beer, with other products entering into our daily food, aye, even into the very air we breathe; products which, when undiluted, are capable of exercising fatally toxic effects. Deprecating the excessive consumption of beer, as being equally as injurious as the excessive use of any other article of food, the author praised its use in moderation as conducive, according to the best and most convincing evidence, to cheerfulness, health and long life. He called attention to the fact that the greater number, if not all of the leaders of the so-called temperance party, are well aware that their arguments cannot be sustained by facts; that they know from experience that all prohibitory laws thus far enacted only tend to increase drunkenness, and that moral suasion, coupled with the removal of restrictions on the use of the milder stimulants, is the only method of ensuring temperance.

Though lacking in statistical comprehensiveness this essay surpassed the Prohibitionists' twaddle in every thing that tends to make an argument logical, strong and convincing.

It must be borne in mind that the advocates of prohibition always viewed the opposition to their schemes as an evidence of the perversity of the German-Americans, and that in transferring their activity to the political arena, they aimed, as has been shown, or endeavored to aim, a blow at this class of voters, who, by the way, took up the gauntlet readily enough. But this new move on the part of the prohibitionists, joined to the more than dubious attitude of the distillers, also exercised a very decided influence upon the course of the brewers' association, and became a determining factor in more than one direction. To begin with, it strenghtened the position of those who at the preceding convention had advocated an open declaration in favor of State laws of the nature and purport of the Worth bill, and it obliterated the last trace of hesitancy that many brewers had hitherto evinced in the matter, fearing a disruption of their relations with the dealers.

In the resolution adopted at the thirteenth convention this mutation in the views and aims of the brewers is clearly reflected; they were drafted by as strong a body of representative men from all parts of the country as the chair could possibly have selected from the list of available delegates. It consisted of F. Lauer, J. Greenway, J. Scheu, H. H. Rueter, J. Obermann, J. F. Betz, J. Gardiner, C. Moerlein, H. C. Bemis, M. Weiss and H. Hofbauer. The passages relating to the subject now under consideration read as follows, viz.:

"*Resolved*, That this Congress emphatically protests against the prohibitionists' attempt to classify brewers and dealers in malt-liquors with distillers and dealers in distilled liquors; and that every member of this Congress pledges himself to defend and maintain a proper distinction between the two lines of trade.

"*Resolved*, That by means of local and general associations, brewers' meetings, public assemblies and private influence, and by the encouragement of publications and the circulation of statements, newspaper articles and general literature, advocating sound views on the malt-liquor question, we endeavor to render nugatory teetotal misrepresentation, and thereby save our business from the serious detriment and annoyance which threatens it; and it is further

"*Resolved*, That this Congress hails with satisfaction the growing public sentiment in favor of relieving malt-liquors from oppressive legislation, and hereby tender their thanks to the editors of the various newspapers and other periodicals who have, in their editorial columns, shown the impropriety of classifying malt-liquors with ardent spirits in the enactment of laws regulating their sale."

So far as a literary propaganda through the newspapers was contemplated, the delegates could not ignore the immense difficulties which would have to be overcome, nor could they fail to see that the pecuniary means of the association would not suffice to accomplish a ten-thousandth part of the work that would be absolutely required. The trade-journals, though ably managed and brilliantly edited, could not serve the purpose, and an attempt to present the brewers' case in suitable form to the editors of the larger newspapers throughout the country would have required a literary force entirely beyond the reach of the trade. It was one thing to determine upon certain desirable measures, and quite another to execute them. Discussions in which T. Straub, C. G. Stifel, A. Stephan, H. H. Rueter, P. Schemm, C. Boss, in short the best minds of the convention participated, only tended to emphasize this difficulty. The only practicable method seemed to be that proposed by Obermann to the effect that the local associations be requested to cause suitable literature to be published at their own expense within their respective cities or districts. This perplexing condition of things, the disparity between aims and means, gave rise, however, to two other propositions of the most far-reaching importance, one of which was carried out immediately, while the other was held in abeyance until a more opportune moment had arrived for its realization. The former emanated from G. Bergner, the author of so many important measures, and was to the effect that as great necessity existed for the publication in the English language, and at the seat of the Federal Government, of a newspaper representing the cause of personal liberty as opposed to prohibitory fanaticism, the Executive Committee should be authorized to expend $2,000; it being understood that Louis Schade, who modestly suggested this small amount, would receive this sum for the purpose of establishing the *Washington Sentinel*. As another surplus of $10,000 over and above the sum already invested in interest-bearing bonds had been reported by the Finance Committee (P. Schemm, G. Ehret and G. A. Bassermann), with the recommendation that it be similarly invested, Bergner's proposition seemed all the more feasible and acceptable. It was adopted then and there, although not without creating considerable strife, which was finally allayed by the conciliatory efforts of H. H. Rueter and Emil Schandein, the latter of whom, subsequently one of the most assiduous workers and most effective speakers of the trade, made his *debut* on this occasion.

The other proposition originated in the Brewers' Association of Long Island and came before the convention through the agency of Joseph Liebmann, then the president of that body. It was virtually to the effect that a central literary bureau be established and maintained by the trade for the very purposes outlined in the resolutions just quoted. The recommendations embraced in this document read as follows:

"1. That a central committee be appointed whose chief duty it shall be to oppose prohibitory and unduly restrictive legislation in all the States represented in the association.

2. That this committee cause to be prepared, printed and distributed suitable literature upon all subjects affecting the industry, and that local associations be requested to co-operate with this committee in every effort designed to secure the most reliable information and statistical material from the various States.

3. That the committee be authorized to employ one or more secretaries capable of preparing scientific essays upon all subjects relating to the trade's interest."

In somewhat rough and general outlines this scheme corresponds, as the reader will have noticed, with the fundamental characteristics of the present literary bureau; hence, to Joseph Liebmann and his local association belongs the credit and the distinction of having given the first impulse towards the establishment of what in after-years proved to be by far the most useful and effective institution of the organized trade. The motion to lay the matter upon the table (made by C. Schmitt of Cleveland), and adopted by the convention, must not be construed as an evidence of the delegates' disapproval of the plan. The association had already undertaken the defrayal of all expenses arising from litigations designed to test the constitutionality of prohibition before the highest tribunal of the land, and the extent of the obligations thus assumed could not be computed beforehand. It would not, therefore, have been in harmony with the conservative, cautious and business-like methods of the Executive to countenance another plunge into expensive ventures, the limit of which could not well be foretold with any degree of accuracy. At any rate the records, which are exceptionally meagre upon this point, show that the Executive Committee recommended a postponement of the scheme on this ground only. But besides this there was another consideration which might have been urged against the plan at that particular time. A political journal was about to be established at Washington, and it remained to be seen in what measure and degree its editor would accomplish the objects enumerated in the resolution, and to what extent he would succeed in securing to the trade a hearing before the American people through the medium of his exchanges.

The casual reference in this and the preceding chapter to the brewers' attempt to test the constitutionality of prohibitory laws might be misconstrued by those unfamiliar with the subject, unless an explanation be given as to the nature of the particular case under consideration. The possibility of such a misconstruction is all the greater, because the average reader's mind will involuntarily revert to more recent test-suits, which are unlike these earlier cases in many respects. The earliest judicial decision on the subject, frequently quoted in prohibitory arguments, is the one rendered by the United States Supreme Court in the year 1847. It did not involve all the essential elements of modern prohibition, nor did it dispose of the question of compensation for property destroyed through the operation of restrictive laws. But the decision clearly conceded to the States the right to restrain the traffic even to the point of entire suppression. A prohibitory law formed the basis of a subsequent judicial decision (1856) by the New York State Court of Appeals in which it was held that the destruction of property in liquors was in direct violation of the constitutional provision that no person should be deprived of property without due process of law. These were the two decisions, bearing on the subject, which previous to the period now under consideration were most frequently quoted and referred to in public discussions. The trade's opponents pretended to believe that it was a waste to time for the brewers to again test the constitutionality of these laws, seeing that the Supreme Court had already decided adversely; but the friends of personal liberty, leaving aside even the points before mentioned, argued differently. They knew, if the chronicler may be permitted to quote himself,* that in those days everything was made subservient to, or sacrificed for, the principle of States' Rights; and, what is more, they recollected (and their adversaries, who constantly prate about a parallel between abolition and prohibition, might occasionally recollect) that from the very same Justice who thus immolated personal liberty upon the sacrificial altar of State sovereignty, also emanated the infamous Dred Scott decision, a piece of judicial despotism, as the Republican party styled it, which the people overthrew together with the institution in whose favor it was perpetrated. Knowing this, they hoped that in a more enlightened period the old decisions might be reversed in favor of the fundamental principles of liberty and natural justice. Besides, as has already been stated, the modern cases involved points of law not previously adjudicated upon.

The case which the Washington Committee had been instructed, at the twelfth convention, to defend on behalf of the association was the first of that series of litigations which in recent years culminated in the well-known decisions in the Kansas cases. It was the suit of Bartemeyer *vs.* Iowa, involving, it was erroneously believed, the rights of private property, and the duty of the government to protect every citizen in the enjoyment of his rights. W. T. Dittoe had originally been retained to defend this suit, and the committee confirmed this appointment under instructions from the association.

---

* See Up to Date under caption "Judicial Decisions."

Both Dittoe's argument and the decision, which latter was not rendered until some time after this convention, will be reviewed elsewhere.

In connection with this matter it is of interest to learn that the Washington Committee at that time labored under the impression that it was the duty of the national body to assume the defense of all suits involving the prohibitory principle even before they reached the United States Courts in the ordinary course of appellate proceedings. This view, differing essentially from present-day methods, came to the surface when H. H. Rueter— whose speeches were then looked upon as an indispensable feature of every convention—narrated the status of the beer-question in Massachusetts. As has been stated elsewhere, the legislature of that State had annulled the law exempting the manufacture and sale of malt-liquors from the operations of the prohibitory law; but in their usual hypocritical endeavor to curry favor with the farmers, they left cider, a far more intoxicating drink than beer, free from any restraint whatever. How this was possible in a State where scientific enquiries, to which the brightest minds of the world contributed, had demonstrated the desirability of encouraging the use of fermented drinks, was explained by Rueter in these words, viz.:

"Owing to political barter and arrangement of reciprocity between our prohibitory organizations and many members of the ruling Republican party, aided by the circumstance that last year's elections included the presidential one, it has become possible for a faction without any great political power in itself, so to shape our legislature, that, notwithstanding earnest endeavors on our part, our State has been put under a most stringent prohibitory law, which puts under the same legal ban all distilled and fermented liquors, with the only exception of cider. Cider with 10 per cent. alcohol is left to our country people to make or to drink *ad libitum*, while beer and ale with 4 to 6 per cent. are taken from our city dweller and put under prohibition, so that virtually we have at present a law which subjects a citizen to fine and imprisonment in the house of correction for an act, which the law sanctions and protects in another citizen of the same State, an injustice and an outrage so glaring that in itself it should be sufficient to condemn this law in the eye of every fair-minded man. But our prohibitionists found it necessary to make this sacrifice of principle, or better this concession, to our farmers and cider producers and drinkers, through whose instrumentality they mainly work their nefarious schemes, because they would not have secured their co-operation for the suppression of all other alcoholic beverages if the list had included their favorite drink—cider."

Lauer immediately proposed that the national association should assume the expense of testing the constitutionality of this law, and Stifel, Schemm and Bassermann coincided with him; the former moving that $2,000, be appropriated for the purpose. Rueter evidently entertained a different opinion concerning the proper functions of the parent association; he probably held that a test case should be brought in the State Courts by the local association, and that the national body ought to assume the further prosecution of it, if by reason of an adverse decision an appeal to the Federal Courts became necessary. At all events, he candidly stated that he had no instructions to ask for assistance, as his association intended to bring the law before the proper courts at their own expense. In spite of this utterance, the convention adopted the following resolution, viz.:

"*Resolved*, That the Committee on Agitation and the Executive are empowered by this convention to bring the local prohibitory law of Massachusetts and the local-option law of Iowa before the Supreme Court of the United States to test their constitutionality."

Concerning the *personnel* of this convention the list of delegates at the end of this chapter affords an excellent criterion. Many new men took a silent part in the proceedings, and not a few, who had hitherto been passive spectators, now took an active part. The membership had increased and the organization had extended its operations to the States on the Pacific Coast. There is perhaps no better or more reliable indication of the growth of the body that the list of the convention officers, and the Agitation Committee. The former, submitted by Kuntz, Schemm, Hull, Obermann and J. Kauffmann comprised these names:

Vice-Presidents: John Greenway, Syracuse, N.Y.; Jacob Ruppert, New York, N. Y.; Jos. Hensler and J. H. Ballantine, Newark, N. J.; John Gardiner, Philadelphia, Pa.; A. J. Springer, Lancaster, Pa.; C. Boss, Cincinnati, O.; Fred. Haltnorth, Cleveland, O.; M. Brank, Chicago, Ill.; Anton Meyer, Bloomington, Ill.; J. Leisy, Keokuk, Iowa; H. Hoffbauer, Buffalo, Iowa; C. Koehler, Wm. J. Lemp, St. Louis, Mo.; E. Schandein, Fred. Falk, Milwaukee, Wis.; R. Portner, Alexandria, Va.; A. Reymann, Wheeling, W. Va.; L. Muth, J. H. Von der Horst, Baltimore, Md.; H. H. Rueter, A. J. Houghton, Boston, Mass.; George A. Bassermann, New Haven, Conn.; Fred. Claus, Bridgeport, Conn.; C. Geissbauer, Covington, Ky.; P. Schillinger, Louisville, Ky.; Chas. Wagner, Lafayette, Ind.; P. Lieber, Indianapolis, Ind.; F. Fortmann, San Francisco, Cal.; J. Hartmann, Wilmington, Del. Secretaries: Gustavus Bergner, Philadelphia, Pa.; Andrew E. Leicht, Chicago, Ill.; A. F. Dobler, Albany, N. Y.; W. H. Hull, New Haven, Conn.

The Agitation Committee was a particularly strong and representative body; it consisted of: Frederick Lauer of Reading, Pa., Chairman of the Committee, and Vice-President of the Executive Committee. William Massey, Gustavus Bergner and John F. Betz of Philadelphia, Pa.; Theo. F. Straub and George Gerst of Pittsburg, Pa.; Adolph Schalk and John H. Ballantine of Newark, N. J.; Henry Clausen and Peter Amerman of New York, N. Y.; J. Greenway of Syracuse, N. Y.; Henry Bartholomay of Rochester, N. Y.; Gerhard Lang, J. Haberstroh, Wm. W. Sloan and M. Beck of Buffalo, N. Y.; Christ. Moerlein, Christ. Boss and J. Hauck of Cincinnati, O.; C. E. Gehring and Fred. Haltnorth of Cleveland, O.; Chas. Stifel, C. Koehler, J. L. Schlossstein, St. Louis, Mo.; Conrad Seipp, M. Brand and

P. Bartholomae of Chicago, Ill.; J. Obermann, A. Blatz and Emil Schandein, Milwaukee, Wis.; R. Portner, Alexandria, Va.; A. Reymann, Wheeling, W. Va.; L. Muth, J. Seeger, J. H. Von der Horst, Baltimore, Md.; John Wahl, Monroe, Mich.; Alfred Werthmueller, Burlington, Iowa; A. Richardson, J. Pfaff, H. H. Rueter, A. J. Houghton, Boston, Mass.; G. A. Bassermann, W. H. Hull, New Haven, Conn.; J. Fehrenbach, Wilmington, Del.; Peter Weber, Louisville, Ky.; Chas. Wagner, Lafayette, Ind.; F. Fortmann, San Francisco, Cal.; G. Auer, New Orleans, La.; Louis Lange, Fernandina, Fla.; F. Rennert, New Braunfels, Texas; J. Seeger, Columbia, S. C.

The association's gain in membership and in affiliated associations; its prosperous condition and the successes achieved during recent years were offset in a measure by the loss of one of its most meritorious, capable, active and disinterested members—Meinrod Kleiner, of Cincinnati, whose name, prominently connected with every important measure, appears upon so many pages of this history. Born in Prussia, he settled in Cincinnati where he soon rose to distinction among his fellow-citizens, honored and respected for the liberality that characterized his participation in every enterprise which had for its object the enhancement of public interest and the welfare of his city. These words are taken from a resolution adopted by the Cincinnati Board of Trade, of which Kleiner had been vice-president. He was, in fact, one of the founders and incorporators of that body, in which were represented all the vast mercantile and industrial interests of the city. Eulogies were delivered by Simpkinson, Macneale, Pierson, Jones and Mitchell, all men of the very highest social and commercial standing in their community. The Brewers' Association placed on record this well-deserved tribute, drafted by Bergner, Portner and Schandein, acting as a committee on condolence, viz.:

"*Resolved*, That in the demise of our member, Meinrod Kleiner, whom most of us remember in the enjoyment of robust health and the full power of manhood, we recognize the proof that an Almighty Power gives us of the uncertainty of life, and submit in resignation to the irreparable loss. *Resolved*, That we mourn over his grave as that of one of the pioneers of our association, at the founding of which he assisted, and one of the most earnest champions, not only of our rights, but of human rights in general."

In advocating the establishment of an English newspaper at Washington, Bergner expressed the apprehension that the prohibitionists would seek to influence Federal legislation in the succeeding session of Congress. He evidently did not know that they had already done so. At their solicitation Vice-President Wilson caused to be introduced into the United States Senate a prohibitory bill for the District of Columbia; it was referred to the District Committee, of which Senator Pomeroy, of Kansas, held the chairmanship. Had not Pomeroy been under a dense cloud by reason of corruption and bribery openly charged against him, the bill would in all likelihood have been reported favorably, although at that stage of its parliamentary progress it would surely have expired like so many similar measures proposed since that time. The mention of this fact will serve to fix the date of the beginning of our opponents' surprisingly persistent and equally unsuccessful Congressional agitation.

In matters relating to the Internal Revenue the new Act, now generally called the brewers' law, worked satisfactorily, leaving scarcely any room for just complaint. True, in its execution, the commissioner promulgated regulations relative to the gauging of vessels and the branding of casks with a United States mark, which would have entailed upon the trade considerable expense and unnecessary hardship and annoyance; but when the brewers' committee, consisting of Amerman, Clausen, Howard, Flanagan, Jones, Schaefer, Ballantine, Schalk, Massey, Lauer, Bergner, Betz, Rueter, Greenway and Lewis, called upon and showed him how useless, unjust and burdensome his regulations would be, if put into operation throughout the country, he immediately rescinded them. At the same time he gave positive assurance that he would neither advocate nor even countenance any of the renewed schemes of speculators who endeavored to foist stamp-cancellers, facetiously styled instruments of torture, upon the industry. Although the convention report does not give the reason for the commissioner's favorable decision in this matter, it is well known that an investigation made by the revenue collectors throughout the country, under instructions from the Commissioner, showed that frauds which the stamp-canceller was ostensibly designed to prevent, were almost unknown;—another evidence of the honesty and integrity of the trade. Reports of collectors, to which the chronicler recently obtained access, proved that losses sustained by the fraudulent use of stamps did not amount to one-twentieth of one per cent.

Both Flintoff and Schade spoke at this convention, the latter dilating in a very able manner upon the spirit of Knownothingism which, as we have seen, played no inconsiderable part in the prohibitory movement. Among other interesting items he presented the following summary of a pamphlet he had published in 1855. and to which we have already referred:

> But does this great and beautiful country belong to the Pilgrims and their bigoted descendants ? I say emphatically, No ! Let these figures speak for themselves. The basis of calculation is the following: In 1790, when the first census was taken the population of the United States, including white and colored persons, was 3,231,930. If all increase from immigration had been cut off, the surplus of births over deaths would have constituted the only growth in our

population. In 1850 that increase was 1.38 per cent. In 1870 it was 1.57 per cent. Now, if we assume that the population of 1790 would have increased every year 1.38 per cent., what would be the white and free colored population in 1870? The following table will explain that:

1790................3,231,930	1840................6,413,161
1800................3,706,674	1850................7,355,423
1810................4,251,143	1860................8,435,882
1820................4,875,600	1870................9,675,164
1830................5,591,775	

The actual population of the United States in 1870, excluding the slave population freed by the last war, was, however, 34,125,999. The immigrants since 1790 and their descendants numbered, therefore, in 1870, no less than 24,450,835.

To prove the correctness of this result I give the actual increase and percentage of several European countries during that period:

		Increase.
England and Wales in 1790	8,675,000	2.61 per cent.
England and Wales in 1871	22,704,108	
Prussia in 1797	8,660,000	2.34 per cent.
Without the new acquisitions in 1866....	20,268,097	
France in 1789.	26,000,000	1.46 per cent.
France in 1866........................	38,192,064	
United States in 1790..................	3,231,930	2.96 per cent.
Without immigration in 1870...........	9,675,164	

It will be seen that if the United States had had in 1870 only 9,675,164, about as many as they in reality had in 1825, they would still have increased more than the most prosperous and progressive nations in Europe actually did. The immigration since 1790 has therefore advanced this country nearly fifty years!

To the brewing industry of the world the time of the thirteenth convention marks the beginning of a new epoch. It was towards the end of the year 1872 that Pasteur's theory on his *bières de la revanche nationale* became generally known through the spirited discussions it evoked in the Academy of Sciences and the Institute. In the preceding year the eminent scientist, who attributed to the use of beer the physical superiority of the German soldiers over those of his native lands, had completed his researches, and now presented to France, as one of his eulogists expressed it, the sublime revenge of genius in the gift of a simple and economical method of brewing. Foreign trade-journals of the period, although they reported in detail the methods of Pasteur, seemed inclined to mildly ridicule the claims of the Frenchman, and this inclination arose probably from the peculiarly Gallic grandiloquence with which the discovery was heralded, and the somewhat incongruous relation between a scientific achievement and the desire for national revenge. To-day the brewers gratefully appreciate the advancement of their art through these efforts, and in brewing circles there is no name more sincerely honored and revered than that of Pasteur. His *Etudes sur la Bière* is a scientific work of the first magnitude, and his contributions to our knowledge of the chemistry and physiology of fermentation; on the micro-organism and secondary products of alcoholic fermentation, pure yeast in brewing, and kindred subjects were really "epoch-making" achievements. The thirteenth convention did not discuss this subject, but there can be no doubt that it had attracted attention in the American trade, always eager and ready to adopt improvements in any branch of brewing.

The utilization of brewers' grains as food for cattle gave rise in 1872 to a controversy which, although the association took neither notice of, nor action upon it, deserves special mention. Complaints had been made, it seems, by residents of the city of New York living in the neighborhood of breweries, that the removal of brewers' grains beyond the city limits was not attended to with sufficient care to prevent offensive odors due to the putrefaction of the material. The Board of Health investigated the matter and found that the complaints were groundless. At the same time the chemist of the

Board analyzed this by-product of the brewery, and in his report declared it to be a most valuable nutriment, particularly for milch-cows, as the grain retains nearly all the phosphates and a large proportion of its fatty and oleaginous compounds. Upon the application of several breweries the Board did, however, formulate rules and regulations for the shipment of malt-refuse by rail. Professor Chandler, the eminent chemist, who lived and had a lecture-room in the immediate vicinity of F. & M. Schaefer's brewery—whence grains were to be shipped on the Harlem Railroad through Park Avenue—published a letter stating that, being personally interested by reason of the proximity of his house to a brewery, he had investigated the matter and felt justified both as "the occupant of a house on that avenue and as one specially interested in sanitary reforms in giving his consent that these grains be sent daily up the Harlem Railroad in open cars to be loaded on the avenue." He added his testimony as a chemist to that of the Health Board relative to the healthfulness and nutritiousness of brewers' grains as feed for milch-cows.—In the course of our narrative this subject will receive further attention, as in after-years it became a source of great annoyance to the trade by reason of the schemes of blackmailers and others.

Excepting the adoption of the usual temperance and revenue resolutions, the appropriation of a subsidy for the two trade-journals, and the formal acceptance of the Boston association's invitation to hold the next meeting in their city, this convention adopted no other measures worthy of note.

The year 1873 is a memorable one in the history of the United States; the events which made it so occurred a few months after this meeting, when the country was suddenly convulsed by one of the most disastrous panics on record. We mention this because at the next convention the brewers felt impelled by the extraordinary condition of affairs to publish a document which ranks very high among the official utterances of the association.*

---

* The following is a list of delegates present at the thirteenth convention:

A. F. Dobler, Albany, N. Y.; J. F. Stoll, Troy, N. Y.; W. Lehmann, Adrian, Mich.; R. Portner, Alexandria, Va.; W. Braun, Amherst, O.; F. Oberholtz, F. Horix, Akron, O.; L. Muth, J. C. Roosmarck, J. Schreier, J. H. Von der Horst, Baltimore, Md.; A. J. Houghton, H. H. Rueter, Boston, Mass.; M. Beck, C. Gerber, J. F. Jost, J. F. Kuhn, Gerhard Lang, Jacob Schen, W. W. Sloan, C. Weyand, D. Bain, John Irlbacher, Henry Diehl, Henry Dilcher, Nicholas Scherf, Felix Berger, Henry Rathman, George Fischer, Joseph Diebold, John Gerriston, C. F. Bitter, John Streich, Buffalo, N. Y.; Anton Meyer, Bloomington, Ill.; J. Baehr, A. Burkhardt, John A. Bischop, Braun & Schneider, John Davis, C. Fovargue, C. Gehring, P. Griebel, F. Haltnorth, J. M. Hughes, Hughes & Rogers, Chas. Jahraus, J. Koestle, J. Kraus & Co., Lloyd & Keys, J. Muth & Sons, J. Mail, William Oppmann, L. Schlather, M. Stumpf, Schmidt & Hoffmann, C. Sutter, E. Akley, Griffith Bros., J. Heinz, P. Mueller & Co., F. D. Phelps, A. Rauchfuss, Putnam; Akley, Stovering & Co., J. B. Smith, M. M. Spangler & Co., Cleveland, O.; George A. Bassermann, W. H. Hull, New Haven, Conn.; C. Boss, John Kaufmann, C. Moerlein, J. Schneider, A. Schmid, P. Weyand, L. Burger, Chas. Berkhemer. J. Geiger, M. Johnson, A. Schwill, Cincinnati, O.; H. Cordes, San Francisco, Cal.; H. V. Bemis, F. Bartholomae, M. Brand, F. Binz, A. E. Leicht, Conrad Seipp, P. Schoenhofen, K. G. Schmidt, J. C. Huck, Chicago, Ill.; R. Quaif, A. Shaw, S. Aub, Cooperstown, N. Y.; C. Schwind, Dayton, O.; H. Fink, Dunkirk, N. Y.; E. W. Voigt, Thomas D. Hawley, Detroit, Mich.; H. Kalcelage, Erie, Pa.; Green & Son, Hubbardsville, N. Y.; H. Hoffbauer, Buffalo, Iowa; J. Leisy, Keokuk, Iowa; C. Muensenberger, Kenosha, Wis.; J. A. Springer, Lancaster, Pa.; F. Wagner, Lafayette, Ind.; G. Doerschuck, Otto Huber, Long Island, N. Y.; L. W. Falk, Jacob Obermann, E. Schandein, Milwaukee, Wis.; J. Prentice, Monroeville, Ohio; John Wahl, Monroe, Mich.; Ott Bros., Norwalk, O.; Jos. Hensler, F. Geissele, L. Angster, Newark, N. J.; Jacob Ahles, Peter Ahles, J. C. Boettner, H. Claueen, W. Eckert, George Ehret, Andrew Finck, August Finck, A. Huepfel, J. Ruebsam, H. Reinhardt, Henry Elias, John Flintoff, A. Geiger, A. Neidlinger, F. Beringer, W. Fontaine, Theo. Krausch, J. Koenigsberg, Moritz Kopp, Albert Meyer, A. Roeck, Chas. Stoll, W. Spittler, F. Uhlmann, W. G. I. Wheeler, R. Katzenmayer, G. Grassmann, J. March, New York, N. Y.; H. P. Luce, J. Ackermann, Oneida, N. Y.; Gustavus Bergner, J. F. Betz, John Gardiner, T. C. Engel, G. Enser, Peter Schemm, Jos. Gormley, W. W. Hughes, George Goldthorpe, J. M. Smith, L. Schulze, Philadelphia, Pa.; V. Frank, Poughkeepsie, N. Y.; William Berger, C. Eberhardt, J. Frauenheim, John Gangwisch, John M. Hammel, Theo. Lutz, John P. Ober, Gottlieb Siedle, Theo. Straub, Pittsburg and Allegheny, Pa.; John Dick, Quincy, Ill.; H. Bartholomay, Rochester, N. Y.; F. Laner, Reading, Pa.; B. Miller, W. C. Schaefer, G. Lang, Steubenville, O.; C. Koehler, Chas. Stifel, Math. Weiss, St. Louis, Mo.; John Greenway, Syracuse, N. Y.; J. Fox, J. Kuebler, Sandusky, O.; Jas. Grasser, A. Stephan, F. Lange, Toledo, O.; Christ. Mueller, Tiffin, O.; George Zent, Tonawanda, N. Y.; D. D. Pier, Utica, N. Y.; H. C. Rogers, Louis Schade, Washington, D. C.; John Daul, Williamsville, N. Y.; A. Reymann, Wheeling, W. Va.

Chapter XII.

NEW ENGLAND ASSOCIATION; FRANK JONES ITS PRESIDENT; PERSONAL NOTE. BREWING AND LIQUOR LAWS IN NEW HAMPSHIRE, MAINE, MASSACHUSETTS, RHODE ISLAND AND CONNECTICUT. THE WOMAN'S CRUSADE; ITS CAUSE AND PLACE OF ORIGIN; MOTHER STEWART; DIO LEWIS ORGANIZES THE WOMEN OF HILLSBORO; WHAT THEY ACCOMPLISHED. LEWIS' THEORY; HIS CHARACTER; ORIGIN OF WASHINGTONIANS. FOURTEENTH CONVENTION, CLAUSEN'S ADDRESS; RECOMMENDS AN APPEAL TO THE PEOPLE; QUOTES *TRIBUNE* ON CRUSADE. DR. HAMMOND AGAINST PROHIBITION AND ON USE AND ABUSE OF DRINK; WISHES TO SEE BREWING ENCOURAGED. BISMARCK'S DRINKING HABIT. MINISTER FRANCIS ON SOBRIETY OF BEER-DRINKERS; PERTINENT STATISTICS. PROHIBITIONISTS' STATEMENT AS TO DEATHS CAUSED BY ALCOHOL, DISPROVED BY STATISTICS; AMUSING INCIDENT. COMMISSION BILL INTRODUCED IN CONGRESS; SCHURZ AND BAYARD OPPOSE IT; CONSISTENT ATTITUDE OF BREWERS TOWARDS IT. INTERNAL AFFAIRS; NEW MEN; W. A. MILES. CONVENTION OFFICERS. FINANCES. SCHADE'S *SENTINEL* EULOGIZED; FORMER APPROPRIATION DONATED. USEFULNESS OF FLINTOFF, SCHWARZ AND LEWIS. REYMANN; PERSONAL NOTE. ATTITUDE OF PRESS. HOP-DUTY; COMBINATION OF INTERESTS FAVORS IT. ALLEGED DISCREPANCY BETWEEN BREWERS' ESTIMATED AND ACTUAL OUTPUT; DISCREPANCY EXPLAINED TO COMMISSIONER, WHO AFFORDS NO RELIEF; BREWERS MUST SUE COLLECTOR; COMMISSIONER SUGGESTS THAT BREWERS PROPOSE NEW METHODS; BERGNER'S PROPOSITION REFERRED TO LOCAL ASSOCIATIONS. THE BARTEMEYER CASE DECIDED; NATURE OF DECISION. RUETER'S ADDRESS. BREWERS' APPEAL TO THE PEOPLE OF THE UNITED STATES.

The invitation to hold the fourteenth convention at Boston really emanated from the New England Brewers' Association, of which the Boston brewers, organized under circumstances described in a preceding chapter, had become the nucleus. Of the latter association we have already given a brief account in so far as it has a bearing on our subject. The president of the former body was Frank Jones, of New Hampshire, a public-spirited citizen and brewer who, by reason of his services as a member of Congress and the prominent part he has always taken in every public enterprise within his State, enjoys an excellent standing in the community, and an enviable reputation of which his colleagues are justly proud. It is probably due as much to Frank Jones' judicious efforts as to any other single cause that the liquor-law of New Hampshire is not to-day the counterpart of the law in the adjoining State of Maine.

From the very beginning the prohibitory law of New Hampshire (1855) differed from the present Maine-model in two essential particulars, viz.: (1) It forbade the sale, not the manufacture, of intoxicating drinks; (2) it exempted not only cider, but also beer and wine—in other words, all fermented beverages. This was the status of the drink-question in that State at the time of the fourteenth convention. The brewing industry flourished in New Hampshire to a greater extent than in any other New England State, Massachusetts excepted, and this exceptional condition may be attributable to the fact that New Hampshire was probably the principal source of supply for Maine, where brewing never did take firm root, and where what little there ever was of it soon succumbed to drunkard-breeding prohibition. Remarkably enough, in 1874 Maine still produced 11,000 barrels of malt-liquor; New Hampshire ranked next to Massachusetts, the latter State producing 493,339, the former 110,075 barrels. Connecticut brewed 55,165 and Rhode Island 19,593 barrels. In Massachusetts a considerable decrease, as compared with the production of 1873, resulted from the unwise law before referred to. In Rhode Island everything seemed to conspire to retard the development of the trade. The drinking-habits of the people who inherited a taste for ardent spirits from ancestors that gave up beer for the drink which the trade with the West Indies brought them; a prohibitory law exempting only native wines and cider, and an almost total lack of immigration; these three causes explain everything. The prohibitory act remained in force until 1863, when a moderate license law took its place. In the year of the fourteenth convention Prohibition, with the usual exempting clause in favor of cider and native wines, gave brewing another setback. Connecticut at that time had a license law, enacted in 1867, which superseded the old cider-exempting prohibitory act. A very large proportion of the malt-liquors brewed in these States was then, as has been stated, of the kind known as ale or porter; but in earlier years a brew known as common-beer, similar to that before described, was in vogue. The first attempt to introduce lager-beer in New Hampshire was made in 1872, but seems not to have been successful.

Although the legal status of brewing was far from being favorable or encouraging, there was really no part of our country where the temperance principle of substituting fermented drinks for ardent liquors had gained so many adherents among the educated, especially the professional classes; and it is from scientists, scholars and statesmen of Massachusetts that the brewing industry received more effective literary and scientific support than from any other State. But here, as elsewhere, the calm, deliberate and unbiased opinions of those best qualified to lead in a great social question could not stem the tide of fanaticism which, in the very year we now write of, had assumed a most pernicious character. We refer to the Woman's Crusade, one of the most peculiar manifestations of zealotism aroused in the breast of hysterical women by the trickery of men who had neither the courage nor the manhood to attack their opponents, save from behind the inviolable bulwark of petticoats. Casual references to this craze in the speeches and reports of the fourteenth convention make it desirable to state briefly the origin and object of the crusade.

The Woman's Crusade originated in Ohio, where the Adair Law, already mentioned elsewhere, was in force, providing for damages caused by drink and giving to the wife or mother of a drunkard the right to bring damage-suit in her own name against the liquor-dealer who sold the drink to her relative. Under this law two suits were brought against a liquor-seller of Springfield, Ohio. The prosecuting attorney introduced a Mrs. E. D. Stewart ("Mother Stewart" as she was afterwards familiarly called) as the legal representative of the injured plaintiffs, and prevailed upon the Justice to permit her to plead the cause of her clients. The defendants were convicted, and this success so elated "Mother Stewart" that she immediately sought to organize the women of Springfield for the purpose of closing all saloons. The ladies she appealed to evidently entertained quite a different view of the functions of true womanhood; and they accordingly refused to join her. The report of these occurrences spread rapidly and thus came to the knowledge of Dr. Dio Lewis, who, after making a futile experiment in the indicated direction in Fredonia, N. Y., at once proceeded to Hillsboro, Ohio, where, preaching his new doctrine, he succeeded in enrolling a large number of women as crusaders against the saloon. His idea was that the saloons could be closed if the women would lay siege to the enemy's stronghold and keep up a fusilade of prayers until the besieged surrendered. On the 23d day of December, 1873, the crusaders assembled in the Presbyterian Church, and thence seventy-five of them sallied forth in double file, visiting every saloon and by force of prayer and psalm-singing compelled some dealers to sign a pledge not to sell any more intoxicants. They then beleaguered the premises of the rest in such an effectual way that the transaction of business became utterly impossible. Suits brought against them for trespass and unlawful obstruction of business could have no effect where the entire female portion of the community was artificially excited to fever-heat by a sense of the heinous crimes which they fancied God had called upon them to exterminate. Defenders of the craze claim that no acts of violence were committed by the crusaders; that the only means they resorted to were the power of prayer and moral suasion. Just as if anything more were needed to ruin the business than an organized body of women invading saloons by squads from day to day, from morning till night, remaining on post, praying, singing, shouting and exhorting, until relieved by a fresh patrol! The craze spread like an infectious disease through the whole country; until the people perceived its dangerous character and sustained the determined efforts made by those affected by it to put a stop to it. The assertion that the crusaders abstained from acts of violence, cannot be maintained. If Dio Lewis could have prevented them, they would not have occurred; but he was not capable of "subduing the spirits he had conjured up." In some towns the crusaders conducted themselves in a manner justifying a comparison with the women of the French Commune; and the term Reign of Terror, which has sometimes been applied to that rule of so-called moral suasion, was amply deserved. Dio Lewis himself, at one time the best-hated opponent of prohibition, certainly did not approve of physical violence. Some of his ideas with regard to prohibition were exceedingly sound; thus he held, for instance, that drinking is a vice, not a crime; that the State must punish crime, but that a vice must be cured. He even conceded the right of every man to drink, or sell drink, and held all laws interfering with this right to be unjust and unreasonable. He believed moral suasion could easily crush the traffic, and that prohibitory laws could never accomplish this. Years after the crusade he wrote these words, published both in his own journal and the *North American Review:*

"I am an old man, but I expect to live long enough to see the friends of temperance turn their backs upon the constable, join hands and hearts in a grand movement combining the tactics of Washingtonianism and the Woman's Crusade, and within twelve months fill the most wonderful page in the history of Christian civilization." He certainly was a sincere and a good man, unusually gifted and endowed by nature with many engaging qualities. Not to him, but to the men who after him took up the crusade, do the words apply by which we endeavored to characterize the instigators of those misguided women. In his numerous controversies with Neal Dow and other eminent prohibitionists he invariably carried off the palm, his arguments being strongly sustained by incontrovertible evidences of the fallacy of prohibition.

The foregoing reference to Washingtonianism calls for another historical digression. The Washingtonian Temperance Society was originally composed of reformed drunkards, a class of men who did not content themselves with their own salvation, but felt an unconquerable desire to rescue other drunkards, and to prevent moderate drinkers from becoming drunkards. This they did by depicting their own former depravity in the most horrible and disgusting colors. The Washingtonians were organized at Baltimore in 1840. A convivial party of six tradesmen, who had been in the habit of meeting in a saloon, were converted to total abstinence by the fervent harangue of a temperance lecturer, and, after having signed the pledge, began to preach the cause. Subsequently, their principal leader, also a reformed drunkard named Hawkins, extended the work, and under his guidance the association acquired some fame and actually succeeded in inducing several thousand sots to sign a pledge of total abstinence. The movement lasted but a short time, and had been almost forgotten when Dio Lewis resurrected its principle of moral suasion.

These brief historical explanations will enable the reader to appreciate more fully the attitude of the brewers' association at the fourteenth convention, a meeting which exercised a far-reaching influence, and left a profound impression not only upon the people of the city and State in which it was held, but upon the people of the whole country. In his address, President Clausen, after thanking Frank Jones for his eloquent and hearty greeting, reviewed the situation in Ohio and other States were the crusade executed a sort of lynch-law, and the prohibitory propaganda throughout the country. He insisted that the time had come for brewers to take a determined stand and to appeal to the common sense, fairness and sense of justice of the American people. He showed by quotations from newspapers, including the *New York Tribune*, which had favored the crusade, that whenever the mass of the people had a chance to express their views at the ballot-box, the craze was voted down. The *Tribune*, for instance, wrote: "The question in the Ohio towns was virtually this: Shall we have Prohibition? It arose in the form of license. The prohibitionists sagaciously attempted to turn the feeling in favor of compulsory total abstinence. The women injudiciously lent themselves to the scheme and the result is an apparent rebuke to them, while it is in reality a simple but emphatic negative to the question the prohibitionists insisted upon propounding to the people of Ohio." This is a garbled statement. The truth is, and Clausen stated it very tersely, that the people of Ohio wanted neither the one nor the other. They had become surfeited and disgusted with the emotional paroxysm of hysterical women and the hypocrisy of would-be reformers, and town after town, including the home of "Mother Stewart," rose in indignant protest against the craze.

In his review of the effects of Prohibition Clausen cited the testimony brought forth by the Massachusetts enquiry and added to it extracts of Pascoe's pamphlet on the subject, and of Prof. William A. Hammond's celebrated inaugural address, delivered on the 4th of May, 1874, when he entered upon his office as president of the Neurological Society, his theme being "Effects of Alcohol." As this address, remarkable in more than one respect, is now out of print, it may not be amiss to reproduce Clausen's quotations from it. While admitting that even the moderate use of alcoholic stimulants may be prejudicial to some persons, Hammond showed that to a majority of human beings such stimulants, used in moderation, are not only beneficial but actually necessary. Dwelling at length upon the results of excessive libations of ardent spirits, he concluded from his own observations and experiences that "chronic alcoholic intoxication very rarely, if ever, ensues on the moderate use of light German or French wines, or of those made in this country, when they are not fortified by the subsequent addition of spirits, and it is *still less* apt to ensue from the temperate use of malt-liquors."

Perhaps the most lucid physiological summary ever published of the whole question of proper use and pernicious abuse is presented in the following statement of Dr. Hammond:

"If asked what constitutes excess I can only answer that, in the abstract, I do not know, any more than I know how much tea or coffee any one of you can drink with comfort or advantage; how many cigars you can smoke without passing from good to bad effects; how much mustard on your beef agrees with you, and how much disagrees, or how much butter you can eat on your buckwheat cakes. For some persons tea and coffee and tobacco and mustard are poisonous. Every person must, to a great extent, be a law unto himself in the matter of food. A single glass of wine may be excess to some individuals, while to others it fills a *rôle* which nothing else can fill.

"That alcohol, even in large quantities, is beneficial to some persons, is a point in regard to which I have no doubt; but those persons are not in a normal condition, and when they are restored to health their potations should cease. I have seen many a weak, hysterical woman drink a pint of whisky a day without experiencing the least intoxicating effect, or even feeling excited by it.

"The exhausted tissue has seemed to absorb it with an energy as though it were its one thing craved, and recovery has been rapid under the use when all other means have failed. I have seen strong men struck down with pneumonia and fever, and apparently saved from the grave by brandy or other alcoholic liquors. I have prevented epileptic seizures by its moderate use. Neuralgic attacks are often cut short by it, and sometimes entirely prevented. It has been efficacious in catalepsy, and in tetanus; it is one of the best antidotes to the bites of poisonous serpents, as I have repeatedly witnessed. In the convulsions of children from teething and other sources of reflex irritation it is invaluable. In the spinal irritation to which women, and especially American women, are so subject, nothing takes its place, and in certain forms of gastric dyspepsia it must be given if we wish to cure our patients."

With reference to the moderate use of alcoholic liquors Dr. Hammond says: "It must be remembered that we are not living in a state of nature. We are all more or less overworked; we all have anxieties and sorrows and misfortunes which gradually, in some cases, suddenly, in others, wear away our minds and our bodies. We have honors to achieve, learning to acquire, and perhaps wealth to obtain.

"Honors and learning and wealth are rarely got honestly without hard work, and hard work exhausts all the tissues of the body, and especially that of the nervous system. Now, when a man finds that the wear and tear of his mind and body are lessened by a glass or two of wine at his dinner, why should he not take it?

"The answer may be:—Because he sets a bad example to his neighbors. But he does not. His example is a good one, for he uses in moderation and decorum one of those things which experience has taught him are beneficial to him. And why should he shorten his life for the purpose of affording an example to a man who probably would not heed it, and who, if he did, is of less value to society.

"The inborn craving for stimulants and narcotics, is one which no human power can subdue. It is one which all civilized societies possess. Among the earliest acts of any people emerging from savagism, is the manufacturing of an intoxicating compound of some kind.

"But if we cannot overcome the instinct by prohibitory laws, we can regulate it and keep its exercise within bounds. My own opinion is that the best way to do this is by discriminating legislation in favor of wines and malt beverages, and against spirituous liquors. I would make it difficult to get whisky, and, at the same time, easy to procure beer, and I would likewise offer every encouragement to the growth of the vine and the hop."

Had Hammond been able to read the speeches delivered and reports submitted to this convention, he might have selected from almost any one of them telling illustrations of his well-defended and now universally recognized theory that to a civilized people, and among them pre-eminently to the best intellects who have "honors to achieve, learning to acquire, and perhaps wealth to obtain," stimulants are necessary and indispensable. He probably would have used the following from the letter of a correspondent of the *New York Herald* who, in detailing the almost incredible number of the most difficult and delicate affairs submitted to the German Foreign Office and disposed of by the Iron Chancellor, wrote:

"When it is remembered that this immense mass of business, and much more, has all passed through the brain of a single man in twelve months, some estimate may be formed of the daily occupation of Prince Bismarck, and his almost superhuman capacity for incessant work. To support him in his labors he eats, like a giant, mighty meals of solid food, washed down with half-a-dozen tumblers of strong Burgundy, enough to upset the wits of an ordinary man for a whole evening. But no sooner is the tremendous dinner over than Prince Bismarck sets to work again, fresher than ever, and drinks quantities of beer while he dictates and decides questions of State policy during the evening, and cuts those grim jokes of his which pass into proverbs."

Coming from the most eminent American physician, and one whose training, studies and practice specially qualified him to speak authoritatively upon the subject, Hammond's words derived particular relevancy and force at that time in view of the fact, before adverted to, that the prohibitionists had just begun to single out malt-liquors for their most virulent attacks, and in this endeavor proceeded in a way that might almost have aroused the suspicion that they were in league with the distillers. President Clausen reiterated his conviction that true temperance would not become the rule until the laws in every State were so changed as to encourage and foster viticulture and brewing; he supported this view by several felicitous quotations from letters and lectures of well-known Americans familiar with European customs and habits, among them John M. Francis, formerly American Minister to Greece, who asserted that in all his travels in Greece, Spain, France and Germany he rarely met a drunken man, although the entire population: men, women and children, used either wine or beer. In their report the Agitation Committee cited a statistical evidence which might have been attached to the foregoing as an apt illustration. It is in the form of a statement of arrests made in New York during twelve years, beginning in 1860 and ending in 1872. Of the total number of persons arrested for drunkenness and disorderly conduct 33 per cent. were native Americans, 52 per cent. of Irish, and 15 per cent. of German birth.

The exaggerations of prohibitionists as to the destruction of life caused by alcohol has always been their chief stock in trade, and as at that time methodical enquiries into this and kindred phases of the drink-question had not yet been undertaken on a comprehensive scale, they found no difficulty in propagating their falsehoods; and it is a singular phenomenon that a falsehood, when once properly launched on its career, grows in proportion to the distance it travels from its starting-point or place of origin. Of this peculiarity Clausen gave a very amusing example, to which he joined an effective bit of statistical argumentation. It seems that *Harper's Weekly*, in an article on temperance and prohibition, had ventured the assertion that in this country over 50,000 people were annually brought to their graves through the excessive use of alcohol. A few days thereafter a member of the Ohio Legislature, in supporting a motion welcoming the crusaders to the city of Columbus, increased the number to 75,000; and within two weeks after this event an ex-Judge of the Ohio Supreme Court, speaking on the floor of the Constitutional Convention in favor of the temperance movement, added still another 25,000. Thus amplified by the glowing imagination of Western enthusiasts, the tale returned to New York, where Rev. E. L. Rexford instantly doubled the dilated number, thus fixing the number of deaths from alcoholism at 200,000. Resisting the alluring temptation to attack this method of pleading by an argumentation *ad risum*, Clausen exploded this fast-breeding falsehood by this dispassionate statement, viz.:

"The volume of vital statistics of the United States Census of 1870, gives the total number of deaths in this country during the year at 492,264; 260,673 of these being males and 231,490 females. Of the males 131,405 were under the age of fifteen years, and of the females 114,116. This leaves a balance of both sexes of 246,745 upward of that age which died from all causes whatever during that year. The census specifies over a hundred different diseases which contributed to this result. Consumption alone took off 21,243 men between the ages of fifteen and fifty; pneumonia 6,864 males of the same age, and also nearly as many females. How many is alcohol charged with? Just 1,161 males and 249 females. A score of other causes of death can be picked out which take off greater numbers, and which could be reduced largely by proper attention to the laws of health, by common foresight, and even reasonable care. These figures certainly do not sustain the exorbitant statements of abstinence mathematicians.

"It may be said that death does not always result so directly from the use of alcohol, that this cause may be charged with it, but that it enters, nevertheless, largely into other diseases, aggravating them. So it is, and at what rate? I have before me an article from a New York paper summarizing the mortality of New York City for the year 1872, giving the details of the cause of the 32,647 deaths which took place in its population of one million. It shows that of the causes referred to alcoholism is accountable for 314 deaths, and that intemperance was certified to as either the direct or complicating cause in, altogether, 826 cases—not quite three times the number of deaths charged directly, which would give for the United States, at the same proportion, about 3,000 men in all. This may certainly be enough in itself, but it will serve no good purpose to obscure the judgment of the people, and to obstruct the proper consideration of the subject by unwarranted representations, giving currency to the notion that two hundred thousand die annually by reason of the excessive use of alcohol. The fact is simply this, that only with the death of *one in every thirteen thousand* inhabitants of the United States liquor has anything to do, and malt-liquors have no share in this at all."

Sincere advocates of temperance undoubtedly believed that all such statements as to the proportion of deaths, crimes, pauperism and insanity, caused by alcohol, were based upon statistical enquiries, but the average writer or speaker on the side of prohibition knew the falsity of them, having himself helped in manufacturing them out of whole cloth. Their pet scheme of having these questions investigated by a Federal Commission to be appointed under authority of a law so framed as to virtually put the investigation into their hands, originated at this time. In the United States Senate the prohibitionists had Wilson whom they could rely upon for assistance in any effort they might see fit to make in the direction of Federal legislation, and it was through the help of this truly good man, whose record in every other respect commands our respect and admiration, that they succeeded in having the Commission Bill introduced for the first time in February, 1874. It was re-introduced at nearly every succeeding session up to 1892, when Congress finally directed that the Commissioner of Labor institute such an enquiry. At its very inception this movement encountered a most formidable opposition, not on the part of the brewers, but of two eminent statesmen, whose soundness of judgment and integrity of motives and purpose no one can question: the Democrat, Senator T. F. Bayard, and the Republican, Senator Carl Schurz.

The words of these two statesmen were quoted by Clausen, and it may be taken for granted that being spoken at the brewers' convention in a city where Schurz had a short time before delivered an oration on the life of his friend Charles Sumner, late colleague of Wilson, the introducer of the Bill, the effect must have been telling and incisive. They are words which surely deserve to be perpetuated in a history of the United

States Brewers' Association. In commenting on the bill Schurz said: "There are many other evils affecting society, which need to be inquired into. For instance, gambling is worse than intemperance. Another subject, the extravagance of the female sex in matters of dress is a great evil, and has ruined many families. How many clerks have been induced to rob their employers, or bank officers to become defaulters, in order to satisfy this love of dress. Indigestion makes a man sour and unsociable, and Congress might inquire into the cause of this, or go on with inquiries until it should be found out what effects the consumption of hot soda had upon society, and establish a bureau of health and public morals." He did not desire to be understood as trifling with the temperance principle. To a certain extent he was a temperance man, and nothing was more disgusting to him than a drunken man, unless it be a drunken woman. Nothing could be more loathsome than a human being degrading himself to the level of a beast. He thought the movement, of which this Bill formed a part, was misdirected zeal, and gentlemen favoring it were taking hold of the wrong end of the subject. Human nature was so constituted that it needed relaxation, and could not be put down. The surest remedy was not the forcible suppression of any indulgence not morally wrong when used moderately, but the substitution of better pleasures for bad ones. He believed that if social enjoyments were introduced among the people, a wholesome social reform would be achieved, and a lasting benefit be conferred upon society.

From Bayard's speech against the proposed measure we quote the following:

"There are some subjects which are clearly within the domain of law. There are others which are as clearly within the domain of morals. There are some

the jurisdiction of which may be considered doubtful.
But there can be no doubt—and this remark applies to
general legislation, not simply to the legislation of the
Congress of the United States, which must be under the
limitations of the Federal Constitution, it applies, as I
say to general legislation—that whether the subject proposed to be acted upon is properly within the domain
of law or the domain of morals is not always easily to
be decided. There can be no doubt that sumptuary
laws are rather within the domain of morals than of law;
and the result has been that they always have been
considered odious among all free peoples; objectionable,
difficult of execution, and their enactment or execution
has generally been abandoned. One difficulty, therefore, respecting this question of enforced temperance,
is that all the laws in relation to it partake in their
nature of sumptuary laws: they are in themselves invasions of that right of individual action, that control of
personal tastes guided by personal predilection, and by
individual constitutional peculiarities, which each man
should be left to judge of for himself, and the interference with which he justly considers an unauthorized
invasion of his personal liberty. It seems to me that
the plain object of this bill and this commission is to
allow the advocates of what I may term the political
temperance movement to obtain a budget of what they
would be pleased to call 'statistics,' to brandish before
the eyes of Congress and all of the State Legislatures,
so as to demand prohibitory legislation in regard to the
sale of alcoholic drinks. I do not understand the
ground upon which this constant interference in the
shape of sumptuary or coercive laws can be justified. I
do not understand how their advocates can expect from
them any other than the usual results—an enforced
obedience that will break into disobedience, and drive

the parties, even while they submit, into hypocrisy and dissimulation. If the vice must be, let it be open. Its horrible, its shocking attendants may do something to prevent it. There is a narrow-mindedness, as it seems to me, in this system of forcing the same class of habits on one man as on another, that I cannot approve. Without regard to his tastes, without regard to his capacity, without regard to his means, without regard to the idiosyncrasies of his constitution, you would say that on this subject all men must be alike. There is no sensible physician, there is no sensible moralist, that will not answer that the proposition is false *per se*. There are scarcely any two constitutions upon whom the same stimulus will have the same effect. To one man the moderate use of alcoholic stimulus may be a source of health and vigor; to the other it is almost a poison. How can we prescribe a law which will enforce the same system as to both?"

From the very beginning the attitude of the organized brewers, as a body, has been thoroughly consistent in this matter. Not only had they nothing to fear from an impartial investigation, but they could readily perceive, on the contrary, that any endeavor promising to throw the light of truth and science upon the subject must inevitably benefit them, showing, as it could not but do, that their opponents did not understand the requirements of true temperance if they opposed the popularization of malt-liquors. The Washington Committee, represented by Lauer, G. Bergner, William Massey, C. Psotta, J. F. Betz. L. Muth and Robert Portner, therefore, did not oppose the general object of the Bill, but suggested to the Senate Committee such modifications as seemed calculated to ensure an impartial investigation; and these suggestions were adopted, much to the chagrin of the prohibitionists, who subsequently caused the original draft to be introduced in the House of Representatives. In view of the fact that this policy was afterwards abandoned by those who represented the association at Washington, but only to be resumed with greater vigor after a brief space of time, it may be well to reproduce the literal text of the Agitation Committee's report upon the subject. It reads that "the Association could perceive no serious objections to the appointment of such a commission, provided fair-play was allowed to the brewers, for we can easily put on record the fact that fermented beverages are necessary, nutritive and harmless; calculated to diminish poverty and crime, and to make a people progressive, temperate, contented and happy."

Concerning purely internal affairs of the association, there is to be noted not only a very considerable increase in membership, but also a more hearty and general co-operation on the part of the members. Thus, for example, we find among the convention officers and committees new names, some of them borne by men who left upon the association's affairs the indelible imprint of their intellectual force and energy of character, and among these none stands forth in bolder relief than that of William A. Miles. In order to enable the reader to judge for himself we give here the names of these officers and committees, the latter appointed by the chair, the former recommended by a committee consisting of T. Carberry, John Eichler, E. Frauenheim, W. H. Hull and H. Ferris.

With Lauer as honorary president, there were vice-presidents George A. Bassermann, New Haven; F. Fortmann, San Francisco; George Juenemann, Washington; J. Fehrenbach, Wilmington; Louis Lange, Fernandina; Conrad Seipp, Chicago; F. W. Anschuetz, Keokuk; P. Lieber, Indianapolis; P. Weber, Louisville; George Auer, New Orleans; Joseph M. Smith, Boston; Jacob Seeger, Baltimore; Charles G. Stifel, St. Louis; John Orth, Minneapolis; E. W. Voigt, Detroit; Frank Jones, Portsmouth; A. N. Beadleston, New

York; Fred. Volz, Newark; Christian Moerlein, Cincinnati; H. Weinhard, Portland; William Massey, Philadelphia; Nicholas Molter, Providence; Jacob Seeger, Columbia; F. Rennert, New Braunfels; David Yuengling, Jr., Richmond; A. Reymann, Wheeling; Jacob Obermann, Milwaukee. Secretaries: Gustavus Bergner, Philadelphia; William Miles, New York; William J. Lemp, St. Louis; Joseph McCormack, Boston.

The Finance Committee consisted of G. A. Bassermann, H. Bartholomay, R. Jacobs; the Committee on Petitions, of G. Bergner, J. C. G. Huepfel and J. Obermann; the Committee on Resolutions of Lauer, W. J. Lemp, C. Moerlein, G. Bergner, H. H. Rueter, J. T. Taylor, E. Penrose, Joseph Schlitz, Peter Schoenhofen and F. W. Anschuetz.

In spite of a rapidly augmenting expense-account, the assets of the association showed a marked increase, the total balance in June, 1874, amounting to $20,000, including, of course, the sums permanently invested in interest-bearing bonds. The expenditures amounted to $9,872, of which an item of $2,000 was accounted for as a "loan." And thereby hangs a tale. The appropriation of this sum for the purpose of establishing the *Washington Sentinel* appears to have been regarded by some as a loan, by others as a gift. The fiscal officers of the association entertained the former view and consequently obtained from Schade a chattel mortgage for the amount. In order to determine the exact nature of this transaction G. Bergner, the author of the original resolution appropriating this sum, recommended, as chairman of the Committee on Petitions, that "the amount paid to Mr. Louis Schade be now confirmed as a donation and the mortgage held by this association against his chattels be cancelled." Schade himself stated in a letter to this committee that he, in common with many members of the association, understood that the sum appropriated was to be considered a donation. He pointed out that the *Sentinel* had already accomplished the purposes for which it was created, namely, to protect the interests of the trade, and that he was entitled to this substantial recognition on the part of the trade.

The report afforded an opportunity for an expression of opinion on the subject, of which P. Schemm, G. A. Bassermann, F. Lauer and J. Obermann availed themselves, speaking in eulogistic terms of the *Sentinel's* efforts;* and the convention accordingly adopted the recommendation, together with the usual appropriation of $200 each for the *Amerikanische Bierbrauer* and the *American Brewers' Gazette*. John Flintoff was still editor of the latter journal. His ability and talent, both as a writer and speaker, qualified him particularly as an agitator, and he was frequently called upon to lecture on subjects pertaining to the trade. In addition to this work he voluntarily assumed executive duties devolving upon the secretary, at that time a very busy official. In fact, the duties of this officer had become so numerous and onerous that this convention authorized the appointment of an assistant secretary, which position was given to Flintoff as a fitting and well-deserved appreciation of his work. At conventions Flintoff usually acted as reading clerk, and a speech from him in his partly satirical, partly humorous style had become quite as much an expected part of the proceedings as Lauer's oration and Schade's statistical exhibits.

In the meantime A. Schwarz performed not only equally meritorious labors in the literary domain, but rendered inestimable services to the trade by his incessant efforts to propagate that progressive spirit in matters

---

* The chronicler, then the editor of the *Washington Anzeiger* and translator in the Post Office Department, had no idea at that time that the best years of his life would be devoted to the brewing industry. Looking back to the time when the *Sentinel* was established, it strikes him as a singular coincidence that he contributed several articles to the earliest numbers of this paper.

relating to the scientific development of the art, which has since become a distinctive characteristic of the American brewer, admiringly and, perhaps, a little enviously acknowledged by the very highest European authorities on the technic and science of brewing. Another exceedingly valuable officer, one whom the association had frequent occasion to compliment and thank officially was James M. Lewis, nominally secretary, but actually the legal adviser of the Ale Brewers' Association of New York; the framer of the Act of 1872, and of many subsequent law-drafts, as well as the author of some of the best arguments submitted to Congressional committees. At this convention his name again appeared in connection with an important revenue-matter, which will presently claim the reader's attention. While on the subject of personal merits the chronicler cannot refrain from mentioning the fact that at the fourteenth convention the secretary read a telegram from A. Reymann, expressing regret at his inability to participate in the association's deliberations. It was the first time that this member failed to attend a convention and, being a member of the Agitation Committee, to which he had belonged from the beginning, he felt that an apology was due his colleagues. Why mention this incident? Because it reveals one of the main causes to which the association owes its strength at the present time; it was this almost punctilious devotion to duty on the part of the older members; their acute sense of the responsibilities and obligations voluntarily assumed by them in becoming members and accepting office, and their absolute unselfishness that made the society what it is. To this very day the older members, at least those of them who are still active, live up to that high standard. If the children and children's children of those pioneers follow such examples—as, in fact, many do—

the brewing industry will never suffer for want of able champions.

The adoption of certificates of membership was first proposed at this convention, a motion to that effect having been made by P. Schemm. A proposition, submitted by W. Eberhardt, to change the time for holding the annual conventions from June to October was not adopted. The relations of the association to the Press received some further attention, and during the deliberations upon the subject it transpired that the newspapers in the cities where conventions were being held, always manifested the greatest willingness to publish detailed reports of the proceedings, while the telegraphic news-agencies rarely ever failed to do justice to the trade. The Boston Press made no exception in this respect, and Rueter's grateful words of praise, coupled with a vote of thanks to the local newspapers, were received with unfeigned enthusiasm. The *New York Staatszeitung*, always very friendly to the industry in those days, had for the first time sent a special reporter in the person of Edward Grosse, who subsequently became one of the stanchest supporters of the cause of personal liberty, and during his successful career as a municipal, State and Federal officeholder frequently assisted the trade in various ways. In concluding this brief mention of purely internal affairs, it may be well to record the fact that the project of a brewers' school was again brought forward at this convention, in an informal way, by the well-known brewmaster Robert Lieber of Boston, who attended the convention as a guest, specially invited by members of the local association.

While the convention was in session (it convened on the 3d day of June, 1874) the Congress of the United States deliberated upon a proposition to again increase the duty upon hops. Lewis was then in Washington and telegraphed that on the 8th of June, brewers would be heard in opposition by the Senate Finance Committee. The careful reader will have noticed that ever since the friendly advice was given to brewers by members of Congress not to send an attorney to represent them, but to personally present their claims, wishes and objections to the proper committees, this course has invariably been pursued by the association through its Agitation Committee, both as to Congressional and Departmental affairs, and the results achieved demonstrated the soundness of the advice. In regard to import duties, the policy of the dominant party precluded the possibility of success, and in this particular instance the task of the brewers seemed specially difficult, because some members of the House, it was said, had a personal interest in the bill, having a large stock of hops on hand from which they hoped to derive large profits if the duty were increased. These men and the grangers made common cause with the domestic vintners who desired an increased duty upon light wines.

Under the new internal revenue law the relations between the trade and the Commissioner assumed a still more favorable and pleasant character, a goodly share of which was due, however, as well to the brewers' conscientious compliance with the regulations as to a spirit of fairness and the friendly disposition of Commissioner Douglass. Notwithstanding these propitious conditions and circumstances there arose a disagreement of a very serious nature on account of that section of the law which had caused so much annoyance to brewers before it was amended in 1872, and now that it was modified in a seemingly equitable and practicable manner, gave rise to still greater worry and perplexity. We refer to the section requiring the keeping of accounts of malt and hop consumed, and the rendering of a monthly account of malt-liquors brewed. Some collectors alleged to have discovered, at the end of the year, a large discrepancy, in many instances, between the estimated quantity produced and the actual quantity sold. The brewers readily accounted for the discrepancy; it arose from defective returns in which they had entered the full quantity contained in the boiling vat or kettle, making no deduction either for waste and evaporation at this stage, or for leakage and waste at other stages of the brewing process. In some cases the alleged difference amounted to 1,500 barrels. The collectors assessed an additional tax, plus the penalty provided for by law in each case. The Philadelphia brewers were principally affected by this course and they sought, but failed to arrive at, an understanding with the local collector. The parent association, at Bergner's solicitation, then took up the matter and submitted it to Commissioner Douglass for decision. In a lengthy correspondence and a subsequent conference with the Agitation Committee he held that his subordinates had acted in accordance with the law, and that the brewers were to blame, as the blank form upon which the returns must be made particularly provide for a statement on the part of the brewer of the quantity of beer wasted, lost by leakage, and consumed on the brewery premises. He could not allow amended returns to be made, but in cases where assessments had been made he would receive statements under oath of the circumstances under which these errors had occurred, and would take such statements into consideration in remitting or mitigating the assessment. If in view of the nature of such statement he should feel constrained to confirm the assessment, the brewers would have to pay the assessed amount. If they felt that they were wrongfully dealt with, they might sue the collector for the recovery of the sum paid.

He proposed that the brewers themselves agree upon a uniform method of determining the quantities to be accounted for, to the end that he might, if the plan be feasible and conducive to a better understanding, instruct the collectors accordingly. Acting upon this suggestion, G. Bergner proposed to the fourteenth convention that " a petition be submitted to the commissioner requesting him to instruct his collectors that brewers shall be required to make returns of the quantity of beer, not after the brewing process is completed, but only when the beer is racked from the fermenting vats into the storage casks, which latter shall be correctly gauged, and the quantity so ascertained shall be returned as the quantity actually brewed, allowing a deduction of 5 per cent. therefrom for waste." C. G. Stifel and C. Moerlein opposed this proposition, and Clausen, yielding the chair to Lauer and taking the floor, spoke very earnestly against hasty action. The association had already assumed the defense of the suits brought by members for the recovery of the amounts assessed under this ruling and paid under protest; and there was, therefore, no need of precipitation. He suggested that the whole matter be referred to the local association with the request that they express their views as to the best method of rendering the accounts required by law. And this course received the sanction of the convention.

Unfortunately, the Bartemeyer case, upon which the association had hoped to obtain a decision determining the question of compensation as viewed in the light of the principle establishing the right of property, proved to be defective in this very essential particular. The United States Supreme Court decided the appeal in a manner which did not in the least alter the legal status of this feature of the question. Concerning it the Court held: "If it were true, and it was fairly presented to us, that the defendant was the owner of the glass of liquor which he sold to Hickey at the time that the State of Iowa first imposed an absolute prohibition upon the sale of such liquors, then we concede that two very grave questions would arise, namely: first, whether this would be a statute depriving him of his property without due process of law; and, secondly, whether if it were so, it would be so far a violation of the 14th Amendment in that regard as would call for judicial action by this Court. Both of these questions, whenever they may be presented to us, are of an importance to require the most careful and serious consideration. They are not to be lightly treated, nor are we authorized to make any advance to meet them until we are required to do so by the duties of our position." This somewhat ambiguous phraseology encouraged both sides in the belief that if a proper test-case could be brought, involving the principle upon which the Court was so exceedingly careful to avoid an expression of opinion, the decision would be favorable to them.

In reference to the Massachusetts test-cases the Agitation Committee had taken no action during the year, neither did they assign any reason for this inactivity; nor can we obtain any explanation of it from the address of H. H. Rueter, who on this occasion spoke in his happiest and most effective style, embellishing and fortifying his arguments with apt illustrations and quotations, all tending to show the errors of prohibitionists, and the correctness of the brewers' view that beer is virtually a temperance agent. Among others he quoted Dr. Chalmers' remark that it was an outburst of nature, when, as was stated upon reliable authority, out of 500,000 men who took the pledge in the United States, 350,000 broke it in six months, a statement to which he joined the pertinent question: "Have the same proportion ever broken vows of chastity or any other solemn obligation?"

From the minority report of a committee of the Massachusetts Legislature, he quoted a statement showing that in spite of the operation of prohibitory laws, intemperance, as indicated by arrests for drunkenness, had increased from 1860 to 1874 at an alarming ratio. The exact data read: "Increase of population $31\frac{1}{2}$ per cent.; increase of drunkenness 326 per cent.; increase of intemperance over increase of population 935 per cent." Referring to Bowditch's celebrated utterance: "I believe that Germans are destined to be really the greatest benefactors of this country by bringing to us, if we chose to accept the boon, their beer," he said: "With such testimony from such a source we need not care for the aspersions, the slurs, the malice and defamation of any prohibition agitator; with the laws of nature on our side, we need feel no apprehension of any permanent injury to our interests through unwise and unjust legislation, nor through the persistent perversion of the laws of God by self-constituted commentators of his word."

Adopting the president's suggestion concerning an appeal to the people of the United States this convention—in every respect one of the most notable gatherings of brewers—adopted the following address, drafted by a special committee, composed of Frank Jones, William Massey and M. Pfaff. It is a most remarkable document, in every way worthy of preservation. In the preceding chapter we have alluded to it and now reproduce its full text:

ADDRESS

Of the Fourteenth Annual Brewers' Congress, in session at Boston, Mass., the 3d, 4th and 5th of June, 1874, to the People of the United States:

In view of the aggressive war against the manufacture of and trade in beverages waged for years by many State Legislatures, and especially of late by some female organizations under the leadership of certain fanatics pretending to seek the advance of the cause of morality and temperance, the Fourteenth Annual Convention of the United States Brewers' Association, assembled in the City of Boston and State of Massachusetts, this 4th day of June, A. D. 1874, desire to address the President and the fellow-citizens of the whole country in words of earnestness and remonstrance, prompted by firm convictions of right and the highest regard for the welfare and prosperity of this great Republic, and not by selfish interest.

The pith of the question in issue is not that of morality as against immorality, nor of temperance as against intemperance. Were it that the whole membership of our association would be found battling with all its might and influence, and by the side of all other organizations, of whatever name or kind, secular or otherwise, to promote morality and temperance throughout the land, and would cheerfully submit to even personal sacrifices in the effort. In their own way, the members of our association, represented in this present Fourteenth Annual Convention, have done as much as lay in their power, by personal example as well as by argument and persuasion, to foster among their neighbors and friends a life of high-toned morality and sobriety. They can point with pride to the fact that many of their fraternity have risen from humble station to prominence, and that in the locality of their residence many of them have repeatedly been chosen by their fellow-citizens to occupy public positions of high trust and responsibility, in which they not only retained but increased that confidence of the people to which they were first indebted for their elevation. A pursuit that can point with truth to such proud instances of distinction accorded to many of those who follow it as a legitimate business cannot be of that degrading character ascribed to it by those that war against it; nor can its influence be such as necessarily to lead to immorality and intemperance. We refer to this with just pride, and as a complete answer to the unwarranted accusations of our enemies, conscious that the sound sense of the American people will not be misled by unfounded clamor.

We propose to submit to the people, in their primary capacity, as the only sovereign source of the governing power in the Republic, the very pertinent and important question, Whether they set any value upon the credit and honorable standing of the United States among the nations of the world? That this is no idle query, a few authentically established historical facts will show. Within the last eight months the country has passed through a most disastrous financial revulsion, which affected the revenues of the National Government to a very serious extent. The President of the United States, at the beginning of the Congress now in session, called attention to the fact that the revenues were decreasing, and that to cover the appropriations made taxation would have to be increased to the extent of $40,000,000 in order to meet current expenses. From the monthly reports of the Secretary of the Treasury the people have ascertained that while during the twelve months ending with the 30th of June, 1873, about $43,000,000 of the national debt had been paid, the total of that immense debt of over two thousand millions had, on the 1st of May, 1874, been actually increased since then, owing to the want of a surplus revenue applicable to its reduction. The Hon. HENRY L. DAWES, an honored and distinguished representative from Massachusetts in Congress, and, as the Chairman of the Committee on Ways and Means, the leader of the House—a gentleman than whom, both from his ability and long official position, no one is better capable of forming and giving a correct opinion on the condition of our national finances, rose in his seat in the House on the 7th of May last, and in the course of a long and carefully prepared speech stated, that while by existing laws the sum of $29,100,000 should have been turned into the sinking fund during the year closing with the present month—sacredly pledged for the ultimate redemption of the debt—not one dollar had yet been paid into that fund, although the year was then nearly past; and this because the revenues were deficient. We ask the people of this country whether they are ready to consent that the revenues of the Government be still further and more largely reduced; that not only the payment of the national debt shall cease, but that the Government should also, without running still deeper in debt, be unable to pay the interest, and thus assume before the world the position of a dishonored bankrupt?

The continued agitation of Total Abstinence, to be forced upon the people by prohibitory laws—by the unseemly parade and self-debasement of female "crusaders," whom we consider to be the unconscious but misguided tools in the hands of unscrupulous men aiming at personal aggrandizement—by forcibly, either by statue law or otherwise, compelling the stoppage of the manufacture of, and all trade in beverages, must, we assure our fellow-citizens, ultimately deal a deathly blow to the finances of the country. We wish to refer to the following official facts, extracted from the last annual report made to the present Congress of the United States by the Commissioner of Internal Revenue:

Total Internal Revenue Receipts for the last fiscal year, $112,747,772.99.

Of this vast amount the following sums were collected during the year from the trade in stimulating beverages:

Fermented liquors, barrel tax..	$8,910,823.83	
Brewers' special tax..........	304,650.21	
Dealers in malt-liquors.......	109,463.80	
		$9,324,937.84
Total from distilled spirits, including tax as manufactured article, and rectifiers' and wholesale and retail dealers' special tax.................		52,099,371.78
Grand total tax receipts from these sources..............		$61,424,319.62

These official statements show the astonishing fact—astonishing as it must be to a vast majority of the people—that this trade, so fiercely denounced, so unreasonably warred against, and the total suppression of which is so clamorously demanded, did actually pay, for the last fiscal year, FIFTY-FIVE PER CENT. of the entire Internal Revenue Tax collected from all sources subject to it throughout the country! The grand total receipts of the Government for the same year from all sources are given by the Secretary of the Treasury in his report to Congress as follows:

From Customs (duties on imports).....	$183,167,838.66
" Internal Revenue...............	112,747,772.99
" Public lands........	2,831,673.95
" Miscellaneous sources...........	15,279,000.99
Grand total from all sources..........	$314,026,286.59

Hence it will be seen that this trade alone contributed *twenty per cent.* to the whole revenue of the Government during a year, when $43,000,000 of the National Debt was paid off; that, in fact, this trade alone paid in one year that enormous amount of the public debt, and left a surplus in the Treasury of nearly $18,500,000 to be applied to the other expenditures of the Government.

Can the people afford to have such an immense sum of money withdrawn from the National Treasury to which it now annually flows in daily instalments? What branch of industry is there in the land that could supply the deficiency? None. The principal officers of the National Government know this well. Occasional complaints and representations that were made by the Executive Committee of the brewers and by others interested in the same trade, as to the injustice, harassment and vexations caused by various Departmental regulations or injudicious provisions of law, have always been respectfully listened to, both in the Departments and in Congress, and, whenever possible, the remedy sought was applied and relief granted. This was done, as we ,are fain to believe, from a settled conviction, that an industry like ours in fermented liquors, which yields nearly ten millions a year of tax, with a steady and regular increase from year to year, ought not to be crippled, but should be encouraged rather for the benefit of the National Treasury, as it adds that much to alleviate the burdens of the people. This industry alone has a capital invested of about $152,776,696, and on that, as the official figures show, it pays an Internal Revenue Tax at the rate of over SIX PER CENT. If any other manufacturing or commercial industry of the country were taxed as high as that, it might linger for a while, but must ultimately succumb to the burden. Hence there is no hope to replenish the Treasury from such sources already taxed to the fullest extent. Take the banks. Their total capital foots up about $1,500,000,000, and they paid during the fiscal year referred to, $3,771,031.46 as Internal Revenue Tax on capital, deposits, and circulation. Were they taxed at the same rate as the trade in malt-liquors—six per cent.—this would require them to pay annually $90,000,000, a strain so overpowering, that every one of them would be compelled to close its doors and stop business. Even if their share of taxation was increased only from the present rate of one-tenth of one per cent. to a full per cent., it would amount to $15,000,000 a year, not enough by three-fourths to cover the falling off in the Treasury caused by the proposed suppression of the trade in beverages, and yet it would cripple them so as to compel them shortly to suspend. The injury to the whole business community, and through it to the people at large, to be wrought by such an event, would be incalculable, and must create widespread dismay, felt in every homestead and at the hearth of every family throughout the land. All would suffer alike, but the bone and sinew of the country, those that till the soil, build our houses, work our machinery, construct our railroads, constituting more than three-fourths of our entire population, would be the greatest sufferers of all. Any financial depression is sorest felt by those whose means are most limited, and the extinction or even decimation of a source of revenue to the Government which no financiering genius, either in Congress or out of it, knows how to replace, would as certainly create havoc and panic in the country as the sun shines at mid-day.

All other branches of industry are now already so heavily taxed, that the demand is universal for a reduction of the burden. Should there be decreed an increase, it would speedily be followed by a contraction, if not a cessation, of production, and thus the smaller quantity to be taxed would neutralize the increase of the tax. Were an addition of some consequence made to the tariff on imports, the whole West and South, in common with the commercial portion of the East, would as with one voice cry out against it. Hence the Treasury would be crippled; funds would be wanting, not only to reduce the National Debt as heretofore, but there would be none to add to the Sinking Fund, endangering the ultimate redemption of the debt; means would fail to pay even the interest thereon as it matures at intervals, and the United States would stand before the world a discredited, dishonored nation. Can the people desire such a result? We have not painted the picture in colors too dark. The official reports disclose themselves, and the foreshadowed result will follow the suppression of the trade, now so vehemently urged, as sure as night follows day.

But, fellow-citizens, the orators employed by those who make war upon us, tell you from every platform and almost in every street corner, in their papers, pamphlets and tracts, which they scatter liberally among you, that our trade is, if not the only, at least the principal source of pauperism and crime. The only true method to reason upon any subject is first to ascertain the facts, and in this matter we have a reliable means to lead us to a full knowledge of the facts in the decennial census of the United States, compiling and presenting official reports from every section of the country. Here we find that the whole number of paupers in all the thirty-seven States and ten Territories comprising the United States were in 1870 exactly 116,102, among a population of 38,558,371, or about just as many as are found on the pauper lists of the single City of London, among a population of about 8,700,000. Of persons convicted of crime in that year the number was 36,562, or less than one in every thousand of population, a smaller percentage than obtains either in England or France, while the pauper rate in this country is about ten per thousand, and in London two per hundred. Even small as this ratio is shown to be here as compared with other countries, we admit that is too large in a land that affords such an abundant and unequalled field for honest toil, but it is beyond question that any violent disorder of the commercial and industrial life of the country, as it now sustains itself under our laws and institutions, any sudden drying up of the springs which furnish the National revenue—as would necessarily follow an even partial success of our violent antagonists—would as suddenly increase the ratio of pauperism and crime in the land, not ten-fold, but more than a hundred-fold. This country would then present to the world the mournful spectacle of repeating in gigantic scale the fate of the man who explained the cause of his death on his tombstone:

> "I was well, would be better—
> Took physic, and here I am!"

There is yet another and a higher than a mere financial issue which we propose to submit to the people of the whole country. It is that of PERSONAL LIBERTY. The principle of the SOVEREIGNTY OF THE INDIVIDUAL was years ago announced by an esteemed Massachusetts philosopher, whose very definition of the term was accepted and embodied in systems of philosophy by eminent European thinkers. The spirit of that principle breathes forth in every line of our own immortal Declaration of Independence. It is the same which urged on and fed throughout the Northern States the increasing agitation against negro bondage in the South and led to its final abolition. UPON THAT SAME PRINCIPLE WE MAKE THE ISSUE NOW. A man shall own himself, be his own master, be owned or controlled by nobody else, have no master or overseer put over him, so long as he regards the like right to individual sovereignty in others. That was the sole aim established by the success of the American revolution, and it ought at last, through the results of our great war, to become the rule in every section of our Union of States. This right to personal liberty no man, and no community of men, has any legal power to interfere with. The "State" being a corporation of thousands or millions of people, has, by the very cause of its existence, the power and duty to protect its members against outlaws; against those who disregard all rights of persons and of property and prey upon society. To repress and punish these is the sole object of criminal legislation. That is the whole extent of it, and it can no further go. The right to pursue any honest calling or trade, to change from one to another, to move from place to place, to live where and how one pleases, are but corollary to this incontestable right to personal liberty. The enjoyment of one's tastes and habits is alike an unassailable right, personal to each individual, and if he be but one in a community of one hundred thousand, the other 99,999 have no just authority to prohibit or restrain him from the full exercise of that right. Whoever, by his acts, offends against public order, becomes amenable to the penal rules for its protection. But he who keeps within the strict limits of his own right stands upon the broad foundation of the sovereignty of the individual, and has all the bright principles of true American republicanism, and all whose faith in a higher manhood is still aglow to guard and defend him.

These fundamental principles we ask the FRIENDS OF LIBERTY in every city, county and State to urge upon the people at every suitable opportunity, and insist upon their spirit being introduced into every political platform, every candidate to be caused firmly to pledge himself to their enforcement, and a strict test to be made upon them at the polls. It were a sad day for this free land of ours, should it ever come to pass that after having given the black man back to himself, and endowed him with the power to govern the country along with his fellow-men, we in the North should be retracing our steps, become recreant to the very principle of personal freedom that broke the chains of slavery in the South, and legalize among ourselves another equally reprehensible and unjust system of bondage, by which the right to his individual sovereignty could be denied to an unoffending citizen by any combination of men or women, large or small.

The opponents of personal liberty being leagued together and acting in concert through every State in the Union, it will become necessary for its friends to do likewise. Men of all pursuits, professions and callings must be aware that their individual freedom being once curtailed in one direction, the meddling spirit that incited the first step will not rest satisfied with its partial victory. Fiercer and fiercer will its onslaught grow, and concession after concession will it demand to its domineering ambition. The foe cannot be fought piecemeal. He must be engaged in all his strength and laid at rest forever. A compact union of all the FRIENDS OF LIBERTY, determined not to sheath the weapons of offence until victory be lastingly secured, will accomplish it at the first trial. The times are propitious for such a movement. Political parties, as they were once known, with their iron grasp and stern discipline, holding their followers in close subjection, are in a state of more or less disintegration. And after all, the FRIENDS OF LIBERTY aim not only not at the destruction, but will strenuously work for the enhancement of those principles of either party, which are truly salutary to the common weal, and in every essential republican. We believe that there is a majority of voters in every village and hamlet, in every town and city in the Continent, ready to join in leagues of freedom for the defence of the credit of the United States, and for the protection of personal liberty.

We appeal to every well-minded journal in the country to aid us by disseminating these views and advocating their purposes.

We appeal to those in every place in the land whither our voice can reach, who believe that the financial honor of the nation should be maintained untarnished, and that the rights of an American citizen to be a SOVEREIGN on the soil of his own country is not to be infringed either by specious legislation nor by mob violence—to gather together and form into local leagues, expressing for their objects the principles here presented, and communicate their organization to our Secretary, and from these incipient organizations State councils may speedily follow.

We appeal to men in all stations of life to come forward in aid of this great movement to save the treasury of the nation from pillage by unreasoning fanaticism, and to protect themselves in the full enjoyment of their God-given rights.

We appeal to the women of the land to give us their succor, for it is to preserve the liberties of true manhood to their children that we labor, and that their sons may not cry out for shame when the name of their country is mentioned in their hearing.

We appeal to all our fellow-citizens not to lag behind in the coming struggle to preserve what the Fathers have bequeathed to us, and to make lastingly true those declarations of the RIGHTS OF MAN, which electrified the world with their glory, revealed to our sires by the immortal spirit of '76.

The standard we unfurl has no doubtful meaning; on its bright folds are emblazoned PATRIOTISM AND DEVOTION TO LIBERTY in their purest meaning. No true American, loyal to the country of which he is a citizen—in whatever clime he may first have seen the light—and loyal to the principles upon which its institutions were founded, can feel indifference at this issue. Churchmen and laymen, employers and employed, are all alike concerned in the issue. Let the watchword be—

MAINTAIN THE CREDIT AND HONOR OF THE UNITED STATES;
PRESERVE THE SOVEREIGNTY OF THE INDIVIDUAL.

And, as the Union and NATIONAL LIBERTY TRIUMPHED, so will the financial stability of the National Government be upheld, the welfare and prosperity of the people be advanced, and PERSONAL LIBERTY be victorious for everlasting.*

---

* The following is a list of delegates present at the fourteenth convention:

Christ. Isengart, W. Schindler, E. Fitzgerald, Albany, N. Y.; E. Flood, J. Montgomery, C. Whiteside (guests), Albany, N. Y.; J. Carmichel, Amsterdam, N. Y.; Thomas M. Dukehart, Baltimore, Md.; Alley & Nichols, G. P. Burkhardt, Thomas Carberry, Isaac Cook & Co., Conrad Decker, Eldredge & Son, E. Habich, A. G. Houghton & Co., Haffenreffer & Co., Frank Jones, Mount Washington Brewing Company, H. & J. Pfaff, Rueter & Alley, John Roessle, Stanley & Co., A. C. Wallace, George W. Wadsworth, Dole Bros., Isaac Pratt, Jr., H. Strater & Co., Mills Bros., George F. Blake Mfg. Co., R. Higgins, William Appleton, Pier Bros., Boston, Mass.; Gen. Sewell, C. Perry (representatives of the Government); Chas. Beck, J. Jost, E. D. S. Shoemaker, Albert Zeigele, William C. Barthauer, Sol. Schen, G. A. Schaefer, H. Diehl, B. A. Lynde, M. Cline, A. F. Wheeler, William Lants, Buffalo, N. Y.; Christ. Moerlein, H. Goeppe, L. Soehnchen, H. Schlosser, A. Schwill, Cincinnati, O.; Philip Bartholomay, Conrad Seipp, P. Schoenhofen, C. Lichtenberger, G. W. Cornell, Chicago, Ill.; L. Schlather, Cleveland, O.; J. G. C. Schmersahl, Charles Schmersahl, Clarkstown, N. Y.; G. A. Bassermann, W. A. Hull, New Haven,

Chapter XIII.

FISCAL POLICY OF THE GOVERNMENT; SIMULTANEOUS REDUCTION OF DEBT AND TAXATION. PANIC OF 1873 IN THE MIDST OF PROSPERITY; ITS EFFECT AND CAUSE; BREWERS' ADDRESS IN RELATION TO IT. PRESIDENT CLAUSEN, SICK AND OVERWORKED, RESIGNS; RUETER SUCCEEDS HIM; PERSONAL NOTES. CONVENTION AT CINCINNATI; STATE OF INDUSTRY PAST AND PRESENT; PERSONAL REMINISCENCE; CAREER OF A CINCINNATI BREWER. PRESIDENT RUETER'S ADDRESS; REVIEW OF ASSOCIATION'S WORK; ELOQUENT PROMULGATION OF GUIDING PRINCIPLES; PROHIBITORY AGITATION DISSECTED. THE WHISKEY-RING, CONSIDERED HISTORICALLY AND IN RELATION TO ATTITUDE OF REVENUE OFFICE TOWARDS BREWERS. THE 2½ BUSHEL DECISION; ARBITRARY RULINGS AND PETTY ANNOYANCES. BREWERS SUE REVENUE COLLECTORS. APPOINTMENT OF A WASHINGTON ATTORNEY; HIS AND COMMITTEES' WORK. CONGRESSIONAL MATTERS; FISCAL POLICY CHANGED; INCREASE OF BEER-TAX THREATENED; BREWERS OPPOSE IT SUCCESSFULLY, ACQUIESCING IN INCREASED HOP-DUTY; NEW TARIFF AND INCREASED INTERNAL TAXES. BREWERS' SUCCESS IN RELATION TO SPIGOT-HOLE CLAUSE; LAW AMENDED; ITS TEXT. SPECIAL-TAX DECISION; BREWERS OBJECT TO IT AND SEEK CONGRESSIONAL REMEDY. OFFICERS OF ASSOCIATION. VOTE OF THANKS TO CLAUSEN, SCHAEFER AND AMERMAN; PERSONAL NOTES. SCIENTIFIC ESSAYS RECOMMENDED; SCHWARZ ON PROGRESS OF BREWING; HIS ATTITUDE CONCERNING UNMALTED CEREALS. CHARGES OF ADULTERATION AND FLINTOFF'S REPLY. LAUER'S SPEECH ON IMMIGRATION; REPELS CURTIS' ATTACK. NATIONAL MALTSTERS' ASSOCIATION ORGANIZED; ITS COMPOSITION AND OBJECTS. REDUCTION OF DUES PROPOSED. DEATH-ROLL. DECREASE OF BREWERIES. LIST OF DELEGATES.

The foregoing address to the people of the United States presupposes, on the part of the reader, a general

Conn.; F. Claus, A. Winter, Bridgeport, Conn.; John Smith, Clyde, N. Y.; Thomas D. Hawley, Detroit, Mich.; F. W. Anschuetz, Keokuk, Ia.; Jacob Schen, Lancaster, N. Y.; Morris Hughes, Pittsburg, Pa.; J. Obermann, Jos. Schlitz, F. Falk, Milwaukee, Wis.; F. Volz, Newark, N. J.; A. N. Beadleston, C. P. Hawkins, H. Ferris, David Jones, William Miles, D. G. Yuengling, G. M. Streeter, Jacob Ahles, George Bechtel, H. Clausen, P. Doelger, Georga Ehret, John Eichler, William Eckert, John Gillig, Christ. Huepfel, Jacob Hoffmann, John Kress, Christ. Koehne, L. F. Kuntz, J. J. Mentges, William Orth, Jacob Ruppart, H. Reinhardt, F. Schaefer, Joseph Setz, H. Zeltner, R. Katzenmayer, William H. Akin, John Flintoff, A. Schwarz, C. H. Brooks, C. W. Standart, S. B. Bettinger, Charles Wagner, William Splitler, J. M. Otto, Joseph Milles, H. Steubing, H. Loewenhelm, G. W. Gillette, M. C. Gillette, J. Robitcher, Joseph Naser, William C. Rogers, W. G. J. Wheeler, August Roeck, A. Pfund, John Weber, W. A. Lawrence, B. B. Sharp, G. W. Turrell, Thomas Gervan, H. C. Smith, N. Tarr, Louis Wolff, F. Twinch, R. Peutlage, H. Wellbacher, James Sparkmann, A. Wittemann, New York, N. Y.; E. Penrose, Thomas Penrose, Paterson, N. J.; J. T. Taylor, Albany, N. Y.; E. Frauenheim, William Eberhardt, Pittsburg, Pa.; N. Molter, Providence, R. I.; D. G. Yuengling, Sr., Pottsville, Pa.; V. Frank, Poughkeepsie, N. Y.; Gustavus Bergner, John F. Betz, John Bower, Peter Baltz, George Enser, Joseph Fielmayer, John Gardiner, C. F. Goldbeck, William Massey, John C. Miller, G. F. Rothacker, Peter Schemm, Sr., Peter Schemm, Jr., Christ. Herter, W. W. Hughes, W. Smith, F. Blackburne, Jr., J. Goldthorp, J. Watson, Philadelphia, Pa.; F. Lauer, Reading, Pa.; Geo. Dressel, Rondout, N. Y.; D. G. Yuengling, Jr., Richmond, Va.; H. Bartholomay, S. N. Oathout, Rochester, N. Y.; William J. Lemp, R. Jacobs, C. G. Stifel, C. F. Hoppe, St. Louis, Mo.; James Shaw, Springfield, Mass.; P. Zent, Tonawanda, N. Y.; R. Portner, Alexandria, Va.; L. Schade, William Metzger Washington, D. C.

knowledge of the events with which it deals; its framers had to take it for granted that the calamities which led to the terrible panic of 1873 were still fresh in the minds of the people and required no explanation. For this reason that part of this statesmen-like document which relates to the financial condition of the country may not be as intelligible to the reader as he doubtless would wish it to be. A few words will explain the situation. The address refers deprecatingly to the persistent policy of the Government to reduce the national debt, simultaneously with a steadily increasing contraction of the internal revenue system and a corresponding reduction of the revenues from this source. Abstractly considered, both of these objects seem highly laudable, assuming a prosperous condition of the country and a financial plethora, such as actually existed previous to the panic; although many citizens believed that while the tax-reduction might go on, the wiping out of the national debt by a generation that had already made extraordinary sacrifices, both of blood and money, in order to maintain the integrity of the Union, might be left in part to posterity. The policy of the Government, however, aimed not only at a complete rehabilitation of the nation's credit, never very seriously affected after the trying years of the civil war, but also at the saving of the enormous sums required for the payment of interest. Within four years (1869–1873) over $27,000,000 had thus been saved, the total reduction of the debt amounting to $383,629,783.

At the same time bonds bearing six per cent. interest were replaced by five per cent. bonds at the rate of $90,000,000 annually; and all this while the list of taxed articles was being contracted from year to year, reducing the revenues at a marvelous rate; and while in every domain of human activity, progress, success and prosperity crowned the efforts of our people.

Without any forewarning there came at this very period of national rejoicing the sudden failure of Jay Cooke & Co. (September, 1873), involving in its downfall a number of houses of the very best standing, who in turn dragged along with them into insolvency many smaller establishments, thus creating a panic which spread rapidly to the furthermost corners of our continent, causing an almost complete cessation of commerce, and the absolute suspension of all manufacturing business, excepting that devoted to the production of the necessaries of life. The cause of it all was over-production. In every direction an uncontrollable spirit of enterprise had outstripped the actual needs and demands of the market, and a terrible reaction became inevitable. The Government, although suffering from the panic both by reason of a depreciation of its notes and a very considerable decrease of revenues consequent upon the stagnant condition of the import-trade, was appealed to for help that could not be given, and the Treasury Department was flooded with the wildest schemes. As soon as Congress assembled (December, 1873,) these schemes assumed the shape of bills, of which there were at one time no less than sixty, all dealing with the results of the panic and presenting in their entirety a most heterogenous mass of conflicting propositions. The discussions and the work of the committees, which lasted until the beginning of April, 1874, led to no tangible result. It was virtually a struggle for the resumption of speciepayment and against inflation. Grant vetoed the bill passed by Congress, because in his opinion it did not go far enough; and thus the session ended without bringing relief or a definite change of the fiscal policy. The whole question remained in its unsettled state and no one could foretell what the future course of the Government would be. At this stage the brewers published the address reproduced in the preceding chapter; a document which added considerably to the intellectual character of the Boston convention. Its immediate effect upon legislation may not have been what had been expected, although even this was very marked; but the impression it made upon the public mind could not be gainsaid. The newspapers discussed it, each from the political standpoint of its editor; some approved, others bitterly opposed the brewers' views, but all concurred in the opinion that it was a highly important and significant document, worthy of careful consideration.

From 1862 to 1875 the brewers of the city of New York uninterruptedly enjoyed the signal honor of holding the office of president of the United States Brewers' Association, and during fully eight years of that period Henry Clausen filled the important place, performing its arduous duties with uncommon ability, and in a manner that redounded to his own credit and the honor and the lasting benefit of the association and trade. In the latter year he retired from office, and in doing so gave another striking proof of his sincere and profound attachment to the cause, and his solicitude for the industry's prosperity by urgently recommending to his colleagues of the Executive the selection of H. H. Rueter as his temporary successor.

This occurred in April, 1875, two months before the fifteenth convention was held at Cincinnati, and, unless everything were to be allowed to drift along in haphazard fashion until the meeting, the Executive was compelled to act promptly. Clausen's health had become precarious and his physician imperatively advised rest. Engaged in many industrial enterprises besides brewing, and participating to a considerable extent in municipal affairs (as his duty as a local legislator compelled him to do), Clausen was indeed an overworked man, and must himself have felt the need of rest, even if ill-health had not interposed a peremptory injunction against continued labor. At first his real motive may not have been appreciated ; at any rate, one might infer this from the urgency with which his colleagues insisted upon his continuance in office. He had always expressed his belief in rotation in office, and may have harbored the idea that his long-continued service might be construed as a monopoly of honors, and thus give rise to discontent. If that had been his motive—and we now know that it was not—the bearing of his fellow-members, and particularly of the man whom he recommended as his successor, would soon have disabused his mind of this delusion. Rueter peremptorily refused to accept the office when first notified of Clausen's intention. Flintoff was sent to Boston to persuade him to reconsider his decision, and his own and Clausen's nearest friends urged him to accept until they finally succeeded in inducing him to assume the responsible office temporarily. As if determined to render a reversal impossible, Clausen did not attend the Cincinnati convention.

Of the state of the industry and the character of the local association in that city mention has been made elsewhere. The former could not but be a prosperous one in view of the habits of the population, of whom a very large proportion regarded beer and wine as necessaries of life. The presence of a deep and broad stratum of the Palatine element at first induced energetic efforts in the direction of viticulture, and an enthusiastic Anglo-American, who during his travels abroad had become familiar with vine-growing on the banks of Old Father Rhine, took a leading part in this matter. But it was not until after many costly experiments had been made that the Ohio wine acquired the reputation it has to-day, and many years elapsed before the product of the transplanted vine yielded sufficient quantities of the golden liquid to cover the demand. In the meantime brewing became firmly rooted. On a very small scale common beer was brewed very early in the first third of the century; but neither local histories nor the Federal censuses afford us more than a superficial view of the state of the industry. Personal recollections, however, enable the chronicler to present at least one highly interesting item. About the year 1832 there came to Cincinnati a well-educated young Franconian, amply provided with money, who had left his native land with the determined intention of establishing a brewery in that city. He had probably read one of the many descriptions, then published in German papers, of the beauty and great wealth of natural resources of the Ohio valley, and concluded to try his fortune there. He had been trained, practically and theoretically, as an agriculturalist in the German sense of the term, and understood the growing of corn and wheat quite as well as sheep-raising or brewing and distilling. He established a brewery at Cincinnati in the year named, but failed shortly thereafter, losing his entire investment. He drifted to Washington, obtained a position in the Patent Office, and soon distinguished himself by a series of publications on agriculture, which attracted the attention of Congress, who, without his solicitation, voted him a compensation of one thousand dollars for an exceedingly valuable treatise on the wool-industry of Hungary. He represented Morse, the inventor of the electric telegraph, in Europe; was subsequently appointed American Consul at Stuttgart; travelled extensively in South Africa, and, returning to his adopted country, permanently settled in Washington, again taking up those literary labors which had established his reputation as an authority upon his chosen subjects of study. Surely, when Karl Ludwig Fleischmann established a brewery at Cincinnati and lost all his wealth in it, he little dreamt what the end of it all would be.

Those who engaged in the business at the same time were probably more successful, because they confined their operations to the old method which reqnired that to a very large extent the brewer should also be his own tapster. Up to the middle of the fifties this was the custom "across the (Cincinnati) Rhine," and there was probably no trans-rhenish brewery that had not a summer-garden attached to its saloon. The production in 1851 amounted to about 128,000 barrels in the city and 200,000 barrels in the entire State, and in 1875 the State's production aggregated 840,000 barrels. Local competition sometimes had proved an almost insurmountable hindrance, in that city, to effective co-operation among the brewers; and it may be that the peculiarly favorable conditions which existed before the temperance movement (there being then scarcely any restraint npon the traffic, for constitutional prohibition was a dead letter), contributed to this state of affairs. Even at that time, however, the brewers of Cincinnati always loyally and strongly supported the national association, and under pressure of adverse circumstances they were soon made aware of the necessity of local co-operation.

When the fifteenth convention assembled in their city (June 2d and 3d, 1875) they were fully organized and had been for some years. G. M. Herancourt was their president, and it was he who greeted the delegates and bade them welcome in the Queen City. President Rueter delivered a most eloquent address, covering fourteen closely printed pages, thus disproving his own apprehension, expressed in his first letter declining the presidency, that he "lacked many of the requisite qualifications, and could not possibly during the short space of time intervening fit himself even for a merely passable discharge of the duties devolving upon the presiding officer." Probably with a view to impressing upon his hearer's minds the vast scope and importance of the work performed by the association under the leadership of his predecessor, he devoted fully eight pages of his address to a succinct review of the convention proceedings, presenting them in their chronological sequence and with such commentaries upon them as the condition of things demanded. To the reader, fresh from the perusal of our detailed account of these very proceedings, a reproduction of this part of the address would probably not be desirable, but to the president's hearers his retrospective synopsis, illumined by the side-lights he threw upon it, must have been exceedingly interesting. The statistical part of his address need not be reproduced either, for the tables contained in this chapter cover them; but there is one of his observations which deserves particular attention. He showed that simultaneously with a marked decrease in the production of malt-liquors between 1873 and 1875, the Revenue Commissioner also reported a diminution of the number of breweries. Whether both these facts were principally due to business-depression, or only partly to this, and mainly to unwise liquor-laws, cannot be determined with that mathematical accuracy which is the pride and boast of the statistician; but no possible doubt can exist that the decrease in both directions was largest in the States having the most stringent restrictions, as in Massachusetts, for instance; whereas in States having liberal laws the production even progressed; the increase being largest in Wisconsin. Pertinent data will be presented in another part of this chapter.

On many previous occasions had the antagonism between the advocates of proper use and the defenders of prohibition been formulated and illustrated, but never before in quite as incisive, succinct and eloquent a manner, nor in diction as clear and unequivocal as President Rueter put it at this convention. He said:

"We believe, first of all, that each man has a right, morally and socially, to choose for himself whether he will use or refuse spirituous liquors, and that the enactment of sumptuary laws is in direct violation of this right and of personal liberty. We believe that the appetite for stimulants is so common, nay, so well nigh universal, that it must be recognized as a desire, a craving which is natural, which is human; that the use of stimulants from the poles to the equator—a fungus in Siberia, betel and hemp in Asia, ava in Polynesia, koumiss in Russia, maté in South America, coca leaf in Peru, tea, coffee, tobacco, opium, alcoholic and fermented liquors in all quarters of the earth—is absolutely inexplicable on any other hypothesis. We believe that prohibition has failed and will ever fail, because it refuses to recognize this natural appetite for stimulants; and that all it can ever hope to accomplish by a suppression of their legal sale, is to drive them into illicit channels. We believe that only such laws are wise and rational which contemplate a proper gratification of the desire for stimulants, which carefully distinguish between use and abuse, and by an intelligent regulation of their sale are calculated to lessen the deplorable effects of their abuse to a possible minimum. We believe that the light and innoxious malt-liquors which the brewer provides are above all others adapted to satisfy the appetite for stimulants with least danger of abuse. We know that other governments recognize this fact, and favor their consumption by removing all restrictions from their sale, by carefully adjusting their taxation with a view to their popular use, and in some instances even exempting them altogether. And we finally and conscientiously believe that our law-makers and our philanthropists do positive harm to the cause of temperance and good morals, so long as they refuse to acknowledge the truth of these tenets, and, arraying themselves on the side of prohibitionists, regard as enemies those who are really their allies."

The question as to how prohibitionists, hopelessly in the minority everywhere, could nevertheless succeed in putting their impress upon the laws of so many States, he answered in these words:

"Whatever victories the prohibitionists have therefore gained at the ballot box, have been won through the votes of sober citizens, who were neither abstinents nor intemperates. Their votes have decided all the prohibitory issues, for they form the overwhelming majority of temperates, and constitute the main bulk of the political parties. A terrible pressure was brought to bear on this great mass of citizens, always moving at half-tide on the moral question of temperance or abstinence. The fierce abstinent said to the temperate: 'Whatever you claim for your own individual right, do you believe the State has a right to make drunkards, to make paupers and criminals, to license iniquity?' It was decent to answer, 'No.' Politically stupid as it was, legally illogical and dogmatic as it was, it became respectable for the average voter to answer, 'No.' 'Then vote prohibition,' the men who were in earnest said, and as earnestness always carries force, they had their way. If to this stupefaction of the moral consciousness and befogging of political intellect be added, the pandering to political passions and motives, political barter and dicker, 'log-rolling,' and 'pipe-laying,' it is clear that there was no moral responsibility for the rank and file in voting at the polls. No one changed his habits by reason of his vote for a liquor law, and each ordered his case of wine, or bought his bottle of whiskey just as coolly as if he had not stood for the principle of absolute prohibition at the polls. Thus were politicians evolved out of the abstinence pressure, when passing from the moral into the political sphere. Men of strong natures, and abounding in animal spirits, the men who govern society, so far as administration goes—the very men who are more likely to drink than the average citizen, the average conference leader or Sunday-school teacher—are driven into a false and pharisaical obeisance to liquor legislation, even if they do not conceal their personal habits. Add to these various elements of honest, if mistaken, conviction, of deluded acquiescence, and enforced compliance, the nasty, foul, hybrid creatures who feign a virtue, when they have it not, and drink secretly, while in public they maintain temperance, prohibition, total abstinence, and the semblance of any virtue their snivelling natures can contain, and we have the combination, or better, the mixture for the administration of law or 'positive morality.'

"It would be folly or self-deception to deny or to cover up the fact, that mainly from the ranks of Republican voters have been furnished the converts and conscripts which were needed to give to the handful of honest prohibitionists whatever influence and weight as a political body they possess to-day, and that under the auspices of the Republican party have been gained whatever victories over sacred rights and personal liberty prohibitionists can to-day flaunt in the faces of freemen. Nothing can be further removed from my purpose, and nothing more alien to the intentions and aspirations, which animated the founders of our Association, than to throw the firebrand of party politics among its members, and thereby jeopardize or destroy its usefulness for its legitimate mission. But as good citizens, whatever our political professions, we must hold to strict accountability a great political party, if by its influence or connivance, through its organization and party machinery, tyrannical and unjust temperance laws are burdened upon the people, or retained upon the statute-book, through State legislation. In doing this, we do not put 'beer' above politics, but place 'principle' above politics, and can rightfully call on every liberty-loving fellow-citizen to join our cause."

In pointing to a strong current of public opinion favoring a license-system, such as had just been introduced in Massachusetts, the president dwelt with force and eloquence upon the necessity of maintaining the brewers' policy of a broad discrimination in favor of malt-liquors, not only in regard to fees, but also in the matter of all other regulative restrictions. In a casual, but none the less effective way he also mentioned some of the more noticeable indications of a general revolt against prevailing corruption and the possibility of organizing a third party, combining the honest men of both political organizations in an effort to purify politics.

In this latter particular he also had to take it for granted that his hearers were familiar with the events to which he referred, and needed no further explanation.

It is different with the readers of this history, who will probably be unable to recall on the spur of the moment the state of affairs to which reference is here made. In the year 1875 official corruption in the highest places seemed to have reached its climateric. The Shepards and Belnaps and McDonalds of the Administration had well-nigh succeeded in besmirching even the name of General Grant, the people's idol, whose honesty no one doubts to-day, but whose loyalty to his corrupt friends, and confidence in their integrity had induced him to do and to omit acts which could not but cast the gravest doubt and strongest suspicion even upon his personal and official motives. And to crown all that had gone before, the year 1875 brought the public exposure of the Whiskey-Ring, an organized band of robbers, who had in their pay court officers, revenue officials, party leaders, and law-makers, and with such assistance succeeded in defrauding the Government and the people to an extent that will never be fully known, because all the criminals were not caught, nor could the whole amount of the defalcations and thefts of those who were indicted ever be fully ascertained. When Secretary Bristow had completed his wonderful work of investigation there were indicted one hundred and fifty-seven distillers, rectifiers and wholesale dealers, and *eighty-six revenue officers*. The distilleries seized represented a capital of $1,500,000, and the illicit spirits seized by the Government amounted in value to $1,600,000. Singularly enough, the only exhaustive history of the Whiskey-Ring was written by one of the convicted thieves, a Col. McDonald, supervisor of internal revenue at St. Louis, Mo., who was appointed in spite of the urgent protest of Senator Schurz, Gratz Brown and other prominent Republicans of that State; and who in this book of his attempts to prove that the Whiskey-Ring was asked to furnish and did furnish the means with which to "fight Schurz and every enemy of Grant even to the death." The testimony of a convicted thief should have no historical weight in the eyes of earnest truth-seekers; at all events, we would not accept it if unsupported by unimpeachable evidence, and even then we should be strongly inclined to discount it, if the motive of the testifier be a desire for vengeance which is glaringly manifest in McDonald's version. But there is ample evidence of a trustworthy character that at one time the thieves had full and free communication with Washington, and exercised an influence which placed them in a position to dictate appointments to, and dismissals from, the service. This does not prove, however, that their influence extended to the President of the United States. The trial proved that officers of the courts and all grades of revenue officials and employees were implicated, each having a price formally fixed and regularly paid for certain stated services. Various methods of frauds were being used; but no difficulty could be encountered in any, so long as store-keepers, gaugers, collectors and supervisors co-operated, as they did, to make these thefts as successful and profitable as possible. The store-keeper, for instance, allowed two quick fermentations within the period prescribed by law for one, the distillers books being manipulated accordingly; the gauger failed to cancel the stamps upon spirits ready for shipment, either allowing the empty vessels to be returned to the rectifier with the stamp intact, to be re-filled; or permitting the removal of the uncancelled stamps to be used again. In this and other ways frauds were rendered perfectly safe and practically illimitable. One firm testified that they manufactured two hundred and twenty-five thousand gallons a month of which fully one-half was sold without payment of tax upon it; and this meant an illicit sale of 750,000 gallons annually, for which the Government received not one cent, although the consumer had to pay the full tax, which went into the pockets of the thieving manufacturers and Federal officers. At a moderate estimate these fraudulent operations alone yielded to their perpetrators no less than five millions of dollars annually, not to speak of the stupendous frauds practiced by distillers at every change in the tax-rate.*

Viewed in the light of these frauds the attitude of some of the revenue collectors towards the brewers in regard to purely technical violations of the law seems strongly suggestive of what Lauer so frequently complained of, *i. e.*, an attempt to blackmail the trade under threat of prosecution or rather persecution. And it is but another proof of the brewers' integrity that they invariably resisted these attempts, appealing directly to the Commissioner, or, failing to find justice there, to the courts. The righteousness of their course inspired them with the necessary courage and back-bone to meet the wiles of corrupt officials by the exercise of their rights as citizens and tax-payers.

This disposition on the part of revenue-officials to harass the trade—perhaps for a purpose other than that of a strict and faithful execution of the law—had again come to the surface at the very time of Bristow's exposure of the Whiskey-Ring. In many districts collectors assessed taxes upon what they alleged to be the difference between the quantity of malt-liquors returned by the brewer as actually sold and the quantity which, judging from the consumption of malt, the collector believed had been produced. Comparing the material-

---

* D. A. Wells proved that even at the lowest tax-rate (20 cents per gallon in 1862) the distillers only paid tax on 16,000,000 gallons, although the census of 1860 showed a domestic production of 90,000,000 gallons.

account with the sale-returns, and allowing a certain quantity of malt for every barrel of beer, they arrived at a basis of computation as arbitrary as it was unreliable. A. Reymann, of Wheeling, paid under protest a small amount ($47.00) thus assessed, and was requested by the Agitation Committee to sue the collector for the recovery of the amount; but shortly after this occurrence the revenue officers at St. Louis, the origin and home, the very hot-bed of the distillers' frauds, called upon the brewers in that city to render an exact account of the material used, to the end that the excess of malt over and above two and one-half bushels per barrel of beer returned as sold, might be taxed at the rate fixed by law for malt-liquors. Simultaneously with this the brewers of Baltimore, New York, Peoria and other places received similar notices. There never has been, was not then, and is not now any clause in the Internal Revenue Act limiting the brewer in the use of his material, or requiring him to make a return of materials used. The requirement as to keeping an account of materials did not justify the collectors to demand such a return, and their assessment of taxes under the circumstances described was clearly contrary to law; yet, although the Agitation Committee, represented by Lauer, Bergner, Portner, Jones, J. C. G. Huepfel, Schade, and Lewis, submitted these cases to the Commissioner with a strong argument in favor of an abatement of these assessments, the Department insisted upon its course, and the brewers were compelled to pay the assessed amounts under protest, and to proceed by process of law against the collectors for the recovery of the money. The Philadelphia brewers were the first to proceed methodically and jointly in this direction, and as it was supposed that their test-case (that of Bergdoll and Psotta for the recovery of $1,419) would establish a precedent for all cases throughout the country, the fifteenth convention, upon Lauer's motion, appropriated $500 for the purpose. The brewers in all other parts of the country adopted the course here outlined, but there were some notable exceptions which deserve particular mention. Under the leadership of Joseph Liebmann, the brewers of Williamsburgh, for instance, peremptorily refused to pay the assessed amounts, and when the collector attempted to enforce payment they obtained an injunction against him, giving the required bond during the pendency of the litigation.

In reading the many unwarrantable interferences with the trade on the part of revenue officials, one is almost tempted to suspect a systematic attempt to divert attention from quarters where stupendous tax-frauds were being perpetrated. In Chicago, Bartholomae & Roesing and Conrad Seipp had been notified by the collector that they must pay tax on malt-liquor consumed by their employees; although, as the reader will recollect, the Department, at the suggestion of the association, had long ago decided that beer so consumed is not taxable. A simple remonstrance, submitted to the Commissioner by Robert Portner and Louis Schade, sufficed to stop the Milwaukee collector in his unlawful course.

Such petty annoyances multiplied and suggested to the Executive and the Agitation Committee the advisability of having a representative of the association permanently located at Washington to whom might be entrusted the task of conferring with the Revenue Commissioner whenever questions of this character arose, as neither the officers nor the members of said committee could afford, nor could they reasonably be expected to devote so much of their time to these minor matters; seeing that, even so, enough remained for them to do at Washington that could not be delegated to an employee.

Robert Portner had of late years voluntarily assumed a goodly share of such work, and during the time which elapsed between the fourteenth and fifteenth conventions his vigilance and activity had frequently been very helpful to the committee, particularly in the cases already mentioned, and in two extremely important legislative matters, in all of which he needed the services of a local assistant. As Schade understood the entire revenue-question, having made it a subject of special study, and was regarded as the natural representative of the trade by reason of his being the publisher and editor of a paper established with the brewers' means, nothing could have been more logical than to call upon him for such assistance. Both he and Portner performed valuable work for the association, and the vote of thanks, proposed by the Executive and cheerfully given by the convention, appears to have been fully deserved by them. We shall presently see what the condition of affairs just described led to.

So far as Congressional matters were concerned the brewers needed all the sagacity, prudence and foresight of their leaders to prevent the imposition of additional burdens, and at the same time to secure a very necessary modification of that part of the revenue law which provided that no package shall have more than one spigot-hole.

The danger of an additional tax on malt-liquors arose from the financial condition described in this chapter. The commercial and industrial interests of the country demanded some action promising to restore confidence and bring general relief; the elections revealed a potent opposition to the ruling party; in fact, the Republican majority in the House of Representatives had been wiped out, and the leaders appreciated the necessity of prompt action. The effort towards the resumption of specie payment, frustrated by Grant's veto because it did not in his opinion go far enough, was now successfully renewed, and an act having that end in view was passed in January, 1875. Grant, in approving it, addressed a special message to the Senate, recommending, among other things, an increase of the revenue as an indispensable requirement of the object aimed at. Instead of the rapid decrease of revenue which had for years characterized Federal legislation, Congress now adopted the very policy which was clearly outlined in the brewers' appeal. And in this change of policy lurked the danger of additional burdens upon malt-liquors. A tax of two dollars upon every barrel of beer was almost the first proposition made in this direction, and the Agitation Committee must have been in a sad quandary when, considering their instructions to oppose increased import duties upon hops, and to ask for lower malt-duty, they found themselves confronted by this new move. Their report is very brief upon the subject; it states that the sub-committee, consisting of Lauer, Bergner, Massey, Portner, Flintoff and Schade, discovered immediately that the proper committees of both Houses were determined that the "brewers must have something to carry in the new revenue bill," and that it would, therefore, have been unwise to oppose an addition of three cents per pound to the duty on hops, or to ask for a reduction of the barley-duty. It is well to bear in mind that the proposition to double the beer-tax made its appearance thus early; it re-appeared on every subsequent occasion, whenever the Government needed additional revenues either by reason of defective fiscal legislation or in consequence of the reckless extravagance of Congress in the expenditure of the people's money. In order to complete our account of the situation it must be stated that the new law (Act of March

3d, 1875,) repealed the clause providing for a reduction of ten per cent. in certain customs duties under the law of 1872; increased the duties on sugars, hops and other articles, and raised the internal tax upon spirits from 70 to 90 cents per gallon, and on tobacco from 20 to 24 cents per pound.

At the same time the revenue clauses relating to the collection of the latter taxes were modified in many respects, and here the Washington Committee had an opportunity of securing a modification of the clause prescribing that brewers' packages shall have but one spigot-hole. Designed to prevent frauds, this provision caused much unnecessary annoyance and inconvenience to the brewers, and could easily have been dispensed with in view of the many other precautionary regulations of the law, and the almost unlimited power of the Commissioner to prevent fraudulent practices—not to mention its absolute superfluity on account of the oft-attested integrity of the trade. Unable to secure the Commissioner's approval of the modification, the brewers finally proceeded without his aid. Through their colleagues of Milwaukee they succeeded in inducing Senator Carpenter to introduce a bill permitting two spigot-holes, and the Agitation Committee at once entered upon a very spirited campaign, as we may infer from the report, in which they dwell upon the assistance they solicited and received from Senators Logan, Bayard, Carpenter, Fenton, Schurz and Sherman—then Chairman of the Senate Finance Committee—and from Representatives Foster (Ohio), Rusk (Wisconsin), Randall and Clymer (Pennsylvania), and E. H. Roberts (New York). Shortly before the enactment of the new revenue law the collectors in Milwaukee had seized 100 kegs of beer belonging to P. Best, and 85 kegs belonging to V. Blatz for violation of this obnoxious clause. Upon proper representation by the Washington Committee, the Commissioner subsequently mitigated the assessment and penalty to one-sixth of the original amount. The section of the law as amended reads as follows, viz. :

> That every brewer shall obtain, from the collection of the district in which his brewery or brewery-warehouse is situated, and not otherwise unless such collector shall fail to furnish the same upon application to him, the proper stamps, and shall affix, upon the spigot-hole in the head of every hogshead, barrel, keg, or other receptacle in which any fermented liquor is contained, when sold or removed from such brewery or warehouse, (except in case of removal under permit, as hereinafter provided,) a stamp denoting the amount of the tax required upon such fermented liquor, which stamp shall be destroyed by driving through the same the faucet through which the liquor is to be withdrawn, or an air-faucet of equal size, at the time the vessel is tapped, in case the vessel is tapped through the other spigot-hole, (of which there shall be but two, one in the head and one in the side,) and shall, also, at the time of affixing such stamp, cancel the same by writing or imprinting thereon the name of the person, firm, or corporation by whom such liquor was made, or the initial letters thereof, and the date when canceled. Every brewer who refuses or neglects to affix and cancel the stamps required by law in the manner aforesaid, or who affixes a false or fraudulent stamp thereto, or knowingly permits the same to be done, shall pay a penalty of one hundred dollars for each barrel or package on which such omission or fraud occurs, and be imprisoned not more than one year.

At this time another revenue-matter claimed the committee's attention. Secretary Noth of the Iowa Brewers' Association informed them that Mr. Glab, of Dubuque, was required to take out a new license upon the dissolution of partnership in the firm of which he had been a member, and of whose brewery he had become sole owner. His refusal to take out a new license brought on a legal contest in the United States Circuit Court, resulting in a decision adverse to the Revenue Department. The collector, nevertheless, insisted upon payment of the special-tax, and when the committee appealed to the Commissioner, referring to the judicial decision in the premises, they were informed that the Court was in error as the section under which the renewal of a license was required as often as the brewery changed ownership, had never been repealed. The only proper remedy lay in a modification of the law, and to that end a representative from Pennsylvania (probably Hiester Clymer) at the brewers' request introduced a bill in the House of Representatives.

Relating to the organization of the fifteenth convention there remains to be said that the nominations submitted in the report by the proper committee, consisting of C. Boss, J. Gardiner, P. Schoenhofen, A. G. Huepfel and J. Obermann, were as follows: Honorary Presidents: Henry Clausen, Fred. Lauer; Vice-Presidents: Ferd. Krug, Ignatz Huber, J. H. McAvoy, P. Lieber, F. R. Herold, John Wieland, George Juenemann, J. Fehrenbach, George Noth, Chas. Geisbauer, George Auer, Charles G. Stifel, Anthony Yoerg, Frank Jones, Jacob Ahles, E. W. Voigt, Joseph Schaller, F. Lang, John Baier, H. Weinhard, William Massey, N. Molter, J. Seeger, George Bauernschmidt, F. Rennert, Robert Portner, A. Reymann, Fred. Pabst; Secretaries: Gustavus Bergner, Andrew E. Leicht, R. Reinboldt.

President Rueter then appointed these committees: On Revenue Resolutions: F. Lauer, G. Bergner, and G. M. Herancourt; on Temperance Resolutions: Fred. Lauer, Charles G. Stifel, J. Kauffmann, John F. Betz, Gustavus Bergner, Joseph Grasser, Robert Portner, P. Lieber, Mathias Dick, L. Schlather, F. Metz; Finance: George Ehret, C. E. Gehring, Gerhard Lang; Petitions: A. G. Huepfel, Jacob F. Kuhn, A. E. Leicht, J. G. Sohn, and George Enser.

To the name of F. Lauer, to whom alone had been given the post of honorary president at every convention since 1863, was now added that of Henry Clausen, Jr., the retiring president. Probably no resolution ever offered in a brewers' meeting reflected more faithfully the sentiments of every delegate than the one which Lauer introduced at this convention anent Clausen's retirement:

"The members of the National Association consider it their imperative duty to express their deep and heartfelt regret that their honored President, Henry Clausen, Jr., has been compelled by considerations of his health to offer his resignation. They will ever remember the valuable and efficient services which he has rendered the association. To him it is chiefly to be ascribed that the Brewers' Association has gained a national reputation and has made its influence felt in the halls of Congress as well as throughout the country."

At the same time the association lost by resignation two other officers both of whom were justly held in the highest esteem, viz.: the treasurer, Frederick Schaefer, and Peter Amerman. Schaefer had uninterruptedly served for fifteen years, ever since the organization of the association, and during this period had managed the affairs of his office with uncommon skill and fidelity. Amerman had always been one of the leading minds of the ale-brewers' association, and long before these two branches of the trade became united with the national body, he had promptly assisted the Washington Committee in the performance of its arduous duties. Subsequently, having been elected to this body, he almost invariably accompanied the sub-committee to the Capital. While Schaefer resigned to make room for a new man, Amerman did so, because he retired from the brewing business. The convention bestowed upon both the well-merited distinction of resolutions of thanks. Honorary membership had not yet been adopted by the association as a mark of recognition and distinction for retiring members and officers of the standing and merits of these two, else it would surely have been conferred upon them.

The vacancies thus created were filled by the election of Henry H. Rueter as president, and Jacob Ahles as treasurer. With Katzenmayer as secretary, Flintoff was re-elected as assistant scribe. The question of appointing a representative at Washington was brought before the convention in the report of the Committee on Petitions, recommending the usual subsidy of $200, each, to the two trade-journals; an appropriation of $400 as a salary for the assistant secretary, and concluding with this proposition: "In the absence of any petition, but in consideration of services rendered and to be rendered, the committee recommends that Louis Schade, Esq., be made counsellor for the association at the Federal Capital at a salary of $500 for the ensuing year." C. G. Stifel warned against hasty appropriations, and this elicited a number of highly eulogistic remarks on the services of Schade. Miller and Massey joined in these and the former proposed to increase the amount to $1,200, but withdrew his motion upon Schade's assurance that the sum named by the committee would be amply sufficient.

An incident which occurred when this report was read shows how well the trade-journals filled their allotted sphere, receiving generous support, and prospering with the industry they served. A. Schwarz, in the name of the *Amerikanische Bierbrauer*, accepted the gratuity of $200, but with justifiable pride pointed out the fact that he no longer needed this assistance, and would give one-half of the sum in equal shares to the brewers' and coopers' benevolent societies of the cities of New York and Cincinnati; while the other he intended to give as a reward to "the foreman who had served longest in one and the same establishment with zeal, diligence, sobriety and good results." Beginning with practically nothing, Schwarz had within seven years succeeded in placing his paper on a paying basis. At this convention he also delivered the first scientific address on brewing, in fact the first speech ever made in a brewers' meeting that related to the process of brewing. It may have been prompted by a circular issued by the Executive in January, 1875, calling attention to the fact that the festivities arranged by local associations of convention-cities, although highly gratifying as evidences of commendable hospitality, generosity and brotherly feeling, tended to interfere with the more serious duties of the meeting, and had thus far had the effect of precluding the possibility of considering technical and scientific matters. The local associations responded encouragingly to this suggestion, and expressed a desire to see a new departure inaugurated. This was probably the reason why Schwarz was called upon to speak on the scientific development of brewing. What he said was timely, and in the eyes of many delegates may have had the charm and advantage of novelty; to our readers it would be "ancient history," hence we refrain from reproducing even its gist. But as an evidence of the mutability of views and opinions under the influence of scientific discoveries, it may interest the present-day brewer to learn that Schwarz advocated the exclusive use of barley-malt, deprecating the admixture of any unmalted cereal. We know that subsequently his own researches and the experiments made in his own laboratory forced upon him the conviction that a better, more palatable and equally wholesome beer can be made of barley-malt, with an admixture of unmalted cereal, than of barley-malt alone. At the Cincinnati convention Schwarz evidently intended to meet, in what he then considered a proper way, the frequent charge of adulteration brought against brewers. The use of rice and corn, in fact, of starch, derived from cereals other than barley, was just beginning to find favor, and prejudice and ignorance at once seized upon this as a welcome opportunity for villifying the brewers and charging them with adulteration. The *Cincinnati Gazette*, in an editorial article, had advised the fifteenth convention to devote its attention to the subject of noxious beer; and it surely must appear a little singular that it was Flintoff, not Schwarz, who took up the gauntlet. The following quotation from his address is a fair specimen of the style, both amusing and instructive, which Flintoff generally used when addressing the conventions. He said:

"This newspaper editor accuses you of using corn instead of barley in brewing. Suppose you acknowledge the corn, what then? Why, he talks about generating fusel oil which the distillers can get rid of, but which the brewers can't. Which, as it happens, is *vice versa*. The brewer does not create it, and the distiller does. But this is a mere bug-bear. I will refer him to any good chemical dictionary as to how fusel oil is created. Beer he evidently knows very little about. Chemistry will inform him that starch is starch, whether obtained from barley, rice, potatoes, or corn; that starch is the base of grape sugar; that sugar is the base of alcohol; that hops are a clarifier and preservative; that alcohol is necessary as a corrective and preservative, and that the combination of the two in boiling water produces a healthy, harmless and nutritious beverage, highly refreshing and gently stimulating. But if the man who wrote that article partakes alternately of water, whiskey and beer, he will find a fight inside of him which will ultimately give him a sore head.

"Gentlemen, amid the seething mass of corruption and fraud by which we are surrounded—rings in business, scandals in theology, venalities in office—amid it all, social, moral, political or theological, the brewers come out the brightest and purest, for they brew honest liquor and they honestly pay their taxes."

Exposed to continual attacks throughout the year, the association, as a rule, lacked adequate means of instantly replying to these assaults at the places where they originated; and it was therefore but natural and perfectly proper that whenever an opportunity offered for a prompt public rejoinder, for a vindication of the trade,

Fifteenth Convention. 397

an exposure of calumnies, or a correction of popular errors and fallacy, the members of the association should eagerly avail themselves of it on the spot—as Flintoff did on this occasion. Lauer had frequently pursued the same course, so had Clausen, and his successors emulated these examples. At the fifteenth convention Lauer singled out an oration by George William Curtis in which the foreign immigration was arraigned for introducing, besides ignorance and vice, "powerful organized influences not friendly to the republican principle of freedom of thought and action." Lauer never delivered a more forceful, incisive and pointed speech, and his words derived particular weight from the fact that he himself belonged to that class of immigrants whose patriotic efforts and sacrifices he cited in refutation of the charge of Curtis. He said:

"Now, in the name of the German-Americans who compose a majority of this Brewers' Congress, in the name of the German immigrants everywhere throughout the United States, in the name of the immigrants from all nations and every clime, I denounce this language as a libel upon them, as false as it is foul. Can Mr. Curtis tell us how many of the men who took the field at Concord and Lexington and repulsed the British General Gage were of foreign birth? Can he tell us how many of the brave soldiers, officers and privates, who fought under Washington and his foreign volunteer Generals, Lafayette, De Kalb, Kosciuzko, Steuben, Montgomery and others, and aided in achieving American independence, were 'foreign immigrants?' Can he tell us how many regiments of the Union Army during the recent war of the Rebellion were recruited from 'immigrants and the children of immigrants?' The answers to these questions will give the lie to his accusation that immigration has 'introduced powerful and organized influences not friendly to the republican principle' more effectively than any words that I could employ.

"Let this beautiful, populous and prosperous city of Cincinnati, appropriately named the 'Queen City of the West,' bear witness against the base libel and the baser libeler. Of her population of 216,000 by the census enumeration of 1870, not less than 80,000 were of foreign birth! Look across 'the Rhine' and see what the German immigrant has done and is doing towards building up the trade and industry of this city. Let Mr. Curtis come with us and mingle among that orderly, quiet, frugal and industrious people, and learn from ocular demonstration what sort of an American citizen the German immigrant becomes when he makes here his home. He may hear another language than the one he is used to speaking, but he will find that the 'immense ignorance,' which he professes to fear so much, has no existence except in his own mind, warped by prejudice and dwarfed by narrow bigotry. The republican principle of freedom of thought and action is as dear to the immigrant as it can be to the native-born citizen; and it is for that very principle, in opposition to the tyranny of Sabbatarian legislation, sumptuary laws and sectarian intolerance, that we, the Brewers' Congress of the United States, contend here to-day. 'Freedom of thought and action,' the unalienable right of man, is guaranteed to us under the Constitution, to which we have sworn allegiance. We know what it means, and, in the future, as in the past, we, 'immigrants and the children of immigrants,' will always be found among its stoutest advocates and defenders."

At this convention the only German speech was that of A. Schwarz, and it was probably the only set speech uttered in that language since the adoption of the bilingual resolution. In fact, not only all speeches and proceedings, but also the reports now appeared exclusively in English garb. German translations of the latter were invariably prepared and printed; but when President Rueter first asked for an expression of opinion as to whether the annual reports should also be read in the German language, the vote upon it showed such a decided majority on the negative side, as to dispel the last trace of doubt concerning the future of this question.

The association's efforts to bring about the co-operation of all kindred trades resulted, as we have seen, in the acquisition of a considerable number of members from the ranks of the maltsters and hop-dealers. Frequent personal contact and intercourse, for which the annual conventions afforded ample opportunities, helped to mature a plan not at all contemplated by the leaders of the parent association when they invited the kindred trades. A comparatively large number of maltsters had attended the Boston convention, and it was there that the project of forming a National Maltsters' Association was first suggested. In September, 1874, the representatives of the trade in eleven of the principal malt-producing States convened at Niagara Falls, and effected this national organization. Its President, B. A. Lynde, of Buffalo, N. Y., addressed the fifteenth convention on the subject, and outlined the objects of the association in these words: (1) To cultivate friendly relations among all who are engaged in the business of malting; (2) to obtain information relative to the extent and quality of the crops of barley and hops, and to exchange views in relation to the same; (3) to examine into the merits of any new inventions; (4) to consult together upon the best methods of malting, with a view to advancing the standard quality; and (5) to promote and protect the malting business in all its interests. Lynde took a higher ground when he dwelt upon the necessity of making common cause with the brewing trade in everything pertaining to the temperance question. He said that every assault of fanaticism and every attempt at unjust legislation which the brewers encounter was aimed, indirectly, but just as certainly, at the interests of the maltsters; and that in resisting injustice and endeavoring to enlighten public opinion the maltster should bear his proper share of the necessary efforts and labors.

This new organization did not diminish the membership of the brewers' body; on the contrary, those maltsters who had been members before induced others to join, and thus what might at the first glance have appeared as a detriment to the further growth and development of the parent body, really inured to its advantage. The financial condition of the association continued to flourish to such an extent that C. G. Stifel felt justified in proposing a reduction of the annual dues to ten cents for every hundred barrels of beer sold. The motion would probably have been adopted if President Rueter had not called attention to the fact that it involved an amendment to the constitution and would, therefore, have to be announced within a stated period before the convention at which it was to be voted upon. Stifel then introduced a formal notice embodying his proposition, which was referred to the Executive for submission at the succeeding convention, if upon enquiry among the local associations such a course appeared desirable.

This convention ordered the adoption of a design for a membership-certificate, selected by J. Gardiner, P. Schoenhofen and H. Schimper, and, upon C. G. Stifel's suggestion, ordered that every certificate should bear the date on which the member to whom it was to be issued, entered the association. The adopted design, graphically descriptive and symbolical of the trade, is the one in use at the present time.

The death-roll of the association embraced three names: C. Isengart of Troy, Joseph Schlitz of Milwaukee, and Joseph Uhrig of St. Louis. The death of J.

Schlitz, and of one of the twin-sons of William Frahm of Davenport, also a member, occurred under singularly distressing circumstances. Both were passengers on the ill-fated steamer "Schiller," which went down off the coast of England on her trip to Hamburg, dragging with her to the bottom of the sea nearly all her passengers.

Concerning the data relative to the decrease in the number of breweries, alluded to in another part of this chapter, we quote the following from Schade's address at this convention, viz.:

"Taking the official reports of the Internal Revenue Department for 1873 and 1874, we find that Mississippi and Florida have each lost, in 1874, all their three breweries; Arkansas, her one brewery; Alabama, three out of five; Georgia, three out of seven; South Carolina, three out of four; Tennessee, five out of seven, and Virginia, four out of ten. Texas, too far away from Cincinnati, lost only eight out of forty-two.

"The Local Option law of Pennsylvania reduced the number of breweries in that State from 500 in 1873 to 346 in 1874, thus destroying 154 breweries in one year. In Michigan, out of 202 breweries in 1873, only 68 remained in 1874. In Ohio the crusaders destroyed 68 out of 296 breweries, *while they increased the number of distilleries from* 51 *to* 56; in Indiana the Baxter law stopped 66 out of 158, or more than one-third of the whole number; Illinois only lost 37 out of 210; Missouri breweries were reduced from 130 to 92; in New York the breweries decreased from 481 to 349, though the amount of beer manufactured was only 7,976 barrels less in 1874 than in 1873; Massachusetts lost 9 out of 49 breweries; in Maryland the breweries were reduced from 74 to 65; in New Jersey the number of breweries has decreased from 81 to 54; in Kentucky, from 53 to

34; in Montana, from 31 to 23; in Kansas, from 55 to 40; in Minnesota, from 132 to 109; in Iowa, from 174 to 129; in Wisconsin, from 280 to 201."*

---

* The following is a list of delegates to the fifteenth convention:

J. F. Story, Albany, N. Y.; Robert Portner, Alexandria, Va.; Henry H. Rneter, Boston, Mass.; G. Banernschmidt, J. H. Vonder Horst, Baltimore, Md.; Charles Gerber, H. Grau, Jacob F. Kuhn, F. J. Kaltenbach, Gerhard Lang, George Luipold, Henry Diehl, B. A. Lynde, A. J. Wheeler, Buffalo, N. Y.; G. M. Herancourt, Hanck & Windisch, Gambrinus Stock Co., Foss, Schneider & Brenner, John Kauffmann & Co., H. Lackmann, Christian Moerlein, M. Muller, Nichaus & Klinkhammer, J. G. Sohn & Co., Schaller & Gerke, Windisch, Muhlhauser & Bro., Albert Schwill & Co., J. Brinkmann, M. Goepper & Sons, Elsas & Fritz, Cincinnati, O.; J. Geisbauer, Lang & Knoll, Covington, Ky.; McAvoy, A. E. Leicht, C. Schoenhofen, L. C. Huck, J. Bullen, C. Cornell, E. W. Bloke, Chicago, Ill.; C. Fenchter, Cairo, Ill.; E. Agate, Cuba, N. Y.; C. E. Gehring, H. Baer, Isaac Leisy, H. Muller, Leonard Schlather, Cleveland, O.; C. Schwind, Dayton, O.; E. W. Voigt, R. Lehmann, W. C. Stoppel, Detroit, Mich.; H. Kalvelage, J. Koehler, Erie, Pa.; F. Herold, Hartford, Conn.; P. Lieber, H. Boas, C. Maus, Indianapolis, Ind.; J. Huber, G. Wagner, Rock Island, Ill.; L. Ebert, Ironton, O.; A. Munzenberger, Kenosha, Wis.; E. Hatzfeld, Lancaster, Pa.; P. Schillinger, Louisville, Pa.; L. W. Falk, F. Obermann, Milwaukee, Wis.; John Baier, H. F. Schimper, C. Immen, Newark, N. J.; Peter Ott, A. Ott, Norwalk, O.; Roesing, New Albany, Ind.; J. Ahles, Henry Clansen, Jr., George C. Clausen, George Ehret, J. G. Gillig, A. G. Huepfel, Fred. Schaefer, D. G. Ynengling, Jr., E. G. W. Woerz, R. Katzenmayer, J. Flintoff, A. Schwarz, E. Grosse, Robert Schroeder, Henry W. Schmidt, W. G. L. Wheeler, W. H. Akin, G. C. Pier, Paul Weidner, Thos. Girvan, M. Gillette, W. A. Lawrence, New York, N. Y.; G. Zoller, A. Pfund, Theo. Krausch, H. Steubing, A. Roos & Son, T. Trageser & Son, C. Schulze, W. Maarks, J. Tovey, G. F. Blake; F. Krug, C. Metz, Omaha, Neb.; John N. Straub, Pittsburg, Pa.; Gustavus Bergner, Peter Baltz, John F. Betz, George Enser, Max Ebels, John Gardiner, William Massey, J. J. Walter, Theo. Bergner, G. J. Burkhardt, George H. Becker, W. W. Hughes, Philadelphia, Pa.; J. Gormley, J. M. Smith, George Goldthorp, C. Harris; Mathias Dick, Quincy, Ill.; Fred. Laner, Reading, Pa., D. G. Ynengling, Jr., Richmond, Va.; F. Feuerbacher, C. Koehler, F. Nolker, F. Prall, C. G. Stifel, John Schneider, A. W. Straub, St. Louis, Mo.; C. Dinkel, Springfield, O.; J. Grasser, F. Lang, A. Stephan, Toledo, O.; C. Mueller, Tiffin, O.; G. Juenemann, L. Schade, William Metzger, Washington, D. C.; A. Reymann, F. Walter, Wheeling, W. Va.

Fifteenth Convention. 403

STATEMENT

SHOWING BY STATES AND TERRITORIES THE PRODUCTION, TAX PAID, IN BARRELS OF 31 GALLONS EACH, OF FERMENTED (MALT) LIQUORS DURING THE YEARS ENDING JUNE 30TH, FROM 1868 TO 1875, BOTH INCLUSIVE.

STATES AND TERRITORIES.	1868. Number of Barrels. $1.00 p. b.	1869. Number of Barrels. $1.00 p. b.	1870. Number of Barrels. $1.00 p. b.	1871. Number of Barrels. $1.00 p. b.	1872. Number of Barrels. $1.00 p. b.	1873. Number of Barrels. $1.00 p. b.	1874. Number of Barrels. $1.00 p. b	1875. Number of Barrels. $1.00 p. b.
Alabama	664	583	719	695	1,117	665	574	401
Arkansas	412	156	190	96	125	321	40	95
California	167,652	159,392	190,369	191,139	192,577	209,055	247,136	302,287
Colorado	2,471	2,260	3,851	7,153	9,172	14,358	20,180	23,517
Connecticut	37,181	38,296	43,707	51,540	57,416	53,557	55,165	52,503
Delaware	4,064	5,297	3,704	3,321	4,209	5,161	6,172	5,647
Florida	....	....	....	88	125	169	25	....
Georgia	2,893	4,384	4,870	6,105	5,303	6,235	5,501	5,631
Idaho	2,347	1,742	1,360	1,178	995	934	846	916
Illinois	494,879	457,407	432,278	465,125	497,977	520,393	651,855	536,619
Indiana	136,718	127,734	124,308	146,939	158,958	177,206	176,873	181,054
Iowa	102,115	110,537	103,637	105,806	121,027	143,045	163,433	180,654
Kansas	18,756	18,944	20,237	24,585	24,886	26,042	27,412	23,593
Kentucky	79,499	65,433	66,640	85,242	101,404	111,253	118,142	114,070
Louisiana	41,288	38,104	48,636	54,022	48,270	48,590	42,263	30,911
Maine	2,729	6,033	4,042	8,669	5,574	5 043	11,447	11,528
Maryland	137,167	130,611	128,433	155,468	173,531	200,083	204,105	191,549
Massachusetts	275,771	294,839	313,950	625,731	570,432	609,923	493,339	479,598
Michigan	128,772	133,549	129,626	141,236	163,768	202,569	196,424	191,275
Minnesota	42,564	44,036	56,720	62,569	69,525	83,922	89,645	68,567
Mississippi	246	34	312	686	840	903	249	7
Missouri	247,883	235,752	249,112	323,850	368,969	401,427	408,161	397,034
Montana	2,675	1,902	3,673	8,527	2,568	2,556	3,608	8,968
Nebraska	7,881	12,174	14,361	14,825	16,559	20,340	23,246	22,867
Nevada	7,673	6,710	7,785	9,420	11,007	18,277	11,943	12,991
New Hampshire	60,765	79,620	77,036	74,845	101,311	121,225	110,075	139,483
New Jersey	372,167	412,017	432,089	514,189	565,152	688.079	545,743	485,600
New York	1,729,046	1,896,119	1,992,959	2,305,145	2,602,505	2,908,343	2,900,375	2,889,777
North Carolina	51	75	96	61	2	126	35	82
North Dakota	511	854	201	944	905	1,143	1,663	1,824
Ohio	563,655	551,623	570,922	656,897	725,610	842,011	852,610	840,115
Oregon	6,128	7,007	6,568	6,208	5,957	5,641	6,670	7,257
Pennsylvania	722,227	755,447	788,034	918,938	1,006,829	1,106,091	1,072 056	964,634
Rhode Island	10,724	9,426	12,589	13,141	17,808	16,169	19,593	18,976
South Carolina	1,120	913	1,304	1,488	1,957	1,964	1,988	1,835
South Dakota	....	....	....	....	....	....	....	....
Tennessee	12,576	8,185	8,911	7,079	6,546	7,103	4,345	1,541
Texas	8,733	6,595	6,906	8,759	15,598	16,307	13,805	14,058
Utah	619	1,436	1,147	1,389	2,271	4,822	5,850	5,830
Vermont	8,294	2,690	1,934	1,757	2,516	2,344	2,253	1,196
Virginia	8,644	9,166	8,181	7,621	10,562	11,514	10,864	14,879
Washington	1,857	2,036	2,141	3,285	4,180	4,879	4,735	5,254
West Virginia	15,379	14,486	14,408	16,130	20,295	24,081	24,171	26,526
Wisconsin	201,448	187,503	189,664	218,544	295,818	367,781	417,313	440,616
Wyoming	....	70	791	493	928	1,465	2,008	2,793
Alaska	....	....	....	....	....	....	....	....
Arizona	120	173	279	163	612	451	442	528
District of Columbia	17,554	14,177	12,058	12,964	15,057	19,328	25,592	21,573
Indian Territory	....	....	....	....	....	....	....	....
New Mexico	355	908	784	701	758	880	865	1,190
Oklahoma	....	....	....	....	....	....	....	....
TOTAL	6,685,664	5,866,395	6,081,517	7,159,742	8,009,971	8,910,820	8,880,831	8,743,747

Chapter XIV.

CENTENNIAL EXHIBITION; ATTEMPT TO EXCLUDE BREWERS; HISTORICAL PARALLEL; BREWERS PROCEED AGGRESSIVELY; APPEAL TO BREWING AND KINDRED TRADES IN FAVOR OF SEPARATE EXHIBIT; ENTHUSIASTIC RESPONSES ENABLE EXECUTIVE TO BEGIN WORK. BREWERS' EXHIBITION COMMITTEE CREATE FIVE DEPARTMENTS AND ERECT SEPARATE BUILDING; MAKE USE OF EDUCATIONAL OPPORTUNITIES; PUBLISH VALUABLE PAMPHLET. DESCRIPTION OF BUILDING AND EXHIBIT. EFFECT OF EXHIBITION. GERMAN BREWERS PRAISE IT; SEND DELEGATE. SIXTEENTH CONVENTION. BERGNER'S SALUTATORY AND RUETER'S REPLY REFLECTING SPIRIT ANIMATING BREWERS. RUETER'S REVIEW OF THE TAXATION AND TREATMENT OF BREWING IN FOREIGN COUNTRIES COMPARED WITH AMERICAN LAWS. PRESIDENT QUOTES BOWDITCH AND OTHERS IN FAVOR OF BEER; REVIEWS INTERNAL AFFAIRS OF ASSOCIATION AND MAKES VALUABLE SUGGESTIONS; PLEADS ELOQUENTLY FOR HARMONY AND DEVOTION TO COMMON CAUSE. LAUER'S ADDRESS INCISIVE AND TO THE POINT, REPLETE WITH TELLING ILLUSTRATIONS. THE ASSOCIATION'S WORK AT WASHINGTON; EXECUTIVE ASSUMES GREATER PART OF LABORS WITH ATTORNEY. THE REVENUE OFFICE PERSECUTE BREWERS UNDER 2½ BUSHEL-DECISION; BREWERS REMONSTRATE, RESORT TO COURTS, AND FINALLY APPEAL TO CONGRESS. KEHR BILL INTRODUCED; ABLE ARGUMENT BY BREWERS; HOUSE PASSES BILL, ALSO SENATE; SENATOR DAWES EULOGIZES BREWERS. TEXT OF ACT. REPREHENSIBLE ATTITUDE OF NEW REVENUE COMMISSIONER; MORE PERSECUTIONS AND ANOTHER APPEAL TO CONGRESS, FOLLOWED BY INTRODUCTION OF ANOTHER BILL. COMMISSION BILL AGAIN PASSES SENATE; SENATOR BAYARD'S SCATHING CRITICISM OF IT. RESOLUTIONS, THEIR GIST AND CHARACTER. CONSTITUTION AND INCORPORATION OF ASSOCIATION. DISCUSSION OF MAXIMUM REVENUE AND RATE OF DUES; REPORT OF COMMITTEES ON SUBJECT; TREASURER'S BOND NOT SANCTIONED; DUES NOT INCREASED. REIMBURSEMENT OF LOCAL ASSOCIATIONS FOR EXPENSES IN GENERAL INTEREST. CONVENTION COMMITTEE AND CONVENTION APPROPRIATION DETERMINED UPON. CAUSE AND RESULT OF ACTION. MEMBERSHIP STATISTICS TO BE PREPARED; UNSATISFACTORY CONDITION OF THEM. MEMBERSHIP AND DEATHS. LITERARY BUREAU TO BE ESTABLISHED. MALTSTERS PROPOSE FIXING OF UNIFORM GRADES OF BARLEY. MINOR MATTERS. ELECTIONS. LIST OF DELEGATES.

The Centennial International Exhibition of 1876, commemorating and celebrating the Declaration of Independence, afforded an excellent opportunity for demonstrating, not only the extent, value and economic importance of brewing, but also its ethical and moral possibilities under a wise, judicious and practicable system of encouragement; and Bergner's invitation, extended in the name of his association, to hold the sixteenth convention in the Centennial City of Philadelphia, was really, as he himself expressed it, a successful effort "to kill two birds with one stone." It certainly is an evidence both of the brewers harmonious and effective co-operation and of their indomitable energy and aptitude for rapid work, that at the fifteenth convention not a single preparatory measure relative to this matter had been adopted and that, nevertheless, when the Exhibition was formally opened by General Grant, the brewing trade had its own building on the grounds, and was represented by an exhibit which, while comparing favorably with that of any other industry, was excelled by none.

The first step towards the erection of this building was taken in January, 1876, when the Executive, justly indignant at an ill-concealed attempt to exclude the trade from the exhibition-group to which it properly belonged, called upon the local associations for an expression of opinion as to the advisability and feasibility of arranging an exhibit separate and distinct from all others and combining with it such educational efforts and pertinent object-lessons as the circumstances and environments suggested and warranted. It would, indeed, have afforded material for a remarkable historical parallel if malt-liquors had been excluded from the Exhibition in the very city in which, in the preceding century, on an equally important and a kindred occasion of national rejoicing, *i. e.*, the celebration of the ratification of the Federal Constitution by ten States (July 4th, 1788), malt-liquors and cider were virtually proclaimed to be the only drinks which patriotic citizens, willing to aid the cause of temperance, should use or permit to be used. The order forbidding the sale of intoxicants,

other than beer and cider, on the grounds wher[e]
celebration took place, really amounted to this,
was issued under the impression of, and in accor[d]
with, Rush's tract on the subject, and its autho[r]
tended it as a pointed demonstration in that direc[tion].

The Executive's appeal to the local association[s]
the trade elicited so many favorable responses tha[t]
cess seemed assured from the very beginning.
meeting held in Philadelphia on the 20th of Janua[ry]
necessary arrangements were completed and sub
tions of money and promises of personal services
in such volume and numbers that the good work
gressed rapidly and smoothly, without the least
drance or friction, up to the day of the opening
thence on to the end of the Exhibition.

For the proper management of so complicat[ed]
exhibit as the industry with all its affiliated and de
ent interests required, the association, adopting a
excellent system of dividing labors and functions,
ized five departments, placing each one in charg[e]
separate committee, and authorizing these comm
to appoint from their own ranks a sufficient num
directors who assumed complete executive charg[e]
control of their respective departments. A g
supervision over the entire exhibit in all its depart
was exercised by an executive committee, consist
H. H. Rueter, chairman; William Massey, trea[surer]
G. Bergner, J. Gardiner, Henry Clausen, Jr., J.
J. F. Betz, F. Lauer; and Richard Katzenmaye[r]
John Flintoff, secretaries. Theodore Bergner ac
special superintendent, and Charles Stoll as superi[ntend]
ent for the erection of buildings. The five depart
were organized as follows, to wit:

---

* Hildreth's "History of the United States of America," Vol. IV, page

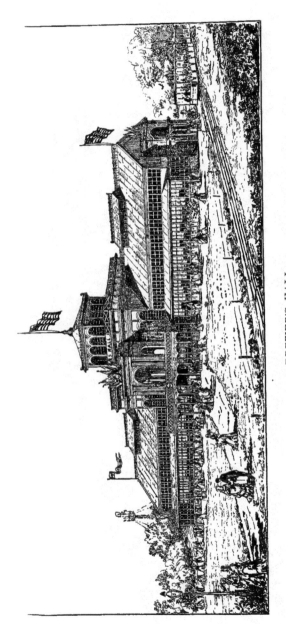

BREWER'S HALL,
CENTENNIAL EXHIBITION, 1876.

Sixteenth Convention. 407

I. Essays and Statistics: A. Schwarz, Louis Schade and John Flintoff. II. Malt-Liquor Department: T. C. Lyman, chairman; George Ehret, James Flanagan, Henry Ferris, J. C. G. Huepfel, W. A. Miles, Philip Merkel, E. J. W. Woerz, William Howard, Joseph Liebmann, Joseph Ruebsam, John H. Ballantine, Adolph Schalk, Charles Engel; Directors: William A. Miles, Joseph Liebmann. III. Machinery Department: Charles Stoll, Theodore Bergner, Ed. Haas, G. J. Burkhardt, John M. Smith, W. W. Hughes, William Orth, F. Spiess, J. Schwarzwaelder, John Farrell, H. Schimper; Directors: Charles Stoll and John M. Smith. IV. Maltsters' Department: B. A. Lynde, chairman; V. C. Sweatman, treasurer; J. T. Story, secretary; H. W. Smith, George Bullen and William Appleton; Director: Matthew White. V. Hop Department: W. H. Akin, chairman; S. Uhlmann, P. Weilbacher, C. H. Brooks, E. Wattenberg, W. Jerome Green, D. Conger, J. F. Scott, H. Goepper, G. W. Elkins, J. G. Hanson, F. B. Dole; Director: P. Weilbacher.

The accompanying picture reproduced from the association's centennial pamphlet, conveys a fair idea of the appearance of the Brewers' Hall. It was designed by H. J. Schwarzmann, the architect of the principal exhibition buildings, and erected by J. B. Doyle. Its length was 272, its width ninety-six feet; the central tower had an elevation of sixty feet, and the wings of twenty-eight feet. The main portion of the building was devoted to the exhibition of all mechanical appliances used in every branch of the brewing industry, and its principal dependent trades. In addition to this, sufficient space and convenience was provided for the storage of malt-liquors both for exhibition and competition. This portion was divided into three separate compartments; one for the storage of ale in bulk, the other for malt-liquors on draught, and the third for the storage of lager-beer, the latter being so arranged as to hold a quantity of ice four feet deep, eighty feet long and twenty feet wide. Samples of malt-liquors were constantly on draught, affording ample means and opportunity for acquainting visitors with the whole-souled hospitality so characteristic of the trade. And with this

food for the body the trade distributed food for the mind
in the shape of a pamphlet of forty closely printed pages
on the drink-question in its various aspects. The essays
it contained, written by two of the three literary gentlemen who composed the first-named committee, explained
the entire question in a clear, concise and lucid manner,
and emphasized the results of scientific investigations
and the opinions of eminent men on the subject. In
addition to a general description of the Exhibition and
its principal buildings, the booklet embraced four essays,
viz.: I. Malt-liquors: the true position of the trade;
statistics of trade; the use and abuse of malt-liquors
considered economically, socially and politically, by
John Flintoff. II. The malt-liquor-question in its
medical aspect. III. Opinions and facts from eminent
physicians, chemists and others in favor of beer as light
wholesome beverages. IV. Statistics and deductions
therefrom relating to malt-liquors, by A. Schwarz. As
an educational means applied on an occasion when
nearly one-fifth of the entire adult population of the
country, bent upon seeing and learning, and in a most
receptive mood, could be reached in a direct and personal way, this pamphlet must have had an effect superior to any effort ever put forth by this or any other
similar body of manufacturers. Thousands of good
citizens who probably had never heard malt-liquors
spoken of except in terms of unmeasured abuse and
execration, were now given an opportunity to look into
the matter practically and theoretically; and they undoubtedly saw in the orderly, pleasant and peaceful
intercourse of unaccountable multitudes of men and
women, among whom not a single intoxicated person
could be discovered, the very best evidence of the absolute truthfulness of all that the brewers' essays urged in
favor of malt-liquors.

An object-lesson of such irresistible force, diurnally repeated during the entire duration of the Exhibition, could not fail to produce a profound and lasting impression upon any mind not hopelessly clouded by preconceived notions and prejudices. Years of systematic agitation could not have accomplished the favorable results achieved by this Exhibition. Under ordinary circumstances such work must be carried from central points through thousands of radiating channels and over vast stretches of territory in order to reach those upon whom it is intended to exercise its influence. On this occasion this process was reversed; thousands of channels brought to this ever-flowing source of information the very persons for whom it was created.

As an industrial exhibit pure and simple, Brewers' Hall exceeded the expectations of its most enthusiastic advocates; it proved that American brewing had reached the highest plane attainable by means of every scientific and technical improvement applicable to the industry at that time; that it was an expanding, growing and progressive industry, up to date in every respect, abreast with every forward movement, and not satisfied even then with its achievements. Competent foreigners admitted all this, and those of them who were not afraid to emulate Professor Reulleau's example of unsparing criticism of their own country's showing, confessed that in science and technic the American brewer was ahead of his European colleague.

In the machinery department there were, in addition to complete model breweries on a diminutive scale, no less than 150 exhibits embracing the principal appliances used in brewing and the kindred trades; nearly every exhibit being the product of a different branch of industry, thus clearly demonstrating to what a great extent the trade contributed to the prosperity of other manufacturers, rarely ever associated in the public mind with the production of a glass of beer. The two other departments, devoted to the malt and hop interests, conveyed to the mind of the husbandman an adequate idea of the intimate industrial relations existing between brewing and agriculture. Malt-kilns, in full operation on both the German and American systems, showed how the grain is converted into malt, and a collection of samples of barley and malt, embracing every known European and American variety, was made to serve as a means of impressing upon the domestic barley-grower the necessity of improving upon his methods of cultivation. In this particular the Maltsters' Committee went so far as to offer five prizes for the five best samples of domestic barley of the crop of 1876, and made known that their national association would in the future permanently continue these competitive examinations, thus offering the strongest possible inducement to the growers to perfect their product. Both this department and the one devoted to the hop-interests contained separate exhibits of the appliances and utensils used in these dependent branches. A very interesting feature of the latter department consisted of an exhibition of every variety of the hop-vine, represented by living samples, which had been planted around Brewers' Hall, and at the proper season produced a most charming and appropriate decorative effect. The total cost of the entire exhibition amounted to $46,287.80.

Long before the association assembled in convention, the work of the brewers upon the grounds of the Exhibition had attracted public attention and was favorably commented upon by the Press at home and abroad. The brewers in other lands manifested great interest in this effort to place their craft in its proper position before the world, and the Brewers' Association of

Germany, gratefully mindful of the hearty and brotherly greeting which their American fellow-craftsmen had sent them when they first organized, deputed one of their members, F. Goldschmidt, of Berlin, to represent them at the sixteenth convention. In Goldschmidt's credentials, a veritable masterpiece of ornamental penmanship, the German association expressed the hope that the friendly relations existing between the two bodies may be perpetuated; they acknowledged their obligation to their American colleagues in these words: "It is an object of wonder on this side to observe the great efforts made by colleagues beyond the ocean to give the brewing trade such a representation, by means of a special exhibition at the World's Fair, as will comport with the importance to which, thanks to unceasing efforts, our trade has been elevated."

This splendid work, the manner in which it was done, and its grand results have never been excelled, and our admiration for the men who performed these labors, so fruitful of beneficent effects upon the industry, becomes all the greater when we consider the motive which dictated their course and action.

On this point we may quote the words of G. Bergner, spoken at the opening of the sixteenth convention. He said that he rejoiced to be able to thank all those with whom he had "labored in the good cause of exhibiting to the world what an important and useful industry brewing had become," and he welcomed "those who, inspired by the good example of their fellow-manufacturers, would yet come forward with liberal hands to offer their share, *knowing that what is being done is not aimed at immediate personal gain, but the moral elevation of our business in the minds of those who have hitherto opposed us.*" This was, indeed, the keynote at this gathering. It must be stated in the outset that the labors of the officers and committees at this meeting were of a two-fold character, as they related to the convention proper, on the one hand, and to the Exhibition, on the other. The convention was opened in Maennerchor Hall, on the 7th of June, 1876, at ten o'clock a. m.; and after the business of the first day had been disposed of, the delegates proceeded by special train to Fairmount Park where, at 2.30 o'clock p. m., the Brewers' Industrial Exhibition was formally opened.

In replying to Bergner's salutatory address, President Rueter said:

"The words of welcome and greetings of friendship, to which we have just listened, and with which it is customary to open the proceedings of our annual conventions, were never more appropriate and timely, were never more significant, than they are to-day, when uttered by the representative of our colleagues of this City of Brotherly Love, where to-day stand reared proud temples, dedicated to peace and goodwill toward our fellow-men, upon whose altars mankind is showering its choicest fruits of civilization and progress. It is a happy concurrence that the sixteenth annual convention of the United States Brewers' Association should be held at the City of Philadelphia, the scene of the centennial commemoration of our country's birth to independent national existence, even if it were for no other reason than that thereby has been secured to us a most gratifying attendance of members and friends. The occasion has, however, added an important feature to our convention, in giving rise to the conception and creation of the Brewers' Industrial Exhibition in connection with our country's International Exposition. The idea was suggested and its realization was taken in hand, from no other motive than the earnest desire to serve and advance common interests; and I beg of my hearers to look upon and judge of the undertaking, and deal with it in no other light but this. If the unusual concourse of people incident to the centennial celebration, tends to give us a more numerous audience at large than we could otherwise reach, we have additional reason for congratulation. Let us bear this in mind, and, while thorough debate is desirable, let us show ourselves, by the absence of all bitterness and the observance of the strictest decorum, to be men temperate in all things."

Again, as in the preceding year, the presidential address partook very largely of the character of a learned essay in its didactic parts, and of a stiring controversial oration in those portions which dealt with the machinations of the industry's opponents. Probably the most interesting and instructive feature of this speech was a comparative statement of the production of malt-liquors and of the revenues derived from this source in the principal beer-producing countries. The reproduction of the statistical table embracing these data may be dispensed with in view of the fact that President Rueter summarized and commented upon its showing in these words, which fully explain the gist of the figures: "You will observe," he said, "that in the United States the production of malt-liquors averages 0.37 hectoliter per head, while the general average of the countries named is 0.49 hectoliter per head. In Bavaria the rate is largest, 2.84 hectoliter per head, or about seven and one-half times as large as in this country. Figured at this rate, our production would be over sixty million barrels. England produces nearly four times as much per head of population as we do here, and furnishes over one-third part of all the malt-liquors produced by the countries mentioned. Russia, Sweden and Norway average less than one-tenth of a hectoliter per head, and intemperance prevails; while all Germany averages one and one-half hectoliter per head, and is sober. England, always held up to public gaze by our temperance orators as steeped in beer, and in refutation of the claim that beer-drinking nations are sober nations, produces only 1.38 hectoliter *per capita*, which is less than all Germany averages, and not half the quantity that Bavaria and Wurtemberg, taken together, produce per head. As England exports very largely, the rate of consumption per head, in contradistinction to that of production, must be considerably less than 1.38 hectoliter per head; so that much of the intemperance prevailing there must be ascribed to the consumption of other alcoholic drinks than ale, porter and beer. The beer-tax in the United States is eight per cent. higher than the average rate of the countries comprised in this statement; and while Rhenish Bavaria, Denmark and Sweden exempt malt-liquors from taxation altogether, the governments forming the German Brew-Tax Confederation impose a tax only one-third as high as ours."

Referring to the refusal of the Reichstag to increase the tax upon malt-liquor, being unwilling to enhance the price of "an article of diet and nourishment most valuable to the poorer classes, and for which no other can be substituted," President Rueter showed that under this fostering policy the consumption of beer had progressed within four years at such a marvellous rate as to increase the revenue from this source from 3,065,519 to 5,785,193 thalers, thus clearly demonstrating that a moderate taxation of malt-liquors not only serves the ethical purposes of a temperance agent, but also commends itself to wise lawmakers as a most excellent fiscal policy from a purely utilitarian point of view. He then contrasted the methods of regulating the retail sale of beer and wine in Germany and in the United States; the one leaving the traffic almost absolutely free, unhampered by taxation; the other hampering and harassing the trade, over-burdening it with local taxes and restricting it by innumerable restraints. And to bring out as forcibly as possible the pernicious results of the latter and the excellent moral effects of the former method, he quoted copiously from Dr. Bowditch's report. As this report—republished since by the association—has frequently been referred to, but never extensively quoted, in the preceding chapters of this book, we may reproduce here that part of President Rueter's quotation in which the showing of Dr. Bowditch's investigation is summarized in his own words, viz.:

"I. Stimulants are used everywhere, and at times abused, by savage and by civilized men. Consequently intoxication occurs all over the globe.

"II. This love of stimulants is one of the strongest of human instincts. It cannot be annihilated, but may be regulated by reason, by conscience, by education, or by law, when it encroaches on the rights of others.

"III. Climatic law governs it; the tendency to indulge to intoxication being not only greater as we go from the heat of the equator towards the north, but the character of that intoxication becomes more violent.

"IV. Races are modified physically and morally by the kind of liquor they use.

"V. Beer, native light grape-wines and ardent spirits should not be classed together, for they produce very different effects on the individual and upon the race.

"VI. Light German beer and ale can be used even freely without any very apparent injury to the individual, or without causing intoxication. They contain very small percentages of alcohol (4 or 5 to 6.50 per cent.).

"VII. By classifying all liquors as equally injurious, and by endeavoring to further that idea in the community, we are doing a real injury to the country in preventing a freer use of a mild lager-beer, or of native grape-wine, instead of the ardent spirits to which our people are now so addicted.

"VIII. Instead of refusing the German lager-beer, we should seek to have it introduced into the present 'grog-shops,' and thus substitute a comparatively innocuous article for those potent liquors which now bring disaster and death into so many families."

Without confining himself to the observations, experiences and opinions upon which these conclusions are based, President Rueter, alive to the necessity of arraying against the prohibitory fanaticism every available bit of testimony from men who have the nation's confidence and whose social standing and intellectual force and attainments lend weight to their words, cited a number of more recent utterances by distinguished persons who had studied the question, or had casual occasion to gather information concerning it. The most prominent among these was Bayard Taylor, who in writing to the *New York Tribune* of his experiences in Maine, where he was both highly pleased and somewhat astonished to have ale served to him, said: "We Americans are a curious, almost incomprehensible race. There is nothing more refreshing, nutritious and wholesome than good ale; there is nothing more discouraging to stomach and soul than the overheated, bitter slops which are usually served to us as tea. Yet we rarely have a chance to get the former; and even when we have such a chance we prefer, for the sake of appearances, to swallow the loathsome substitute." Concerning prohibition Taylor uttered these memorable words: "It is melancholy to see so much honest, conscientious effort misdirected, as in the case of temperance reform. The root of the evil lies deeper than any prohibitory law can reach. The human race *never* will submit to so intimate an interference with its personal habits. Neglect in the training of children, a low selfish ideal of manhood, intellectual narrowness, intolerance, bigotry, suppression which provokes excess, these are the sources of that tendency to intemperance which has become a national shame."

Turning to the internal affairs of the association President Rueter gave an account of the officers' and committees' labors, disclosing an activity as energetic, varied and manifold as has rarely, if ever, been equalled before or since that eventful year. In addition to the work required by the Exhibition, and many Congressional matters and several revenue-questions, the Executive Committee undertook a thorough revision of the constitution; enquired into the question of adulteration; again considered the project of establishing a brewers' school;* determined upon and outlined a new departure in the matter of literary labors, and discussed and acted upon Clausen's suggestion that the reading of scientific and technical essays should form part of the convention proceedings, taking the place of the expensive festivities usually arranged by the local associations of convention cities. Upon all these points President Rueter submitted pertinent recommendations. He suggested, among other things, that in view of the accumulation of funds in the treasury a fixed sum be expended annually for the services of able writers. Referring to the desirability of a brewers' school he said: "The history of the world's industrial pursuits notes the slow progress attained until the aid of science was invoked: they slumbered for ages until science called them to new life, and started them on the race for industrial honors which marks our present epoch. Merely empirical knowledge is no longer sufficient for lasting success in an age wherein Nature's laws of the survival of the fittest finds such general application. The question, therefore, is not any longer as to the need of a thorough theoretical and practical knowledge, but simply as to where and how it shall be obtained." Aware that a mere admonition against the lavish expenditure of money for convention festivities did not and would not have the desired effect, he proposed that the association should peremptorily prescribe a uniform limit for them and simultaneously provide for the dis-

---

* No action was taken on this question at this meeting, but brewmaster R. Lieber of Boston, delivered an impressive speech in favor of establishing a school.

cussion of scientific and technical subjects to which should be devoted the time usually alloted to these entertainments.

From his peroration, couched in words of incisive force, deep earnestness and glowing enthusiasm, one might almost infer that a spirit of discord or of selfishness and indifference had crept into the ranks of the association and threatened to destroy its usefulness. He hinted that his short official career had imbued him with a vague sense of danger that the harmony which had thus far characterized the labors of the parent body might be disturbed, and the bonds of friendship be loosened and broken, "because we may some day forget that our association was formed for the *common* good." Whatever cause may have induced this apprehension, it certainly was turned to good account, when the speaker made it the occasion for an appeal that can never lose its force or freshness so long as there is need, and there always will be, of stimulating harmonious and unselfish co-operation. He said:

"Friends of the West, friends of the East, let there be no East and no West in your councils and in your fealty to a common cause. Citizens all of one country, let not sectional prejudice take root in your hearts—and members all of the same time-honored calling, let no mere technical distinction stand in the way of unity of purpose and harmony of action. Let this centennial year witness a regeneration, in us all, of that spirit of unanimity, of that active, persistent and determined interest in the welfare of our association, which characterizes the early history of our organization, and which still imbues many earnest members. Let this spirit and this active interest extend far and near; let us put the hand to the plough, and not look back; let us crush out from among us all dissension, and let us look upon him as a common enemy who would sow the seeds of discord in our midst. Let us carry home with us the firm resolution never to break this new covenant, and let us ingraft it in the hearts of the rising generation, as a sacred legacy to be transmitted from father to son long as barley and hops thrive on our broad acres, and refreshing beer is quaffed by grateful millions."

Even if the convention report did not record the enthusiastic ovation which followed Joseph Kuntz's motion for "a vote of thanks to the President for his magnificent address," the reader could not fail to feel that this concluding appeal of a speech, so full of high-toned sentiments, valuable information and timely suggestions, must have produced a deep impression.

Not only the president, however, but all other speakers "rose to the occasion," and the reports fairly mirror a predetermined effort to make the best possible use of the grand opportunities offered by this convention, held at so propitious a time and at a place and under circumstances so exceedingly favorable to an effective propagation of liberal views and the correction of popular errors concerning the nature of the trade and the character of the men engaged in it. F. Lauer supplemented, so to speak, the president's address by an historical review of the Knownothing movement in which he again, as on previous occasions, demonstrated how much of its growth, power, wealth, moral and intellectual progress our country owed to immigration. He traced the retarding influence of this movement upon the inflow of labor and capital, and, drawing a parallel between it and the prohibitory crusade in the Western States, sought to prove, and did prove, that this more recent manifestation of intolerance and nativism could not but have the same effect. In dealing with the question of crime caused by alcohol, he cited Kingsmill's work on "Prisons and Prisoners," in which this eminent clergyman and philanthropic reformer, formerly chaplain of Pentonville Prison in England, sums up his observations and the results of his enquiries in almost the same words used by Bayard Taylor, as herein quoted. He also cited a recent enquiry into the increase of crime in the City of New York which revealed the fact that the most potent cause of the lamentable moral status of the metropolis was due to the corruption and inefficiency of the police force, a result of the unprecedented venality which prevailed throughout the municipal government. He touched upon the "two-wine theory" in a controversial allusion to the attempt, made at a conference of Methodist ministers, to substitute unfermented grape-juice for the communion-wine then in general use. He had no idea, of course, that this was the beginning of a serious agitation which divided the clergy of this country into two hostile camps, led to protracted and acrimonious controversies in the pulpit, the lecture-room and the Press; and was not settled and disposed of until twenty years later. As has been stated before, Lauer always evinced a remarkable aptitude in bringing to bear upon the questions of the day every contemporaneous utterance that tended to lend to his words a local coloring or direct personal relevancy. On this occasion, in pleading with his usual impressiveness the cause of malt-liquors, he quoted from the *Hartford Courant*, edited by General Hawley, the president of the Centennial Commission, a letter from Munich by Charles Dudley Warner, in which occur these significant sentences:

"Perhaps the temperance question is not exactly solved in Munich; I don't know if it was ever raised; indeed the *in*temperance question has made so little progress that the other has probably not been reached. You wouldn't say that the Munichers are moderate in the use of beer. * * * * If one were disposed philosophically to study the temperance problem, Munich would be a good field for it, for one can see here exactly what is the effect of unrestrained liberty. * * * * Probably you could not find in the whole city a man or a woman who has ever thought of what we call total abstinence, and they could not comprehend the idea. But there are plenty of temperance people—that is, people who drink beer regularly and never over-step the bounds of moderation. The observation that one makes in Munich is that drunkenness is a rare exception. In a residence here of many months I have never seen more than one or two intoxicated people, and they were not marked by the wildness or viciousness of our strong-liquor inebriety, but seemed rather good-humored carls who had lost their way and didn't seem to care whether they ever found it. But this seems very remarkable, when there is a beer house every half block, and you cannot select a residence in any part of the town that is not as handy to a *keller* as it is to a public school or to a church. *And I cannot see that the freedom of beer tends to any habit of over-drinking. I have known strangers to indulge freely in beer here the whole season and be just as good temperance people at the end as they were in the beginning.*"

Justly rebuking and criticising the hypocrisy of lawmakers who yield to the clamorous demands of prohibitionists, although they themselves drink and know the futility and perniciousness of sumptuary laws, Lauer quoted parts of a lecture on over-legislation delivered by J. H. Bromley before the Yale Law School, showing that under prohibitory laws there was not less, but rather more liquor sold in Massachusetts and other States, and that of an execrable quality. When asked by Bromley what he thought of such a condition of things, a Massachusetts politician replied: "That is all right; everybody seems satisfied; the temperance men have the law and the other fellows have the liquor."—

The appointment of an attorney charged with a sort of general surveillance over Washington matters had a tendency to transfer a considerable portion of the labors and functions of the Agitation Committee to the care of the Executive. The division of labor had not been quite logical from the very beginning, as has been pointed out on several occasions. Under Clausen's administration the most glaring incongruities were eliminated, as, for instance, the anomalous position assigned to the president at the conventions, when any member, totally unfamiliar with the work of the committees, might be elected to preside over the meeting. Yet there remained many defects and shortcomings, and one of them was the practice of leaving all Congressional and Departmental matters to the Agitation Committee, although the Executive Committee was the only body who had a permanent office and place of business, who attended to all correspondence with the members and thus came into possession of all information requiring action and calling for an exercise of the very duties assigned to the Agitation Committee. Virtually there were two executive bodies, as there were at an earlier period two presidents. Towards the end of Clausen's administration the two committees began to attend to Washington matters jointly or alternately; and when Rueter assumed office and had sufficiently familiarized himself with the work, the Executive frequently proceeded independently, especially when the urgency of pending cases demanded immediate action.

It was in the nature of things that the newly appointed attorney should communicate with those whom he could at all times reach with as little delay as possible; and from this it followed that all his correspondence must be with the Secretary. As a result of this inevitable and timely change in the *modus operandi* the Executive Committee assumed the supervision over a large part of Washington matters, which during the year 1875-1876 exacted particular vigilance and care. The Revenue Office, ignoring the remonstrances of the association and unwilling to await judicial decisions upon contested cases, continued, through its collectors throughout the country, to assess additional taxes on the quantity of malt consumed over and above two and one-half bushels per barrel. A change in the chiefship of the Office— Pratt having succeeded Douglass—may have caused this course. The matter had dragged along in its unsettled condition ever since the preceding convention, and it was understood that the Department would allow brewers to give bond during the pendency of the litigation. When it became known that this policy had been abandoned, a special meeting was held in New York (October 31st, 1875) at which a determined opposition was agreed upon. A deputation of brewers, consisting of H. H. Rueter, William A. Miles, G. Bergner, A. E. Leicht, Louis Muth and Robert Portner, accompanied by Schade and Flintoff, called upon the Commissioner at Washington and submitted a memorial protesting against these assessments upon the ground of their utter illegality, and requesting their discontinuance. Rueter, Miles, Bergner and Leicht took part in the discussion upon the various points urged by the Commissioner in favor of his interpretation of the law, and it seemed as if their arguments had had their effect, although no formal assurance was given that the objectionable order would be withdrawn. Instead of that the Commissioner simply "pigeon-holed" the brewers' memorial, and held the question in abeyance until the following December, when another attempt was made to enforce the assessment under threat of seizure. In this instance, W. A. Miles, Frank Jones, James Liebmann and R. Katzenmayer remonstrated with the Commissioner and secured a postponement of proceedings.

This state of affairs had now become intolerable; the Commissioner stubbornly refused to rescind his regulations on the ground that such a course would also apply to tobacco manufacturers and distillers. Although President Rueter refuted this fallacious, unjust and arbitrary reasoning in a very able rejoinder, no relief could be expected from this quarter and the association, therefore, appealed to the lawmaking power. In January, 1876, Representative Kehr (of Missouri) introduced a bill nullifying the Commissioners' decision in explicit terms. After having passed its second reading, this measure was referred to the Committee on Ways and Means, when a delegation of brewers (Rueter, Lauer, Ahles, Jones, Clausen, Massey, Bergner, Gardiner, Portner, Schandein, Schade, Katzenmayer and Flintoff) argued before the Committee in favor of its immediate enactment—Rueter, Clausen and Massey acting as spokesmen. The Revenue Office, represented by the two Deputy Commissioners Cushing and Holmes, acknowledged the correctness of the brewers' argument and offered no objection to the bill. Yet, strangely enough, a few weeks after this hearing the collector at Milwaukee again insisted upon payment of the illegal tax and threatened seizure of the breweries. At this juncture the Chairman of the Ways and Means Committee, Col. Morrison, interceded and brought about a formal agreement that action should be suspended until the Kehr Bill should be decided. It was not until two months after this occurrence (March 3d) that the House passed the measure. In the Senate General Logan, Chairman of the Finance Committee, accelerated its consideration and succeeded in having it passed within a few weeks. During the discussion on the subject, Senator Dawes, who while Chairman of the Ways and Means Committee of the House, had ample opportunity of becoming acquainted with the trade's attitude in all matters relating to the revenue, lauded the brewers' patriotism and integrity, and indirectly rebuked the Revenue Commissioner for his course.

Among other flattering things, he said: "*I think the views of the Brewers' Association should have great weight, and in any further legislation we should confer with these men, just as we did when the law originated.*"

Determined not to permit the miscarriage of their plans through inadvertence or a lack of attention to the happenings within official circles, the Executive maintained daily communication with Washington, and Emil Schandein, who was just beginning to make his strong personality felt in association matters, remained at the Capital for fully two weeks. With Portner and A. W. Straub he materially assisted the attorney in this matter. The new act read as follows, viz.:

"That nothing contained in section 3,337 of the Revised Statutes of the United States shall be so construed as to authorize an assessment upon the quantity of materials used in producing or purchased for the purpose of producing fermented or malt-liquors; nor shall the quantity of materials so used or purchased, be evidence, for the purpose of taxation, of the quantity of liquor produced; but the tax on all beer, lager-beer, ale, porter or other similar fermented liquor, brewed or manufactured, and sold or removed for consumption or sale shall be paid as provided in section 3,339 of said Statutes and not otherwise. Provided, that this act shall not apply to cases of fraud. And provided further, that nothing in this act, shall have the effect to change the rules of law respecting evidence in any prosecution or suit."

The new Revenue Commissioner, unlike his immediate predecessor, appeared to be rather unfriendly to the trade, and being unfamiliar with the duties of his office, he was apt to allow full sway to his subordinates, whose occasional abuse of official power has already been adverted to. L. Schade, in his address to the sixteenth convention, complained bitterly of Pratt's arbitrary and unjust bearing, and his inclination to set the ponderous machinery of his office in motion upon the slightest provocation and frequently without any justification whatever. Without any direct or indirect cause, he changed several minor regulations governing the traffic and thereby caused much annoyance to the brewers ; in several instances he also sanctioned undue severity in the literal execution of the law on the part of collectors. Conspicuous cases in point were those of F. &. M. Schaefer, Schmitt & Koehne, F. A. Neumann and J. F. Betz, who were charged with illegally removing malt-liquors from their breweries to their storage cellars. Of course, the removal of malt-liquors from brewery premises without permit was a violation of the literal text of the law; but as the collector could not fail to perceive the absence of fraudulent intent, the beer having been removed in an unfinished condition, not for consumption, but for storage, and in vessels other than those intended for the market, the Commissioner should have discountenanced further proceedings. Instead of that, he approved the collector's course; promising, however, to hold the charges in abeyance in order to afford the association an opportunity of having the law modified in a suitable manner. Recent experience in the case of the Kehr Act had probably convinced him that he could not expect to persecute the trade with impunity, and seeing that the association was determined to again appeal to Congress, he even promised to assist them. His deputies actually did aid the brewers' attorney in drafting the following amendment to section 3,345 of the Revised Statutes :

"Any brewer having cellars or vaults not on the brewing premises, but described in his annual notice to the collector, as used in connection with his brewery for the storage of unfinished fermented liquors produced by him, may remove such fermented liquors in an unfinished condition, to such cellars or vaults, or from thence to the brewery; in packages unlike those ordinarily used for fermented liquors, without affixing to such packages the tax paid stamps, or the *permits* mentioned in this section."

The Commission Bill again came to the surface and was passed by the Senate in spite of Senator Bayard's repeated protest. To show the insincerity of the prime-movers of this scheme, Bayard offered an amendment including the use of opium in the proposed investigation. Senator Sherman, in opposing this amendment, facetiously claimed that this would open the Chinese question, to which Bayard replied in these significant words:

"Now, sir, the examination of the relative use of the stimulant of opium in all its shapes with the use of alcoholic and fermented drinks is so far from being a Chinese question that, I am sorry to say, it is formidably an American question. I have thought of this subject; I have studied this subject with a very earnest desire to arrive at correct opinions in regard to it, and to benefit the unhappy victims of these vices; and I say now to the Senator from Ohio, if he did not know it before, that any respectable physician, either in the large cities of this country or in the small towns of the country, will tell him that, when you have by coercive laws prevented the sale and use as a beverage of intoxicating liquors, you instantly have caused a most terrible increase in the use of opium as a stimulant, and being more secretly sold, and to women and to childen, it is capable of more secret use, and it is far more deleterious in its results. I say that, when you propose to examine the question of intoxication upon the ground of public morals and public health, and you find that the disuse or prohibition of the use of those drinks is followed inevitably by a recourse to a far worse species of stimulants, you turn your back upon your duty, and show that you are not hearty in the performance of that duty when you do not make an inquiry which ought to be made a subject of coincident examination."

The members of the association had ample cause to congratulate themselves upon the exceedingly able and signally successful management of Congressional matters; yet they appreciated that without the friendly disposition manifested by the leading lawmakers, the ablest efforts would probably have failed to realize all that had been contemplated. It was this consideration, and a laudable desire to make public acknowledgement of fair treatment, that prompted the Committee on Resolutions (consisting of H. Clausen, Jr., W. Massey, A. Schalk, C. G. Stifel, F. Lauer, J. Obermann, C. Moerlein, G. Bergner, P. Schoenhofen, R. Portner and H. Dick) to submit, among others, this resolution: "*Whereas*, The Brewers of the United States have received, at the hands of the present members of both Houses of Congress, impartial hearing and prompt relief from Internal Revenue rulings which unjustifiably embarrassed them in the pursuit of their trade, and *Whereas*, On the floor of the Senate the opinion has been expressed that new legislation in the revenue laws relating to the manufacture and sale of malt-liquors should only be had after conferring with the officers of the United States Brewers' Association, as men whose opinion is entitled to great weight— *Resolved*, That the members of the United States Brewers' Association hereby manifest their appreciation of such relief granted and opinion thus expressed, and declare it as their unanimous purpose that they will, as heretofore, present to Government only such claims, measures, amendments and alterations of the Internal Revenue laws as are just and equitable, and to urge their adoption on their merits only."

The remainder of the resolutions deviate from former emanations of this character in that they are much more concise, brief, and to the point, and pertain chiefly to the actual needs and requirements of the trade. Formerly two separate committees were appointed, one submitting temperance resolutions, and the other, resolutions relating to the revenue and kindred questions. Both these tasks were now performed by one body, who in regard to the former subject-matter endeavored to express the association's sentiments and aims in language less florid, but not less impressive and eloquent than that erstwhile used for similar purposes.

During the six years which had elapsed since the adoption of the first constitution the internal affairs of the association assumed a more systematic character, and had in many respects expanded beyond the rather narrow sphere to which constitutional limits confined them. These considerations, and the manifest expediency of legally incorporating so important a body of manufacturers and thus placing it in a position to more effectually maintain its rights and guard its interests, prompted the Executive to submit a new constitution, together with the draft of a Congressional Act of Incorporation, which the convention, upon R. Portner's motion, referred to a charter committee, composed of H. Clausen, J. M. Lewis, C. Moerlein, C. G. Stifel and J. Obermann. In the charter the maximum annual income was fixed at thirty thousand dollars, but even the Charter Committee could not fully agree upon this, and C. G. Stifel, probably one of the minority, inclined to the opinion that it would not be wise to fix upon so large a yearly revenue, as it would reveal in Washington and elsewhere the power of the association. Although the President explained that the fixing of a maximum income was a mere matter of form and that the amount might at any time be decreased or increased, Obermann also believed that a lower sum ought to be fixed, particularly because a reduction of the rate of dues had been proposed and would probably be adopted. That the fixing of the maximum annual revenue at $30,000 was merely a matter of form, as President Rueter explained, could not have escaped the observation of so clear-sighted a man as C. G. Stifel, if he had read the report of the Finance Committee (J. C. G. Huepfel, Robert Portner and Herman Mueller) showing that the total annual dues did not exceed $7,500; while the entire assets, representing both this sum and the surplus funds accumulated during sixteen years, amounted to but $22,878, of which $6,000 was invested in United States securities and $8,000 in New York City bonds. Obermann's remark precipitated the discussion upon the question of annual dues, raised at the preceding convention, and now brought forward by the Charter Committee in their report embodying the alterations proposed by them.

The proposed amendments provided (1) that the annual dues be decreased from twenty to ten cents; (2) that the initiation fee be increased from two to ten dollars; (3) that all moneys exceeding $3,000 be invested in United States bonds; (4) that the treasurer should give a bond in the sum of $3,000; and (5) that all printing, the cost of which exceeded twenty-five dollars, should be given to the lowest bidder. P. Schemm objected to the amount of the treasurer's bond on the ground that if the securities were to be entrusted to the safekeeping of this officer this sum would be utterly insufficient. C. Moerlein believed that if a bond should be required, the clause compelling the treasurer to deposit the association's funds in a bank was superfluous; R. Portner held that unless the treasurer received a fixed salary his bond would not entail upon him any legal obligations. Counsellor Schade, called upon by the president to give his opinion on this point, confirmed Portner's contention, whereupon the latter moved to strike out the bond-clause. Schalk spoke in favor of this motion and expressed the opinion that the Finance Committee should be vested with power to invest the surplus funds. H. Clausen combined the two motions into one, which was thus adopted. The question of reducing the annual dues evoked quite a spirited discussion. Schalk opposed it, announcing at the same time his determination to propose the expenditure of a sufficient sum of money for literary purposes. E. W. Stiefel (Baltimore) could see no necessity for reducing the dues so long as the members cheerfully paid the present rate, confident that the best use would be made of it. Obermann, Lackmann, Herancourt and O. G. Stifel argued in favor; Lauer, Kuntz and Portner against the reduction. The final vote showed twenty-eight members for the proposition and thirty-four against it. Upon Joseph Kuntz's motion the initiation-fee was raised from two to five dollars. With these slight amendments the new constitution was adopted. Its full text will be reproduced in the next chapter, the reason for thus shifting it from what might appear to be its proper place being that it was again submitted to the association for re-adoption at the seventeenth convention. Upon closer enquiry into the subject the Executive had ascertained that it would be preferable in every way not to secure a Congressional charter, but to incorporate the association under the laws of the State of New York. This required a modification of the constitution adopted at this convention; and from the historical point of view, nothing of importance having occurred within the year to change the status of the matter, the amended constitution only ought to form part of the association's permanent record.

The extent of the parent body's obligation to reimburse local associations for expenses incurred by them in any effort they may have made, of their own accord and without consulting the former organization or its officers, to protect the trade's interests, had never been definitely settled; in fact, it was an open question whether such an obligation could logically be deduced from any provision of the constitution or any convention resolution. The utmost that one might infer from relevant reports and discussions was that a tacit understanding justified the national body to so reimburse local associations whenever the latter, unable on account of the urgency and stress of circumstances to consult the parent body, performed labors properly belonging to the province of the United States Brewers' Association; and that in all such cases the final determination of the claims rested with the convention. At this meeting the Committee on Petitions (C. Best, Jr., J. Kuntz, J. G. Sohn and P. Baltz), in recommending the payment of $500 to the Chicago Brewers' Association to cover expenses incurred in contesting the $2\frac{1}{2}$ bushel decision and in laboring for the Kehr Act, suggested that "hereafter local societies should be reimbursed only for such expenses as have been incurred by them in matters which have first been submitted to the Executive Committee." J. Obermann objected to the reimbursement in this particular case on the ground that other local associations had expended money for the same purpose, but had lodged no claims against the association. This precedent would entitle them to present their claims, and on behalf of his own association (Milwaukee) he reserved to himself the right to do so. Lauer, Clausen, Kuntz and Schemm spoke in favor of the entire report. Its adoption by a very large majority indicated, in a measure, the wishes of the association with regard to this important question; and the subsequent adoption of Clausen's conciliatory motion that the just claims of the Milwaukee Association be referred to the next convention, left no doubt as to what would be the prevailing policy.

The delegates of the Chicago Association (Gottfried, Schoenhofen, Seipp and Schemm) evidently did not relish the responsibility which this precedent placed upon them, for they immediately requested J. Kuntz to move, in their name, that the appropriation in their favor be rescinded. Obermann, however, again objected, holding that in relinquishing their claim the Chicago brewers could not prevent the members of his association from availing themselves of Clausen's motion. Thus the matter remained in its former state.

The origin of the Convention Committee dates back to this meeting. H. Clausen, Jr., with the tenacity of purpose so characteristic of his whole career, determined to force the issue he had raised several years ago in relation to the lavish expenditure of money for convention festivities. He now offered this resolution, which, by the way, was strongly recommended in President Reuter's address:

Resolved, That there shall be appointed annually a committee of three, called a Committee of Arrangements, whose duty it shall be to make the necessary arrangements for the entertainment of delegates at annual conventions; and be it further *Resolved,* That an amount, not exceeding fifteen hundred dollars, shall be paid into the hands of such committee from the treasury, to be expended for such entertainment.

His object was to limit the total convention-expenditures to this sum and to discourage the spirit of emulation which had prompted local associations to excel each other in the splendor and munificence of their entertainments. Clausen deprecated this tendency because he deemed it extremely unwise, hurtful to the serious objects of the association, calculated to create discontent, and to produce unnecessary friction and rivalry. His own words convey his ideas very clearly:

"This may become by-and-by a dangerous rock, on which the useful actions of our General Association may split. The number of places where our annual meetings may be held is rather limited. There are many small places where brewers are not able to bear the costs of the convention; or, on the other hand, if we would throw the burden of the expenses on such small organizations, the delegates might find fault with the reception tendered them. In order to encourage those local associations which have only a small number of members, it seems to me wise to have the proposed Committee of Arrangements appointed. The costs of the convention have to be borne by all, and should be paid from our treasury. We don't hold these conventions for the purpose of amusement, but to discharge business. I think every one of us has sufficient means to take care of himself."

As the reader knows, the Convention Committee became an integral part of the administration, and the convention appropriation remains to this day what Clausen's motion made it in 1876; but the main object for which both were called into existence have not been realized and in all likelihood never will be. This is one of the few instances where Clausen's efforts did not accomplish the result aimed at. As a rule his propositions arose from the actual requirements and needs of the association and, therefore, proved lasting and effective. At this very convention, referring to the confused and confusing condition of the statistics of membership and dues, which caused disagreements and dissatisfaction whenever a division of votes was ordered, he proposed that henceforth the Secretary should prepare an exact statement of the membership and dues of each association, so as to enable him to determine, when called upon by the presiding officer, how many votes each body is entitled to. This innovation was necessary for more than one reason, and received the convention's approval.

From accessible records it is impossible to state even the number of members of that or any previous period; we only know that the association was constantly increasing, but exact data cannot be obtained. An indirect criterion of the growth of the body may be derived from the composition of the Agitation Committee at this gathering. It consisted of:

F. Lauer, Reading; Frank Jones, Portsmouth; H. H. Rueter, Boston; William Massey, Gustavus Bergner, John F. Betz, Philadelphia; A. Schalk, J. H. Ballantine, Newark; H. Clausen, W. A. Miles, New York; John Greenway, Syracuse; Henry Bartholomay, Rochester; Albert Ziegele, Buffalo; C. Moerlein, Christ. Boss, Cincinnati; Charles Stifel, A. W. Straub, St. Louis; Conrad Seipp, Andrew E. Leicht, Chicago; E. Schandein, Jacob Obermann, Milwaukee; W. H. Hull, New Haven; F. Fortman, San Francisco; Jacob Seeger, Columbia; George Auer, New Orleans; H. Koehler, Davenport; R. Portner, Alexandria; L. Schlather, Cleveland; A. Reymann, Wheeling; L. Muth, Baltimore; William E. Voigt, Detroit; J. Fehrenbach, Wilmington; P. Lieber, Indianapolis; P. Schillinger, Louisville; Morris Hughes, Pittston; F. Krug, Omaha.

Naturally enough, with the growth of the association, the death-roll grew larger every year. At this convention the Condolence Committee (F. Lauer, C. Moerlein and G. Bergner) reported eighteen deaths:

William Eckert, New York; Philip Metz, Omaha; John A. Boppe, G. Hill, Christ. Trefz, Newark; Charles W. Schindler, Albany; Jacob Huebner, Boston; Charles Boehmer, Philadelphia; John G. Gerke and Peter Weyand, Cincinnati; P. Constans, Newport; Henry Reinhardt, Staten Island; Jacob Dold and A. Schaefer, Muscatine; John Schittenhelm, New Orleans; A. Geiger, Iowa City; A. Huenervogt, Baltimore; Paul Linck, Hartford.

The project of establishing a literary bureau, which had been held in abeyance for several years, was again brought up by A. Schalk in the form of a resolution empowering the Executive Committee to "engage competent literary men in order to contradict the false assertions of the enemies of the trade, and to expend an amount not exceeding $3,000 for this purpose." P. Schemm doubted the practicability of the scheme; it appeared impossible to him to contradict all the innumerable falsehoods disseminated through hundreds of channels in every part of the country. President Rueter explained that such an agitation was not contemplated; that the method to be adopted would include well-directed efforts to supply liberal newspapers with information and pertinent data requiring special study and enquiry on the part of literary men more or less familiar with the social, moral and economic aspect of the question. No other objection was urged and no further opposition manifested; hence, when J. Kuntz proposed to invest the Executive with full power in the premises, the convention assented almost unanimously, the result of the vote showing forty-seven delegates in favor and only seven against the plan. The necessity for such work must have been clear to any brewer who knew the systematic methods by which the prohibitionists propagated their absurd ideas, and who understood the shameless manner in which they manufactured or falsified statistical evidence in support of their assertions.

The Maltsters' Association, through their president, B. A. Lynde, invited the brewers to co-operate with them in establishing and permanently maintaining uniformly high grades of barley, their experience having taught them that unless the principal consumers of this agricultural product were properly represented in the inspecting committees of Boards of Trades where barley is bought and sold, grades would constantly be changed to suit the quality of successive crops, and a uniformity of such grades in *all* markets could never be attained. This proposition, and an appeal from the German Hop Growers' Union soliciting the American brewers' assistance in arranging an international hop exhibition at Nuremberg, were handed to the Executive Committee for suitable action.

With the re-election of the entire Executive, augmented, in accordance with the newly adopted constitution, by the election of two vice-presidents (F. Lauer and H. Clausen, Jr.,) the Centennial Convention was closed.*

---

* The following is a list of delegates and guests present at the sixteenth convention:

Albany: F. Dobler, Fred. Hartmann, Fred. Hinkel, Jr. Alexandria: Robert Portner. Alleghany City: Damas Lutz. Baltimore: George Bauernschmidt, George Brehm, T. Dukehart, Carl Hertlein, Louis Muth & Son, George Roasmark, F. Schneider, Joseph Schreier, Jacob Seeger, E. Stiefel, L. Strauss, S. Strauss, John H. von der Horst, John F. Wiesner & Son, John Boyd, H. Dantrich, H. Ellenbrock. Bennett: F. Klusman. Boston: Robert Lieber, John Rossle, H. H. Rueter, John A. Kohl. Bridgeport: F. Klauss. Buffalo: Chas. Gerber, Christ. Geyer, Joseph L. Haberstro, F. X. Kaltenbach, Jacob Kuhn, Gerhard Laug & Bro., John M. Luippold, Jacob Scheu & Son, John Schuessler, Christ. Weyand, Albert Ziegele & Sun, D. Bair, Henry Diehl, John Irlbacher, John Kamm, B. A. Lynde, A. M. Marsch, Marvin & Cline, A. McLeish, J. O. Meyer, G. A. Schaffer, Solomon Schen, Conrad Sueber, A. G. Wheeler, Jno. W. Wigand. Burlington: A. Bosch, C. G. Bosch. Chicago: M. Gottfried, Peter Schoenhofen, Conrad Seipp, Otto A. Sommer. Cincinnati: G. M. Herancourt, Frank Kauffman, John Kauffman, H. Klinkhamer, H. Lackman, Chr. Moerlein, Geo. Moerlein, Jr., Peter Schaller, C. G. Sohn & Son, Geo. Weber, J. C. Brickmann & Son, Louis Burger, John Kirby. Clarkstown: Carl Schmersahl, J. G. C. Schmersahl. Cleveland: C. E. Gehring, John Gehring, Jacob Mall, Herman Mueller, Leonard Schlather, A. Zetle. Davenport: M. Frahm, H. Koehler, G. A. Schlapp. Dubuque: Tschirgi & Schwind. Easton: Seitz Brothers. Erie: Helur. Kalvelage. Guttenberg: W. Kamena. Hartford: C. Herold. Hoboken: A. Zoller. Humboldt: H. C. Brendecke. Indianapolis: Aug. Erbrich. Lancaster: Ed. Hatzfeld. Louisville: Ph. Schillinger, John Zeller. Milwaukee: Carl Best, Jr., Jacob Obermann, Fr. Ruschhaupt. Newark: Gottfried Krueger, A. Schalk. New Haven: Wm. H. Hull. New Rochelle: Andreas Luckhart. New York City and Vicinity: J. Ahles & Son, J. C. Boettner, Henry Clausen, Herman Clausen, Jos. Doelger, Peter Doelger, Geo. Ehret, H. Elias, And. Fink, Geo. I. Gillig, J. Hoffmann, J. C. Huepfel, Chr. Koehne, John Kress, Wm. A. Miles, Fr. Oppermann, Wm. Orth, Jacob Ruppert, Jos. Schmid, Geo. Schmitt, N. Stenger, D. G. Yuengling, Jr., A. Schwarz und A. Geiger, editors of the *Am. Bierbrauer;* Edw. Grosse, special representative of the *New York Staats Zeitung*; Dr. A. Hofer, special representative of the *Sunday Mercury;* R. Katzenmayer, secretary; J. Flintoff, assistant secretary; J. Arras, W. H. Akin, J. Becker, Fr. Beringer, Wm. H. Fonntain, Louis Frank, E. Kussmaul, W. A. Lawrence, J. Naser, A. Pfund, Geo. W. Pier, A. T. Roeck, Fr. Schmidt, H. W. Schmidt, Wm. Schmiedel, Edw. Schweyer, C. W. Standart, Aug. Strassburger, John Trageser, John Tovey, S. Uhlman, W. G. I. Wheeler, P. Weilbacher, C. H. Zindel, Ang. Zinsser. Morrisania: W. Ebling, John Eichler, Jos. Kuntz, H. Zeltner. Staten Island: Geo. Bechtel, Chas. Bischoff, Emil Bischoff. Brooklyn: Jos. Burger, J. G. Fuller, Wm. Howard, Otto Huber, Jos. Liebmann, S. A. Bernhelmer, Chas. Stoll, Ang. Wohlfahrt. College Point: Jos. Setz. Omaha: Wm. Krug. Oswego: Louis Broesmer. Philadelphia: Lorenz Aurrhein, J. & P. Baltz, Geo. H. Becker, Bergdoll & Psotta, Bergner & Engel, Jno. F. Betz, Cary & Riehl, Chas. Glass, Eble & Herter, Euser & Theurer, A. Erdrich, G. Esslinger, F. Fielmeyer, John Fritsch, John Gardiner, Geo. Gindele, Jos. Gindele, Goldbeck & Boehmer, John Grauch, Robt. Gray, Louis Gross, J. Hohensdel, Hensler & Flach, Geo. Keller, Klumpp & Co., F. Kohnle & Son, G. Manz, Wm. Massey, Henry Mueller, Francis Orth, F. A. Poth, G. F. Rothacker, P. Schemm, L. Schlotterer, Chr. Schmitt, Louis Schweizer, L. Specht, John Stein, Theiss & Co., Henry Walther, Anton Waltz, John Weymann, Peter Arnold, Aschenbach & Muller, Gottlieb Bauer, Heury Bayard, A. Benignus, Theo. Bergner, Betz Bros., Wm. Birkenstock, F. Blackburn, Patrick Bonner, Brauer & Bruckmann, Brook & Fin, Brown & Woelpper, Geo. J. Burkhardt, W. Charolden, H. R. Crawell, Dickson & Lauten, Chas. Dittmar, John Doyle, M. Ehret, G. W. Elkins, N. Erick, French, Richards & Co., M. H. Graef, Ed. Haas, P. Hausmann, J. H. Heaton, C. B. Himpel, F. Hindrmeyer, Hoff, Fonntain & Co., W. Hughes & Son, Victor Kalk, John Karrer, Ketterer & Scherer, Kline & Bro., Knickerbocker Ice Co., John Kramer, John Linck, J. McCauley, Geo. Mitchell, Morgan & Orr, John Muffler, Jos. Oechsle, Perot & Son, Jacob Rech, O. Schada, Chr. Schantz, John Shirpert, Chr. Schroeder, F. Shove, J. Smith & Son, Ph. Spoeter, B. C. Sweetman, Trottman & Ott, John Velt, Louis Walther, John Waschler, G. Wehn, Chas. Welker, J. & L. Wenkenbach, J. G. White, Work & Drewn, Jacob Zaiss. Pittsburg: Leopold Vilsack. Pittston: H. R. Hughes. Pottsville: F. G. Yuengling. Poughkeepsie: Frank Valentine, Sr., Frank Valentine, Jr. Quincy: Hermann Dick. Reading: Peter Barbey, Fred. Lauer. Richmond: David G. Yuengling, Jr. Rochester: H. Bartholomay. Rock Island: J. Huber, Fr. Hass. Rondout: Geo. Dressel. Schenectady: Peter Engel. St. Louis: Adolph Busch, Chas. G. Stifel, A. W. Straub. St. Paul: Anton Young. Syracuse: John Greenway. Titusville: C. Schwartz. Toledo: J. Grasser. Wabash: R. F. Lutz. Washington: L. Schade, C. Heurich, M. Metzger. Wheeling: A. Reymann, F. Walther. Wilmington, Del.: J Fehrenbach.

Chapter XV.

ATTITUDE OF PROHIBITIONISTS TOWARDS TRADE; OPPOSE BREWERS' EXHIBIT AND BOYCOTT EXHIBITION; THEIR VOTE 1872 TO 1876; ANALYSIS OF THEIR POLITICAL WEAKNESS; THEIR PRESIDENTIAL VOTE; PLATFORM. PLATFORM OF REPUBLICAN AND DEMOCRATIC PARTIES. TILDEN'S OPINION ON PROHIBITION. THE DRINK-QUESTION IN PRESIDENTIAL CAMPAIGN. PROHIBITIONISTS DEMAND FEDERAL PROHIBITION. BLAIR OFFERS PROHIBITORY AMENDMENT TO CONSTITUTION. SEVENTEENTH CONVENTION. ORIGIN, DEVELOPMENT AND STATUS OF BREWING IN MILWAUKEE AND WISCONSIN; PERSONAL NOTES. NEW DEPARTURE; OBERMANN AND THE MAYOR GREET DELEGATES AT A "COMMERS." RUETER'S ADDRESS; QUOTES GOV. RICE'S VETO MESSAGE; EXTRACTS OF MESSAGE; COMMENTS THEREON; VALUABLE HISTORICAL MATERIAL; CHARGE OF ADULTERATION EXPLODED. SCHADE ON UNCONSTITUTIONALITY OF PROHIBITORY LAWS; THINKS SECTION 8, ARTICLE I, COVERS POINT; DEFECTS OF HIS OPINION; WHAT CONSTITUTION REQUIRES AND PROHIBITORY LAWS AIM AT WITH REGARD TO FEDERAL TAXATION. SECTION 3,243 OF REVENUE ACT TO BE AMENDED, BECAUSE INCONGRUOUS, ILLOGICAL AND UNJUST TO THE TAXED TRADES. RUETER'S CLAIM THAT TAXATION SANCTIONS; LAUER ON SAME SUBJECT, BOTH REFERRING TO SAID SECTION. MINOR REVENUE MATTERS PROMPTLY SETTLED BY NEW COMMISSIONER G. B. RAUM. RAUM'S RECORD; HIS FAIRNESS AND EFFICIENCY; ALLOWS 2½ BUSHEL CLAIMS; BREWERS APPRECIATE HIS COURSE. DUTY ON HOPS AND MALT; AMERICAN HOP-GROWERS UNDERSELL FOREIGN GROWERS IN FOREIGN MARKETS, YET INSIST ON PROTECTIVE DUTY; INTRODUCTION OF HOP-EXTRACT WEAKENS THEIR ABSOLUTE CONTROL OF MARKET. OFFICERS OF CONVENTION. CHANGES EFFECTED BY NEW CONSTITUTION IN NATURE OF MEMBERSHIP, FUNCTIONS OF OFFICERS AND COMMITTEES, AND THE CHARACTER OF ASSOCIATION; OTHER FEATURES; ITS WEAK POINTS. LIABILITY OF ASSOCIATION FOR EXPENSES INCURRED BY MEMBERS; CLAIMS OF MILWAUKEE AND BALTIMORE ASSOCIATIONS; DISCUSSION ON SUBJECT; DRIFT OF OPINIONS; DANGEROUS PRECEDENTS. ATTEMPT IN MICHIGAN TO IMPOSE EXTRA TAX ON OUTSIDE BREWERS; MISUNDERSTANDING AS TO MICHIGAN BREWERS CLEARED AWAY. APPROPRIATIONS, DUES, MEMBERSHIP, ETC. DEATHS. ADULTERATION. NEW JOURNALS. OFFICERS AND DELEGATES. TEXT OF CONSTITUTION.

Concerning prohibitory endeavors in the direction of Federal legislation as well as respecting the movements of the national organization of prohibitionists since the presidential campaign of 1872, a few words will suffice to describe the situation. Their general policy of singling out malt-liquors as being most dangerous to their scheme, because productive of true temperance, remained unchanged; and they made use of every opportunity for villifying or injuring the brewers. Thus, for instance, the strongest opposition to the brewers' exhibit, described in the preceding chapter, naturally emanated from their national camp. The attempt to exclude the industry from the class to which it properly belonged may really have been but the reflex action of prohibitory antagonism, brought to bear upon the authorities vested with supreme power and control in all matters relating to the Exhibition. At any rate, when the association, instead of undertaking the futile task of disproving the technical quibbles and subterfuges with which they would probably have been confronted in any effort to obtain proper classification, proceeded independently, determined to have a separate building, the prohibitionists conceived the shrewd scheme of preventing the selling or giving away of malt-liquors, and in this endeavor they claimed to have on their side at least the letter, if not the spirit, of a State law forbidding the sale of intoxicants in Fairmount Park. Unfortunately for them, the commissioners did not view the matter in that light, and by their refusal to exclude the trade provoked a resolution, adopted at the National Prohibition Convention (May 17th, 1876), in which "all good citizens and religious men of the nation" were exhorted "to refuse to encourage the Exposition by their presence unless the drink concessions be revoked and annulled." Well, these concessions were neither revoked nor annulled; all temperance and religious men of the nation probably obeyed the boycott-appeal addressed to them; and yet—*mirabile dictu!*—the Exposition proved to be a magnificent success.

In spite of their most strenuous efforts the prohibitionists in all this time never succeeded in changing public opinion to any considerable extent, yet, for reasons repeatedly explained in the course of this narrative, their demands frequently influenced the action of professional politicians who, eager for votes and blind to the lessons of experience, allowed themselves to be deluded by false representations concerning the moral power of the cause and its supposed effect upon the result of the elections. True, compared with the presidential vote of 1872 (5,607), the State elections showed a marked increase of strength, the total prohibition vote being 18,723 in 1873, 39,351 in 1874 and 42,185 in 1875; but at the presidential election in 1876 the total vote shrunk to less than 10,000, the exact number of votes cast for Smith, the prohibitionists' candidate, being 9,737. The vote at these three State elections fluctuated very materially in the various States; for example, in Ohio the prohibitionists in 1873 polled 10,000 out of the total of 18,723 votes cast throughout the country; but in 1875 the same State gave the cause but 2,593 ballots. Nebraska gave the prohibitionists 1,346 votes in 1874, and none in 1875; Illinois gave 516 in 1874, and none in 1875; Kansas, 2,277 in 1874, and none in 1875. The exact figures are as follows, viz., 1873: Connecticut, 2,541; Minnesota, 1,050; New Hampshire, 1,779; New York, 3,272; Ohio, 10,081—total, 18,723. 1874: Connecticut, 4,960; Illinois, 516; Kansas, 2,277; Michigan, 3,937; Nebraska, 1,346; New Hampshire, 2,100; New York, 11,768; Ohio, 7,815; Pennsylvania, 4,632—total, 39,351. 1875: California, 356; Connecticut, 2,932; Massachusetts, 9,124; Minnesota, 1,600; New Hampshire, 773; New York, 11,103; Ohio, 2,593; Pennsylvania, 13,244, and Wisconsin, 460—total, 42,185.

No less than nineteen States contributed to the total vote of 9,737, cast in 1876 for the presidential candidate of the prohibition party, and neither Maine nor New

Hampshire nor Vermont were among them. Iowa gave 36, Kansas 110, Massachusetts 84, and Rhode Island 68 votes. New York contributed 2,329, Ohio 1,636, Pennsylvania 1,319, Kentucky 818, Michigan 767, and Connecticut 378; the strength developed in each of the remaining States was below 200 votes.

In their platform the prohibitionists demanded legal prohibition in the District of Columbia and the territories of the manufacture, sale, importation and exportation of alcoholic beverages; an amendment to the Federal Constitution to the same effect, and treaty stipulations with foreign countries designed to prevent the exportation and importation of intoxicants. The Republican platform afforded scarcely any clue to the policy of that party on the subject; while the Democrats openly espoused the cause of "personal liberty unvexed by sumptuary laws," and denounced "the policy which discards the liberty-loving German, but tolerates a revival of the coolie trade in Mongolian women imported for immoral purposes."

Tilden's views on the subject, expressed in 1855, supplemented these declarations and were often quoted during the campaign. While running for the office of attorney-general on the ticket of the "Soft Shell" Democrats, Tilden received an indirect offer of support from the prohibition party, conditioned upon his countenancing sumptuary legislation. The implied offer took the form of a request to give his views on such laws. To this Tilden replied in a strong letter from which the following is a literal extract:

"Prohibitory legislation springs from a misconception of the proper sphere of government. It is no part of the duty of the State to coerce the individual man except so far as his conduct may affect others, not remotely and consequentially, but by violating rights which legislation can recognize and undertake to protect. The opposite principle leaves no room for individual reason and conscience, trusts nothing to self-culture, and substitutes the wisdom of the Senate and Assembly for the plan of moral government ordained by Providence. The whole progress of society consists in learning how to attain, by the independent action or voluntary association of individuals, those objects which are at first attempted only through the agency of government, and in lessening the sphere of legislation and enlarging that of the individual reason and conscience. * * *

"While in favor of sobriety and good morals, the Democratic Party disowns a system of coercive legislation which cannot produce them, but must create many serious evils, which violates constitutional guarantees and sound principles of legislation, invades the rightful domain of the individual judgment and conscience, and takes a step backward toward that barbarian age when the wages of labor, the prices of commodities, a man's food and clothing, were dictated to him by a government calling itself paternal."

Although the principal issue of the presidential campaign overshadowed all minor questions which formed the subject of contention between the four political parties then in the field, there can be no doubt that the sumptuary planks in the platforms of three of the parties exercised a very much greater influence upon the voters than all other minor issues combined, including that of the Greenback party. Viewed in this light, the popular vote demonstrates not only the weakness of the prohibition league, but also the moral and numerical strength of their opponents; the only difference being that the former is expressed in exact figures, while the latter requires an analysis of the popular vote in the different States. For present purposes it suffices to give, in connection with the foregoing platform declarations, the bare figures showing the popular vote as follows: For Tilden 4,285,992; Hayes 4,033,950; Cooper (Greenbacker) 81,737, and Smith (Prohibitionist) 9,737. Out of a total of 8,411,416 the prohibition party polled 9,737 votes, while the advocate of personal liberty received four million two hundred and eighty-five thousand votes, *i. e.*, a clear majority of 160,568 over all other candidates.

Seventeenth Convention.

As the years rolled by the pretensions of the party increased in inverse ratio to the growth of their numerical strength. In the face of an aggregate popular force of 9,737 votes, they had the unblushing effrontery to claim that they represented the moral sentiments of the American people, and demanded that this sentiment be embodied into the Federal Constitution. In December, 1876, H. W. Blair accordingly introduced in the House of Representatives a joint resolution proposing a constitutional amendment to the effect that "from and after the year 1900 the manufacture and sale of alcoholic beverages, except for medicinal, mechanical, chemical and scientific purposes shall cease, and that the exportation and importation of the same shall forever thereafter be prohibited."

This was the status of prohibition when the association assembled in its Seventeenth Convention at Milwaukee, on the 6th of June, 1887.—Among the younger cities of the Northwest, Milwaukee has always been remarkable for the rapid development of its brewing industry. The introduction of the trade into what was then the territory of Wisconsin dates back to 1840, and so far as Milwaukee is concerned brewing is almost coeval with the first settlement of white men on the estuary of the river from which the city derived its name. The pioneer brewers were a German, Riedelshoefer, and three Britons, Owens, Pawlett and Davis, who, in 1840, began business with the most primitive utensils and on a diminutive scale. In 1842 Jacob Best engaged in brewing with his four sons, (Charles, Jacob, Philip and Lorenz,) and, like the earlier brewers in the older States, managed the entire establishment in all its branches without hired help. His annual output did not exceed 500 barrels during the first three or four years. It was this enterprise, though not this identical establishment, which, under the subsequent management of Philip Best aided by his sons-in-law, Capt. F. Pabst and Emil Schandein, became one of the largest breweries in the world. In 1843 David Gipfel established a brewery; after him came F. Neukirch and C. F. Melms in 1845, and John Brown in 1846. Between the latter year and 1850 there may have been a few more new breweries of which we have no accessible record. J. Schlitz, V. Blatz, J. Obermann, A. Krug, C. Wehr, C. Foster, G. Schweickhart, F. Falk, F. Goes, P. Altpeter, Borchert and Jung—all these embarked in the industry during the succeeding decade; and still later came those whose names, not mentioned here, appear in the list of delegates appended to this chapter. Throughout Wisconsin brewing followed closely in the wake of the pioneer settlers, an exceptionally large proportion of whom were Germans, accustomed to the use of beer as a part of their daily diet, which to some extent answered the purpose of both food and drink. Wherever these immigrants settled, whether in the depths of Wisconsin's virgin forests, on the banks of her rivers, or the shores of her lakes, one was sure to find a brewery corresponding in size and capacity with the extent of the settlement. Since the fourth convention, which was held in Milwaukee, in September, 1864, the production of malt-liquors in the State had increased from 102,564 to 443,064 barrels. In the city of Milwaukee the brewers maintained a strong and effective organization, which, since the death of C. F. Melms and Joseph Schlitz, was usually represented, at the meetings of the parent association, by J. Obermann, Emil Schandein, the Uihleins and several others whose names have been mentioned before. At the time of the seventeenth convention, Obermann was president of the local association, and it was he who welcomed the delegates in a manner and under environing circumstances which signalized and initiated a new departure in the mode of reception. Hitherto the salutatory address was delivered by a resident brewer at the opening of the convention, and constituted the initiatory part of the proceedings. At Milwaukee the reception of the delegates assumed the character of a semi-social function, which took place at the Grand Opera House on the evening before the convention; and it was not only the local brewers' association, through Obermann, but also the city of Milwaukee that welcomed the delegates, extending to them through the Mayor, Hon. A. R. R. Butler, the ancient courtesy of the "freedom of the city." Butler spoke strongly in favor of malt-liquors; he said that he had recently visited all the principal cities of Germany, and that his observations confirmed the uniform testimony of all intelligent travellers to the effect "that while beer is universally used by all classes of German people, there is no drunkenness in Germany;" and he expressed the hope that the introduction of the German national beverage into this country, productive of sobriety as it must be, "would also be accompanied by that respect for law and order which characterizes the German people." This innovation, which could not but impart prestige to the brewers' meetings and afforded an opportunity for social intercourse and a free interchange of ideas and experiences, found great favor among the members and became a part of nearly every subsequent convention.

In his address at the opening of the meeting on the following day, President Rueter, after a brief excursion into the realm of brewing statistics, dwelt with great force and lucidity upon the fallacy of prohibitory legislation and the inconsistency of its advocates. As an example he cited the attempt made in Massachusetts to enact a local-option law in place of the license-law, and quoted the message in which Governor Rice vetoed the bill. Both the text of the quoted extracts, and President Rueter's comments upon and deductions from them, are in the nature of valuable historical material bearing on our questions and should be preserved for future use and reference. In his veto message Governor Rice said:

"It appears to me that upon a subject lying so near the morals and habits of our people as does the social use of intoxicating liquors, one upon which there is a wide diversity of opinion, and in respect to which we are compelled to seek the best practical results rather than to solve questions of casuistry, legislation ought not to be fitful and intermittent, and the statute ought not to be changed unless some palpable form of evil is resulting, or unless the change proposed is clearly demanded by public opinion. The existing law to regulate the sale of intoxicating liquors has, in its present form, been in force only about twelve months, and has been only partially tested. * * * I trust that it is only to declare your own opinion to say that this subject is too weighty an one to be made a plaything in politics; and thousands of suffering women and children are looking with beseeching solicitude to the State authorities to deal with the evils of intemperance only with patient investigation and wise discretion. There are no evidences of flagrant evils resulting from the present law; but, on the contrary, the sale of spirituous liquors, to be drunk on the premises, has been constantly diminishing; and there is, so far as I know, no public opinion demanding new legislation on the subject. I respectfully submit that the fact that a majority of the members of a legislative assembly is so constituted as to be able to pass laws not demanded by the public welfare, is not of itself sufficient to justify such legislation; but, on the contrary, as has been wisely said, 'every act of authority of one man over another for which there is not an absolute necessity, is tyrannical.' It is a settled fact that no legislation can perfectly extirpate the use of intoxicating liquors as a beverage, and all the forces of Christendom have not been able by any means to accomplish that result; and if there be Pagan or non-Christian countries whose abstinence from the use of spirituous liquors has been enforced by absolute authority, even those people have other stimulants not less hurtful and pestiferous in their indulgence. It is a fact of history in the experience of the Commonwealth that extreme laws on this subject have not been effective, and their impotency has not always arisen from indisposition to enforce them on the part of those charged with that responsibility, but from inherent difficulties which lie in the way of their administration. Any other conclusion than this supposes that some of the purest men who ever held executive and judicial offices in this State have been false to their own previous belief, to their open avowals of opinion, to their personal honor and to their oaths of office. There is nothing else in the known character of these men, nothing discernible in any other of their relations to society which tolerates the suspicion either of their dishonor or dishonesty, and they stand acquitted in the public judgment of any dereliction of duty in this particular also.

"Turning to the consideration of the proposed act, one fact developed by its passage is too important to be passed without special notice, as indicating an essential change in opinion upon the whole subject under discussion. Hitherto the culminating objection to the present and to all similar laws urged by earnest advocates of that side, has been against any form of license ; yet notwithstanding the act now proposed involves direct provisions of license at local option, I observe upon analysis of votes upon two bills of the present session, that a large majority of those voting for the Prohibitory bill (so called) in April, voted for the principle of license embodied in this bill of May. It may therefore be assumed that by general consent the principle of license has been eliminated from future discussion and legislation upon this subject, and that the most serious objection that has been urged against the present law has been abandoned.

' I have not full returns from the cities and towns where licenses have been authorized, but from returns furnished by the Chief Detective of the Commonwealth at the beginning of the present year from the 235 towns and cities, or from some more than two-thirds of the whole number, it appears that the whole number of arrests for drunkenness in these places in the year 1874 was 25,740
In the same places like arrests in 1876 18,696

Showing a decrease of 7,044
between the last year of the prohibitory law and the first year of the license law, in these 235 towns.

"The Chief of Police of Boston sent in the following statistics of results in this city for the year 1876:
Number of arrests for drunkenness in 1874 11,880
Number of arrests for drunkenness in 1876 8,564

Showing a decrease of 3,316
Total number of prosecutions under liquor law.............. 4,028
Total number of gallons of liquor forfeited 26,888
Total number of places abandoned as to sale in 1876......... 619

"That visible drunkenness has diminished in our streets will be admitted by every candid observer; indeed, an intoxicated person is now seldom seen abroad, and there is a growing sentiment against intemperance. Drunkenness is no longer condoned in respectable society, and the fashion of the times as well as the moral sentiment of the people of all classes is forming against it. The use of liquors is no longer considered essential to occasions of public hospitality; and recent significant examples have been given of their entire disuse. It would not be true to attribute the whole of this gratifying progress of temperance to the existing laws; but the law is one of the conditions of society wherein this awakening has taken place; and to me it seems inexpedient to supplant so serviceable and so acceptable an instrumentality in order to try chances in a new field of experiment, with the hazard of losing all that has been gained and all that may be reasonably hoped for."

In reference to this excellent public document President Rueter said:

"Nothing truer was ever said, than that the fact that a majority of the members of a legislative assembly is so constituted as to be able to pass laws not demanded by the public welfare, is not of itself sufficient to justify such legislation; but that on the contrary, every act of authority of one man over another, for which there is not an absolute necessity, is tyrannical. It is just on such an accidental make-up of our State legislatures, that the passage or defeat of tyrannical sumptuary laws hinges. It is not a matter of wise and dispassionate deliberation, but, much like the throw of the dice, a mere question of chance. If votes in sufficient number can be obtained by pledge or bargain, by cajoling, hectoring or persuasion, the leaders will gain their point by securing the passage of their pet law. That a large and important industrial interest may thus be tossed about, and be at the mercy of hirelings to a pretended cause; that investments made this year under the sanction of the law of the State, may the next year be jeopardized by an arbitrary change of the law; that a business may be considered legal to-day, but be outlawed to-morrow; that in the pursuit of precisely the same business, a man may retire one night with the comforting thought of being a law-abiding citizen, while the very next night, owing to a despotic law, he must seek rest as a law-breaker—all at the whim or chance-vote of men whom mere accident has placed in brief authority—is a wanton abuse of republican prerogative that should bring the blush of shame to the brow of every patriot and lover of republican institutions. During the recent discussion of the liquor question just such men, with whose help these tyrannical laws are passed, were openly charged on the floor of the Massachusetts House of Representatives with freely indulging in intoxicants at a prominent Boston hotel, of which fact the accuser had positive and personal knowledge, and then going and voting for prohibition; not a resenting voice was raised. Is it at all strange that such men pass laws, which offer a premium on rascality, by providing that debts owing for goods bought and received, contrary to the prohibitory law, may not only be repudiated, but that the purchaser, although he himself has re-sold the goods and pocketed his money, in violation of the same law, may come into court, and even recover all moneys paid for purchases made and goods received contrary to the provisions of the prohibitory law? To be sure, the victim may glean consolation, if he is only philosophical enough, by calling to mind the fact, that he has right and justice on his side, whatever the State law may say; does not his cash account tell him that the Federal government pronounces his business perfectly legitimate, for it surely must not for a moment be supposed that the government of a great and enlightened people would deign to participate in the gains of a business, at the rate of sixty-six millions a year, if deemed illegitimate."

450   *History U. S. Brewers' Association—Chapter XV.*

Referring to a number of extremely absurd charges of adulteration against the brewing industry, instigated by prohibitory agitators and disseminated by biased newspapers, President Rueter summarized the second annual report of the Massachusetts Inspector and Assayer of Liquor* in the following words:

"Nine samples of lager-beer and ale were analyzed and carefully examined for adulterations. The report says: 'The results showed that all of the samples were absolutely free from cocculus indicus, picric acid, strychnia *or any other bitter except that of hops and malt.* All the samples were found to be pure and as free from injurious substances as alcohol in any form can ever be.' In the general remarks on beers and their adulterations, contained in this report, the State Assayer quotes Dr. Hassall, of London (Food and its Adulterations. By Arthur Hill Hassall, London, 1876); Dr. G. Wittstein, from a paper upon the Examination of Beer for Adulterations, published in '*Archiv der Pharmacie*,' 1875; Prof. A. B. Prescott, from his works on the Chemical Examination of Alcoholic Liquors, 1875; Dr. Andrew Ure, from his Dictionary of Arts and Manufactures, 1872; Prof. C. F. Chandler, of the New York Board of Health; Prof. J. M. Merrick, from the Second Annual Report of the Board of Health of the City of Boston, 1874; Prof. Wm. Ripley Nichols, of the Mass. Institute of Technology, from a report made to the Board of Health of the City of Boston, 1875—all in order to show the improbability and the entire want of evidence of the adulteration of malt-liquors, as demonstrated by the examination of a great number of samples in England, Germany and in this country. The author, Prof. James F. Babcock, concludes his remarks on malt-liquors by stat-

---

* Published as House Document No. 266. 1877.

ing, that the results of a number of analyses of beer from different brewers, made by him during the past year, fully agree with the conclusions of all the chemists quoted above. In the light of such evidence mere assertions to the contrary lose all significance, and based thereon, *a resolve, adopting public refutation and challenge of proof as a matter of self-defense, has nothing of ostentation about it.*"

A comprehensive review of many important affairs, including the new constitution, the project of establishing a brewers' school, a retrospective summary of the Exhibition and its incalculable advantages to the trade, and the fiscal policy of the Federal Government in its bearing on the liquor-revenue in prohibitory States, constituted the remainder of President Rueter's address. In regard to the latter subject the association, at the suggestion of counselor Schade, adopted a policy which, if its premises had not in some respects been precisely the reverse of the actual state of affairs which they were supposed to reflect, might have produced a strong impression; but even then could scarcely have been expected to accomplish the desired result.

Schade held that article I, section 8, of the Constitution of the United States, virtually forbids the enactment of prohibitory laws. Section 8 reads: "The Congress shall have power to lay and *collect* taxes, duties, imports and excises to pay the debts and provide for the common defense and general welfare of the United States; but all duties, imports and excises shall be *uniform throughout the United States.*" Schade believed that the italicised words sustained his view. In his report, submitted at this convention, he said: "Thus it will be seen that the Constitution expressly gives the Federal Government the right to lay and collect *throughout* the United States a *uniform* internal revenue tax to pay debts and carry on the Government. *That right is supreme above all State laws.* No State can rightfully adopt any enactment or exercise authority by which the Federal Government will and can be prevented from collecting that *uniform* internal revenue." The weakness of this argument lies in the erroneous assumption that prohibitory laws prevent either the uniformity or the collection of the tax. In the exercise of the police power conceded to them by judicial decisions, prohibitory States simply forbid the manufacture and sale of intoxicants. If prohibitory laws destroy the brewing industry, wipe it out of existence, as they actually do, the Federal Government cannot, of course, derive any revenue from the manufacture of malt-liquors in prohibitory States; but that fact does not impair either the uniformity of the tax or its collectibility. With regard to these States the Federal Government stands in precisely the same position which it occupied in the case of most of the Southern States at the time when brewing did not exist therein. If prohibitory laws cannot prevent the sale of ardent spirits and other intoxicants, as in fact they cannot and do not prevent it, the Federal Government rigorously insists upon the payment of the tax by retailers in these States, and neither the State legislatures nor the State officers have ever attempted to forbid the collection of this tax, or even to question the absolute right of the Government to lay and collect internal taxes. That prohibitory laws favor the illicit traffic cannot be gainsaid; but this feature of the question has no more bearing on the constitutional argument than, for instance, the fact that it is more difficult to collect the tax on ardent spirits in the "moonshining" districts of the mountainous wilds of Kentucky or North Carolina than in New York or New Jersey. There are other constitutional provisions which the Brewers' Association, in common with many eminent jurists and a minority of the Supreme Court Judges, regard even to this day, and in spite of contrary decisions, as direct injunctions against prohibitory laws in their ultimate effect upon the rights of personal property and personal liberty; but in regard to the issue raised by Schade, the Federal Constitution, and more particularly the section just quoted, could not logically be so construed as to sustain Schade's reasoning. This defective premise naturally attenuated the force of the brewers' argument against section 3,243 of the Revised Statutes, which Schade believed should be so amended as to prevent the enactment of prohibitory laws. This section provides that—

"The payment of any tax imposed by the internal revenue laws for carrying on any trade or business shall not be held to exempt any person from any penalty or punishment provided by the laws of any State for carrying on the same within such State, or in any manner to authorize the commencement or continuance of such trade or business contrary to the laws of such State, or in places prohibited by municipal law; nor shall the payment of any such tax be held to prohibit any State from placing a duty or tax on the same trade or business, for State or other purposes."

Aside from any constitutional or legal reasoning, this section always appeared to unbiased critics as an unnecessary concession by which the Federal Government of its own accord assumed an illogical, incongruous and anomalous position, incompatible with its own dignity and extremely unjust to the industries from which it derived a disproportionately large share of its revenue. President Rueter came very much nearer than Schade to the core of the question, and its ethical and common-sense aspect, when he said:

"Spirits, fermented liquors and tobacco yielded, during the last fiscal year, ninety per cent., or $105,792,985.70, of the internal revenue receipts for the year, which were $117,237,086.81, leaving but $10 in every $100 collected, or $11,444,101.11, coming from other sources.

Upon such a showing may justly be based a claim for intervention by the Federal Government against State enactments which deprive two of these three classes of taxpayers of the benefit and protection of the law, declare them criminals, render their persons and property liable to seizure, and which, if enforced, would ruin their business. No prevarication and no Congressional enactment, such as section 3,243 of the Revised Statutes, can in the least affect *the truth and the force of the maxim that taxation sanctions.* Is government justified in setting aside the common sense and simple justice of this principle, in deference to the 'higher law,' sometimes claimed by prohibitionists, or because the question of State rights presents legislative perplexities? Need Congress heed the noisy claim for the 'principle' involved, if the very framers and promoters of these prohibitory State laws never hesitate to sacrifice principle to expediency?"

The elimination of section 3,243 would not have affected the right of the States to restrict or forbid the traffic, but it would have done away with the unnecessary disavowal of the "maxim that taxation sanctions;" and while this would not have been of any practical value to the trade, it would at least have removed from it the moral stigma which it implied. It is certainly illogical to impose a tax upon a business and at the same time prescribe that the payment of this tax shall not authorize the tax-payer to commence the business so taxed. The only logical and honest course would be not to collect the tax where the business so taxed cannot be commenced or continued. Lauer, who usually supplemented the report of the Agitation Committee by a speech, also took up this question and said this about it:

"Now, when it is considered that nine-tenths of all internal revenue taxes are raised from the manufacture and sale of fermented and spirituous liquors and tobacco, the folly of enacting State laws such as have been mentioned will be at once seen. Without the revenue derived from the source indicated, the Government could not go on for a week, and would be bankrupt. It is, therefore, worse than ridiculous that a set of fanatics should constantly hamper and persecute the tax-payers. Either the manufacture and sale of these articles are all wrong and a crime, and then the Government becomes *particeps criminis* by fostering and taxing the same, or they are branches of legitimate business, and as honorable and necessary as any other, and then the Government is bound to protect those citizens, at least as long as it compels them to pay taxes, against any obnoxious and destructive interference by anybody, whether it be a legislature or a body of citizens."

Thus it will be seen that the officers of the association fully understood both the strength and the weakness of their case. Its strength was in its direct appeal to common sense and common justice, and in its bearing on the fiscal and economic value of the industry; its weakness was in the Constitutional premise upon which Schade had placed it.

While he erred in this particular, the attorney performed meritorious work in many other respects and strengthened his standing in the association by a number of propositions calculated to avoid injustice and unnecessary friction in the execution of the revenue laws. Certain Iowa brewers had been compelled to take out dealers' licenses because they had bought beer from other brewers. Under the provisions of section 3,349 which, as the reader will recollect, formed part of the bill drafted by the association and enacted by Congress, a special tax was not required for such transactions, but the Revenue Office nevertheless demanded it under section 3,244 which provided that a brewer should not pay special tax by reason of selling malt-liquors *manufactured by him*. The intention of the lawmakers was made manifest when they enacted section 3,349; but the Revenue Office availed itself of the former provision, which Congress had failed to amend by the addition of the words "or bought by him." Contradictory provisions of this and a similar nature gave rise to many petty annoyances; but, fortunately, a new Commissioner, actuated by a more friendly spirit and a juster sense of his official responsibility, had taken Pratt's place and in consequence of this change technical quibbling and hair-splitting no longer interfered with the prompt and satisfactory settlement of these cases.

Green B. Raum, the new Commissioner, was not only a most painstaking, honest and conscientious officer, whose record has never been excelled, but he was also a liberal, just and fair-minded man, who accorded to the tax-paying industries that considerate treatment which their fiscal and economic importance warrants and demands. In inviting the Commissioner to attend the seventeenth convention, the association expressed this sentiment: "There never was a time when the brewers entertained as friendly a feeling to the Commissioner and the officers of the Internal Revenue Division, as at present. This is chiefly due to the liberal, fair and just construction and execution of the laws by yourself and your officers." Under Raum's administration all pending claims for the abatement or the refunding of assessments under the $2\frac{1}{2}$ bushel decision were allowed, much to the chagrin, it seems, of some collectors, who had continued to harass the brewers of their district, in spite of the understanding that, pending litigation, all cases should be held in abeyance. The friendly disposition of the Commissioner justified the hope that in their endeavor to have the laws amended in those minor provisions which have before been referred to, they might depend upon the assistance of the Revenue Office, and the convention therefore adopted the attorney's suggestions and instructed that officer to take such steps as the circumstances required.

If the Federal lawmakers were not unduly influenced by the executive officers to whom they naturally applied for advice upon purely administrative details of the revenue-law, no difficulty could be apprehended in this direction, more especially in view of the fact that the association had no intention of seeking any modifications of existing laws which would reduce the revenue, except perhaps, in the matter of import duties upon hops, barley and malt. As to the latter subject the position of the brewers remained unchanged so far as the underlying principle was concerned, while their arguments against the imposition of a hop-duty derived additional force from the fact that American growers had for a number of years exported large quantities of their product, successfully competing with European growers in the latter's own home-markets. Exporting their hops to England free of duty, while protected at home by an almost prohibitive duty against foreign competition, the American grower enjoyed the singular advantage of being able to dictate prices at home, and thus, although underselling his foreign competitors in foreign markets, yet sell his product in England at a lower price than he demanded from the American brewer. Fortunately, the latter was no longer altogether at the growers' mercy, for ever since the company represented by W. A. Lawrence, a member of the association, had succeeded in preserving hops in the form of an extract, the surplus of one year's abundant crop could be used to cover a possible shortage in the crop of the next or a succeeding year.

At the fifteenth convention Lawrence had demonstrated that the extract contains all the valuable qualities of the hop without leaves, stems or any extraneous matter; the proportion of ingredients in an average sample being, according to reliable analyses, 17.94 aromatic essential oils, 31.63 pure lupulin, 40.41 hopresin, and 10.02 extractive matter. Practical tests made by brewers soon convinced the trade that the extract is at least equal to the hops, and thus the general use of the former substance in some measure mitigated the hardship which an unwise protective tariff inflicted upon the industry— a fact that could not, however, weaken the brewers' argument in favor of the free importation of their raw-material. We shall presently return to, and trace the devious course of, this question.

As an illustration of the force of habit and the coercive force of a long-established custom, it may again be mentioned that in spite of the enormous augmentation of the business brought before the conventions for consideration or final action, the association still adhered to the old practice of interrupting the first day's proceedings by a recess for the sole purpose of giving the nominating committee an opportunity to name vice-presidents and secretaries, who were supposed to assist in conducting the proceedings. At this convention the committee, composed of J. Obermann, P. Schemm, H. Grau, W. Eberhardt and L. F. Kuntz, submitted these names:

Honorary Presidents: Frederick Lauer, Reading, Pa.; Henry Clausen, New York City. Vice-Presidents: Fred. Krug, Omaha, Neb.; Fred. A. Thieme, Lafayette, Ind.; W. H. Hull, New Haven, Conn.; John Wieland, San Francisco, Cal.; C. Heurich, Washington, D. C.; Conrad Seipp, Chicago, Ill.; Joseph Stoeckle, Wilmington, Del.; Rud. Lange, Davenport, Ia.; Ph. Schillinger, Louisville, Ky.; George Auer, New Orleans, La.; Chas. G. Stifel, St. Louis, Mo.; Anthony Yoerg, St. Paul, Minn.; Hon. Frank Jones, Portsmouth, N. H.; Albert Ziegele, Buffalo, N. Y.; George Ehret, New York City; E. W. Voight, Detroit, Mich.; H. Wagener, Salt Lake City, Utah; H. C. Brendecke, Humboldt, Kan.; Christian Moerlein, Cincinnati, O.; Joseph Grasser, Toledo, O.; Hermann Schalk, Newark, N. J.; H. Weinhard, Portland, Ore.; William Massey, Philadelphia, Pa.; Nic. Molter, Providence, R. I.; F. Giesecke, New Braunfels, Tex.; Robert Portner, Alexandria, Va ; Thos. M. Dukehart, Baltimore, Md.; Val. Blatz, Milwaukee, Wis.; A. Reymann, Wheeling, W. V., and John Roessle, Boston, Mass. Secretaries: Aug. Uihlein, Milwaukee, Wis.; Andrew E. Leicht, Chicago, Ill.; Wm. A. Miles, New York City; Adolph G. Hupfel, Morrisania, N. Y., and Richard Katzenmayer, Secretary.

The special committees appointed by President Rueter were constituted as follows, viz.:

Constitution and By-Laws: H. Clausen, E. Schandein, P. Schoenhofen, A. Reymann and L. Muth. Life Membership: C. Moerlein, F. Lauer and W. Massey. Resolutions: F. Lauer, H. Clausen, R. Portner, J. Obermann, I. Huber, A. E. Leicht, W. A. Miles, J. C. Miller, T. M. Dukehart, P. Schillinger, L. Schlather, H. Bartholomay and C. Moerlein. Petitions: C. G. Stifel, F. Pabst, P. Schemm, O. Huber and F. Jones. Condolence: F. Lauer, W. Massey and A. G. Huepfel.

The Finance Committee consisted of J. C. G. Huepfel, George Ehret and W. A. Miles; it was no longer appointed by the president, however, as we shall presently show.

The Committee on Life Members and that on Contingencies had just been created; the latter, upon President Rueter's suggestion, (1) because the Committee on Petitions, to whom all contingencies had up to this time been referred, could not dispose of the rapidly augmenting matters of this character, and (2) because contingencies, in the strict sense of the term, did not properly belong to this committee. The other new committee was created under the constitution, adopted at the preceding and re-confirmed, with slight amendments, at this convention. This new constitution, which is appended to this chapter, provided for three classes of members; while the superseded constitution, adopted at the Davenport convention, recognized only two classes, viz.: active and associate members. The term "associate member" was not used, however, until a later period.

Under the new classification the somewhat inapt designation of "honorary members" was assigned to maltsters, hop-dealers, etc.; while the term "life members" was reserved for those upon whom the association conferred the distinction now known as honorary membership. Life membership was conferred, at this convention, upon J. A. Huck and George Metz, Chicago; G. Klotter and R. Reinboldt, Cincinnati; R. Amerman, S. Sommer, Franz Ruppert, A. Schmid, A. Huepfel, M. Kuntz and M. P. Read, New York; Adolph Schalk and John Baier, Newark; F. Collins, Philadelphia, and Augustus Richardson, Boston.

In regard to the annual dues the status of the newly created honorary members remained unchanged; that is to say, they continued to pay a uniform sum ($30), without regard to the quantity of malt or hops sold by them —an obviously unjust and inequitable arrangement, both to the association and many of these members. The new constitution completely changed the character of the parent body, inasmuch as it eliminated what for the sake of brevity has been styled the representative system. Instead of a federation of local associations, such as the Davenport constitution provided for, the national body now became an association composed exclusively of individuals or firms, each one of whom was entitled to one vote. A Board of Trustees took the place of the Executive Committee; the Agitation Committee, instead of being appointed by the president, was now elected by the convention, and instead of being an independent body, exercising certain executive functions, now became subordinate to the Board of Trustees. The Finance Committee became a permanent organization, deriving its power from the association through the Trustees. The office of the association was permanently located at New York; and for this reason the new constitution provided that certain officers, as, for instance, the treasurer and the Finance Committee, shall reside at or near that city. Some very essential matters, in regard to which the association had on various occasions taken action or adopted resolutions enunciating a definite policy, such, for example, as the one relating to literary agitation, found no place in the new constitution, because the powers of the Trustees were now sufficiently enlarged and augmented to cover the entire field and to warrant any course or line of action demanded by the welfare of the trade.

The only really weak point of the new constitution, and the very one upon which the association had on a previous occasion expressed a very decided contrary opinion, was in that provision of Article VIII of the By-Laws which recognized the right of local associations or members to take independent measures in the interest of the whole body, and to demand reimbursement of expenses incurred in such efforts.

When this question was discussed at the preceding convention, the association recognized this right, but wisely sought to limit its exercise by adopting the committee's report, to the effect that in future no claim for reimbursement should be entertained, unless the claimant had, before undertaking the contemplated work, obtained its approval and sanction by the executive officers of the parent body. The new constitution ignored this very essential and necessary safeguard, and thus placed the association in a rather dangerous and irksome position. The pertinent provision reads: "Whenever any local association or active member thereof has rendered direct and valuable services in the interest of this association, the association, at its annual meeting, shall upon application for indemnity for expenses incurred thereby, and satisfactory proof being given, fix the amount of such indemnity, and the trustees shall direct the treasurer to pay the amount so fixed to the treasurer of such local association or active members thereof."

No sooner had this policy been promulgated than it gave rise to acrimonious discussions which plainly revealed its dangerous character, and must have convinced its advocates that the precautionary limitation before referred to could not safely be ignored. Among the eleven petitions submitted to the proper committee at this convention, two were in the nature of such claims; one from the Baltimore association for $250, the amount of expenses incurred in contesting the $2\frac{1}{2}$ bushel decision; the other from the Milwaukee association for $1,705, expended in defeating an attempt made in the Legislature of Michigan to impose an extra tax of one hundred dollars upon all dealers selling malt-liquors not brewed within the said State. As to this latter petition the report of the committee read as follows, viz.:

"On petition of Milwaukee local association, and in consideration of the fact that the recent attempt of certain brewers in the State of Michigan to restrict the sale of malt-liquors brewed in other States, within said State of Michigan, by imposing by legislative enactment, an extra tax of one hundred dollars upon all dealers in such foreign malt-liquors, is strongly to be condemned as a narrow-minded, short-sighted, and selfish measure, most injurious, as a precedent, to the best interests of the brewing trade, and the harmonious existence of our association — to reimburse said local association for actual expenses incurred in preventing the passage of such enactment, and furthermore, to pass a resolution of censure upon all brewers and other interested parties, engaged in promoting said ill-advised movement.

In submitting this recommendation President Rueter spoke warmly in favor of its adoption, closing his remarks with these words: "In this particular case all the brewers of the United States are confronting the brewers of Michigan, and for this reason the expenses ought to be defrayed by our association." M. Martz, of Detroit, indignantly repelled the charge lodged against the brewers of his State; they had not, he said, asked for the enactment of such a law; but, on the contrary, when the bill had been introduced without their knowledge, they opposed it more strongly than the Milwaukee association, and in proof of this Martz produced a printed copy of the Michigan brewers' remonstrance, which, upon Clausen's motion, was read then and there by A. E. Leicht, of Chicago. A very able document it was, indeed; firmly opposing the extra tax; treating the question in a thoroughly scientific manner from the moral, the sanitary and the economic point of view, and strongly urging upon the legislature the wisdom and expediency of liberally encouraging and protecting the manufacture and sale of fermented beverages. Emil Schandein, who had acted for the Milwaukee association in defeating this obnoxious measure, unhesitatingly admitted that a mistake had been made; that his petition must have been misunderstood, for in it he explicitly exonerated the Michigan brewers from any complicity in this attempt. In this report Schandein made use of this phrase: "It is not here charged that the brewers of Michigan were the prime movers in this matter; but if any one of them saw fit to furnish aid to the enemy it was the *individual*, and not the Michigan *brewer*, who forgot his country and remembered his State." The hypothetical part of this sentence probably gave rise to the misunderstanding. President Rueter immediately offered an apology to the Michigan brewers and to their spokesman, Martz, who supplemented his previous remarks by the statement that the measure had been proposed and advocated by the temperance party.

J. H. McAvoy opposed the appropriation of the sum required for reimbursing the Milwaukee association upon the ground that all brewers' associations throughout the country were compelled, for self-protection, to expend large sums of money locally, and that any one of them might bring similar claims. His own association had expended $10,0C0 to defeat the temperance party at elections. Frederick Pabst showed that Milwaukee brewers had also expended large sums in this manner for which they did not ask reimbursement. Clausen, while admitting the dangerous character of such a precedent, spoke in favor of the appropriation, as the enactment of the law would have affected the brewing industry in every State, Michigan excepted. He also pointed out the fact that the brewers of Michigan had in good faith petitioned for a reduction of the fees for beer-licenses, and that the Legislature, willing to grant this petition, sought to cover the deficiency by imposing an extra tax upon the sale of malt-liquor brewed outside of the State. Rueter, speaking for the Executive, explained that the case under consideration differed in every respect from the example cited by McAvoy; that the national association never had defrayed expenses of local campaigns or efforts to defeat State legislation; but in the present instance, an encroachment upon the entire industry having been attempted and successfully prevented, that provision of the new constitution which recognizes the justice of claims of this character should be held to apply. W. J. Lemp, of St. Louis, protested against the claim of the Baltimore association on the ground that nearly every local association, his own included, would be justified in presenting similar claims, because they, also, had contested the $2\frac{1}{2}$ bushel decision and incurred considerable expense in doing so.

The far-reaching significance of the quoted provision of the constitution made it appear desirable to record as fully as possible, the discussions upon the first concrete cases that arose under its operation, in order to demonstrate not only the intention of its authors, as expressed by Rueter and Clausen, but also the view taken of it by the members generally. In relation to the latter point our material is rather meagre, unless we accept the result of the vote as a criterion; and that vote clearly indicates acquiesence in the views expressed by the officers and committees, for the entire report of the Committee on Petitions, including the contested claims, was accepted by the convention.

Among other appropriations recommended by this Committee was one for $5,000 to cover the remaining liabilities of the Fair Committee. It will be recollected that the total expenditures for the brewers' magnificent exhibit amounted to $46,678.80, of which $41,657.51 had been raised by subscriptions, leaving a balance of just claims against the Committee to the amount of $5,000. Had there been a surplus it would have been paid into the treasury of the association, and as all the incalculable advantages of the Exhibition redounded to the benefit of the whole trade, it was no more than fair and right, as the chairman of the Exhibition Committee (H. H. Rueter) emphasized, that the association should cover the deficiency. Among the other money-matters submitted by the Committee was an increase of the attorney's annual salary to $1,500, and an appropriation of $1,500 for the Milwaukee association, who thus became the first beneficiary of the new rule under which legitimate convention expenses are being defrayed by the parent body. All these appropriations exceeded, in the aggregate, the total revenue of the association from annual dues, which in the year 1876–77 amounted to $9,345. It was probably this consideration that prompted the Committee on Petitions to report adversely upon a request of the German Hop Growers' Society that the association donate a prize to be competed for by growers at the International Hop Exhibition, mentioned in the preceding chapter. The total assets of the association amounted to $27,619.63. In the absence of statistics of membership, it is impossible to determine whether the total receipts, other than those accruing from interest on bonds and initiation fees, represented the exact amount of the revenue that should have been derived from annual dues. There may have been included in the stated sum arrears paid up; and, on the other hand, a considerable sum of arrears may have been outstanding; in either case conclusions drawn from the data given would be defective. Nor would a converse deduction as to membership, upon the basis of these data, be any more reliable. Be that as it may, at any rate the financial condition revealed a marked increase of members, which must have been particularly large between the years 1874 and 1877, and which was not appreciably affected by losses either through resignation or death.*

The aggressive policy recommended by President Rueter in regard to unfounded charges of adulteration was promptly adopted by the Committee on Resolutions, who reported the following, viz.:

Whereas, In spite of the extraordinary endeavors of our association to define the true status of our trade, to inform those who are

---

* The Committee on Condolence at this convention reported the following deaths, viz.: John Hohenadel, Philadelphia; Franz Binz, Chicago; Andreas Schinnerer, Schenectady; Adolph Meckert, Guttenberg; J. G. Sohn, Cincinnati; Jacob Dick, Quincy; Joseph Baumann, Omaha; John Kress, New York; Philip Neu, Belleville; John Noth, Davenport.

ignorant as to the honest and healthful ingredients employed in the manufacture of malt-liquors, and to deny the dishonest aspersions continually made by our enemies, much still remains to be done. Be it *Resolved*, That every member sign, and cause to be circulated as extensively as possible, a declaration to the effect that the malt liquor by him produced is made from pure material, and that no obnoxious ingredient is allowed to enter or be used in his brewery. *Resolved*, That all persons who question or deny this statement be invited to inspect the whole process of manufacture in the establishments of members of this association.

To this Henry Clausen added another resolution, reaffirming the association's determination to expel any member found guilty of adulteration, and to investigate all charges of this character, to the end that the offending parties may be dealt with according to their offense. This resolution also appeals to the Press not to publish such accusations unless supported by sufficient evidence, and, as a matter of simple justice, to publicly retract charges not corroborated by facts.—The trade journals had hitherto rendered good service in this matter, and as the working force was increased during this year by the establishment of two new journals, viz.: The *Western Brewer*, published by S. Rich & Co., and the *German and American Brewers' Journal* (A. E. J. Tovey, Manager), the chances of a successful campaign of enlightenment appeared very promising.

The National Maltsters' Association, in a letter addressed to Secretary Katzenmayer, suggested the advisability of holding the brewers' annual convention in September, instead of May or June, as the two bodies could then meet at the same time and place. Massey made a motion to that effect, and Lauer, Schemm, Schillinger and President Rueter spoke in favor, Stifel and Lemp against it. The latter expressed the conviction that many valuable members would not attend conventions in September, because those of them who manufactured their own malt were compelled to remain at home in the Fall in order to secure their supply of grain. The vote on Lemp's amendment to Massey's motion, to the effect that the time for holding the conventions remain unchanged, was almost unanimously adopted.

The election of officers and committees under the new constitution resulted as follows, viz.:

President: H. H. Rueter; First Vice-President: F. Lauer; Second Vice-President: Henry Clausen, Jr.; Secretary: Richard Katzenmayer; Treasurer: Jacob Ahles; Trustees: J. C. G. Huepfel, W. A. Miles, Henry Bartholomay, William Massey, William J. Lemp, Christian Moerlein, Conrad Seipp, Jacob Obermann.

Agitation Committee: Fred. Lauer, Reading, Chairman; Henry Clausen, Jr., William A. Miles, George Ehret, John C. G. Huepfel, David Jones, James Flanagan, New York; William Howard, Brooklyn; John Greenway, Syracuse; Henry Bartholomay, Rochester; Albert Ziegele, Buffalo; Henry H. Rueter, John Roessle, Boston; Hon. Frank Jones, Portsmouth; Hermann Schalk, Newark; Wm. Massey, Gustavus Bergner, John F. Betz, Peter Schemm, Philadelphia; Chas. G. Stifel, Wm. J. Lemp, St. Louis; Christian Moerlein, H. Lackmann, Cincinnati; Leonard Schlather, Cleveland; Conrad Seipp, Andrew E. Leicht, J. H. McAvoy, Chicago; Emil Schandein, Jac. Obermann, Milwaukee; E. W. Voigt, Detroit; P. Lieber, Indianapolis; H. Koehler, Davenport; Ignatz Huber, Rock Island; F. Krug, Omaha; John Wieland, Fred. Fortmann, San Francisco; J. F. Stöckle, Wilmington; Louis Muth, August Beck, Thos. M. Dukehart, Baltimore; Robert Portner, Alexandria; A. Reymann, Wheeling; Jacob Seeger, Columbia; John Debus. Covington; Jos. Miller. Chicago: J. H. McAvoy, Ph. Bartholomae, Frank Binz, M. Gottfried, John A. Huck, Louis C. Huck, Andrew E. Leicht, John M. Leicht, Geo. Metz, Conrad Seipp, Peter Schoenhofen, H. S. Glade, A. Magnus, J. Liginger, Wm. B. Orcutt, F. W. Wolf, Geo. Bullen, L. C. Epps, Geo. B. Cornell, C. W. Bayinton, Chas. Pope, C. Kattenidt, Chas. Kastner T. J. Lefens, E. W. Barnes, T. J. Will, E. D. Northrop, representative of the *Chicago Times*; J. M. Wing and H. S. Rich, representatives of the *Western Brewer*; J. A. Koenig, representative of the *Illinois Staats-Zeitung*. Decatur: H. Schlaudemann. Dubuque: M. Tschirgi. Detroit: Mich. Martz, Bernhard Stroh, E. W.

* The following is a list of delegates and guests present at the seventeenth convention:

Alexandria: Robert Portner. Albany: Wm. Story, J. F. Story. Boston: Henry H. Rueter. Baltimore: Th. M. Dukehart, Henry von der Horst, Louis Muth. Buffalo: Donald Bain, S. J. Brauer, Hermann Grau, G. F. Kuhn, Theo. Kleinschmidt, B. A. Lynde, John Schnessler, Ed. Schnessler, C. G. Voltz. Burlington: Alfred Werthmneller. Boone: F. M. Herman. Burlington, Wis.: Wm. Fink. Cleveland: F. H. Brann, Hermann Mueller, Leonard Schlather. Cincinnati: Henry Foss, H. Lackmann, John Kauffmann, Christ. Moerlein, Geo. Sohn, Joseph Schaller, John Debus. Covington: Jos. Miller. Chicago: J. H. McAvoy, Ph. Bartholomae, Frank Binz, M. Gottfried, John A. Huck, Louis C. Huck, Andrew E. Leicht, John M. Leicht, Geo. Metz, Conrad Seipp, Peter Schoenhofen, H. S. Glade, A. Magnus, J. Liginger, Wm. B. Orcutt, F. W. Wolf, Geo. Bullen, L. C. Epps, Geo. B. Cornell, C. W. Bayinton, Chas. Pope, C. Kattenidt, Chas. Kastner T. J. Lefens, E. W. Barnes, T. J. Will, E. D. Northrop, representative of the *Chicago Times*; J. M. Wing and H. S. Rich, representatives of the *Western Brewer*; J. A. Koenig, representative of the *Illinois Staats-Zeitung*. Decatur: H. Schlaudemann. Dubuque: M. Tschirgi. Detroit: Mich. Martz, Bernhard Stroh, E. W.

The following is the text of the Constitution and By-Laws, viz. :

CERTIFICATE OF INCORPORATION.

We, the undersigned, Henry Clausen, Jr., William Massey, Jacob Ahles, John Gardiner, Gustavus Bergner, Richard Katzenmayer, James M. Lewis, George Ehret, Jacob Ruppert, George Winter, J. Chr. G. Hüpfel, Fred. Schaefer, Wm. A. Miles, John Geo. Gillig, George Schmitt, Henry Elias, Martin Schwaner, William Howard, Phil. Ebling, Fred. Lauer, Chas. C. Clausen, Joseph Kuntz, John Eichler, George Bechtel, Joseph Rubsam, Joseph Burger, Otto Huber, Andrew Finck, D. G. Yuengling, Jr., W. T. Ryerson, George Ringler, Joseph Schmid, Jacob Hoffmann, Peter Doelger, David Jones, David Mayer, Chas. Bischoff, Jos. Liebmann, Frank Jones, Jacob Pfaff, Henry H. Rueter, Louis Muth, Christ. Moerlein, Peter Schemm, Wm. J. Lemp, Chas. G. Stifel, L. Schlather, H. Lackmann, Jacob Obermann, Emil Schandein, John Greenway, Hermann Schalk, Ed. W. Voigt, H. Bartholomay, John F. Betz, Conrad Seipp, And. A. Leicht, A. Reymann, Joseph Stoeckle, John Kauffmann, Phil. Schillinger, Robert Portner, all being of full age, and citizens of the United States, do hereby certify, that we desire to form a Society pursuant to the provisions of an Act entitled, "An Act for the incorporation of Societies, or Clubs, for certain lawful purposes," passed May 12, 1875.

NAME.

First.—The corporate name of the said Society is, *The United States Brewers' Association.*

Voigt, T. D. Hawley. Erie: C. M. Conrad. Highland: Martin Schott. Kenosha: C. Muentzenherger, A. Mnentzenberger, John Pettit. Lafayette: Fred. A. Thieme. Louisville: Phil. Schillinger, John Zeller. Milwaukee: F. Pabst, E. Schandeln, Chas. Best, Jr., Henry Best, Val. Blatz, John Blatz, Alb. Blatz, Franz Falk, Sr., Louis Falk, Franz Falk, Jr., Max Fueger, Adam Gettelmann, Fr. Miller, Jac. Obermann, Phil. Obermann, Fred. Obermann, Anguet Uihlein, Henry Uihlein, Alfred Uihlein, Ed. Uihlein, Chas. Westhofen, manager Milwaukee Brewing Association; Prof. Ruschhaupt, editor of the *Brauerei;* Wm. Gerlach, J. Enes, Otto Zwietusch, G. J. Hanson, Louis Aner, H. Wiegand. Monroe: Jacob Heftey, G. Lesenherger. New Albany: Paul Reising. Nurnberg, Bavaria: J. Kohlenberger. Newark: Chr. Felgenspan, Wm. Laible. New York and Vicinity: Jacob Ahles, Fred. J. Ahles, John F. Betz, Henry Clausen, Hermann Clausen, G. Ehret, John Eichler, Philip Ebling, John G. Gillig, Otto Huber, Ad. Hupfel, L. F. Kuntz, Wm. A. Miles, E. Schaefer, R. Katzenmayer, John Flintoff, editor of *American Brewers' Gazette;* Edw. Grosse, special representative of *New York Staats-Zeitung;* A. Schwarz, editor of *Americanische Bierbrauer;* John Tovey, manager of *German and American Brewers' Journal;* Anthony Pfund, Garrett A. Pier, Chas. Stoll, S. J. Bartol, Chas. Schickedantz, Paul Weidner, Jos. Boll, M. E. Edson, E. Mauer, Jas. Naser, J. McKinney, A. Zoller, H. C. Schulz, Geo. Chatillon. Portsmouth: Frank Jones, M. C. Philadelphia: John F. Betz, John Bergdoll, Theo. Bergner, Chas. Glass, Max Eble, John Fritsch, Henry Flach, Chr. Halsch, Wm. Massey, John C. Miller, Germantown; Peter Schemm, Jos. Theurer, Felix Geiger, John Birkenstock, Ernst Derkum, Jos. Gormley, Ch. Osner. Pittsburg and Alleghany City: Wm. Eberhardt, W. K. Walter. Reading: F. Lauer. Rockford: John Peacock. Rock Island: J. Huber, Fr. Haas (guest). Rochester: Henry Bartholomay. St. Louis: W. J. Lemp, Chas. G. Stifel. Terre Haute: Anton Mayer. Titusville: Chas. Schwartz. Toledo: Jos. Grasser, Rob. Lehmann. Toronto: W. D. Matthews. Wilmington: Jos. Stoeckle. Wheeling: A. Reymann. Washington: Louis Sehade, Chas. Henrich, Jacob Roth, Wm. Metzger. Waukegan: E. D. Besley, Wm. Besley, A. Michels.

BUSINESS AND OBJECT.

Second.—The objects for which the Society is formed are: the improving the Art of manufacturing Malt-Liquors, the dissemination of valuable information and useful knowledge relating to the mode, manufacture, sale, and consumption of Malt-Liquors, the advancement, development, and protection of the brewing and Malt-Liquor interest in the United States, and for purposes of sociability and culture.

TRUSTEES.

The number of Trustees to manage the affairs of the Society shall consist of the President, First Vice-President, Second Vice-President, Treasurer, and Secretary for the time being, and eight members of the Society.

The names of the Trustees for the first year are: Henry H. Rueter, President; Fred. Lauer, 1st Vice-President; Henry Clausen, Jr., 2d Vice-President; Jacob Ahles, Treasurer; Richard Katzenmayer, Secretary; J. C. G. Hüpfel, Wm. A. Miles, Henry Bartholomay, W. J. Lemp, Wm. Massey, Christian Moerlein, Conrad Seipp, and Jacob Obermann.

OFFICE.

The office of the said society shall be in the City, County and State of New York.

CONSTITUTION.

ARTICLE I.—NAME.

The name of the Association shall be the "UNITED STATES BREWERS' ASSOCIATION.'

ARTICLE II.—OBJECTS OF THE ASSOCIATION.

The United States Brewers' Association is established to secure co-operation among the Brewers of the United States in furthering and protecting the interests, general welfare and prosperity of the brewing trade. More especially to guard their interests, as affected by Federal and State legislation; to protect themselves, as far as possible, against an oppressive, arbitrary or unjust administration of the Internal Revenue Laws relating to the manufacture and sale of malt-liquors; to aid the United States Government in the collection of the tax on fermented liquors, lawfully due, by discountenancing all evasion and imparting desired information as to the best system of taxation and modes of collection; to encourage and forward in every way all improvements in the manufacture of malt-liquors; to gather and disseminate practical and useful information relating to the brewing trade in all its bearings; to refute and repel the unjust aspersions and ill-advised action of the so-called temperance party against the manufacture and use of fermented malt-liquors, and to vindicate the truth, based upon the experience of all civilized nations, that by the popular use of fermented beverages the cause of rational temperance is most surely advanced and best sustained.

Finally, to promote social intercourse among the members of the association, cultivate friendship and good-will, encourage all good qualities of head and heart, and keep good-fellowship with all true friends of civil and religious liberty.

ARTICLE III.—MEMBERSHIP.

MEMBERS.—Any person or firm or corporation carrying on a brewery on his own account, and being of good character, may become a member, and be entitled to vote (a firm, however, shall be entitled to but one vote), on application to the Secretary, either individually or through a local Association, and payment of the initiation fee and assessment, as provided by Section 8 of the By-Laws.

HONORARY MEMBERS.—Any person in close connection with the brewing trade may be admitted as honorary member on like application, and payment of the initiation fee and dues, as provided in Section 8 of the By-Laws, but shall not be entitled to vote, nor have any interest in the property or effects of the Association.

Any member, or honorary member, may be suspended or expelled, as may be prescribed in the By-Laws, and all interest in the property of the Association of persons ceasing to be members shall vest in the Association.

LIFE–MEMBERS.—Any person, upon the recommendation of the Executive Committee, may be elected a life-member of the Association. Such life-members shall not, however, be entitled to vote or have any interest in the property or effects of the Association (unless specially provided), neither shall such members be subject to any dues or assessments.

ARTICLE IV.—OFFICERS.

The Officers of the Association shall be a President, two Vice-Presidents, a Secretary and a Treasurer, to be elected annually at the Annual Meeting or Convention. There shall also be elected from its members thirteen Trustees. The President, two Vice-Presidents,

Secretary and Treasurer for the time being shall be Trustees, making the whole number thirteen.

There shall be two standing committees, viz., an Agitation Committee and the Finance Committee. The Agitation Committee shall be elected annually by the Association, and be composed of members from the different States, with one of the Vice-Presidents as Chairman, who shall reside at or near the City of New York.

The Committee on Finance shall consist of three members of the Trustees, who shall also reside at or near the City of New York, and be chosen annually by the Trustees.

ARTICLE V.—ELECTIONS.

All elections shall be decided by ballot, unless otherwise ordered by a majority of the members present at the meeting. The Officers elected shall continue in office until their successors shall be chosen.

ARTICLE VI.—CONTINUANCE OF THE ASSOCIATION.

A motion to dissolve the Association shall not be entertained by the Association unless seconded by two-thirds of the members present at a regular meeting, and shall require for its adoption a two-thirds vote of the members present, or represented as precribed in Section 13 of the By-Laws. It shall not take effect in any case until six months from the date of its passage, and shall be null and void and of no effect if, within three months of such passage, one hundred members, entitled to a vote, shall enter a written protest over their signatures against the dissolution of the Association and deliver the same to the Secretary.

ARTICLE VII.—THE CONSTITUTION—HOW AMENDED.

It shall be required that a written notice of any motion to amend this Constitution shall be given to the Secretary of the Association three months previous to the assembling of the Annual Convention, signed by a member, and stating the character of the proposed amendment; and a two-thirds vote of the members present in person or by proxy in favor of such amendment shall be necessary for its adoption.

ARTICLE VIII.

The Association shall annually hold a convention or meeting. The time and place for holding the same shall be determined and fixed at the annual convention or meeting.

BY-LAWS.

I.—Duties of the President.

The President of the Association shall preside at all its meetings and appoint all Special Committees, unless otherwise ordered by the meeting over which he is presiding. He shall decide all points of order raised, and appeals to the meeting from his decision shall be put to vote without debate. In case of his absence or inability to perform his duties, the Convention shall be opened by one of the Vice-Presidents, and a Chairman shall be chosen by the members present. The President is, *ex-officio*, a member of all Committees.

II.—The Secretary.

The Secretary shall keep a record of all meetings, and of all other transactions and affairs of the Association, of which a record is commonly kept; issue all official notices; keep a roll of the members; conduct the correspondence and perform all other duties incident to his office.

III.—The Treasurer.

The Treasurer shall collect all moneys due to the Association, and disburse and invest the funds under the direction of the Trustees. He shall deposit all moneys received by him to the credit of the Association in a bank which shall be designated by the Trustees, and shall pay such bills as may be audited and passed, by check drawn by him and countersigned by the Chairman of the Finance Committee. He shall keep an accurate account of all moneys received, expended and invested, and submit a quarterly statement with vouchers to the Trustees, and make an annual statement to the Trustees.

IV.—The Trustees.

The Trustees shall have general charge of the affairs, finances and property of the Association.

Section 1.—It shall be their duty to carry out the objects and purposes thereof, and to this end they may exercise all the powers of the Association, subject to the Constitution and to such action the Association may take at its annual meeting, and shall have power to call special meetings or conventions whenever they shall deem it necessary.

Sec. 2.—The Trustees shall cause to be prepared annually a detailed statement of the financial condition of the Association, showing its receipts and expenditures for the current year, the number of members and other matters of general interest to the Association; all of which must be submitted to the Association at its annual meetings or conventions.

Sec. 3.—The Trustees shall annually elect from their number a Finance Committee. A quorum of the Trustees shall consist of seven of its members.

Sec. 4.—The Trustees shall have power to fill any vacancy which may occur from death or resignation among the officers of the Association for the unexpired term of their office.

V.—FINANCE COMMITTEE.

It shall be the duty of the Finance Committee to carefully examine and audit all accounts presented for payment. The Chairman shall countersign all checks drawn by the Treasurer in payment of accounts duly audited and passed. They shall make quarterly examinations of the Treasurer's accounts, and they shall report to the Trustees, whenever required, the condition of the Treasurer's accounts, the assets and liabilities of the Association, and such other matters as the Trustees deem proper.

VI.—AGITATION COMMITTEE.

It shall be the duty of the Agitation Committee to watch over the interests of the entire brewing trade, and to keep themselves informed of all inimical influences, and especially as far as possible as regards the enactment of oppressive, arbitrary and unjust laws, affecting the manufacture and sale of malt-liquors; the hostile machinations of political parties, and the ill-advised attempts of individuals and organizations, ostensibly in the interest of the good cause of temperance, to prejudice the public against our business and the popular use of our products. And further, to make such suggestions and recommend such measures and proceedings to the Trustees as they deem necessary or be advised will be instrumental in overcoming or nullifying such influence and laws, and of protecting the brewers' interests generally.

The Committee shall annually make a report of their labors to the Association, at its annual meeting or convention.

VII.—RIGHTS AND DUTIES OF MEMBERS.

All members shall be entitled to the protection of the Association and shall enjoy the rights and privileges secured through membership, as fixed by the Constitution, equally and impartially.

In return each member and honorary member binds himself to abide by the enactments of the Association; to pay all dues promptly and to respond efficiently to all demands which may be properly made upon him by the Executive in furtherance of the ends and aims of the Association.

VIII.—INITIATION FEES, DUES AND ASSESSMENTS.

An initiation fee of Five Dollars shall be paid by every person, who shall be admitted a member of the Association, payable on admission.

Every member shall pay a yearly assessment of twenty cents for each one hundred barrels of malt-liquors by him brewed and sold during the year next preceding the date when such assessment becomes due.

In case of need an extra assessment may be laid on all members by resolution, passed at any annual convention or meeting.

Honorary members shall each pay the sum of Thirty Dollars as annual dues.

If any member or honorary member shall fail to pay his annual dues for two years, his name shall be stricken from the roll of the Association, and he shall cease to be a member.

Whenever any local Association or active member thereof has rendered direct and valuable services in the interest of this Association, the Association at its annual meeting shall upon application for indemnity for expenses incurred thereby, and satisfactory proof being given, fix the amount of such indemnity, and the Trustees shall direct the Treasurer to pay the amount so fixed, to the Treasurer of such local Association or active member thereof.

IX.—CENSURE, SUSPENSION AND EXPULSION OF MEMBERS.

If any member shall be guilty of conduct prejudicial to the interests or character of the Association, or in violation of its Constitution or By-Laws, such member may be, by vote of two-thirds of the members present, censured, suspended, or, by ballot, expelled at the Annual Meeting or Convention. Charges against any member shall be preferred in writing, and delivered to the Secretary, within one month prior to the meeting of the Annual Meeting or Convention, and a copy thereof shall be delivered to the member against whom such charge is made, within the same time; unless such alleged offence or misconduct has been committed within one month preceding the assembling of such Meeting or Convention, in which case such charge may, in like manner, be made to the Convention, and a copy thereof delivered to such member.

X.—Any person or firm who shall cease to be a member of the Association, shall forfeit all rights or interests in the property of the Association.

XI.—ORDER OF BUSINESS.

The following shall be the order of business at the Annual Convention:

Opening by the President.

Election of Vice-Presidents and Secretaries to officiate during the Convention.

Report of credentials presented and examined, and reading names of delegates present.

Report of Agitation Committee.

Report of the Trustees.

Reports of Special Committees.

Reading of Communications.

Any business legitimately before the Convention, bearing on the affairs, aims and objects of the Association and the interests of the Brewing Trade generally.

Election of Officers for the ensuing year.

Appointment of the place of meeting of the next Annual Convention.

The usual parliamentary rules shall govern proceedings at the Convention or Meeting.

XII.—QUORUM OF THE ASSOCIATION.

Thirty members, entitled to vote, shall constitute a quorum for the transaction of business.

XIII.—MANNER OF VOTING.

The voting shall be by *viva-voce*, except as otherwise provided. Members shall be entitled to vote by proxy.

The action of the Convention is binding on all members of the Association.

XIV.—SALARIES AND TRAVELING EXPENSES.

The Secretary shall be remunerated for his services, and the amount of his salary shall be fixed by the Convention.

The Officers of the Association shall have their traveling expenses, in attending the Convention, paid from the treasury.

XV.—SEAT OF THE EXECUTIVE.

The seat of the Executive of the Association shall be in the City of New York, unless otherwise ordered.

XVI.—BY-LAWS—HOW AMENDED.

These By-Laws may be amended, or new By-Laws adopted, by a vote of two-thirds of the members present, in person or by proxy, at the Annual Convention or Meeting; provided that two months' previous notice of such intention, stating the nature of the proposed amendment, be given in writing to the Secretary of the Association.

END OF PART II.

Milton Keynes UK
Ingram Content Group UK Ltd.
UKHW022029250224
438379UK00005B/581